THE ETIQUETTE OF EARLY NORTHERN VERSE

MEDIEVAL
INSTITUTE

UNIVERSITY OF NOTRE DAME

The Conway Lectures in Medieval Studies 2010

The Medieval Institute gratefully acknowledges the generosity of Robert M. Conway and his support for the lecture series and the publications resulting from it.

PREVIOUS TITLES PUBLISHED IN THIS SERIES:

Rosamond McKitterick
Perceptions of the Past in the Early Middle Ages (2006)

Jonathan Riley-Smith
Templars and Hospitallers as Professed Religious in the Holy Land (2010)

A. C. Spearing
Medieval Autographies: The "I" of the Text (2012)

Barbara Newman
Medieval Crossover: Reading the Secular against the Sacred (2013)

John Marenbon
Abelard in Four Dimensions: A Twelfth-Century Philosopher in His Context and Ours (2013)

Sylvia Huot
Outsiders: The Humanity and Inhumanity of Giants in Medieval French Prose Romance (2016)

William J. Courtenay
Rituals for the Dead: Religion and Community in the Medieval University of Paris (2019)

Alice-Mary Talbot
Varieties of Monastic Experince in Byzantium, 800–1453 (2019)

Anne D. Hedeman
Visual Translation: Illuminated Manuscripts and the First French Humanists (2022)

THE ETIQUETTE OF EARLY NORTHERN VERSE

ROBERTA FRANK

University of Notre Dame Press

Notre Dame, Indiana

Notre Dame, Indiana 46556
www.undpress.nd.edu

Published in the United States of America

Library of Congress Control Number: 2021948753

ISBN: 978-0-268-20252-1 (Hardback)
ISBN: 978-0-268-20254-5 (WebPDF)
ISBN: 978-0-268-20251-4 (Epub)

For Walter

CONTENTS

ACKNOWLEDGMENTS

"There is a sort of greatness to your lateness," says Fiona, rebuking Hugh Grant's tardiness in *Four Weddings and a Funeral* (1994). To which he responds: "Thanks, it's not achieved without real suffering." The chapters of this book began life as the Robert M. Conway Lectures in Medieval Studies, delivered at the University of Notre Dame on November 1, 3, and 4, 2010. It would be nice to claim that my thinking took that long to jell. Nice, but not true. It was retirement that made possible the turning of three fledgling talks into a monograph.

It was an honor to give these lectures. I am grateful to the late Remie Constable, then director of the Medieval Institute at Notre Dame, along with Kathryn Kerby-Fulton, John Van Engen, Thomas Noble, Thomas Hall, and Margot Fassler, for their hospitality; special thanks also to Roberta Baranowski of the Medieval Institute for her kindnesses during my visit. I am grateful to the two anonymous readers of the manuscript for wise and generous counsels, and to the staff of the University of Notre Dame Press for the work they have put into producing this book, most particularly to Managing Editor Matthew Dowd, and to Scott Barker for his skillful and meticulous copyediting.

This study explores the manners of a long-lived poetics, its formal subtleties and social signaling. "Who is this book aimed at?" marketing heads ask, as if it were poised to hit someone gazing in the opposite direction. I envisage two audiences: specialists, for whom notes on past and current academic debates are provided; and generalists, readers attentive to the play of sound, to the styles and verbal art of poets who made words sing more than a millennium ago.

So many years, so many accumulated debts of gratitude. Summoning up all the voices that have contributed, knowingly or unknowingly, to *The Etiquette of Early Northern Verse* would quickly drain the pool of possible reviewers. Two ongoing international editorial and lexicographical projects made this study feasible: for *dróttkvætt* stanzas, the volumes of *Skaldic Poetry of the Scandinavian Middle Ages*; for Old English verse, the *Dictionary of Old English* and its web corpus. Six decades ago at Harvard, Theodore M. Andersson introduced me to Old Norse and the wilderness of skaldic verse. At the Centre for Medieval Studies at the University of Toronto (1968–2000), I worked alongside colleagues such as Angus Cameron and Antonette diPaolo Healey, founder and longtime editor in chief of the *Dictionary of Old English*, respectively. Russell J. Poole, my first Toronto doctoral student, taught me far more about skaldic verse than I taught him; Haruko Momma's PhD dissertation illuminated the subtle interactions between Old English poetic syntax and meter. At Yale, a cohort of graduate medievalists brightened my days and opened new paths: I'm thinking of you, Irina Dumitrescu, Eric Weiskott, Anya Adair, Alexandra Reider, Andrew Kraebel, Shu-han Luo, Sarah Novacich, Denis Ferhatovic, Jordan Zweck, Justin Park, and Joseph Stadolnik, among others too numerous to name. I owe special gratitude to the above-mentioned Alexandra Reider for compiling the index. My distinguished colleague Alastair Minnis, now resident in the Scottish Borders, stepped forward at a crucial moment, read the whole manuscript, and made invaluable suggestions. Endnotes record with thanks specific debts to individuals such as Ross G. Arthur, without whose wide-ranging knowledge this study would have been the poorer. My deepest gratitude as always is to Walter Goffart, life partner of a half century, to whom this book is dedicated.

CONVENTIONS

Tradition divides Old Icelandic poetry into eddic and skaldic verse; the former is generally anonymous, undatable, and relatively straightforward in syntax, meter, and diction; the latter, which includes *dróttkvætt*, by named poets, boasts exceedingly complex syntax, meter, diction, and internal rhyme schemes and is to some extent datable. In both Old Norse and modern Icelandic, *skáld* means "poet"; modern Icelandic usage sometimes refers to skaldic verse in general as *dróttkvæði* (lit. "court poetry"). Citations from the *dróttkvætt* corpus (and short forms for individual poems and skalds) are from *Skaldic Poetry of the Scandinavian Middle Ages* (*SkP*), in progress; editors of individual poems are named in the text and/or notes; editors of the separate volumes, in the list of abbreviations. References (e.g., Bragi *Rdr* 3/3, ed. Clunies Ross; *SkP* 3.1:31) identify in order the skald, poem, stanza, line, and editor, followed by the *SkP* volume and page number. I cite skaldic stanzas not yet housed in *SkP* from *Den norsk-islandske skjaldedigtning* (*Skjd*), eddic verse, from Neckel-Kuhn, *Edda*.

As a navigational aid, I recast in prose order the words of *dróttkvætt* stanzas before supplying a translation. Old Norse (ON) refers to variants of Old West Norse spoken in Norway and its North Atlantic colonies during the long Viking Age (ca. 700/800–1030/1125, the dates varying according to where and who you are); ON also refers to the language of Scandinavian newcomers to the British Isles. With the exception of runic inscriptions, the ON vernacular left few records until after the Viking Age and then chiefly in Iceland; current practice, followed here, cites Old Icelandic forms as representing ON. The designation "Viking Age" is capitalized when referring to a historical period (cf. the Middle Ages), but lowercase when used adjectivally (viking-age verse) or with reference to shipborne ruffians (vikings). Information about ON word frequency and distribution has been extracted from the skaldic project web corpus at http://skaldic.abdn.ac.uk/db.php and from the *Ordbog over det norrøne prosasprog: A Dictionary of ON Prose* (Copenhagen, 1989–) at http://onp.ku.dk/onp. ON dictionaries consulted include the *Lexicon poeticum* (*LP*), Fritzner's *Ordbog* (*Fritzner*), and Cleasby, Vigfusson, and Craigie, *Icelandic–English Dictionary* (*CV*). See the abbreviations list for full information.

Citations of *Beowulf* are from *Klaeber's Beowulf* (*Kl* 4); all other citations of Old English poetry are from *The Anglo-Saxon Poetic Records* (*ASPR*). Old English (OE) is the term used for the English vernacular before 1100; the adjective "Anglo-Saxon" in scholarly titles refers to the history, archaeology, and material culture of England during the same period. OE lexicographical material is from the *Dictionary of Old English: A to I Online* (*DOE*), and from Bosworth and Toller, *An Anglo-Saxon Dictionary* (*BT*). Statements about OE word frequency and distribution are based on the *Dictionary of Old English Web Corpus* (*DOEC*). The short titles used for individual poems are those of the *DOE*. See the abbreviations list and bibliography for references to these and other research tools.

The Roman alphabet was used for writing OE and ON with a small number of additional letters. Two symbols, *ð* (uppercase *Ð*) and *þ* (uppercase *Þ*), represent the sounds written *th* in English. After a consonant, ON final *r* is never syllabic. In current practice, consonants are articulated as in modern English; vowels, both long and short, as in modern French or German. The vowel *æ* (*Æ*) represents approximately the sound of *a* in English *cat*; ON *œ* (*Œ*) and *ø* (*Ø*), approximately the vowel of English *fur* or French *œuf*; ON *ö*/*ǫ* is similar to the vowel sound in English *bough*; the diphthong *ei* to the *ai* in English *stain*. Readers will pronounce other modified vowels (*å*, *ä*, *ü*, etc.) as best they can. For the sake of consistency, I retain ON spellings of place-names and personal names as they appear in the nominative case: Óðinn rather than Odin, Othin, or Othinn; spellings of OE place-names and personal names follow standard academic practice: Æthelred rather than Ethelred, Athelred, or Æðelræd; Alfred, king of Wessex, but Ælfric, abbot of Eynsham. The bibliography lists Icelandic scholars under first names.

Following current conventions, I set out *dróttkvætt* verse in short lines; OE in long; the term "a-verse" refers to the first half-line of the alliterative long line; "b-verse," to the second. I refer to skalds by name when known; in discussions of OE verse, the use of singular "poet," with or without a gendered pronoun, is shorthand for the complexities of poetic authorship. In general, punctuation, spelling, capitalization, and textual emendations of OE and ON poems follow the edition cited. Translations throughout are my own, but rest on centuries of scholarship.

MAKING AN ENTRANCE

THREE ETYMOLOGIES AND A PLAN

Walk on air against your better judgement.

—Seamus Heaney, "The Gravel Walks"

Nicholas Howe once observed that a lifetime of reading poetry in the elegiac mood—scattered ruins, lonesome roads, lost homelands—creates ears "finely attuned to the blue note."[1] Melancholia also thrives in academic areas jettisoned from the grand narratives of progress. Vikings are popular as ruffians, not as aesthetes, while students of Old English verse forever find themselves on the wrong side of the Norman Conquest. In 1897, W. P. Ker, northern enthusiast and Tory Radical, chose 1100 as the date separating the medieval from the modern.[2] René Wellek observed eighty years ago that the field of Old English lay outside the movement toward literary history that began in late seventeenth- and early eighteenth-century England.[3] *The Cambridge History of Medieval English Literature* (1999) begins in 1066 and ends in 1547. The essays in *Cultural Reformations: Medieval and Renaissance in Literary History* (2010) play nice-nice with early modern authors, not with tenth-century Benedictines. The first volume of *The Oxford English Literary History: Conquest and Transformation* (2017), covering the years 1000 to 1351, naughtily proclaims that even before the millennium, Old English poetry was in a state of decline, of premature senescence; in the face of crisis, its "belated aesthetic . . . became a fragility which could not be repaired."[4] The beat goes on. Old English verse and its northern relatives represent starts that stopped, a poetics discontinuous with what came later.

Literary expectations based on post-Renaissance traditions have rendered the ways of early northern verse foreign—its flexible temporality, startling sound effects, reticence, and cryptic allusiveness. The three chapters forming this book have a loose thematic connectedness: all seek the codes of a now-extinct verse technique; each peers intently into the northern poet's workshop, trying to identify the tools on his bench and their purpose. An early inspiration was Anne Carson, *Economy of the Unlost: Reading Simonides of Keos with Paul Celan*, her Martin Classical Lectures of 1999. The age difference between the two verse corpora—Old Norse and Old English—interacting throughout this book is less extreme. Still, anatomizing a distant poetics on the basis of the fragments that have survived is like walking into a theater halfway through the film, and leaving before the end, and what we can see on the screen is not only partial but sometimes sputters, as if poorly spliced.

The poetry surviving from pre-1066 Scandinavia and England is verse on a strict diet, determinedly light, intent on saying less than it means. Its removal of weight from things and from language brings uncertainty as well as pleasure. The passage of time has worn away the circumstantial details (dates, local habitations, influences) that literary scholars in later periods take for granted. Franco Moretti's distant reading, alert to data and aloof from stylistic analysis, has limited application to a corpus in which style alone remains as a signpost to poetic practice and community expectations.[5] Formal elements—the multiple means by which an effect is achieved, the structures that language conveys aurally and makes sense-perceptible—are inextricable from their historical context and carry with them no little sociopolitical heft.[6] Texts, even when not authorial, are still authentic.[7] In the pages that follow, I set two early alliterative corpora side by side, and listen as they slowly reveal their craft secrets, how they blend and slice and stir with panache, and how they say "no" to oblivion.[8]

A "style" was once a tool, Latin *stilus*, a slim, pointed instrument used to write on wax tablets. Subjected over the years to metonymic expansion, the word put on weight. Now it encompasses almost everything.[9] Style is form and history, the general and the particular. It is the common denominator among a group; it is the impress of an individual. It is the use of repetition to create artful patterns on cloth or canvas, wood or stone; it is an author's choice of words, syntax, punctuation, meter, expressions, gestures, and rhythm. It is how something means (Benjamin, *Art des Meinens*) as distinguished from what is meant. Style is the man; style is the mask; style is voice. It is artless, natural, fresh, grand, fancy, and worn; style has gone away. Style is loose and cramped, plain and high, early and late, decorous and rude, personal and traditional, attractive and repellent, period, generic, historical, national, and authorial. Style is Middle Minoan, Hellenistic, Gothic, mannerist, baroque, Ciceronian, Proustian, Spenserian, and Miltonic. Style is ingratiation; style is character. Adjectives larded with thick, greasy syllables front and back cluster around the term: bureaucratic, managerial, entrepreneurial, incandescent, even "vulnerably preposterous."[10] Style is the beatitude of Thelonious Monk at the piano, the scalp-tingling vocals of Billie Holiday. Style, says Italo Calvino, dissolves the apparent solidity of the world, conveying meaning "through a verbal texture that seems weightless, until the meaning itself takes on the same rarefied consistency."[11] Style, says Victor Hugo, "is the essence of a subject, constantly called to the surface."[12] Style plumbs the depths, walks the line, and soars without wings. Style has a dancing gait and refuses to be put in a corner. Style says unoriginality is nothing new. Style generates expectations.

The poetries whose etiquette is portrayed in these pages—Old Norse *dróttkvætt* 'court meter' verse and Old English alliterative poetry—form an odd couple, distinct in makeup, dress, speech, and self-presentation. *Dróttkvætt* is syllable-counting with a fixed cadence and system of internal rhymes; its stanzas are often attributed in much later manuscripts to known skalds in the service of named princes. Old English verse, run-on and attached to four basic metrical positions, prefers, with rare exceptions, anonymity. Both corpora derive from an earlier, Continental Germanic alliterative tradition, a poetics that in England enjoyed a continuous, although evolving and at times invisible existence from circa 650 to 1550 CE, and in Iceland, down to the present.[13] During the last quarter of the first millennium, both poetries flourished (and were preserved) within a patronage culture—royal and ecclesiastical courts, aristocratic chieftain and monastic establishments, sites of power whose members competed to legitimize political ambitions, curate historical memories, and acquire cultural cachet and capital. And both, like a *New Yorker* editor, imposed a distinct house style on contributors.

The manners of the two corpora—their exquisite courtesy and public relations savvy, how they say "no" nicely, their heroic indirection, the thoughts they almost hide, their stylistic ecology—reveal a family likeness, a shared frame of reference. Etiquette is social and situational: it always has an audience in mind. The Indo-European root of the word "style," **steig-*, like *stilus* itself, is associated with puncturing and pain. (Asterisks call up a single forgotten progenitor who cannot be proved to have lived but, if she had, might explain the resemblances among her multitudinous descendants.) The same root is behind learned Latin terms for "to prick, prod" (e.g., "instigate"), and stars in domestic Old Norse *steikja* 'to roast on a spit' and Old English *sticca* 'stick' and *stician* 'to stab, pierce, prick, transfix.'[14] "It isn't etiquette to cut any one you've been introduced to," the Red Queen warns Alice, who was hankering for a slice of that leg of mutton she had just curtsied to.[15] The speakers of alliterative verse talk the talk, and it is a refined, pointed, and statesmanlike idiom. Poetry tattles on society: the lines of early northern verse document mores, but also change them, remaking history in the image of poetic language. Sociologists report with dreadful solemnity that "variations in interactional style" relate to different cultural experiences.[16] Old English and Old Norse poets knew something just as important, that what is spoken without care is heard without pleasure. The pages that follow track the complexity and vivacity of an originally preliterary northern art, its gamesmanship and mannerisms, the mobility and nimbleness of its words, their pursuit of things and each other as they knit and knot under formal pressure.

Gregory the Great described the operations of scriptural exegesis as a form of intimate conversation: "For in the same way as we discern the faces of strangers and do not know their hearts, if we join with them in intimate speech, by this very use of conversation we track their thoughts."[17] The two poetries interrogated here are reluctant informants; they give little away. Yet placed side by side in a windowless room, they sometimes, inadvertently, end up tattling on one another, each serving as a surface against which the other emerges in sharper focus—the way the shape, speed, and direction of a ship out at sea become clearer if a second vessel is on the horizon. Certain stylistic aspects of the two seem to rhyme across the nautical miles separating them. When ensconced within the same frame as *dróttkvætt*, Old English verse sails into view as a more intricately designed craft than formerly perceived, one supersensitive to aural signals. So, too, *dróttkvætt* art, for all its verbal extravagance, complex rigging, and aerial leaps, when set next to Old English verse shows itself to be an efficient, practical, and capacious vessel, conveying all that is needed and more. *Dróttkvætt* stanzas accustom our ears to the syntactical patterns and aural carpentry of Old English poetry, the extra sound effects that ornament perhaps a third of its lines. In turn, the habit of indeterminacy characterizing Old English verse, its maze of crisscrossing, resonant formulas, its lack of interest in specifying externals (e.g., colors, textures, size, weight, time, place), and its "intermingling of symbol and the thing symbolized"[18] shed light on skaldic devices such as the *kenning*, a kind of periphrasis whose flickering nouns hint that the world as it seems is not the only reality, that things could have been made (and perhaps were) otherwise.[19]

In these pages, as in an epistolary novel, the two poetries take turns speaking. Chapter 1 introduces them and identifies some of their basic features and moves. These include a tendency to compose in small units (half-stanza and verse paragraph), a dedicated poetic vocabulary, a fondness for compounds, a focus on sound effects, a distinctive handling of interlace, ring, and envelope patterns, the use of vagueness as a poetic dialect, and a type of brevity that precludes explanation.[20] In each corpus, formal requirements act as a mesh or net for capturing and salvaging words, as engines for generating meaning. Chapter 2 retrieves and compares the aural patterns favored by both poetries. Chapter 3 counts the ways in which each corpus employs negative contrast, even well-bred insolence, in orienting itself toward reality and toward an audience trained in the arts of indirection and careful listening.

Each chapter differs from the others in length and approach, forming—like Caesar's Gaul—a lopsided trinity. Triadic structures rarely fail to impose a plot. Each of these three, by serendipity, embodies a reflex of the Indo-European root **(s)lei* 'slippery.' Chapter 1, with its focus on poetic carpentry, recalls Old Norse *sléttr* 'smooth, crafted, artistic,' a word used by the skald Hallfreðr circa 1000 to describe his *dróttkvætt* offering.[21] Chapter 2, devoted to the lost-in-the-mists aural games of the two poetries, evokes Latin *oblivisci* 'to slip away, wipe from the mind.' Chapter 3, probing the reticence of both corpora, summons up Greek *litotes* 'plain, simple,' a rhetorical scheme allied to modesty, courtliness, and propriety, as well as to self-interest, self-censorship, and self-celebration.[22] This Janus-face figure of speech, despite its negative reception in recent centuries,[23] had a productive and long-lasting career in the early medieval North.

A poem is a human voice and a set of formal practices; for an early medievalist, the conversation and the courtesy revealed are heard from far away. Listening to such verse is like receiving a visitor from a distant country. Where is this guest coming from? Why is his dress so outlandish, his speech so full of tongue twisters, a jabberwocky mix of the familiar and the strange?[24] His verbal restraint exudes politesse. But is it mannerly to skew syntax with such relish, to leap about like a frog? Why does he break decorum at this particular moment?[25] Why this glance back while moving forward? What fear or weakness of intellect makes him say "no" while silently nodding "yes"? Would a quick and dirty diagnosis—"thou ailest here, and here"[26]—be impolitic? Under what circumstances does this stranger reach out and pluck a perfect rhyme or discard an expected alliteration? What are his favorite words? Why does he keep repeating himself? Some questions may be too boring, personal, or direct to ask your visitor ("How old are you really?" "Where did you get your facelift done?"), but genuine curiosity and wonder, even about apparent defects, tend to be rewarded. The relationship between reader and text is that of distant pen pals who may never fully reach each other's shores, but who nevertheless grow in each other's company.

Fields are conservative, and the tides of continuity run deep. Periodicity varies according to national traditions. In Icelandic scholarship, the term "medieval" is not normally used for tenth- and eleventh-century skaldic verse; "viking-age" is the adjective preferred by many (but shunned by some) for pre-1100 *dróttkvætt* compositions. We treat disciplines as we do landscape, subdividing the terrain available into plots suitable for individual or team cultivation, leaving the crags and sinkholes alone. (Pre–Norman Conquest alliterative poetry is a small, much trampled on cabbage patch.) Ideas get codified and tend to stay that way, even when the discipline itself has moved on. Tradition has us print Old English verse as long lines; skaldic, as short.[27] Yet both were written out across the manuscript page, largely unformatted, with no ragged right-hand margins.

The pigeonholing of early alliterative poems into types is fraught. Genres of one tradition do not map easily onto those of another. Still, we follow in the tracks of predecessors, reluctant to abandon established distinctions, even when we recognize them as outworn cultural artifacts.[28] We sort poems chiefly by subject matter, each item categorized as scriptural, heroic, elegiac, lyric, commemorative, eulogistic, ekphrastic, liturgical, genealogical, epic, hagiographical, allegorical, didactic, aphoristic, gnomic, or proverbial, with charms hovering mysteriously in the distance—not a native vernacular term among them; only the riddle (OE *rædels*), a thriving Anglo-Latin wisdom genre, is flavored local. Individual works get titles according to whether their subject is living or dead, animate or inanimate, divine or mortal, whether the speaker is female or male, whether the site or individual featured has a name, or, in Old Norse, whether the work has a surviving refrain. Tradition quickly becomes evidence: familiar interpretive frames ease access, bring the foreign home, and assimilate difference. Stasis, fixity, stillness, binding, and order are calming; their opposites—loosening, motion, arbitrariness, chaos, surprise, flux, life—shake things up. In *A Night in Casablanca*, Groucho Marx as hotel manager decides to change the numbers on all guestroom doors. "Think of the confusion," his bosses gasp. "Yes, but think of the fun," Groucho responds.[29]

OPENING DOORS

Are we a pair?

—Stephen Sondheim, *A Little Night Music* (1973)

Viewing a painted canvas calls for understanding something of the formal conventions of the period, the specific choices made by artists, their techniques of brushwork and of mixing pigments. E. H. Gombrich, when he wanted to learn how Constable's *Wivenhoe Park* created its illusion of reality, placed a grid upon the painting and then looked at each little square, deliberately thwarting the integrating tricks of the human eye.[30] Morphological evidence—a characteristic brushstroke, a distinctive rendering of a wrist, or a paint smudge on an angel's wing—lets a curator infer that this or that canvas is a Rembrandt or a copy. Paleographers are able to attribute artifacts to particular hands, moments, and places on the basis of personal, period, or scriptorium style. Classical archaeologists confidently assign their pots to particular workshops and artisans. But the words, half-lines, and shapes of early northern poetry refuse to be neatly pinned down. Three centuries of scholarship have catalogued and classified almost every last verse, but nearly all context for this poetry—the literary/historical equivalent of tree rings, chemical variations in pigments, grave-deposits with coins—has been lost. Only a few short Old English poems are securely datable to before the Viking Age; the tenth- and eleventh-century manuscripts containing most of the remaining verse rarely attribute pieces to specific authors.[31] The authenticity and localization of Old Norse verse are only slightly more secure.[32] Much of the formal court poetry likely goes back to the time it tells of and represents at some distance an original oral performance, but we cannot determine what, if anything, suffered a sea change during centuries of textual transmission. "Probably," "possibly," "perhaps": little about these corpora is not hedged with uncertainty.

Old English alliterative and Old Norse *dróttkvætt* verse were going concerns for more than five centuries—a span longer than that of the Roman Empire and about half that of all succeeding periods of English poetry combined. The 30,000 extant lines of Old English poetry are largely anonymous: individual works are reticent about revealing age, place of birth, title, or gestational traumas. (More data might have meant fewer dates.) Most survive in a single medieval copy and sometimes not even that.[33] Nine manuscripts contain 90 percent of the Old English poetic corpus, a thin margin of survival. Approximately 1,500 *dróttkvætt* 'court meter,' stanzas have emerged from the Viking Age. This poetry steps onto the world stage in late ninth-century Norway and maintains star status in Iceland into the fourteenth; its stanzas are strewn, largely in the form of singlets, over scores of prose texts preserved in more than 500 Icelandic vellums from the late twelfth to the fifteenth century. In medieval Iceland, as in Heian Japan (794–1185), the centrality of poetry in society seems a given—status could be demonstrated by how much poetry one knew by heart. Both Norway's Theodoricus Monachus and Denmark's Saxo Grammaticus confirm that by the end of the twelfth century, Icelanders had a reputation in Scandinavia for the depth and breadth of their historical knowledge, encapsulated in their verse.[34] But the fragmentary *dróttkvætt* compositions that have managed to cross the sea of centuries are but the tips of icebergs that calved long ago. We cannot assume that the extant poetry of either corpus is representative of what once existed (just as we can never know the percentage of undiscovered murders).

The social worlds that produced the two poetries remain mysterious. No matter how delicately we approach these topics, inquiries concerning orality, performance, literary indebtedness, schools, genres, patronage, textualization, or court politics receive few intelligible answers. Divergent styles coexist in the same time and place: contemporaries do things in different ways, whether out of orneriness, absentmindedness, genetic determination, or early bonding with a particular person or parakeet. Attempts to sort out viking-age English and Scandinavian literary relations can end up sounding like Shakespeare's Fluellen: "There is a river in Macedon and there is also moreover a river in Monmouth, . . . and there is salmons in both" (*Henry V*, 4.7.25–31). Sometimes literary influence is so subtle as to be invisible. A. E. Housman's English poems in *A Shropshire Lad* reveal no obvious carryover from the Latin verse he spent his life editing. Other writers are great copiers, if not plagiarists, reminiscent of humpback whales who apparently follow the latest singing styles like fashionistas. These whales spend their summers feeding in cold, high-latitude areas; in winter, they return to the exact spot in the tropics where they were born, supposedly bringing with them the traditional songs of that particular breeding ground. But on the way there, or so recent research indicates, some pods stop at an island hangout and mix it up, incorporating into their native repertoire tunes sung by other whales traversing the same sea roads, a way perhaps to improve their courtship chances, like British pop stars putting on American accents when recording.[35] Viking-age skalds, English churchmen, early northern mercenaries, traders, and artisans of all persuasions were travelers too, people in motion who left behind a past life and those who knew them, and who were transformed by the journey. The earliest known inscription of Old Norse in the Roman alphabet comes not from a Norwegian harbor town but from northern England: a penny struck in the reign of Olaf Guthfrithson (939–40), Scandinavian king of York.[36] For both verse corpora, the trajectories of poetic composition, performance, recording, circulation, and loss are largely irrecoverable.

Forty years ago, R. I. Page, reviewing a volume of essays on the Viking Age, reported: "On the whole, the literary efforts linking Old

English with Old Norse literature . . . are the least impressive. The tools they use are too blunt to attack the problems of a pair of literatures surviving in random sample and with a complete absence of chronology."[37] Archaeological information has continued to pile up, revealing that individuals in any one region of northern Europe at any one time thought about and did things in a variety of ways.[38] Studies of textile production and leather- and bone-working in early medieval York show native English craftsmen adopting Scandinavian techniques and styles while retaining traditional elements of their own.[39] The metalwork in parts of ninth- and tenth-century England reflect a creative and ongoing fusion of Scandinavian and English artistic tastes.[40] Hybrid sculptural monuments, such as the Gosforth cross in Cumbria with its "pagan" iconography, suggest a similar assimilation. By the tenth century, the meaning of an Old English noun might be influenced by that of its Norse cognate (e.g., OE *eorl* 'man,' ON *jarl* 'a Danish under-king'); a Norse verb might similarly acquire the special sense of its Old English cognate (e.g., ON *meta* 'to estimate, value,' OE *metan* 'to traverse [a path]').[41] So, too, the increased use of extra rhyme and extra alliteration in both poetries during this period and their apparent shared delight in litotes and downtoners suggest that aspects of literary style might also be contagious.[42]

These and other features of verbal decorum and patterning remained deeply imbedded in the two verse forms. Both corpora are chips off the Old Germanic block; both were subjected over the centuries to counterflows, minglings, fusions, intertwinings, seesawings, Indra's nets, interpenetrations, and feedback loops. Local traditions, trade routes, diplomatic embassies, raids, intermarriage, and cross-cultural quotation within a vibrant North Sea setting all played a role in defining their similarities.[43] Over the centuries, each absorbed influences from culturally dominant centers with their own multiple and interacting literary systems.[44] So, too, the hip-hop movement that in the 1970s coalesced in the South Bronx and quickly spread around the world seeded so many variants that some historians of music no longer speak of a single hip-hop culture but of separate schools or dialects of hip-hop with distinctive regional forms. Tracing such vertiginous to-ings and fro-ings is difficult in the case of modern printed texts, many of which are now written and circulated online long before their publication date; some, locally ignored, end up exerting influence far from their time and place of composition. Not surprisingly, the meanderings and far-flung networks of viking-age oral genres are largely hidden from view. The one certainty is that the geographical and cultural range of *dróttkvætt* poetry was broader than its current preservation in Icelandic manuscripts indicates.

Cicero tells us what really counts when addressing an audience: delivery, delivery, delivery.[45] Intonation matters, as every actor knows. The speech rhythms and gestures of those who performed early northern verse are now irrecoverable, along with audience reaction, which must have varied considerably depending on who was listening. What information we have about recitation tends to come from unimpressed outsiders, such as the merchant from Moorish-ruled Tortosa who visited Danish Schleswig around 962 and compared the evening entertainment to the barking of dogs.[46] (Recordings of their own verse by William Butler Yeats, Ezra Pound, David Jones, and Édouard Glissant—in a high-pitched key, with stretched-out vowels and final falling cadence—can also alarm.) As for the poet in society, confident statements about him are everywhere, hopeful speculations hallowed by repetition. Ask "who dunnit" and the answers might include a farmhand suffering from singer's block, a seer maintaining a direct line to Óðinn, a prophetess wearing gloves of white catskin, a minstrel in rags and tatters, a wanderer on the whale's mean streets, a silver-tongued advertiser, an outlaw, bishop, priest, cantor, lawman, diplomat, trader, or scribe, or a lady with a mead cup chanting while weaving a shroud.[47] (Not exactly the Algonquin Round Table.) Blurred outlines elicit from interpreters a series of revealing self-portraits: "ogni dipintore dipinge se" (every painter paints himself), concluded Leonardo. As in a murder mystery, a lack of information excites interest and sets the imagination in motion. We become speculative archaeologists, devising precarious reconstructions on the basis of chance remains, forced to use the language of the present to describe the past.

The nineteenth century investigated the constraints of alliterative verse and the work continues. But not even the *terra firma* of meter feels all that solid these days: its cracked stepping stones, much patched and repaired, seem at times *skandala*, 'stumbling blocks'; the workings of "resolution" still fuel debate.[48] We struggle to understand why undisplaced poetic finite verbs frequently alliterate in Old English poetry while nonpoetic finite verbs in that position rarely do,[49] or why in *drótt-kvætt* resolution is avoided after the onset of a line and forbidden in the cadence.[50] The accentuation of words within the alliterative line remains controversial, along with much else.[51] The prosodic rules of the two corpora are various, poorly attested, and in part beyond resuscitation; their styles, elliptical and compressed, bound up with unknown social settings. We are ignorant of how northern poets learned their art, or what they thought good or bad.[52] Intertextual quotation and subtle appropriation in the verse of both traditions suggest strong awareness of the work of competitors.[53] We possess no early local guide to versification or poetic vocabulary, no preconquest Emily Post or Millicent Fenwick to report that "costly" may describe a battle but not a fur coat. Poets may or may not have been conscious of contemporary visual art, of the designs wrought by local metalworkers, manuscript illustrators, carvers, and embroiderers.[54] One twelfth-century *clavis metrica* from Orkney and four Old Icelandic treatises composed between 1150 and 1350, the heroic age of the Latin *ars poetica* in England and on the Continent, gave the study of *dróttkvætt* an academic head start over that of other European vernaculars, and provided modern scholarship on alliterative verse with most of its terminology and principles of analysis and interpretation.[55] But their authors' outlook and tastes, based on a mixture of learned grammatical and native poetics, take much for granted and get some things wrong.[56] We grope in the dark for a light switch.

Dróttkvætt probably began life as a stylized form of Old Norse *fornyrðislag* 'old-story meter' with internal rhyme.[57] Farmers in the flat expanses of Lincolnshire and East Anglia and fishermen in the Norwegian settlements of northwest England may have known poems in this latter "eddic" meter, a relative of the Old English alliterative long line.[58] Old Norse verse persisted for centuries in the northern isles of Orkney and Shetland, politically Scandinavian until 1468–69. At various times during the Viking Age, Icelandic poets visited, resided, and performed in the British Isles; *dróttkvætt* stanzas attributed to a half-dozen skalds praise tenth- and eleventh-century English rulers such as Æthelstan, Æthelred, and Cnut, along with Earl Þorfinnr of Orkney (d. 1064), reared in Scotland.[59] The Norwegian missionary kings had the financial and political support of English royalty and clergy; the same Icelandic skalds eulogized rulers in both nations.[60] By the tenth and early eleventh centuries, five hundred years after groups of Angles, Saxons, and others arrived in England speaking a language barely differentiated from Old Norse,[61] a new North Sea culture zone had reemerged. The so-called Viking Age was a second site of extensive English/Scandinavian contact, with both lay and clerical involvement in patronage.

It is now generally accepted that Old Norse and Old English were to some degree mutually intelligible tongues in late Anglo-Saxon England, even if the precise extent remains controversial. Contemporary references to the Norse language in England survive, in both Anglo-Latin (e.g., Æthelweard's *Chronicle*), and Old English (e.g., Ælfric's homily *De falsis diis*, subsequently reworked by Wulfstan).[62] The twelfth-century Icelandic author of the *First Grammatical Treatise* noted with reference to England that "we are of the same tongue, although one of them has changed greatly or both somewhat."[63] A passage in *Gunnlaugs saga*, perhaps composed in the late thirteenth century, famously if credulously posited that in the late tenth and early eleventh centuries "the language in England was the same as that spoken in Norway and Denmark."[64] Old English loanwords occur in *dróttkvætt* verse from the Viking Age;[65] Norse borrowings into English prose occur during the same period, notably in works by Wulfstan, archbishop of York (1002–23).[66] A. H. Smith was neither the first nor the last to propose that viking-age England possessed a *lingua franca*, a dialect he called Anglo-Scandinavian.[67] Seventeenth-century English and Danish scholars seem to have assumed easy verbal communication between natives and newcomers. The skalds were hailed as a particularly poetic tribe, despite their habit of drinking from skulls, and chanting the same set pieces over and over again;[68] a rumor quickly spread that vikings had inflicted rhyme on the English along with blood-eagling.[69] A print-saturated eighteenth century, obsessed with oral poetry, regularly elided Saxon poet and Norse skald, calling them "brethren": what was true for one was true for the other.[70] Early historical poetics, as Richard Morris has said of early medieval archaeology, was part hard-core analysis and part Gothic romance.[71]

Three Thomases (Percy, Warton, and Gray), along with Walter Scott and George Ellis, insisted upon the cross-fertilization of Norse and Anglo-Saxon bardic cultures;[72] the first two introduced the term "alliterative" into English historical poetics.[73] George Hickes had earlier written about the kinship of the two literatures and compared their alliteration, semirhymes, poetic words, kennings, and variation techniques; he proposed that this verse had been brought to England by the Danes.[74] His association of one Old English poetic style ("Dano-Saxonica") with the northern Angles and another ("Norman Saxon" or "Semi-Saxonica") with southern England was much repeated at the time.[75] A century later, the historian and anti-Jewish polemicist Christian Friedrich Rühs went so far in the other direction as to declare that Old Norse poetry had originated in Iceland in imitation of Old English verse.[76] Sir Walter Scott's *Ivanhoe* (1820) neatly elided Scandinavians and Anglo-Saxons by giving the name Beowulph to the father of the English swineherd Gurth.[77] The Conybeare brothers' introduction to *Illustrations of Anglo-Saxon Poetry* (1826) spoke of "the systematic use of alliteration" in northern verse, and compared its employment in the two corpora.[78] The Icelander Grímur Jónsson Thorkelin's conclusion that *Beowulf* was pure Danish—composed in Old Norse before being brought over to England—found favor in Denmark, if not across the North Sea.[79] Thomas Wright, in a short essay on Old English verse, noted formulaic correspondences between the two poetries.[80] Early nineteenth-century Icelandic scholars such as Þorleifur Guðmundsson Repp and Eiríkur Magnússon, both long resident in Britain, promoted medieval literary and linguistic ties between England and Iceland as a way of challenging Danish authority over their native land.[81] Later, in a Denmark nervous about the German states to the south, Frederik Hammerich confirmed his country's close literary relations with early England; Frederick Metcalfe in England soon rejoiced over the same filiations.[82] Between the two World Wars, in step with William Craigie, R. W. Chambers observed that "the earliest Scandinavian poetry we possess, or of which we can get information, differs absolutely from *Beowulf*, in style, metre, and sentiment."[83] This poem was English to its core. Political preoccupations and philological activity partnered then as now.

Taste is a notoriously fickle guide to the verse of former days. From the seventeenth century on, writers and readers returned again and again to the old texts, only to find that they repelled as much as enchanted.[84] Henry of Huntingdon in the course of translating *The Battle of Brunanburh* noted the "strange words and figures of speech" of that poem.[85] Milton famously characterized the style of the same Old English ode as "over-charg'd."[86] Joseph Bosworth in 1823 called Old English verse and its makers "rude" and warned his readers against mistaking the extant texts for "those delightful beauties which we call poetry."[87] Sharon Turner's much reprinted *History* described Old English poetry as "the rude exclamation of a rude people, with a rude language."[88] Hippolyte Taine found *Beowulf* rude.[89] A century and a half later, Philip Larkin labeled the same corpus "ape's bum-fodder."[90] (Now that was rude.) W. P. Ker described *Genesis* as "mere flat commonplace, interesting as giving the average literary taste and the commonplace poetical stock of a dull educated man."[91] Among the adjectives thrown at *Andreas* in living memory are "tasteless and inapposite," "ludicrous," "clumsy," "bizarre," "incongruous," and "lacking in invention."[92] A few Old English poems and most *dróttkvætt* compositions are, like certain people, magnets for abuse.[93] The philologist Anatoly Liberman scolds the skalds for trivializing "the information poetry had conveyed from time immemorial . . ., for speaking banalities tied to the current moment."[94] Thomas Love Peacock, friend of Shelley, had condemned *dróttkvætt* as "mere trash . . . little more than a rhapsody of rejoicing in carnage, a ringing of changes on the biting sword and the flowing of blood and the feast of the raven and the vulture, and fulsome flattery of the chieftain, of whom the said skald was the abject slave, vassal, parasite and laureate, interspersed with continual hints that he ought to be well paid for his lying panegyrics."[95] W. P. Ker noted drily that "the nature of the two forms of poetry is revealed in their respective manners of going wrong."[96]

Others responded more sympathetically to northern sounds and to formal techniques that seemed at once unfamiliar yet at home in English. Gerard Manley Hopkins declared the alliterative line "a vastly superior thing to what we have now."[97] He slipped a *dróttkvætt* imitation composed by George Marsh into his *Journal*.[98] W. H. Auden recalled his introduction to Old English at Oxford: "I was spellbound. This poetry, I knew, was going to be my dish."[99] He slipped a *dróttkvætt* imitation of his own into *The Age of Anxiety*.[100] J. R. R. Tolkien inserted three of his into his personal copy of *Heimskringla*.[101] Jorge Luis Borges excitedly instructed his translator: "Simplify me. Modify me. Make me stark. . . . I love Anglo-Saxon. I want the wiry, minimal sound. I want monosyllables. I want the power of Cynewulf, Beowulf, Bede. Make me macho and gaucho and skinny."[102] The supreme fiction that the Old

English language was preponderantly monosyllabic can be traced at least as far back as George Puttenham's *The Arte of English Poesie* (1589).[103]

Writing a book is like designing and constructing a dwelling, an edifice with a largely preordained shape and design. A foundation is laid and roof beams raised, strong enough to support an ornamental pinnacle or two. The author maps out a wide entrance way and at least three display galleries, connected to one another by irregular, twisting passageways. Small rooms not part of the original house showcase interactive spaces that urge visitors to "Please Touch." In subchambers beneath the structure, a brood of notes, some misbehaving, huddles for warmth. The writer, her work finished, departs by the back door, exiled forever from the premises. She leaves behind a poetry whose human noise and odd reticence compete in inviting hearers to break and enter the past.[104]

CHAPTER 1

Rules of the Game

The past is a foreign country; they do things differently there.
—L. P. Hartley, *The Go-Between*

WHAT WE TALK ABOUT WHEN WE TALK ABOUT STYLE

Comparing poetries is a little like marriage: you begin by stressing mutual affinities and end up accentuating differences. As in lawful wedlock, the relationship between Old English and *dróttkvætt* verse encompasses stylistic mirroring and variation on multiple levels, a family resemblance reinforced by several periods of proximity and intercourse.[1] The two vernacular poetries connected, even if it was an on-again, off-again affair. Like many couples, they developed horizontal intimacies outside the immediate family. The Old English verse that has come down to us took shape within a culture of literacy; for some poems, a long-lasting attachment to Latin predecessors was an open secret.[2] The postpositioning of prepositions hints at an acquaintance with the ways of Latin verse.[3] The earliest *dróttkvætt* stanzas were not immune to the charms of Carolingian poetic ekphrasis and other courtly literary forms.[4] Both vernacular corpora weathered various forms of inequality; a range of economical, ideological, geographical, and cultural disparities all left a mark. Still, despite their distinct public personalities, the list of compatibilities confirming Old English verse and viking-age *dróttkvætt* as a viable pair is long.[5]

Dróttkvætt verse presents itself as lean, tight, neat, and close-mouthed; Old English, as run-on, messy, and expansive. The former is notably abstruse, devious, and unnatural, committed to maximizing gain at minimal cost and energy; the latter, warm, repetitive, and seemingly open. Handbooks teach that *dróttkvætt* verse is recondite, occasional, subjective, arrogant, formal, convoluted, esoteric, self-conscious, self-seeking, elitist, and situation-bound, that Old English poetry is uncomplicated, narrative, objective, leisurely, expansive, and dignified, concerned with religious/heroic tradition and wisdom.[6] One member of this couple underpays; the other overtips. Nevertheless, they manage to get along and to demonstrate good manners in the other's presence, a familial code of etiquette based on the tenet "if you can't be kind, at least be vague." Frankness, relevancy, logical fullness, staid clarity, a desire to be informative: the modern conversational principles set out by Grice are rarely in sight.[7] Meaning in both poetries is cunningly camouflaged, half-hidden within a flow of compliments, negations, weasel words, and stray observations. In each, dignity, emotional minimalism, restraint, civility, even stealthy one-upmanship take precedence over the communication of facts. Urbane detachment and politeness rule.

From a distance, the underlying architecture of the two bear a resemblance, the deep framework alluded to by the twelfth-century Chinese writer Jiang Teli, whose poem on how to do plum blossoms advised: "Painting plum blossoms is like judging a horse. You go by bone structure, not by appearance."[8] In northern verse, these limbs are often artfully scattered. The disjointedness of the *dróttkvætt* stanza is notorious: within each quatrain, clauses are segmented and placed discontinuously, the sense dispersed over four lines. Old English half-lines do not undergo such drastic dismemberment, but they, too, are mobile; parenthetical clauses, syntactic retroversions, and other unnatural behavior abound. Fifty years ago, T. A. Shippey pointed out that, although subordinate clauses beginning with "when," "since," and "after" are free to come before or after a main clause, in *Beowulf* such clauses almost invariably come second; the fact or emotion comes first, the explanation, cause, or time indication trails behind.[9] The surviving stanzas of the first extant Old Norse praise-poem in regular *dróttkvætt*, Þorbjǫrn hornklofi's *Glymdrápa* 'Resounding-*drápa*' (ca. 890), consistently and similarly subordinates the second half-stanza syntactically to the first, using conjunctions such as "before" or "when"

(*SkP* 1.1:73–91). The cumulative effect of this stylistic habit—"they rejoiced . . . until"—seems meaningful. Nothing in life is certain until the last word is in.

The pair sometimes even lurch alike. The two poetries share a distinctive gait, one marked by twists and turns and startling irregularities of pace, their progress impeded by gaps, ruptures, and stops, by "violent and abrupt transitions."[10] George Ellis commented on the "almost unlimited power of inversion" that Old English poets employed, "a universal characteristic of savage poetry."[11] Some particularly acrobatic half-lines look in two directions at once.[12] Scholars in Germany early bemoaned this poetry's disconcerting *Sprünge* 'leaps,'[13] its *Sprunghaftigkeit* 'erratic jumps,'[14] and *Stilwirrwarr* 'stylistic mishmash.'[15] In 1875, Richard Heinzel noted a "restless energy and submerging of ideas."[16] In 1885, Frances B. Gummere described the jumpiness of Old English poetry: "There is an eternal leaping back and forth, but there is very little actual advance."[17] The avoidance of linear causality in *Beowulf*—its teasing flash-forwards and strategic withdrawals— is advertised in the section of Friedrich Klaeber's edition headed "Lack of Steady Advance."[18] In 1871, Lewis Carroll had introduced an Anglo-Saxon messenger whose odd way of progressing down a path—forward, twist, pause, wriggle, leap—drew Alice's attention.[19] Arthur Brodeur conscientiously revealed the presence of "an unpleasing jerkiness of pace."[20] Michael Alexander observed that "the sense often seems to dance as it advances. A sentence of any length can unfold by taking two steps forward and one step back . . . a minuet-like movement."[21] As one reader observed: "This is not a narrative style for the impatient."[22] Richard Lanham has called this type of sentence syntax "the running style," a choice that "imitates the mind in a real-time interaction with the world . . . as it lurches from crisis to crisis, first tripping over one argument, then bumping into another, unbalanced and unsymmetrical," a mind making the best of things in the moment,[23] a poetics with a turbulence warning stamped on its boarding pass.

On rare occasions the two poetries seem to be impersonating one another, making use of similar verbal fillers and idioms, the same rare words, compounds, and kennings, and displaying identical metrical quirks.[24] Each publicly and frequently indulges in onomastic play.[25] Both dress to be noticed, their glinting ornaments catching the light: here, a hint of golden moss under a firedrake, there, a burning hall or pyre, and, just beyond, mysterious underwater gleams.[26] Individuals in both corpora stride, sit, or speak "under helmet."[27] The noun *mæl* 'time' behaves rather oddly (that is, like an adverb) in each.[28] The compound *garræs* 'spear-onslaught' (*Mald* 32) occurs once in Old English, in a viking messenger's taunting speech; the single attestation of Norse *geirrás* 'spear-onslaught' occurs in Einarr skálaglamm Helgason's *Vellekla* (27/4; *SkP* 1.1:317), a eulogy composed for the powerful ruler of northern Norway around the same time as the Essex battle. Words for some military actions may have been time-sensitive.

In a poem from the 1020s, the skald Óttarr svarti refers to the ancestors of the Norwegian king Óláfr Haraldsson (ruled ca. 1015–30) using the *hapax legomenon þjóðskjǫldungar* 'great-kings' (*Hfl* 20/2; *SkP* 1.2:766); an identical compound, *Þeod-Scyldingas*, occurs in *Beowulf* 1019a, and nowhere else in Old English.[29] Shared origins in Germanic can be assumed for the parallel poetic compounds ON *þjóðkonungr* and OE *þeodcyning* 'king of a people, king (over wide dominions)'; common ancestry need not, however, exclude later cultural reinforcement.[30] The Old Norse epithet occurs in purportedly early eddic and *dróttkvætt* verse, but was used with special vigor by court poets composing in the first half of the eleventh century, skalds such as Sigvatr, Þórarinn loftunga, Þormóðr Kolbrúnarskáld, and Arnórr Þórðarson;[31] the Old English compound occurs fifteen times in poetry (eight of these in *Beowulf*), and twice in (poetic) prose. Words come in and out of fashion. The apparent popularity of *þjóðkonungr* during the reigns of Óláfr Haraldsson, Cnut the Great, and Magnús the Good may have had something to do with changing attitudes toward rulership and with the intimacy of Norse–English geopolitical relations during that period.[32]

The occasional syntactic parallels puzzle. When Sigvatr praises around 1027 a hero who terrifies jarls (Sigv *Erlfl* 9/3; *SkP* 1.2:640), he uses the transitive weak verb *ægja* 'to terrify' with an understood but unstated object ("them"). When the *Beowulf* poet describes Scyld's rule-by-terror over neighboring tribes, he employs the related transitive weak verb *egsian* 'to terrify,' again without a stated direct object: *egsode eorl* 'the hero terrified [them]' (*Beo* 6a).[33] In a subsequent half-line, *lange ahte* '[he] long possessed, had' (*Beo* 31b)—with presumed reference to a kingdom or nation—the verb again seems to lack a direct object. Sigvatr's short sentence *víkingar ǫ́ttu* 'the vikings possessed'—with understood reference to a destroyed building—appears to be a similar kind of ellipsis (Sigv *Víkv* 10/6; *SkP* 1.2:549).[34] There are likenesses in imagery too. When the poet of the Old English *Andreas* envisages waves as hills, hills as heads, a storm as an assault by armed warriors, and a flood as an after-hours mead party, he seems to be echoing familiar *dróttkvætt* conceits or kennings.[35] Sometimes the two corpora flirt openly, as when the Old English poet of *Exodus* calls God's shielding pillar of cloud a net, board, cloud, sail, and tent in rapid succession (71–85), standard base words in Old Norse shield-kennings.[36] Nordicisms have been located not only in the viking messenger's speech in *The Battle of Maldon*,[37] but also in the description of raven ("chooser of the slain") and eagle ("grey plumaged, white-tailed war-hawk") in *Exodus* and *The Battle of Brunanburh*.[38] Still, proof remains elusive: one reader's skaldic shorthand is another's synesthesia.[39] Chronology, too, is often a mug's game. One scholar argues for the influence of the Old Norse *Bjarkamál* on the Old English *Maldon* while another drags the former poem, kicking and screaming, into the twelfth century.[40]

We probe with wonder the fact that the first skald whose verse survives may have had British relatives, and that lines 108–10 of *The Wanderer* are echoed around 966 by Eyvindr skáldaspillir, the last Norwegian skald—"cattle die, kinsmen die, land and realm are emptied" (*Hák* 21; *SkP* 1.1:193)—and recall *Hávamál* 76–77.[41] The material culture of the two poetries—their cups, swords, shields, boar-helmets, halls, and historical backdrops—bears, unsurprisingly, a family resemblance.[42] The *hringiren* 'ring-irons, mail shirts' singing in *Beowulf* 322b have a non-identical twin in a praise-poem by the skald Óttarr svarti (ca. 1020–25): *járnhringar* 'iron-rings, mail shirts' (*Hfl* 8/8; *SkP* 1.2:750). Semantic looseness means that in both corpora "different beverages [e.g., ale, wine, mead, beer] are spoken of indiscriminately."[43] So much is missing from the record, so blurred are the details we can retrieve, that almost any argument for a literary connection, whether the link put forward is specific or vague, lateral or vertical, is challengeable. One scholar proposes, another disposes. This, as Árni Magnússon long ago observed, keeps everyone busy.[44]

A GUIDE TO EXCRUCIATINGLY CORRECT BEHAVIOR

Here is a verbal contraption. How does it work?

—W. H. Auden, "The Dyer's Hand"

The *explications de texte* in this section trace the formal conventions of alliterative poetry over a half millennium and more, stressing the stability within constant change. These analyses, like prescription drugs, come with a warning: each extract differs from the others in its own way, responding to wrinkles in society and to popular modes that we know little or nothing about. Style itself is subject to swift shifts, spasmodic meltdowns, reflecting changes in politics, personal circumstances, or medium. It steps up and slides back in quick time. In 1929, Charley Patton, epic artist of the Delta blues, recorded his first sides, one looking back to life after the Civil War, the other to the great flood of 1927. In 1954, just twenty-five years later, young Elvis Presley from Tupelo, Mississippi, launched his career with "That's All Right."[45] Like today's rappers, the alliterative poets of the North constructed new verses and new rhymes on the rhythmic foundations of their predecessors, the original context sometimes serving as a shadow or second meaning.[46] "Art is long," noted Henry Wadsworth Longfellow, picking up and running with a tag current in the middle of the first millennium BCE.[47]

Three centuries of study of alliterative poetry inform our current understanding of metrical practice in Old English, Old Norse, Old Saxon, and Old High German, a verse technique rooted in the tradition of early Germanic oral poetry. Each line consists of two parts, or half-lines, linked together by alliteration (a repetition of the same sound at the beginning of two or more stressed syllables) and divided by a metrical caesura. A consonant alliterates only with itself (for example, an *f* with an *f*; an *r* with an *r*); each of the consonant clusters *sc-*, *sp-*, *st-* alliterates only with itself (modern Icelandic versification refers to this trio as *gnýstuðlar* 'rumbling staves'),[48] while all vowels (including diphthongs) promiscuously alliterate with all other vowels. The number and position of the alliterating syllables are established by rule: no more than two alliterating syllables in the a-verse (in *dróttkvætt*, the odd-numbered line), and only one in the b-verse (in *dróttkvætt*, the even-numbered line), or so we tell our students. Each half-line in standard Germanic alliterative verse has four metrical positions, as illustrated in the runic inscription below.

Proto-Scandinavian and Early Viking-Age Verse

Around the first half of the fifth century, a carver incised a metrical line on a drinking horn constructed of two layers of gold sheet; the horn emerged from the soil a millennium later in Gallehus, a village in what is now southwest Jutland, just north of the Danish-German frontier. In the mid-nineteenth century, with the clash of Germany and Denmark over Schleswig, the linguistic provenance of the inscription became a political hot potato.[49] The runic inscription, copied before the horn was stolen and melted down in 1802, recorded the signature of the donor or designer in the form of an alliterative long line.[50] The number of nonmanuscript inscribed verses from Anglo-Saxon England (most from the north of the country, and not all in runes) currently stands at eighteen.[51] The Gallehus verse is the earliest of about 150 known metrical runic inscriptions from Scandinavia:[52]

> Ek HlewagastiR Holtijar   horna tawido.
>
> ---
>
> I, **H**lewagastiR son of **H**oltiR,   **h**orn made.

Longfellow influentially compared the sound of northern poetry to the crashing of weapons: "The very meter is rough . . . the verses fall like sword-strokes in the thick of battle. . . . The short emphatic lines . . . ring like blows of hammers on an anvil."[53] (Michael Alexander put it succinctly: "bang, bang, bang . . . crash.")[54] So, too, Walter W. Skeat: "Our older poems remind one of the ringing of hammer-blows on an anvil."[55] The image of Germanic verse "raining its blows on the same spot," "cadenced by the crashing blows of sword and axe,"[56] popular in the same decades as the metrical studies of Eduard Sievers, has been repeated many times since.[57] Such language helps to primitivize Germanic alliterative verse, attributing to it the beat of drum-language, the metronomic pulse of rap. This accentual paradigm, the "thumps" of syllables careening into other syllables, seems slowly to be giving way to a different view of the metrical organization of early northern verse, a morphological one underlying the "stress peaks."[58] The prosodic structure of this poetry seems composed of multiple embodied acts of attention.

The two half-lines of the Gallehus inscription, separated by a caesura, are bound together by alliteration on the three stressed lexical items beginning with *h*, the formal structure of the Germanic long line. Triplets are a known device in the rhetorical arsenal, from Caesar's "veni, vidi, vici" to the toy advertisement "Gotta Getta Gund," the third item signaling completion. (Compare "Safe, small, Scottish," the slogan devised by the University of St. Andrews on the heels of COVID-19.)[59] "Down-step" or "down-drift," the descending torque or slope of the long line, similarly structures genealogical listings such as *Heorogar ond Hroðgar ond Halga til* 'Heorogar and Hroðgar and Halga the good' (*Beo* 61). Alliteration is frequent in languages in which stress is on the first syllable of a word, as in the Germanic, Finno-Ugric, and Mongolian families. In the Gallehus runic line, alliteration falls on the initial stressed syllables of words of high semantic content, here the two names in the first half-line (or a-verse) and on the stressed syllable of the noun opening the second half-line (or b-verse).[60] Double alliteration in the a-verse occurs in about half of Old English a-verses and all *dróttkvætt* odd-line verses. The Gallehus carver placed no word divider (four vertical dots) between the proclitic *ek* and the initial stressed syllable. In northern poetry, the first half of the long line tends to have more prosodic and metrical freedom than the second half. Cognitive psychology research reports that "first letter" cues are at least as effective as rhyme in aiding recall,[61] which helps to explain why words or meanings that have otherwise disappeared from a language live on within alliterative formulas such as "neither kith nor kin" and "time and tide."

The different prosodic weights of the two half-lines in the Gallehus inscription foreshadow the metrical asymmetry of Old English and Old Norse alliterative verse whose two halves are more often rhythmically contrasted than identical, creating an effect "more like masonry than music," "more like Coltrane than Chopin."[62] The Gallehus poet's relegation of the verb to final (nonalliterating) position, after the object it governs, is a pattern frequent in early northern poetry, in which the last word reverberates, briefly, in its solitude.[63] In *dróttkvætt*, the typical inclination of each verse is toward a descent, the trochaic beat of the last two syllables signaling a sinking, a falling. To ears accustomed to Chaucer's European verse—end-rhymed, with predictable metrical patterns and colloquial or educated diction—the alliterative line sounds guttural, harsh and irregular, like surf beating upon hollow rocks.

Four centuries later, a mourning father arranged for up to 750 runes and other characters to be incised on a massive 5.5-ton granite stone in south-central Sweden, its five visible sides recording a complex narrative. The stone stands close to where it was presumably first raised, near the churchyard of Rök in Östergötland.[64] The inscription begins: "In commemoration of Vamoð these runes stand. And Varin drew them, a father in memory of his doomed son." The first narrative section features a stanza about Theodoric the Great, king of the Ostrogoths (ca. 474–526); its form suggests that syllable-counting alliterative poetry using a specialized vocabulary had developed in Norse territory as early as the first half of the ninth century. The normalized text presented below marks the alliteration in bold, possible internal rhymes in italics:

r*éð* **Þ**j*óð*rekr enn **þ**orm*óð*i
stillir fl*ot*na **st**rǫnd Hr*eið*m*ar*ar
s*it*r nú **g***ǫr*r á **g***ot*a **s**ínum
skjaldi um f*at*laðr **sk***at*i M*ær*inga.

Theodoric the bold, prince of the sea-warriors, ruled the shore of the Hreið-sea; now he sits outfitted on his (Gothic) horse, shield strapped on, the lord of the Mærings.

The Hreið-sea probably refers to the Adriatic, near whose shores Ravenna, Theodoric's capital, stands; the name *Mæringa* is also attached to Theodoric and his Italian realm in the Old English poem *Deor* (18–19a). The odd lines (a-verses) in this stanza are sometimes trisyllabic (*réð Þjóðrekr*; *sitr nú gǫrr*); the following even lines (b-verses), tetrasyllabic (e.g., *enn þormóði*; *á gota sínum*), an alternation reminiscent of the early skaldic meter *kviðuháttr*.

The extra alliteration and rhymes in the stanza are not likely to be accidental, nor is the use in quick succession of the relatively rare *st-* and *sk-* alliterative clusters.[65] Rich sound effects like these were standardized and made a formal requirement in *dróttkvætt*. The familiar "once" and "now" opposition structuring the stanza (Theodoric used to rule; now he sits on a horse) occurs in several tenth-century *dróttkvætt* memorial stanzas. At least four of the words employed (*stillir* 'prince,' *flotnar* 'sea-men,' *goti* 'horse,' and *skati* 'lord') are poeticisms, terms that occur in verse, but never or very rarely in prose. Nautical imagery dominates these four lines: the emperor rules over sailors on a seastrand; the *goti* '(Gothic) horse' he bestrides is a base word in ship-kennings ("horse of the sea"). Such terms, while filling out the alliteration, serve a purpose beyond the purely mechanical.

A connection is frequently drawn between this stanza and the famed equestrian statue of Theodoric the Great that once stood in Ravenna. Agnellus of Ravenna writing in the 830s and early 840s recalled how almost thirty-eight years earlier Charlemagne had seized this immense gilded bronze statue and transported it to Aachen, relocating it outside his palace where it could be seen by all comers: "a horse made of bronze washed with yellow gold and his rider is King Theodoric, who carries on his left arm a shield and holds in his raised right arm a lance."[66] Various Scandinavian legates visited Charlemagne in Aachen; envoys of the Danish king Hemmingus brought gifts there in 811;[67] the royal exile Herioldus (Haraldr klakk) repeatedly sought refuge in the Carolingian heartland.[68] The borders between Aachen and Rök were porous, with goods and information seeping through, even before the Viking Age was in full swing.

The earliest extant poem recognizable as *dróttkvætt*—syllable-counting with trochaic cadence and internal rhymes—is Bragi's *Ragnarsdrápa*, a poem in ekphrastic mode describing legendary and mythic scenes on an ornate shield presented to the Norwegian skald by his patron:[69]

> Knátti **e**ðr við **i**llan
> **J**ǫrmun*rek*kr at *vak*na
> með **dr**eyrfáar **dr**óttir
> **d***raum* í sverða f*laum*i.

> Jǫrmunrekkr knátti eðr at vakna við illan draum með dreyrfáar dróttir í flaumi sverða.[70]

> Jǫrmunrekkr then awoke to an evil dream among the blood-stained troops in the eddy of swords [BATTLE].

This is the first half-stanza (of nine) in which the skald depicts the vengeance of the brothers Hamðir and Sǫrli upon the Gothic king Ermanaric (d. 375 CE). The sequence begins with the king awakening from a drunken sleep to a bloodbath in his hall. Each line has six syllables; the syntax is relatively straightforward (except for the withholding of *draum* until the final line), the alliteration (here in bold and including the cluster *dr-*) regular, and the rhymes (in italics) irregular from the perspective of classical *dróttkvætt*. Rhyme was still an optional adornment in the ninth century; the systematized alternation of half- and full-rhymes became a formal requirement only in the tenth.

Old English Poetry

> *There's no getting around the fact that setting words on paper is the tactic of a secret bully, an invasion.*
>
> —Joan Didion, "Why I Write"

After Beowulf has slain Grendel, Danes, old and young, journey back, *fram mere modge mearum ridan* ("from the lake brave ones riding steeds") (*Beo* 855), praising the hero in words that sound like recycled vernacular song:

Đær wæs Beowulfes
mærðo mæned; monig oft gecwæð
þætte suð ne norð be sæm tweonum
ofer eormengrund oþer nænig
under swegles begong selra nære
rondhæbbendra, rices wyrðra.
(856–61)

There Beowulf's glory was told; many often said that neither south nor north between the seas, over the vast ground, under the sky's expanse, was another shield-bearer better, worthier of a kingdom.

Each half-line in this verse is filled by a syntactic unit of four positions, sometimes constituted by two words stressed on their stem-syllable and followed by an unstressed ending: *mærðo mæned, oþer nænig, selra nære, rices wyrðra*. In the a-verse, alliteration must occur on the first syllable possessing metrically significant weight; a second stressed syllable may also alliterate ("double alliteration"). In nominal compounds such as *eormengrund* and *rondhæbbende*, both stem-elements receive stress. The single alliteration required by the second half-line has to fall on the first stressed syllable; the second strong position must not join in. The final word of the line bears stress. Like the Gallehus verse and unlike *dróttkvætt*, Old English verse does not strictly regulate the number of syllables in a half-line, which can range from four to nine or more; in *Beowulf*, the average number of syllables per half-line, as in this excerpt, is just under five.[71]

The *Beowulf* poet avoids combining two half-lines of the same metrical type.[72] Half-lines of identical type are sometimes stacked in successive lines, such vertical patterning often marking the end of the poem (3181–82) or of a verse paragraph, as in lines 859b, 860b, and 861b above. In the passage cited, one a-verse has double alliteration (857) and one long line, vowel alliteration (859), featuring, as usual, different vowels. Rhyme, although an optional feature of Old English poetry, is nevertheless present.[73] The line *fram mere modge   mearum ridan* (*Beo* 855) exhibits two skaldic-type slant- (or half-, oblique-, sprung-, or para-) rhymes, that is, different vowels with similar postvocalic consonants: with alliteration, *mer-/mear-* (cf. current English "sing-song," "tell-tale," "tit for tat," "riff-raff," "flimflam," "mishmash," "TikTok," "ping-pong"); and without alliteration, *mod-/rid-* (cf. "Walpole," "think tank," "kickback," "sit tight," "soul/all," and Bragi's *rek-/vak-*). To the slant rhyme on *mæn-/mon-* (*Beo* 857), *tweon-* and *næn-* in the next two lines might be added, along with the triplets *-cwæð/suð/oð-*, *mærð-/norð/wyrð-*, and *-grund/rond-/und-*, repeated syllables suggesting the swirling interconnectedness of things.

Vernacular authors had two distinct lexicons at their disposal, one for verse, the other for prose, separated from each other by a semantic shift as far reaching as any sound change.[74] Poetic words generalize, ignoring the superfices of things; the inherent sense of "blue" is blueness, not indigo, azure, or turquoise. The prose word details a specific shade or mood, the shifting color of eyes or of the sea and sky; its range is its *curriculum vitae*, where it has traveled, what it has done, its desire for distinctiveness. Theoretically, the poetic word favors speakers, whose ideal economy consists of a few general terms, prose words, auditors, whose ideal economy consists of a vast, precise vocabulary.[75] Borges's Pierre Menard could have been contemplating the dedicated lexicon of northern verse when he proposed "a monograph on the possibility of constructing a poetic vocabulary of concepts which would not be synonyms or periphrases of those which make up our everyday language, 'but rather ideal objects created according to convention and essentially designed to satisfy poetic needs.'"[76] Old Norse and Old English poetic words are recording and storage media, time-travelers whose pasts are legible only down to the waterline.

This excerpt from *Beowulf* features four terms that never occur in prose: two compounds (*rondhæbbend(e)* 'shield-holder, warrior' and *eormengrund* 'vast ground, earth') and two simplices (*mearh* 'steed, mount' and *swegl* 'sky, heaven'). These poetic words bear an antique patina, hinting at buccaneering days of long ago and suggestive of obsolescence, like rotary phones or manual typewriters; they may also be indicative of the general poetic northernism of the Old English verse corpus. None of the four has survived into modern English. *Rondhæbbend* is a verbally derived compound, each of whose elements combines readily with other nouns and present participles, forming half-lines of the same metrical type: e.g., *bordhæbbend* (*Beo* 2895a), *daraðhæbbend* (*Jul* 68a), *lindhæbbend* (*Beo* 245a, 1402a), *randwiggend* (*Exo* 426a, *Jud* 11a, 20a, 188a).[77] Such compounds belong to a metrical type that separates the rhythm of poetry from that of prose. *Eormengrund* 'spacious earth' never appears again in Old English; its Norse cognate *jǫrmungrund* 'vast land' occurs three times in verse: in the tenth-century *dróttkvætt* poem inscribed in runes on the Karlevi stone (see below), in the eddic poem *Grímnismál* (st. 20/3), in which Óðinn's ravens, like Beowulf's fame, fly *jǫrmungrund yfir* 'over the vast ground,' and in *Hrynhenda* (Sturl *Hryn* 16/4), composed in 1263 by Sturla Þórðarson, Snorri Sturluson's nephew.[78] The *eormengrund* of the Danish riders in *Beowulf* may derive from common Germanic stock (the first element occurs in Old Saxon and Old High German) or reflect contact with Norse speakers on the ground. If the latter, the influence could have run either way. In disentangling Old English and Old Norse poetic strands, who owns what is rarely clear.

The noun *mearh* 'steed' is employed more than twenty times in Old English verse as a simplex and an additional seven times as the second element of compounds meaning "sea-steed" = "ship"; it is used once to gloss Latin poetic *cornipes* 'horn-footed.'[79] Cognate Old Norse *marr* 'steed,' also a poetic term, is frequent in *dróttkvætt* circumlocutions for "ship," the viking "wave-steeds," or seagoing vessels, infesting English and other coastlines.[80] An English chronicler recording Sveinn Forkbeard's campaign of 1003–4 uses gilded language to describe the invaders' carefully honed, grimy nobility. Avoiding everyday prose words for "ships," he speaks instead of *yðhengestas* 'wave-stallions,' a conspicuous use of local color and a signal that this passage has veered into verse.[81]

The northern poet's fundamental building block is the half-line. Half-line patterns in the *Beowulf* passage above repeat within that poem and in others. Compare *under swegles begong* (*Beo* 860a) with *under swegles begong* (*Beo* 1773a), *ofer geofones begang* (*Beo* 362a), *garsecges begang* (*And* 530a), or *þisses giddes begang* (*Fates* 89a).[82] The formula *be sæm tweonum* (858b) recurs three more times in *Beowulf* and in poems preserved in three other manuscripts.[83] A distinguishing feature of Old English verse is its fondness for parataxis (apposition or variation), the presentation of the same scene or basic concept in successive statements and restatements without an expressed connection between them.[84] The parallel half-lines in the *Beowulf* passage cited—"between the seas, over the vast ground, under the sky's expanse"—convey, like a sequence of snapshots, a sense of physical and mental motion, of immediacy, while underlining the extreme reach of the hero's glory. The riders fortify their praise with a shield-wall of "no's": *ne*, *nænig*, and *nære*.[85] Neither south nor north, nobody does it better than Beowulf. When *dróttkvætt* poets praise a leader, their evaluations, too, run to the negative: "no warrior more without blame will rule land in Denmark" (Run Öl 1); "king, another prince loftier than you will never be born under the sun" (Arn *Hryn* 20/1–2); "a more illustrious prince will not die" (ÞSkall *Valfl* 2/7). The conjuring up of possibilities *not* to be expected is a recognized feature of northern politesse,[86] as is the use of various aurally derived techniques of repetition and framing.[87]

The *Dróttkvætt* Stanza

A runic inscription carved around 1000 on a porphyry stone near Karlevi, a village on the Swedish island of Öland in the Baltic Sea, includes a *dróttkvætt* stanza, the sole verse in this meter preserved in writing in a contemporary setting.[88] An introductory prose passage explains in three formulaic lines of runes the purpose of the memorial: "This stone is set in memory of Sibbi the good, son of Foldarr, and his retinue set." The name Foldarr is not recorded again in medieval Scandinavia.[89] The individual credited with commissioning the stone remains oddly anonymous, perhaps, it has been suggested, because his relationship to the dead man was known to contemporaries;[90] anonymous, too, are the carver and skald (if they were, indeed, separate persons). The rest of the prose inscription is illegible.

The poetic section that follows this introduction occupies six lines of runes. Italics and underlining distinguish below the separate clauses, bold letters display the kennings.

> Folginn liggr, *hinn's fylgðu*
> (flestr vissi þat) *mestar*
> *dæðir*, **dolga Þrúðar**
> **draugr**, í þeimsi haugi.
> Munat **reið-Viðurr** ráða
> rógstarkr í Danmǫrku
> **Endils jǫrmungrundar**
> ørgrandari landi.

> Dolga Þrúðar draugr, hinn's mestar dæðir fylgðu—flestr vissi þat—liggr folginn í þeimsi haugi; ørgrandari rógstarkr Endils jǫrmungrundar reið-Viðurr munat ráða landi í Danmǫrku.

> The **warrior [tree-trunk of the Þrúðr (goddess) of battles]**, *whom the greatest heroic acts followed*, lies hidden in this mound (most men knew that). A **ship-captain [chariot-Viðurr (god) of the enormous ground of Endill (sea-king)]** more blame-wary, strife-strong, will not rule land in Denmark.

Writing on stone was hard work. The message inscribed by the anonymous carver is stark, direct, and budget-minded. (Economical, too, is the lack of phonetic precision in the sixteen-character runic script employed.) Not only do the skald's discontinuous clauses suggest the brokenness of grief, but the very process of engraving was emblematic of mourning: you cut away from the stone what you want to keep; you peer to see what is no longer there. Engraving an oral *dróttkvætt* stanza in runes masked it under a second code, making it more secure and permanent.

Each *dróttkvætt* stanza consists of eight lines that fall into two syntactically independent halves, the second of which usually completes or supplements what has been said in the first. Each line consists of six metrical positions, three strong and three weak, ending in a cadence of a long syllable followed by a short (= the basic Old English half-line plus a trochee). The odd line has two alliterating staves, placed in two of the three strong positions; in the even line, a single alliterative stave must fall on the first syllable. In the first couplet above, *folg-* and *fylg-* chime with *flest-*; in the second, *dæð-* and *dolg-* with *draug-*; in the third, *reið-* and *ráð-* with *róg-*, while in the final couplet, *en-* and *jǫr-* alliterate with *ør-*, an ingathering of three different vowel sounds. *Dróttkvætt* verse rhymes: each line contains two internal rhymes, the second of which must fall on the fifth (penultimate) syllable. Odd-numbered lines have half-rhyme, in which different vowels are followed by identical consonants (e.g., *dæð-/Þrúð-*, *End-/grund-*); even lines have full rhyme, that is, both vowels and following consonants are identical (e.g., *flest-/mest-*, *draug-/haug-*).[91] The Karlevi stanza is rich in extra half-rhymes, both within a line (*reið-*, *Við-*, *ráð-*) and, in the final couplet, between adjacent lines (*End-*, *grund-*, *grand-*, *land-*). Beowulf's opening vow in Heorot was based on a similar slant-rhyme involving the *gr*-cluster: *for**grand** gramum ond nu wið **Grendel** sceal* . . . ("I crushed the hostile ones and now against Grendel shall . . .") (424). The monstrous "grinder," or so the speaker's sound-association predicts, will be "ground to pieces."[92]

All forms of linguistic expression involve constraints, but few meters are more like a strait jacket than *dróttkvætt* is. Of the forty-eight syllables in a stanza, normally twenty-four were metrically long and stressed, twelve bore alliteration, eight had to form half-rhyme, and eight, full rhyme; there was no choice in the placement of eight rhyming and four alliterating syllables. Each significant word in the eight lines is linked in one or more ways to others in the same or adjoining lines.[93] Henry Sweet dismissed *dróttkvætt* as "a purely mechanical art, valued only in proportion to the difficulty of its execution."[94] But the skald's knottiness had a function beyond aiding in memorization. Prose and looser verse forms can pretend that things are as they seem. In *dróttkvætt*, where meter and patterning form the overriding truth, the skald, tuned in to the mathematical high frequencies of the universe, says things that he did not know he was capable of saying. "I set myself rules in order to be totally free," affirmed Georges Perec.[95] To compose poetry in *dróttkvætt* wiped out an infinite number of possibilities, but there was at the same time a compensatory gain—the conjuring up of the unexpected and unprecedented.

Like Old English poets, the skalds drew from a special lexicon of poetic words, vague, inexplicit, traditional counters that had "a weight and value of their own, instead of referring indifferently to reality."[96] Examples of such terms in the Karlevi inscription include *dolg* 'enmity, battle' and *jǫrmungrund* 'vast ground' (cf. *Beo* 859a: *eormengrund*). The word *róg* appears in both poetry and prose, but with a different meaning in each register: in verse it signifies "strife, war, aggression," in prose, "slander, backbiting"—just as Old English *glæd* means "shining, gleaming" in verse and "cheerful, glad" (about something) in prose. The poetic sense is generalizing and metaphorical ("this is that"): it has global meaning, not tied to local or individual circumstances; the prose sense is referential and particularistic, and tends toward metonymic expression ("this is put for that"). *Rógstarkr* in line 6, like most Old English and Old Norse poetic compounds, never occurs again.[97] This potentially "new" combination evokes something old, even though it may not have existed in the language before and is attainable through this stanza alone. Just as epitaphs insert a vanished past into the present, rescuing the dead from oblivion, so poetic words, like a bridge, seem to reach back to a stratum of time separating what has perished from what is current.

Dróttkvætt stanzas, at least in the early period, were carried in their makers' heads (and in audience memory) in an unchanging state, intact and unbreakable, "a little machine for remembering itself."[98] Repeated sounds opened up a mysterious world of verbal magic. The first line of the Karlevi stanza notes the phonological convergence of death and great deeds on a windswept island: ***folginn*** 'hidden' alliterates and rhymes with ***fylgðu*** 'followed,' as in a game of hide and seek. The Old Norse verbs *fela* 'to hide' and *fylgja* 'to follow, accompany' do not share the same Indo-European root, but it hardly matters: the etymological or charm effect is as strong as if it did. The same applies to the chiming *reið-* 'chariot' and *ráða* 'to rule' in line 5, near-homophones in a restricted space.[99] The English words "enduring" (Latin *durus* 'hard') and "duration" (Latin *durare* 'to last long') do not share the same root either, but this did not stop Paul Éluard's expression of outreaching time by dint of creation—"le dur désir de durer"—from working its magic.[100]

Sibbi, the man who ruled land in Denmark and who held the governance of the sea-king's vast expanse (= the sea) is now himself held in check. The syntax of each half-stanza forms a kind of envelope pattern that seals within itself the life of the man praised, immobilizing his corpse in its bonds. In the first half stanza, a thought begun in line one is completed only in line four. The two halves of this main sentence are sundered by a parenthesis and a subordinate clause and placed as far as possible from each other; the opening words—"he lies hidden"—are left hanging until the last syllables of the fourth and final line are reached—"in this mound." In the second half-stanza, the negation in the first line ("shall not rule") does not find its object until the last word in the last line is reached ("land"), while the two adjectives modifying the noun *Viðurr* in line 5 are placed in lines 6 (*rógstarkr*) and 8 (*ørgrandari*), respectively, a skaldic mode of variation. Discontinuous syntax encourages phrases to resonate semantically with more than one clause: the parenthesis "most men knew that" works with both statements in the first half-stanza. Verbs, normally minimal in *dróttkvætt*, completely disappear from the stanza after line 5. Each quatrain inscribed on the Karlevi stone contains a litotic expression: "most" = "all"; "more damage-wary" = "more circumspect." The first word in the second half-stanza provides the expected "not." The deceased was incomparable: "A ship-captain more prudent will *not* rule."[101] "He was among men the greatest *óníðingr* 'un-dastard,' 'un-wretch' (= admirable, generous one)," observe four runic inscriptions honoring others on memorial stones from the same period.[102] The northern poet maintains good manners in a message shorter than a tweet.

Skaldic art is characterized by a peculiar kind of circumlocution, the "kenning," variously described as a multiexpandable nominal compound, as a periphrastic description of an unnamed referent usually composed of two nouns or a compound noun, or—more simply—as a "characterization."[103] Borges called it "one of the most brazen aberrations in the history of literature."[104] First used as a technical term by Snorri Sturluson, "kenning" was a Victorian innovation in descriptions of the occasional nominal periphrasis in Old English verse.[105] The Norse kenning is based on a system of paradigmatic substitution or variation. Skalds constructed entire systems of interlocked circumlocutions, devising a separate language that often depended on previous knowledge and training for its comprehension. To each element, each kind, was assigned a genus (the base word) and a species, the defining epithet that singled out a salient characteristic, a local habitation, or a name. The ocean is the ship's plain and the whale's riding place, the meadow of the halibut, the field of the salmon, and the isle-studded girdle of earth. It is the wounds of the giant's neck, evoking an image of the dying Ymir, whose blood as it gushed from his neck created the wine-dark sea. Silver is the ice of the head or arm, snow or flour of the purse, glaciers, drifts, or cargo of the crucible. Kennings change shape more swiftly than Leda's Jove. Gold is expressed by more than six hundred circumlocutions, many involving the world of gods and heroes: it is fire of the Rhine and of the sea-gods Ægir and Rán; it is the sun of the ocean current, pyre of the lagoon, surf-flame, fjord-gleam, stones, rocks, embers, or sun of the arms, the shingle of the hawk-beach; it is the moon of the sea-king, the serpent's dell, the feather-bed or payment of the otter, the bed of the snake, the loft of the whale of the heath. It is Freyja's tears, the words and voice of giants, the chant of chieftains of the heath, the foliage of the shining tree Glasir, the dew (or precious sweat, rain, drippings, offspring) of the ring Draupnir; it is the hair and scalp-cords of the goddess Sif, the seed of Fýri's plain, the snow and corn of Hrólfr kraki, the cargo and fair burden of Sigurðr's horse Grani, the headband of the goddess Fulla, the flour of Fróði, the barley of the mill Grotti, the hard toil of the giantess Fenja—image after image mining dark histories. Chemists know gold as a soft, yellow, irreducible element, atomic number 79 in the Periodic Table. The *dróttkvætt* poet's kennings dissolve the surface solidity of the world. They also provide a way of thinking in images.

Any member of a circumlocution might be expanded by further kennings. Periphrases of five parts were within the bounds of good taste, but not those of greater length, or so Snorri Sturluson cautioned aspiring poets. Unraveling a long kenning is like grabbing onto the tail of a slithering sea-beast without knowing what you'll find at the other end. It is not courteous to rush helter-skelter toward the head, to reduce a serial kenning to a one-word solution. Italo Calvino urged with regard to myths: "It is better to let them settle into the memory, to stop and dwell on every detail, to reflect on them without losing touch with their language of images."[106]

The trick to unpacking the man-kennings in the Karlevi stanza is to proceed as if opening a series of nested gift boxes, beginning with the outermost one and working your way in. The kenning in the first half-stanza—*draugr dolga Þrúðar* 'tree-trunk (or 'companion' or 'ghost') of the goddess (the god Þórr's daughter Þrúðr 'strength') of battles'—consists of two boxes: the "goddess of battles" is a valkyrie; her "tree-trunk" or "companion" is the warrior. In skaldic verse, any masculine tree name can serve as the base of a man-kenning: warriors are trees with helmets on.[107] *Draugr*, signifying a fallen or cut-down tree-trunk, is a natural emblem of grief, one suitable for an epitaph: "nous n'irons plus au bois / les lauriers sont coupés." But the poet's rhyming association in line 4 of *draugr* and *haugr* 'mound' calls up another meaning for the former term: "ghost, dead body, inhabitant of a cairn."[108] Proper skaldic etiquette involves teasing and tormenting your listeners: traditional collocations, such as "hand and hawk" or, here, "ghost and mound," are likely to end up attached not to each other but, unexpectedly, to different segments of the sentence. Things may not be as they seem. Kennings not only reflect on and sometimes effect the main "message" of a stanza, but do so concisely, by standing in for a subordinate clause, such as "Sibbi, of famed memory, who fell in battle." In the first half-stanza of the Karlevi inscription, the presence of a valkyrie ("goddess of hostilities" and female agent of death in battle) as the definer in a warrior-kenning offers a strong hint that Sibbi did not die in bed. Verbs in this first half-stanza are in the past tense; in the second half-stanza there is a shift to the future, as if a door has opened.

Our imaginations assemble the scattered parts of a kenning, tracking its nature and direction through its spore. Like Paleolithic hunter-gatherers, we connect visible traces with an absent cause, attempting to make sense of the terrain. The kenning in the second half-stanza of the Karlevi inscription can be assembled as follows: *Endils jǫrmungrund* 'the enormous ground of Endill (a sea-king)' is the sea; the *reið* 'chariot, rider' of the sea is a 'ship' whose *Viðurr* (an Óðinn-name) is the ship's skipper, a powerful chieftain. The kenning connects two categories opposed in nature, water and earth: the land traversed by a sailor is the sea; the horse-chariot in which he rides is a ship. Siggi is depicted as a sea-captain. But the poet's extended circumlocution may signify something more. Kennings in *dróttkvætt* sometimes mark the spot where the skald has forced a crossing, unveiling, momentarily, a landscape glowing with meaning. Gotland, an island further out in the Baltic, boasts numerous viking-age memorial stones, including a number probably contemporary with the Karlevi inscription. Several of these carved doors feature a repeated iconography, a female figure (usually identified as a valkyrie) standing before or above a horseman or a sailing ship, wafting the deceased warrior to the afterlife.[109]

In both half-stanzas of the Karlevi epitaph, the skald calls up powerful figures from the mythological deep past to denote the warrior commemorated. The first half-stanza names Þórr's daughter Þrúðr, base word in a valkyrie-kenning; the second employs the Óðinn-name Viðurr along with one Endill (about whom little is known except that he appears elsewhere in kennings for sea), both forming with *reið* (the *r* or "journey" rune) a kenning for sailor. Names from pagan antiquity lend gravity and cosmic significance to the life of the warrior depicted; *forn minni* 'old traditions,' like silver inlays on a hilt, added value. Viewed together, the valkyrie and sailing ship seem verbal counterparts to the myth carved wordlessly on the stones of Gotland.[110] In the Karlevi *dróttkvætt* inscription as on the picture-stones, the causal connection between the two figures, female and male, is left in half-darkness—a display of poetic good manners. The sequence of alliterating consonants in the stanza—the first couplet chiming on *f–l*; the second, on *d*; the third, on *r*; the fourth, on a salad of assorted vowels—may be a kind of mnemonic, evoking, aurally, the rare name Foldarr (ON *fold* 'land'), that of the deceased's father and possible patron of the inscription.[111] But is this a compliment to the boss, a memorization aid, or the play of chance? Language is accident-prone. In Vladimir Nabokov's short story "The Vane Sisters," the narrator manages to find a hidden name in Shakespeare's sonnets—that of President Taft, twice.[112]

The *dróttkvætt* line, with its trochaic endings, the downward declination of both stress and pitch, sets up a literary context for itself, just as a frame around a painting nudges the beholder to view the scene in a particular way. This syllable-counting form is distinctive and immediately recognizable. In *Astérix et Cléopâtre*, when the Gauls arrive by ship in Alexandria, an Egyptian greets them with these words: "Je suis, mon cher ami, très heureux de te voir." Astérix explains: "C'est un Alexandrin."[113] *Dróttkvætt*, too, has a characteristic sound, one that can be heard even at this distance.

COMPLETING THE CIRCLE

The physician Alcmaeon of Croton (ca. 500 BCE) observed that men die because they cannot join the beginning to the end.[114] *Dróttkvætt* skalds and Old English poets, employing a geometry all their own, drew circles in which each design seemed to move in concord with something else, a pattern imitative of the general human trajectory. Ring- or frame-patterning finds the end of a *dróttkvætt* half-stanza curving back to its beginning, so that the first and last lines encircle the middle, like a fetter.[115] The skald Hallvarðr háreksblesi praised Cnut the Great in half-stanzas whose last words complete its opening words: the main sentence in each is sundered and the two parts placed as far as possible from each other. Not only does the syntax tie beginning to end, but—wrapped around by the two sentence segments—the skald's two kennings, themselves entwined, end up mirroring each other:

> Rauðljósa sér ræsir
> (rít brestr sundr in hvíta)
> baugjǫrð brodda ferðar
> (bjúgrend) í tvau fljúga.
>
> Ræsir ferðar brodda sér rauðljósa baugjǫrð fljúga í tvau; in hvíta, bjúgrend rít brestr sundr.[116]
>
> ———
>
> The impeller of the journey of missiles [BATTLE > WARRIOR] sees the bright red ring-earth [SHIELD] split in two; the white, curve-edged circle breaks apart.

Each half-stanza in Hallvarðr's string of verses forms a kind of double knot, here two interlaced round shields (or one multicolored shield mentioned twice) are split in battle, as in the skald's syntax, but reunited in the final assemblage. The entire scene almost seems staged in imitation of his patron's name, Knútr 'knot.' Other northern poets achieve a similar sense of completion or inevitability by alluding, slantingly, not to a single image, as here, but to natural cycles familiar to their audiences.

Fertility of Soil

The Norwegian skald Eyvindr skáldaspillir Finnsson was in the service of Hákon góði 'the Good' Haraldsson, a ruler fostered at the court of Æthelstan, king of the English (927–39). When Hákon was killed around 960, the kingship passed to the sons of Eiríkr blóðøx 'Bloodaxe' Haraldsson (last of the Scandinavian kings of York). Centuries later, sagas introduce the following stanza with a note that under the reign of Haraldr gráfeldr 'Grey-cloak' Eiríksson the seasons were always bad and the crops failed. Famine and distress were widespread, and snow lay on the ground until midsummer:

> Bǫ́rum, Ullr, of alla,
> ímunlauks, á hauka
> fjǫllum Fýrisvalla
> fræ Hǫ́kunar ævi.
> Nú hefr folkstríðir Fróða
> fáglýjaðra þýja
> meldr í móður holdi
> mellu dolgs of folginn.

> Bǫ́rum fræ Fýrisvalla á fjǫllum hauka of alla ævi Hǫ́kunar, Ullr ímunlauks. Nú hefr folkstríðir of folginn meldr fáglýjaðra þýja Fróða í holdi móður dolgs mellu.[117]

> We bore the seed of Fýrisvellir [GOLD] on the mountains of hawks [ARMS] during the whole of Hákon's lifetime, Ullr <god> of the battle-leek [SWORD > WARRIOR]. Now the afflicter of the people [= Haraldr] has hidden the flour-meal of the little-mirthful bondswomen of Fróði <legendary king> [= Fenja and Menja > GOLD] in the flesh of the mother of the enemy of the giantess [= Þórr > Jǫrð (*jǫrð* 'earth')].

Eyvindr contrasts Hákon's generosity with the meanness of his successors: his forty-eight syllables (a skaldic tweet) are daggers pointed at Haraldr, a weaponization of traditional language. His stanza is no passive complaint about getting gifts from one patron and not from another, but provides grounds for impeachment proceedings. The kennings of *drótt-kvætt* are not standard-issue tiles used to pretty up a stanza or present something ordinary in a covert way. Like compounds, they derive meaning from their context, gain their strength from a kind of photosynthesis. And they sometimes seem to comment obliquely on the politics of the day.

The initial kenning in Eyvindr's first half-stanza, "Ullr of the battle-leek," designates a warrior, the anonymous addressee of the verse; Ullr, stepson of Þórr and the god of duels, seems to have been favored (if one can trust place-names) in districts of Norway opposed to Haraldr. The skald's invocation of a "sword-Ullr" may be an alarm bell. The second kenning, "seed of Fýrisvellir," designates gold, a circumlocution based on the legend of the Danish king Hrólfr kraki (Hrothulf in *Beowulf*), who on the plains of the River *Fýri* famously scattered a gold collar and other treasures to delay the Swedish king (Aðils) pursuing him. Saxo refers to Hrólfr *qui Firsuallinos auro conseuerat agros* ("who once sowed gold in the fields of Fyrisvallar").[118] The third kenning, "mountains of hawks," denotes the arms of the poet himself. Eyvindr's first quatrain can be paraphrased: "Warrior, I bore gold on my arms during all of Hákon's lifetime."

A kenning in the second half-stanza alludes to another legend: the "flour-meal of the little-mirthful [= incensed] bondswomen of Fróði" refers to the gold milled for that Danish king by two enslaved giantesses bent on sabotage. They ensure Fróði's destruction by grinding out an army to depose him.[119] The "enemy of the giantess" is Þórr, whose mother is Jǫrð 'earth'; her flesh is the ground violated by Haraldr, who hides his wealth within her womb. Eyvindr's choice of *hold* 'flesh' for "ground" recalls the creation of *jǫrð* 'earth' from *Ymis holdi* 'Ymir's flesh.'[120] The second half-stanza reports that the people's afflicter has secreted gold in the bowels of the earth, charging the king with financial misconduct.

Eyvindr's two circumlocutions for gold, one in each stanza, suggest in sequence renewal (seeding gold upon the fields evokes fecundity) and death (milled flour hidden in the cavernous earth will never sprout or multiply, just mold away). The poet could have expressed much of what he wanted to say directly, in Keynesian terms. The royal economy rested on a complex system of forced presents, "necessary generosity":

by hoarding gold, by producing a budgetary surplus, Haraldr was deflating the economy and creating unemployment and hardship; by circulating wealth, by deficit spending, Hákon had inflated the economy and achieved full employment and prosperity. Vikings were reputed to be versatile moneyers. However, Eyvindr here speaks not as an economist but as an inspired seer, whose agricultural imagery was directed to king and farmer-soldier alike. A prose summation—"Hákon shared, Haraldr self-deals"—poorly represents eight lines brimming with images of sword, seed, leek, hawk, mountains, battle, flour-meal, bondswomen, flesh, earth, giantesses, gods and men. The skald is making a situated case for popular resistance.

The sustained din of alliterative and consonant syllables, of allusion and apostrophe, the esoteric lore and linking of past and present in Eyvindr's kennings showcase both his artistry and slipperiness: "backward ran sentences until reeled the mind."[121] Enjambed alliteration on *f* links lines 4 and 5, marrying the two quatrains.[122] The two stressed verbs of the stanza—*bera* 'to wear, flaunt' (1) and its near-opposite *fela* 'to hide, bury' (8)—occupy respectively its first and final two syllables. The poet forms two interior aural rings by making the last word of each half-stanza repeat the alliterative staves of its opening verse (*Ullr/ævi*; *folk-/folg-*). The rhymes denouncing Har*aldr* grá*feldr* circle from one *l*-sound to the next (*Ullr*, *all-*, *fjǫll-*, *vall-*, *meldr*, *hold-*, *mell-*, *dolgs*, *folg-*). The contrasting yet rhyming land-words of line 3, *fjǫll* 'mountains' and *valla* (from *vellir* 'plains'), give way in the final couplet to the final terrain-concept, "earth." The *dróttkvætt* template draws words out of the skald, compelling him to speak what he might not otherwise dare to say; it covers him in a cloak of deniability and provides him with an escape clause: "I was praising your love of the land, sir." Traditional metrical and phonological rules generated this tweet, not the poet.

Hydrocycles

A few years later, the skald Einarr skálaglamm ('scales-tinkle') Helgason composed *Vellekla* 'Lack of Gold,' a poem in honor of Earl Hákon the Great, pagan ruler of Norway (ca. 975–95). The wholeness of Einarr's vision—his depiction of a reciprocity existing between warfare, poetry, and kingship—takes the form of a continual circulation of water from land (as springs and rivers) to sea, from sea (through evaporation) to air, and thence back to land, as dew and rain. A deluge of interrelated streams swamps the listener. Stanza 11 celebrates a battle in which Hákon slew three high-ranking opponents:

> Hjalmgrápi vann hilmir
> harðr (Lopts vinar) barða
> (því kom vǫxtr í Vínu
> vínheims) fíandr sína.
> Ok forsnjallir fellu
> fúrs í Þróttar skúrum
> (þat fær þjóðar snytri)
> þrír jarls synir (tírar).

> Harðr hilmir vann fíandr sína barða hjalmgrápi; því kom vǫxtr í Vínu vínheims vinar Lopts. Ok þrír forsnjallir synir jarls fellu í skúrum fúrs Þróttar; þat fær snytri þjóðar tírar.[123]

> The stern ruler had his enemies pelted with helmet-hail [rain of missiles, BATTLE]; therefore, a swelling came to the Vína <river> of the wine-abode of the friend of Loptr <Loki> [= Óðinn > VAT > POEM]. And three very bold sons of a jarl fell in the showers of the fire of Þróttr [= Óðinn > SWORD > BATTLE]; that brings glory to the mentor of the nation [RULER = Hákon jarl].

Hákon's conquest of Norway is depicted as in line with the will of the gods, as ecologically correct: all media mentioned—air (*loptr*), land (*þjóð*), fire, water, and poetry itself—are under Óðinn's tyrannical sway. The subject that is of most import to the skald gets the longest, most sinuous and enveloping circumlocution: his own verse. Einarr's four-part kenning for poetry drums on *vinr* 'friend,' *vín* 'wine,' and *Vína* 'river,' the long *í*-sounds picked up and echoed by *því*, *í*, *fiandr*, and *sína.* The wine of the "friend of Loptr" (Óðinn) is the poetic mead, whose abode is a vat, and the river of that vat is the poem pouring out of the skald. According to Snorri Sturluson, Óðinn's intoxicating drink consists of spittle, blood, honey, and vomit; he never mentions its taste.[124] Hákon's hail (of weapons) makes his skald's cup run over; men fall in a downpour orchestrated by the great god himself. One hand washes the other in this charmed hydrocycle as the poet's kennings gather up directional force: "Like a drink through thirst, gravity plunges through him."[125] The present tense of the verb *fá* in line 7 and the prominent final-word position of *tírr* 'glory' in line 8 confirm that Hákon has "It," the god-given charisma that ensures success. Whatever Hákon wants, Hákon gets.

The skald's final parenthetical clause is a shameless commercial: "Hákon wins good like a bold ruler should." The deeper significance of Einarr's stanza resides in its extras, the excess that does not survive prose paraphrase, the skald's instinct for hidden relationships. Audiences of early northern verse had to dive beneath its surface sense, to swim with the poet's verbal designs, mimetic rhythms, and metaphors, his leaping, dancing orchestration of sounds and figures, in order to hear what was being said. In both corpora, *dróttkvætt* verse and Old English poetry, language is placed under extreme pressure and urgency—by measure, sound, and sense—until something fuses and, flaring, lights up a corner of the darkness.

A Leaf Falls

Even when following a Latin source text closely, English vernacular poets employ a stylistic technique—the half-line formula—that, like the skald's kennings, brings a broader canvas into view. One section of the Exeter Book poem *The Fortunes of Men* catalogues the way men die, beginning with death at the jaws of a wolf.[126] In a much discussed passage, lines 21–26, an anonymous man meets his death by tumbling from a tree.[127] The stages of his fall are drawn out, allowing him to defy for an instant, whirled and wafted by the breeze, the universal laws of gravity:

> Sum sceal on holte   of hean beame
> fiþerleas feallan;   bið on flihte seþeah,
> laceð on lyfte,   oþþæt lengre ne bið
> westem wudubeames.   Þonne he on wyrtruman
> sigeð sworcenferð,   sawle bireafod,
> fealleþ on foldan;   feorð biþ on siþe.

———

> A certain one shall fall from a high tree in the forest, wingless; he is nevertheless in flight, he sports in the air, until he is no longer a fruit of the tree. Then he sinks, mind-dark, onto its root, robbed of his soul, he falls to earth; his life-force is on a journey.[128]

The half-lines in this passage are relatively short; the metrical patterning, like the subject, falling: the two verses that do not end with a relative drop (22b, 23b) depict the doomed man sporting for a brief moment in the air. The final three half-lines are metrically identical and replicate the falling pattern of 22a and 23a. The alliterative formulas in these lines evoke other times, other places. They represent the shared or representative experience of poet and audience, seemingly inserting a chance, if common, fate into an orderly design. The half-line *lacan on lyfte* 'to sport in the air, to fly' occurs at least eight times in the corpus: birds do it, devils do it, even fire-breathing drakes do it. The slant-rhyming half-line *feallan on foldan* 'to fall to earth' is used at least ten times, variously denoting the death of heroes, a bowing down before God, the falling of leaves, and the silent descent of a sword to earth, a multicolored quilt of chance and contingency. The first element of *fiþerleas* 'wingless,' a *hapax legomenon*, alliterates elsewhere with *fliht* 'flight'; here the compound forms a riddling conjunction: a thing *without* feathers that nevertheless flies. The final half-line, *feorð biþ on siþe* 'life-force is on a journey,' recalls the death of the phoenix atop his tree a few manuscript pages earlier: *lif biþ on siþe* ("life is on a journey") (*Phoen* 220). The poet's formulaic phrasing gradually cues listeners in, urges them to connect this single accidental death to a broader interpretive framework. "A tree on earth shall lose its leaves, its branches mourn, the ready shall journey," reports *Maxims I*, 25b–27a, preparing us for Thoreau, whose falling, fluttering leaves "teach us how to die" as they "decay at the foot of the tree."[129] "For a little while leaves are green," says Solomon to Saturn (*MSol* 314). A man up a tree is slowly, insidiously brought home, back to his roots and beginnings, his death mapped as an opening, a migration, a movement toward something resembling meaning: "The mobile and the immobile flickering / In the area between is and was are leaves, / Leaves burnished in autumnal burnished trees / And leaves in whirlings in the gutters, whirlings around and away, resembling the presence of thought."[130] So, too, the final stress, *siþ*-, of the Old English passage returns through alliteration to its opening keynote, *sum*, closing off one life and season from the next.

Sunset, Sunrise

> *Painters had found it difficult to distinguish in their art a rising from a setting sun.*
>
> —Benjamin Franklin, remarks after the signing of the U.S. Constitution, Philadelphia, Pennsylvania, September 17, 1787

Quintilian called it *emphasis* "whereby we excite some suspicion to indicate that our meaning is other than our words would seem to imply; but our meaning is not in this case contrary to that which we express, as in the case of irony, but rather a hidden meaning which is left to the hearer to discover."[131] Something subterranean, some latent sense, is dug out from something said. The situation can seem ordinary in the extreme, even a king and queen retiring at sundown and emerging in regal majesty the next morning.

The evening before Beowulf's fight with Grendel, at the beginning of a new fitt or sectional division, Hrothgar, the aged king whose bedtime is regularly noted (*Beo* 645–46a; 1236–37a; 1318–20; 1791–92a), departs the hall with his retainers to seek out Wealhtheow, "the queen as bed-fellow":

Ða him Hroþgar gewat mid his hæleþa gedryht,
eodur Scyldinga ut of healle;
wolde wigfruma Wealhþeo secan,
cwen to gebeddan. Hæfde kyningwuldor . . .
(662–65)

Then Hrothgar departed with his troop of heroes, protector of the Scyldings, out of the hall; the war-leader wanted to seek Wealhtheow, the queen as bed-fellow. The king-glory [God] had . . .

Hrothgar is called "protector of the Scyldings" as he abandons the hall and hands over his role as defender to Beowulf.[132] The king's choice of sleeping quarters at some distance from his royal seat is no surprise: for twelve years, Heorot has emptied out after the sun went down. Age is weighing on Hrothgar: he is no longer able do everything a king should do. A bed, even a broken-down settle in the women's quarters, probably looked good.

The tonal uncertainties of this passage along with its jaunty rhythm have produced a spectrum of readings whose emphases range from marital sex to geriatric frailty: "The war-leader was ready to be with Wealhtheow / his consort and queen";[133] "Then Hrothgar left that hall, the Danes' / Great protector, followed by his court; the queen / Had preceded him and he went to lie at her side, / Seek sleep near his wife";[134] "The war-leader sought Wealhtheow his queen, / the companion of his bed";[135] "The war-chief would seek the bed of Wealhtheow the queen";[136] "The great man wanted to find Wealhtheow, his bed-companion";[137] "The old warrior wanted to seek his wife, his consort Wealhtheow";[138] "The war-chief wished to seek Wealhtheow, his queen's bed-chamber";[139] "The war-chief wished to join Wealhtheow, his queen, as consort";[140] "[He] left the mead-hall to lie with Wealhtheow, / his queen and bedmate";[141] "Their warrior lord would follow Wealhtheow his queen as the companion of his couch."[142] Or alarmingly, "[he was] bound to Wealhtheow's bed for comforts—his wifely strife-soother."[143] The Danish king is neither a "skulking or faint-hearted coward,"[144] nor a lady's man; no leafy grotto tempts him from his daily round of gift-giving and wisdom-talk. Still, without blaming Hrothgar or puffing up Beowulf, these lines may hint that top-dog status was not only losable, but also visible in the female company that an aged warrior keeps.[145] In viking-age *dróttkvætt* verse, skalds contrast "real men" winning their spurs in the thick of battle with effeminate homebodies snuggling on a couch with the ladies.[146] If the *Beowulf* poet were discreetly evoking this northern motif, his attempt has gone unrecognized. The most recent edition of *Beowulf* neatly skips the issue and supplies an archaeological gloss on the construction of royal beds (*Kl* 4, 156–57).[147] Etiquette means knowing what to leave out and what to suggest indirectly. Virgil's decorum in describing the coupling of Venus and Vulcan (*Aeneid* 8.406) was praised by Isidore of Seville (*Etymologies* 1.37.15), among many others.

When poets mean more than they say, their verse sometimes appears off-kilter. Two related issues in line 665 puzzle. The first has to do with the poet's choice of the compound *kyningwuldor* 'king-glory' (usually glossed as "God"), a *hapax legomenon*; the compound epithet *wuldorcyning* 'God,' with at least forty occurrences in the Old English poetic corpus, appears with its two elements reversed only here.[148] The second curiosity is the half-line *cwen to gebeddan*, with *cwen* alliterating and half-rhyming with *kyningwuldor* over the caesura and producing a prosodic anomaly.[149] A verse such as *beorht* ('bright') *to gebeddan* or *bryd* ('wife, bride') *to gebeddan* would have been unexceptional, but when the second lift of the a-verse contains a proclitic, such as *ge-*, "the absence of double alliteration . . . ruptures the norms of the metrical grammar and may have been intended to emphasize the unusual nature of the moment."[150] Meter and alliteration pressurize, putting a torque on words. The presence of two oddities—*kyningwuldor* and *cwen to gebeddan*—in one alliterative line seems, well, odd.

Gebedda, like *cwen*, has a wide semantic range: "queen" or "lover," "consort," "spouse," or "woman."[151] The term "bed" (OE *bedd*), from an Indo-European root meaning "to dig" and related to modern English "fosse" and "fossil," is central to a small flock of Old English words for cohabitation: for example, *gebeddscipe* '(carnal) intercourse' (*GenA* 1148, 2218, 2468; *ChristA* 76).[152] Old English *gebedda/gebedde*, a mostly masculine weak noun, occurs as a simplex around forty times, only five of these in poetry. The word in *Genesis A* is used once with reference to the two wives of Lamech (1091b) and twice to designate Abraham's wife Sarah (1775a, 1828a); in each appearance, it translates Latin *uxor* 'wife.' The term *gebedda* is never used of Hagar, the Egyptian princess who is Abraham's slave and concubine and Sarah's double.[153] The final poetic appearance of *gebedda* (outside *Beowulf*) is in the Old English *Rune Poem* (93a), whose poet grimly describes the *hruse* 'earth' (f.) as "bedfellow" of a pale corpse.

The remaining occurrences of the word are chiefly in homiletic prose, where worms serve as bedfellows to the buried, and in prose biblical narratives, where Eve is Adam's *gebedda*; Rebecca is Isaac's; and Noah's wife of multiple names is his. In the chronicles and charters of late Viking-Age England, the term attaches itself to various historical queens and noblewomen.[154] A chronicle entry for 965 reports that King Edgar took a nobleman's daughter *him to gebeddan* 'as his consort';[155] this queen, Ælfthryth, the future mother of Æthelred the Unready, is named in a second text as the king's *gebedda* 'spouse.' A charter identifies Æthelred's (and later Cnut's) queen as *thoro consecrata regio* ("consecrated to the royal bed").[156] Eadgyth, wife of Edward the Confessor, the woman seen in the Bayeux tapestry weeping at the foot of her husband's deathbed, is referred to as his *gebedda* '(royal) consort.'[157] The same epithet honors Lady Godiva (Godgifu), who had considerable wealth and standing independent of her husband: "Earl Leofric and his *gebedda*," wording that "may have sounded less indelicate to Anglo-Saxon ears than its sexual bluntness seems today."[158] The first royal Danish princess mentioned in *Beowulf*, Hrothgar's sister, is introduced as the Swedish king's *healsgebedda* 'cherished (lit. 'neck') bed-fellow' (*Beo* 62–63); her name is unaccountably erased. With the exception noted above (*MRune* 93a), *gebedda* in poetry is restricted to sixth-century Danish noblewomen and Old Testament wives, "first ladies" of former days.

Beðja, the Old Norse cognate of *gebedda* and a word for "woman" in modern Icelandic and Faroese, appears a handful of times in extant skaldic verse (and never in Old Norse prose) as a name, or *heiti*, for a powerful female figure, invariably defined by a male partner: Óðinn's *beðja* is Jörð 'earth,' Þórr's much put-upon mother.[159] The skald Skúli Þorsteinsson (ca. 970–1040) composed for Eiríkr jarl Hákonarson (r. 1000–1012), who had been summoned to England to assist Cnut. A stanza attributed to Skúli by Snorri Sturluson portrays the setting sun as a divine *beðja* retiring to her chambers:

Glens beðja veðr gyðju
goðblíð í vé síðan . . .

síðan goðblíð beðja Glens veðr í vé gyðju . . .[160]

Then the divinely cheerful bed-mate of Glenr [partner of Sól 'sun'] strides into the goddess's mansion.

This *dróttkvætt* couplet, twelve syllables in all, includes the required alliteration (on *g*-), and the prescribed half-rhyme (*beð-/gyð-*) and full-rhyme (*blíð/síð-*). The skald's basic aural design is buttressed by the chiming *veð-* and *goð-*, *goð-* and *blíð*, *gyð-* and *síð-*, *veð-* and *vé*; even the preposition *í* supports the full rhyme in line 2. The verb *veðr* 'strides, steps,' were it audible, would make a full rhyme with *beðja* 'bed-mate, woman, mistress, wife,' already enjoying extra alliteration with *blíð* in the even line. In multiple ways, the sounds of this couplet spell out *beðja*, an Old Norse word belonging, or so it would seem, to the language of the gods; *Sól* 'sun' is the *beðja* to whom all heliotropic syllables here turn their heads.

By the time *Beowulf* was written down, Old English *gebedda* 'bed-mate' had, like *bedd* 'bed,' a surrounding circle of friends and relations; it would have shared associations with the flatness and fertility of a cornfield, the softness of feathers, a coat of snow, the silence of the grave, or, prompted by the poet's *kyningwuldor*, solar radiance, as in Skúli Þorsteinsson's couplet. Beowulf's vow earlier that evening in Hrothgar's hall had culminated in sun-imagery: "He who may will go brave to mead after the morning-light of another day, the sun clothed in brilliance [*swegl*, cognate with Old Norse *sól*] shines from the south over the children of men" (603b–606). Night brings this happy-hour scene to a close; combat has been impending from sunrise to dusk; now "darkening night came gliding, the shapes of covering shadows black under the clouds" (648–51a). Things go bump in the night; all is blurred, vague, uncanny.

After Beowulf's successful "night-work" (*Beo* 827), morning celebrations begin with high-spirited men on horseback riding from the lake: "fram ***m**er*e ***mo**d*ge ***m**ear*um *rid*an" (855); bold type marks the alliteration; italics, the two double half-rhymes.[161] With dawn *scofen ond scynded* 'impelled and hastened' (917b–18a), the riders momentarily reappear, trailing the same pattern of doubled half-rhymes: "*hwil*um *flit*ende *feal*we *stræt*e / **m**earum ***m**æt*on" (at times, competing, they measured the dusky road on horses) (916–17a). At this moment, Hrothgar emerges from the *brydbur* 'bridal chamber' (921a) *tirfæst* 'full of glory' (922a); he and his queen with their respective retinues hasten to the high hall.[162] The narrative moves at breakneck speed in several directions at once. Time seems to start and stop, its flickering lending a sense of simultaneity to the glimpses of horsemen, celebratory song, and royalty rising. Threads of discourse appear and reappear as sudden, discontinuous flashes.

The self-alliterating *brydbur* 'bridal chamber' (*Beo* 921a), a compound found only here in Old English poetry, occurs more than thirty times in prose and glosses; in the latter group, it usually translates *thalamus* 'bridal-bed,' as in Psalm 18:6, where the sun, like a bridegroom, hastens from its *brydbur*, glorying in a bright new day.[163] In the first of the Blickling homilies, *brydbur* occurs an extraordinary four times, translating the *thalamus* of the psalm verse and accompanying the poetic word *wuldorcyning* 'glory-ruler, God.'[164] In the *Beowulf* passage, as in the psalm, radiance conquers darkness; shadows slip-slide away, and the diurnal circle resumes.

The royal couple's procession to the hall at fitt's end (*Beo* 920b–24) is carefully choreographed, each a-line fortified with double alliteration, as if to signal approaching closure. The paired stately progress of king and queen has the effect of aestheticizing the violence, the vengeful, testosterone-fueled scoretaking that had just taken place and that culminated in Grendel's bloody body parts dangling under Heorot's roof. The rippling muscles of etiquette break through the clouds of grudge and pain:

> My manners are tearing off heads—
> The allotment of death.
> For the one path of my flight is direct
> Through the bones of the living.[165]

As the scene progresses, hope and history seem briefly to concur.[166] The queen measuring the mead path with her troop of maidens (*Beo* 924) echoes the happy warriors measuring paths with their horses a few lines earlier (916–17a). The last word in the episode—*hos*, the queen's "troop" (of maidens)—is an oddly angled term, a *hapax legomenon* in Old English with a scattering of Continental Germanic cognates.[167] The word is novel, as if evoking a distant (in time or space) collectivity, a female military escort. And it leads into the next movement, for its initial *h* establishes through enjambed alliteration the first line of the following fitt: ***H****roðgar maþelode—he to* ***h****ealle* ***g****eong* ("Hrothgar made a speech—he went to the hall") (925), a line in which crossed alliteration links the sonic patterning of the king's dithematic name (h–g) to that of his destination (h–g), an onomastic "ticket to ride."

Only connect. The narrative moves both forward and sideways, blurring the line between history and myth, juxtaposing the levee of a triumphant ruler and the rising of the sun of Norse story and biblical psalmody. Early northern verse was skilled in throwing curve balls, elliptical lines that thwart and resist easy tracking. Hearers are left to make sense of the ways the poet tried to make sense of the shape of things, tying beginnings to ends, concluding one circle while drawing another.

CHAPTER 2

Secrets of the Line

The line amazes itself

eluding the hand
that fed it . . .

—Seamus Heaney, "Viking Dublin, Trial Pieces"

ROOTS AND RHYMES

"Something deeply hidden had to be behind things," observed the youthful Albert Einstein;[1] "behind the cotton wool is hidden a pattern," mused Virginia Woolf.[2] Words, those strange linguistic cards dealt to us before we can play, have pasts. Real or imagined roots draw phonemes back to distant shores, like Idaho salmon that travel 900 miles and climb 7,000 feet to find the freshwater stream in which they hatched.[3] Early northern poets deployed rhyme and alliteration to divine the links between word and thing, guiding words back to their secret springs.[4] But history, like jam streaks in a pudding, does not come together again when stirred backward.[5]

Sound is central to poetry.[6] Written instructions for composing alliterative verse were unavailable in the early medieval North: no "*drótt-kvætt* for dummies," no "how to sing like Cædmon." Óðinn outlined his method of aural instruction in an eddic long line sparkling with half-rhymes, one of which reunited cognates: ***Mál** er at **þylja** **þul**ar **stóli** á* (it's time to orate from the orator's seat) (*Hávamál* 111/1). Poetry in medieval Iceland meant *samfǫst orð* 'bound words'; in *Beowulf,* a poet's words are *soðe gebunden* 'truly fastened' (871a). The Old English *Genesis* opens not with the first verse of the biblical book but with a prelude, a threefold play on "word":

Us is **r**iht micel ðæt we **r**odera ***w**eard*,
***w**ered*a **w**uldorcining, ***w**ord*um *her*igen . . .
(*GenA* 1–2)

It is our great duty to praise in words the guardian of heaven, the glory-king of hosts . . .

Enjambed alliteration (*weard/wered*) is reinforced by alliterating half-rhymes (*weard, wered, word*), with *her-* , the penultimate syllable, supporting the rhyme chain. This opening section of the poem concludes with a parallel paronomastic construction “oðþæt þeos *woruld*gesceaft / ðurh **word** ge**wear**ð *wuldor*cyninges” (until this world-creation came about through the word of the glory-king) (*GenA* 110–11), capping the *woruld/wuldor* anagram with an allusion to the first verse of the Gospel of John and the mysterious identity of *Deus/Logos*. The next two lines announce the start of world history, the first by echoing *Cædmon's Hymn* (4a, 5a), the second, ***h**elm **ea**llwihta,* ***h**eofon and **eor**ðan*, by crossed alliteration: “Here [the eternal lord], protector of all creatures, [first shaped] heaven and earth.” Creation has begun.

The *Genesis* poet subsequently highlights potential Christological episodes in Old Testament history through multiple plays on “word/Word,” hinting at typological correspondences without ever leaving the literal level of narrative.[7] The Old English *Exodus* casts a quick glance at Noah on his ark, enveloping him with sounds and rhythmical effects worthy of a Cole Porter or Leonard Cohen:

Niwe*flod*as **No**e oferlað
þrymfæst *þeod*en, mid his **þrim** sunum . . .
(*Ex* 362–63)

Noah sailed over new floods, the glorious prince with his three sons . . .

The coupling of *þrymm* ‘majesty, glory’ and *þry* ‘three’ caught on and probably lies behind the Middle English blend *þrimness* ‘Trinity.’[8] The repetition of similar syllables linking related things, like the binding through alliteration of one half-line to the next, conveys the sense of an underlying hidden order in history. Alliterating half-rhymes, like initial light half-lines, sometimes serve as aural punctuation, beginning poems, setting off verse paragraphs, or marking, as in the Noah passage above, particularly significant sections of longer poems.[9]

Poets long before the millennium strove to harvest the truth from words, to reunite through sound-similarity things disjointed by time. In doing so, they converted a style associated with pagan sympathetic magic (*similia similibus* 'like produces like') into an acceptable associative rhetoric. Ælfric spelled this out in balanced alliterative prose: "Ne sceal nan man mid **g**aldre ***w**yrte* **b**esingan, ac mid **G**odes ***w**ord*um hi ge**b**letsian" (No one shall enchant herbs with a charm, but shall bless them with God's words).[10] Half-rhymes lift more than their weight in both poetic corpora. In *dróttkvætt*, a *baugr* 'ring' is by nature *bjúgrendr* 'curve-edged' (Hallv *Knútdr* 4/4); in Old English verse, *gold* 'gold' attracts a *galdor* 'spell' (*Beo* 3052), while *lof* 'praise, glory' is won by not caring about *lif* 'life' (*Beo* 1536). The call of the phoneme was loud in the early North.

Vernacular poets in early medieval Europe had learned support for joining syllables that sounded alike. Isidore's *Etymologies*, the *Roget* of late Romanitas, guided the literati of early England in channeling the words and things of classical antiquity into the medieval present.[11] *Cervi* 'deer' are so-called from their horns, *a cornibus* (*Etym.* 12.1.18); *Heorot* 'hart,' the Danish royal hall in *Beowulf*, is *horngeap* 'wide-horned' (*Beo* 82), a majestic *hornreced* 'horn-house' (704), perhaps indicative of prominent gables. "A mouth [*os*] is so called, because through it as if through a door [*ostium*] we bring food in and throw spit out" (*Etym.* 11.1.49); Grendel opens *recedes muðan* 'the mouth of the hall' when he is ready to dine (*Beo* 724). A mail-shirt (*lorica*) is so called because it 'lacks [leather] thongs' (*loris carere*); "it is made only of iron rings" (*Etym.*18.13.1); noisy *hringiren* 'iron-rings' (= mail-coats) sing out in *Beowulf* (322b–23a).[12] A river (*flumen*) is called from flowing (*fluendo*) (*Etym.* 13.21); the rising river (*flod* 'current') in *The Battle of Maldon* (65) is streaming (*flowende*), a relationship certified by modern etymology. Isidore's books were plundered by the author of the *Liber Monstrorum*, quoted in Alfredian circles, and mined by Wulfstan of Winchester.[13] Anonymous hands added Isidorian glosses to Anglo-Latin texts and Latin–English glossaries and provided an interlinear gloss to at least one text by Isidore.[14]

This chapter explores some of the techniques used by early northern poets to retrieve and organize the sound-and-sense symmetries of language. The structure of alliterative verse is well designed to reunite word families, to recall former ties, whether these relatives are brought together in a half-line or, minding the gap, in a long line or couplet. In both *dróttkvætt* and Old English verse, when an item is expressed by a particular phoneme, similar-sounding words rapidly gather around, as if for nourishment, consolidating the group: "You shall know a word by the company it keeps."[15] Congruencies of sounds can have real-life consequences: people move faster when they hear "quicksand."

Extra Rhymes in *Dróttkvætt* Verse

The early skalds were masters of rhyme.[16] Snorri Sturluson outlined several subcategories of extra rhymes, but not even he could net them all.[17] Sometimes all three alliterating words in a *dróttkvætt* couplet exist in a paronomastic (or pseudo-etymological) relationship. In such cases, the two odd-line alliterating syllables are linked by half-rhyme (Old Norse *skothending* 'inserted rhyme') both to one another and to the full rhyme of the even line.[18] Around 995, the Icelander Úlfr Uggason composed *Húsdrápa* 'House-poem,' one section of which concerns Þórr's fishing expedition. The skald describes how the World Serpent glared at the god:

En **stirð**þinull **starð**i
storðar leggs fyr borði.

En stirðþinull storðar starði fyr borði.[19]

And the stiff cord of the earth stared by ship-side.

By chance, but not really by chance, all three *st-* words assembled by the skald share the same Indo-European root, one suggestive of stiffness, stubbornness, sternness.[20]

In the next stanza, Þórr uses similar triple paronomasia to insult the giant cowering beside him in the rowboat:

þjokkvǫxnum kvað **þykk**ja
þikling firin mikla . . .

kvað þjokkvǫxnum þikling þykkja firin mikla . . .[21]

[he] said it seemed an exceeding danger to the heavy-set fat one . . .

The god, no mean trencherman himself, directs congruent sounds to fat-shame his opponent. Here *þjokkr* 'thick' and *þiklingr* 'thick man' (= chubby, a hulk) are obvious soul mates. In the following stanza (*Húsdr* 6/1–2), the skald again employs triple alliterating half-rhymes, this time with reference to Þórr's physicality: "**full**ǫflugr lét **fellir** / **fjall**-Gauts hnefa skjalla" (the extremely powerful feller of the mountain-Gautr [GIANT] let his fist clatter). Similar paronomastic runs occur in the section of the poem in which the skald describes Baldr's funeral (sts. 7–11).

Another *dróttkvætt* rhyme type not catalogued by Snorri involves the reuse of a nonalliterating penultimate odd-line half-rhyme to initiate the full rhyme (here *a* with *ǫ*) of the even line. The poem *Haustlǫng* 'Autumn-long' by the Norwegian skald Þjóðólfr ór Hvini (ca. 900) exemplifies this technique:

ern at ǫglis **barn**i
arnsúg faðir **Mǫrn**ar.

Faðir Mǫrnar [lagði] ern arnsúg at barni ǫglis.[22]

The father of Mǫrn [= the giant Þjazi] laid an energetic eagle-gust at the falcon's child [= Loki].

An eagle chases a smaller bird. The exact nature of the sucking wind of the giant (in eagle costume) is unclear, perhaps an avian Dyson. The occasional linkage of an odd and even line through rhyme as well as alliteration could be an accident; the hundreds of occurrences of such rhymes in tenth- and eleventh-century *dróttkvætt* suggest purposefulness.

Viking-age *dróttkvætt* compositions exploit the power and mnemonic potential of pseudo-etymological play, employing a range of rhyming techniques to join odd and even verses tightly. Sometimes such pairings served to clarify the structure of a verse whose odd line lacked *skothending*, as in the following couplet from Bragi Boddason's *Ragnarsdrápa*:

þats á **Leif**a landa
laufi fátt—at **hauf**ði.

Þats fátt á laufi . . . landa Leifa . . . at haufði.[23]

That is painted on the leaf [of the trees] of the lands of Leifi [SEA > SHIPS > SHIELD]—head-first.

The alliterating half-rhyme formed by Leifi, a sea-king name, and *lauf* 'leaf' recalls the Old English *l–f* sound-chain and links the two lines in a tight embrace. Because shields were hung along the wooden sides of ships (= trees of the sea), the skald depicts his gifted armor as a painted leaf, a living organism with shape and color and movement. The nonalliterating cadence of the final line (*haufði*) is tied by half-rhyme to *Leifa* in the first.

In another couplet whose odd line lacks *skothending*, Bragi repeats the penultimate alliterating syllable of that line as the first syllable of the following line. The resulting three full rhymes hint at a (possibly etymological) relationship between hardworking draft animals (*raukn*) and the steam (*rjúka* 'to reek') they emit:[24]

svát af *ren*ni**rauk**num
rauk, *Dan*markar **auk**a.

Svát rauk af rennirauknum—auka Danmarkar.[25]

So that steam rose from the rushing oxen . . . the increase of Denmark.

Elsewhere Bragi links the *skothending* of the odd line to the full rhyme of the following even line, tying the two together by half-rhyme more securely than Þórr's fishing rope ever did the world snake:

hrøkkvi*ál*l of **hrokk**inn
hekk V*ǫl*sunga **drekk**u.

Hrøkkviáll drekku Vǫlsunga hekk of hrokkinn.[26]

The coiling eel of the drink of the Vǫlsungar [POISON > Miðgarðsormr] hung coiled up.

Bragi's kenning for poison alludes to the ability of the Volsung hero Sigmundr (Sigemund in *Beowulf*) to drink venom to no ill effect.[27]

Þórðr Kolbeinsson, born in Iceland in the last quarter of the tenth century, composed in classical *dróttkvætt* style. The first couplet of his half-stanza below, reporting Cnut's invitation to Earl Eiríkr to join him in England, begins with an *l–f* slant-rhyme that extends through the first syllable of the even line, exploiting the collocation set used by both Norse and Old English poets:[28]

Enn hefsk **leyfð**, þars **lofða**
lofkennda frák sendu
at **hjalm**sǫmum **hilmi**
hjarl**s** dróttna boð jarli.

Enn hefsk leyfð, þars frák lofða lofkennda sendu boð at hjalmsǫmum hilmi hjarls dróttna jarli.[29]

Again praise begins, there where I heard praise-famed men to have sent a message to the helmet-adorned ruler, to the jarl of the princes of the land.

Skalds, like their English counterparts, set sounds loose to hunt for significant others. In the first couplet, men (*lofðar*) are associated with praise (*leyfð*, *lof*). In the second, the poet refers to Earl Eiríkr as a ***hjalm****samr* ***hilmir*** 'helmet-adorned chieftain,' a frequent *figura etymologica* in *dróttkvætt* verse with more than a dozen examples from the tenth and early eleventh centuries.[30] Repeated pairings like these probably aided recall. In line after *dróttkvætt* line, a *fylkir* 'war-leader, ruler' leads his *folk* 'people, army':

folkeflandi **fylk**ir (Eskál *Vell* 24/7)
folk réð of sik **fylk**ir (Sigv *Austv* 19/1)
folkorrostur **fylk**ir (Sigv *ErfÓl* 22/3)
of **folk**snaran **fylk**i (Arn *Hardr* 13/7)
folkrakkar um vann **fylk**ir (Glúmr Lv 1/7)

fylkir gleðr í **folk**i (Gízsv Frag 1/1)
fylkir . . . **folk**sveimuðr (Ótt *Knútdr* 1/3–4)
folkþorran **fylk**ir (Þorf Lv 1/7)
folk-Rǫgnir getr fregna / **fylk**is sveit (Þfagr *Sveinn* 6/3–4)

A *lofðungr* 'prince' is *leyfðr* 'praised' (ÞjóðA Lv 11/7), a *mildingr* 'prince' is *mildr* 'gracious' (Arn *Hardr* 13/5–6), a *konungr* 'king' is *kœnn* 'skillful, wise' (Hfr *ErfÓl* 27/7–8), a *skjǫldungr* 'prince' is a *skjǫldr* 'shield' (Ótt *Knútdr* 10/1), a *dǫglingr* 'prince' is *dyggr* 'worthy' (BKrepp *Magndr* 11/7–8, Þloft *Glækv* 1/3–4), and a *gœðingr* 'ruler, valiant man' is *góðr* 'good' (Hfr *ErfÓl* 27/5–6). Knútr, the *yngvi* 'king,' was obviously fated to rule *England* (Hallv *Knútdr* 6/1). A *gramr* 'ruler' has authority over *gumnum* 'men' (Eskál *Vell* 28/7). *Aldir* 'men' praise the *allvaldr* 'mighty ruler' (ÞKolb *Eirdr* 10/1), a *siklingr* 'ruler' directs a *sókn* 'onslaught' (Sigv *Nesv* 2/1–2), a *þengill* 'prince' heaps up a *þungr* 'heavy' pile of corpses (Ótt *Hfl* 9/1), while a *mæringr* 'leader' wins *mærð* 'glory' (ESkál *Vell* 37/4–5).

A skald who disposed his rhymes in a distinctive way created a stylistic signature.[31] Connoisseurs of this art claim the ability to distinguish with some confidence an early Bragi from a late Sigvatr, a Hallvarðr from a Hallfreðr, the real Gísli or Egill from later imitators. Some designs, like some tattoos, are more intricate, expensive, and expressive than others. The poem *Glymdrápa* (*glymr* 'clattering'), attributed to the early tenth-century Norwegian skald Þorbjǫrn hornklofi, lives up to its name with tongue-twisting cross-rhyming lines such as "**bryng*ǫgl* í dyn *Skǫgl***ar" (byrnie-goslings [ARROWS] in the din of Skǫgul <valkyrie> [BATTLE]) (5/4).[32] This earliest known *dróttkvætt* praise poem sometimes repeats the second rhyming word in an odd-line *skothending* as the first syllable of the following even line, thereby creating an end-rhyming couplet. Continued *g*-alliteration throughout the half-stanza below harps on the initial sound of the poem's name:

Grennir þrǫng at **gunn**i
gunnmǫ́s fyr haf **sunn**an
(sá vas **gram**r) ok **gumn**um
(goð*varðr*) und sik *jǫrðu*.

Grennir gunnmǫ́s þrǫng jǫrðu ok gumnum und sik at gunni fyr sunnan haf.[33]

The feeder of the battle-mew [RAVEN/EAGLE > WARRIOR] pressed earth and men under him in battle south of the sea.

At other times, the two alliterating syllables forming an odd-line *skothending* (*hjalm/hilm*; *lind/land*) form half-rhymes with the two rhyming syllables of the following even line (*holm/olm*; *lund/bund*):

Ok **hjalm**tamiðr **hilm**ir
holmreyðar lét **olm**an
lindihjǫrt fyr **landi**
lundprúðr við stik **bund**inn.

Ok lundprúðr holmreyðar hjalmtamiðr hilmir lét olman lindihjǫrt bundinn við stik fyr landi.[34]

And the proud-minded prince, accustomed to the helmet of the island-rorqual [SNAKE = helmet of terror], had the wild mast-hart [SHIP] tied to a stake at the shore.

In both couplets, the penultimate syllables form half-rhymes with one another. Maintained through this clamor of multiple, interwoven full and half-rhymes is the image of an untamed Norwegian deer tied to a post—that is, a viking warship at anchorage in a foreign harbor. The skald's two sound-chains here outperform most Old English long-line alliterative runs, such as "**hæl**eð under **hel**mum of ðære **hal**igan byrig" (men under helmets from that holy fortress) (*Jud* 203) and "liðmen to **lande** **linde** bæron" (sailors bore shields to shore) (*Mald* 99), but a family resemblance is still perceptible.

The Icelandic skald Einarr *skálaglamm* 'hall-noise' Helgason is often irregular in his rhyme placements, shifting rapidly from too few chimes (for example, odd lines without *skothendingar*) to too many.[35] The first couplet of his praise poem for Hákon jarl Sigurðarson of Norway (r. ca. 970–99) repeats the word "hear" twice, linking odd and even lines as tightly as Þorbjǫrn did in the *gunn-/gunn-* rhyme just cited. Einarr clearly wants his patron to drink it all in. The second couplet goes overboard with three half-rhymes and two full:

Hug**stór**an biðk **heyra**
—**heyr,** jarl, Kvasis **dreyra**—
foldar **vǫrð** á **fyrð**a
fjarð-leggjar brim **dreggjar**.

Biðk hugstóran vǫrð foldar heyra á brim dreggjar fyrða fjarð-leggjar; heyr, jarl, dreyra Kvasis.[36]

I ask the strongminded guardian of the land to hear the surf of the yeast of the men of the fjord-bone [ROCK > DWARFS > POEM]; hear, jarl, the blood of Kvasir [POEM].

The jarl, as coast guard, is to hearken to the poetic mead, a roaring, oncoming wave that the poet is furiously bailing out of his craft. Half-rhymes that transition into full rhymes in the even verse are a recurrent design in Einarr's praise poem. Here he repeats the fifth syllable of an odd line (carrying half-rhyme and alliteration) as the first syllable in the following even line (bearing full rhyme and alliteration):

fyr **ǫrþeysi** at **aus**a
austr vín-Gnóðar **flaust**a.

At ausa . . . vín-Gnóðar austr fyr ǫrþeysi flausta.[37]

[I must] bail out the bilge-water of [Óðinn's] wine-ship [POETRY] for the bold impeller of fleets [Hákon].

The cognate words *ausa* 'to bail' and *austr* 'bilge-water' firmly link odd to even line while extending the skald's "drink" metaphor in a nautical direction.

The following couplet from the same eulogy represents a *dróttkvætt* variant in which the alliterating penultimate syllable of the odd line forms a *skothending* not only within its own line but also with both rhyming syllables in the next line:

randar **lauk**s af **ríki**
rœkilundr of **tœki**.

Rœkilundr lauks randar of tœki af ríki.[38]

[before] the heeding-tree of the leek of the shield [SWORD > WARRIOR] seized with power.

The syllables *rand-* and *lund-* are linked by half-rhyme; *lauk-* and *lund-*, by crossed alliteration.

Einarr returns to *dunhent* in the following couplet, seemingly associating the sword-name *Laufi* 'leaf' and *líf* 'life' only to indicate their burgeoning antagonism:

Laufa veðr at **lífi**
lífkǫld Hǫars **drífu**.

Lífkǫld veðr Laufa . . . at lífi . . . Hǫars drífu.[39]

[He let] the life-cold wind of Laufi [BATTLE] [grow against men's] life in the snow-shower of Hárr [= Óðinn] [BATTLE].

The triple paronomasia behind Einarr's image of a wind-tossed leaf in a ferocious blizzard suggests something fiercely inimical to life, the inevitability of warriors falling to earth in a wintry hail of spears. In a similar way, the sound effects of the previous couplet subtly link a ruler's deft handling of a sword to his seizure of power, artistry masking a military coup. The skald's exuberant rhyme play sometimes reveals a joy in sound for its own sake; at other times, it suggests what must not be said directly. The demanding structure of *dróttkvætt* was a spur to accessorizing, for performing meaning within strict confines following established rules of poetic etiquette. The diverse rhyming schemes on display in the viking-age skaldic corpus are purposeful, illustrating Georg Lukács's dictum that "the truly social element in literature is the form."[40]

Half-Rhyme in Old English Verse

I tell the tale that I heard told . . .

—A. E. Housman, *A Shropshire Lad*

Speakers of Germanic languages are accustomed to forms of vowel alternations that result in alliterating half-rhymes. English verbs provide pairs and triplets such as drive/drove/driven, ride/rode/ridden, spring/sprang/sprung, speak/spoke, choose/chose, bid/bade, bear/bore, feed/fed, hold/held, heave/hove, hang/hung, drink/drank/drench, knit/knot, grow/grew, fall/fell, swim/swam, sit/sat/set, wind/wound/wend, bind/bound/bend, full/fill, even cool/chill; nouns and adjectives produce sets such as year/yore, food/feed/fodder, hale/health/whole, pride/proud, foul/filth, slow/sloth, long/length/lingering, broad/breadth, and wide/width, along with plurals such as goose/geese, mouse/mice, child/children, brother/brethren, and man/men, all historically explicable.

The alliterating half-rhymes of *dróttkvætt* verse sometimes reunited etymological or pseudo-etymological couples, such as *gǫmlum/glamma, rauða/ryðs, hilmir/holm, lýsa/ljósgarð, landi/lund-, fyll-/full-, yngva/ungr, myrðir/morð-, þunga/þings, afli/efla, segjǫndum/sagna, segls/siglur, sóknþorinn/søkja, knekkt/hnakka, mál/mæla, tala/telja, lofþa/lifði, hefnt/hefna, ofr-/efni, skaft/skifti, lýgr/lægir, lyfti-/lofti, harða/hǫrðum, mǫrk/markar, gengi-/ganga*, and *girði-/garðar*. Old English poets worked similar magic with pairs such as *rad/ræd, hana/hæn, lof/lif, mod/medu, heold/hilde, neode/nyde, naman/nemnan, sprang/sprengde, word/wyrd/geworden*, and *dwæl/gedwilde*. Alliterative verse, like a machine tossing out tennis balls, fills the air with bouncy half-rhymes. Speakers of Old Norse and Old English shared a talent for coining fresh words on old models. Tenth-century England even devised a new noun, *pryde* 'pride,' to accompany a recent Continental loan adjective *prud/prut* 'proud,' imitating a sound change that had occurred centuries earlier (cf. OE *hlud* 'loud,' *hlyd* 'noise'; *ful* 'foul, *fylþ* 'filth').[41] (Later English speakers, following the first-class strong-verb pattern "ride/rode," cavalierly invented a new past tense for the medieval French loanword "to strive.") In England as in the Scandinavian North, interest in the fabric of language, in fossicking among the roots of words, was, like the wind over Iceland, general.

Stylistic traits typical of *dróttkvætt* composition, such as half-rhymes in odd lines, are present, fleetingly, in some of the earliest Old English poems extant. Cædmon, unlettered tender of livestock in seventh-century Northumbria, neatly forms an alliterating *skothending* by coupling heaven and roof (***heof**on to **hrof**e* 'heaven as a roof,' 6a), noting simultaneously, in an alliterating etymological half-rhyme, how the creator (***scyp**pend*, 5a) created (***sceop***, 6b) this firmament. His final verse is particularly skald-worthy: ***firum** **fol**dan **frea** **æl**mihtig* (9), with the ***æl-*** discreetly chiming with the ***fol-*** of the preceding half-line.[42] Bede had confided that it was not possible to translate verse from one language to another "without some loss of beauty and dignity" (*decoris ac dignitatis*); vernacular half-rhymes vanish in his Latin paraphrase of the herdsman's poem.[43] The sound effects audible in Cædmon's inaugural hymn had a past and went on to enjoy a productive future. Old English verse embraces a wealth of glittering and internally chiming lines, still largely uncharted. Here a rowboat arrives to convey news of a saint's death:

. . . þæt se **hærnflota**
æfter **sund**plegan **sondlond** ge**spearn**,
grond wið **greot**e.

(*GuthB* 1333b–35a)

. . . so that the ocean-floater, after sporting in the sea, kicked upon the sandy shore, ground against the gravel.

The mud of the fens is here transformed into the open sea.[44] *Sund* makes a half-rhyme with *sond/lond/grond*; other half-rhymes in the passage include *hærn/-spearn* and *flot-/greot-*. In addition to the two alliterating poetic compounds (one of which is self-rhyming), the poet's doubled *gr*-cluster, a phonestheme from the semantic fields of grimness and grief, suggests the groan of the skiff as it grates upon pebbles.[45]

The nonalliterating half-rhymes of *dróttkvætt* (e.g., ***dæð**ir dolga **Þrúð**ar*) alert us to their half-hidden existence and function in Old English verse. In the latter corpus, rhymes such as ***geor**ne **hyr**don* (*Beo* 66a), *wið **man**na **hwon**e* (*Beo* 155a), *ofer **hleorber**[g]an* (*Beo* 304a), *ac **her** **forþ** **berað*** (*Finn* 5a), *ne **hry**re ne **car**u* (*JgD2* 262a), *þæs **dim**man **cym**e*

(*JgD2* 14a), and ***godum dædum*** (*Wald* 23a) are modest and, like good deeds, slip by unobserved. We jump at jingles such as ***flod blod*** *ge**wod*** (*Ex* 463b),[46] ***folc*** *æfter* ***wolcnum*** (*Ex* 350b), ***flod blod****e weoll* (*Beo* 1422a), ***hlynede*** *ond* ***dynede*** (*Jud* 23b), even *þa middan**geard** manncynnes* ***weard*** (*CH* 7a-b), but our ears barely register pairs such as ***flot****/ge**wat*** (*Brun* 35a-b), ***wind-/stand-*** (*Wan* 76a-b), or **manncynn**es (*CH* 7b). Listen to Beowulf's "decorous and extremely well-measured" reply to Wulfgar's request to identify himself—and that courtier's subsequent response:[47]

"We synt Higelaces
beodgeneatas; Beowulf is min nama.
Wille ic asecgan sunu Healfdenes,
mærum þeodne min ærende,
aldre þinum, gif he us geunnan wile
þæt we hine swa godne gretan moton."
(342b–47)

"We are Hygelac's table-companions; Beowulf is my name. I will tell my errand to the son of Healfdene, the illustrious lord, your ruler, if he will be so good as to grant that we may approach him."

Ic þæs wine Deniga,
frean Scildinga frinan wille,
beaga bryttan, swa þu bena eart,
þeoden mærne ymb þinne sið,
ond þe þa andsware ædre gecyðan
ðe me se goda agifan þenceð.
(350b–55)

"I will ask the friendly ruler of the Danes, the prince of the Scyldings, distributor of rings, about that, as you request, the illustrious lord, about your venture, and make known to you at once the answer that that good man thinks to give me."

Here is a performance of etiquette as understood today. This polite exchange is marked by the elegant variation (or parallelism) of synonyms for the Danish king; the syntactic suspension and vertical placement of these nominals recalls the similar disposition of kenning elements in *dróttkvætt* royal encomia.[48] Like the apposed kenning-parts of Old Norse praise poetry, the variation of poetic words in these two passages does more than fulfill alliterative requirements; the density alone of these noun phrases lends value both to the individual and the regal rank so designated. Repetition artfully patterned signified.

Each of the speeches above occupies five and a half lines; neither speaker is so boorish as to name the king directly; each resorts to polite circumlocutions. Wulfgar's response repeats key words from Beowulf's speech in the same relative positions: *mærum þeodne/þeoden mærne* (three lines from the end); *swa godne/se goda* (the final line); the last two lines of both speeches alliterate alike, first on vowels and then on *g*. Wulfgar matches Beowulf's bold crossed alliteration and subsequent half-rhymes (***beo**dge**ne**atas*; ***Beo**wulf is min **nama***; ***aldre þin**um*, *gif he us ge**unn**an **wile***) with a comparable line of half-rhymes, one pair alliterating and one not (***frean** Sci**ld**inga* ***frin**an wi**ll**e*). A similar mixed format triumphantly concludes *The Battle of Brunanburh* (73):

> **eor**las **ar***hwæ*te **ear**d be*geat*on.[49]
>
> ———
>
> glory-keen men conquered the land.

Patterns of alliterating and cross-alliterating half-rhymes adorn the Old English poetic corpus. These rhymes reunite cognate words in the *Paris Psalter*: *be**heald** min ge**bed*** ***hold**e **mod**e* ("look upon my prayer with a gracious mind") (*PPs* 60.1.2, 118.168.1); *beoð his **wint**er **eac*** ***wyn**num **ic**ed* ("his winters/years, too, will be replete in joys") (60.5.2); ***cum**að nu to**gæd**ere,* *wutun **cwem**an **god**e* ("come together now, let us praise god") (94.1.1); *a**hyld**e ic mine heortan* ***hold**e mode, / þæt ic þin **soð**fæst **weorc*** *symble **worhte*** ("I inclined my heart in faithful manner, so that I always performed your righteous work") (118.112.1–2).

The tonal elegance of a repeated line like ***enge anpaðas, uncuð*** *gelad* ("narrow single paths, a strange passage") (*Beo* 1410, *Ex* 58) is in large part attributable to its mixture of alliterating and nonalliterating half-rhymes. In addition to the three (different) alliterating and half-rhyming nasalized vowels (*en-*, *an-*, *un-*), there is slant-rhyme on *pað-* and *cuð*.

As the men move single file over mountainous terrain to reach, respectively, Grendel's mere and the Red Sea, the verse mirrors a staggered climb down by moving from high front vowel (*e*) to low back vowel (*a*). The same trick of darkening sound, the same sonic mimicry, is present in Thomas Nashe's "brightness falls from the air." Reducing the number of syllables and piling on nominal compounds seems to slow down the pace, as in *guð**rinc** **goldwlanc** græs**moldan** træd* ("the warrior gold-laden trod the greensward") (*Beo* 1881). The poet's triple *g*-alliteration and the heaviness of the three compounds are audible as the hero, weighed down by treasure and sadness, departs Denmark. *Dróttkvætt* art alerts our ears to the subtle half-rhyme of *-rinc* and *-wlanc* (reinforced by *sinc* 'treasure' in the next line), and the full rhyme of *gold-* and *-mold*, sites in later English poetry where we do not expect rhyme to reside.

The nonalliterating half-rhymes bracketing the Sigemund/Heremod episode of *Beowulf* (867–915) seem to signal not closure but enclosure, the end echoing the beginning.[50] The scene opens with warriors racing horses in competition:

Hwilum heaþorofe hleapon **let**on
on ge**flit** **far**an **feal**we **mear**as.
(864–65)

———

At times the battle-bold ones let their dun steeds gallop, compete in a race.

After the king's retainer finishes his tale of Sigemund and Heremod, the narrator returns to the horse race in progress:

Hwilum **flit**ende **feal**we **stræte**
mearum **mæt**on.
(916–17a)

———

At times, contending, they measured the dusky road with their steeds.

Fealu 'pale, dun-colored' appears in both passages, in the latter transposed from horses to path;[51] *geflit* and *flitende* are also repurposed, while nonalliterating half-rhymes (here in bold) inhabit both couplets.

Alliterating half-rhymes attract attention. In *dróttkvætt* odd lines, whenever the two syllables carrying the *skothending* also alliterate, they form pairs such as the following, extracted from stanzas attributed to late ninth- and tenth-century skalds; half-rhymes are in bold, secondary sound effects, italicized:

segls *nag*lfara **sigl**ur	Bragi *Rdr* 5
til **fár**huga **fœr**a	Bragi *Rdr* 8
bauða sú til **bleyð**i	Bragi *Rdr* 9
girðiþjófr í **garð**a	Þjóð *Haustl* 9/3
reiði-Tys it **rauða**	Þjóð *Haustl* 20/3
*il*lts við **ulf** at **ylf**ask	Hildr Lv 1/5
*haf*nið **Nef**ju **naf**na	Hildr Lv 1/1
þvít **ríkr** konungr **rek**ka	Jór *Send* 3/1
þar gekk **Njǫrð**r af **Nirð**i	GSind *Hákdr* 6/5
lystr gekk **herr** til **hjǫr**va	ÞSjár *Þórdr* 1/3
naustr blakks it **næst**a	ÞSjár *Þórdr* 1/7
hafði **fǫr** til **fer**ju	Glúmr *Gráf* 2/1
blakkríðandi **bakk**a	Glúmr *Gráf* 2/3
gumna vinr at **gamn**i	Glúmr *Gráf* 3/3
foldar rauð, ok **felld**i	Glúmr *Gráf* 3/5
val*galt*ar lét **vel**ta	Glúmr *Gráf* 7/5
hein*þyn*ntan lét **hvína**	Glúmr *Gráf* 9/1
sendir fell á **sand**i	Glúmr *Gráf* 11/5
vel *hef*r **hefn**t, en **hafn**a	Glúmr Lv 1/1
folkrakkr of vannt **fylk**ir	Glúmr Lv 1/3
es **dǫkk**valir **drekk**a	Glúmr Lv 1/5
ok **gangs** *Van*ir **ging**u	Eil *Þdr* 5/1
né **djúp**akǫrn **drǿp**u	Eil *Þdr* 11/1
ok **dauðs** vallar **dáð**ar	Þklypp Lv 1/5
byggði **lǫnd** en **lund**a	Eskál *Hákdr* 1/1
hljóta munk, né **hlít**ik	Eskál *Vell* 5/1
herjum kunn of **herj**uð	Eskál *Vell* 19/3
gnótt flaut **nás** fyr **nes**jum	Eskál *Vell* 22/7
þrøngvimeiðr of **þryngvi**	Eskál *Vell* 24/3
gengiligt at **genga**	Eskál *Vell* 27/3
þrymr varð **logs** þars **lǫgð**u	Eskál *Vell* 28/1
ok **hald**boði **hild**ar	Eskál *Vell* 29/5

þás **hring**fǫum **Hang**a	Tindr *Hákdr* 1/5
*hruð*usk **rið**marar **Róð**a	Tindr *Hákdr* 1/7
dreif at **Viðr**is **veðr**i	Tindr *Hákdr* 3/1
þars í **sundr** á **sand**i	Tindr *Hákdr* 3/5

When double alliteration occurs in an Old English a-verse and both initial staves share the same root-final consonant(s), the resulting half-rhymes resemble the alliterating *skothendingar* of *dróttkvætt* verse displayed above:

rodera **ræd**end	*And* 627, 816, *Beo* 1555, *EgD* 23
rad and **ræd**de	*Mald* 18
wuldres **wald**end	*And* 193, 539, *Beo* 17, 183, 1752, *Dan* 13, *Sat* 24
lofigen ond **luf**igen	*Az* 100
lufode on **life**	*And* 597
wuniað in **wyn**num	*Sat* 506, 592
wunian **wyn**dagum	*Fort* 61
wynnum be**wun**den	*Sat* 648
ne ge**feah** he þære **fæh**ðe	*Beo* 109
sund wið **sand**e	*Beo* 213
stonc ða æfter **stan**e	*Beo* 2288
to **med**o **mod**ig	*Beo* 604
modig ond **med**ugal	*Jud* 26
mæg ond **mag**oðegn	*Beo* 408
læddon to **leod**um	*Beo* 1159
heold **hild**edeor	*Beo* 2183
hare **heor**owulfas	*Ex* 61, 181
wean on **wen**an	*Deor* 25, *GenA* 1027, *Ex* 213
wean on**wen**dan	*Beo* 191
ge**grem**ed **grym**me	*GenA* 61
wærleas **wer**od	*GenA* 67
locum be**luc**an	*El* 1026
manna **men**io	*Ex* 334
weollon **wæl**bennum	*Ex* 492
neode ond **nyd**e	*ChristC* 1071
stodon **stæd**efæste	*Mald* 127

dwæl on ge**dwil**de	*GenA* 23
his **boda** **beod**an	*GenB* 558
be **nam**an **nem**nan	*Jud* 81
hreas on **hrus**an	*Beo* 2831
wulf in **wal**de	*Jud* 206
hæðenes **heað**orinces	*Jud* 179
scines **scon**can	*MSol* 101
heolstre be**hel**med	*MSol* 104
feðerhoman on**foð**	*MSol* 151
heaf under **hef**onum	*MSol* 468
bearnes ge**byr**de	*ChristB* 724
synnum a**sun**drad	*GuthA* 515, *Phoen* 242, *El* 1309, *And* 124
haligra **hel**m	*ChristB* 529
haligra ge**hyld**	*Az* 169
hæleð in **heal**le	*Dan* 728, *Mald* 214
hæleð to **hil**de	*GenA* 2061
hæleð **hell**fuse	*And* 50
gyld of **gold**e	*Dan* 175
cyninga **cyn**ost	*KtPs* 3

In a-verses with double alliteration, full and half-rhymes involving the second element of a compound seem particularly artful and distinctive:

gomen gleo**beam**es	*Beo* 2263
nacod nið**drac**a	*Beo* 2273
hreðre hyge**með**e	*Beo* 2442

Half-rhymes in both corpora often link cognate words: Old Norse *mál* 'speech' joins *mæla* 'to speak'; *tala* 'to talk,' *telja* 'to set forth'; *þǫgn* 'silence,' *þegna* 'to be silent'; *set-* 'seat,' *sitja* 'to sit'; *rammr* 'strong,' *remma* 'to strengthen'; *lyfti-* 'lifted,' *lofti* 'aloft'; *afli* 'might, power,' *efla* 'to support'; *land* 'land,' *lendr* 'landed'; and *myrk* 'dark,' *mǫrk* 'forest'; *þverrir* 'diminisher' attracts *þverra* 'to recede'; *harðr* 'hard,' *herðar* 'shoulders'; and so on. These *skothending* pairs sometimes have twins in Old English verse: Old Norse *konungr* 'king'/*kœnn* 'wise' replicates Old English *cyning* 'king'/*gecynde* 'innate, skillful.' Nonetymological matchmaking is not always celebratory. Old Norse *mein* 'harm'/*mann* (acc.) 'man' mirrors Old English *man* 'crime'/*mann* 'man.'[52] Repeated linkages in both corpora can represent a social norm, a basis for stability and order in the world. In *dróttkvætt* verse, the noun *hjaldr* 'battle' and the valkyrie *Hildr* 'war' eagerly reunite. The *forn* 'ancient' should be *firnum* 'vehemently' praised; a *reiðr* 'angry' ruler raises *rauðar* 'red' (shields).[53] In Old English poetry, *god* 'good' goes with *god* 'God'; *hæleð* 'man' with *halig* 'holy'; and *healdan* 'to hold' with *hold* 'trusty.' More realistically, a *maga* 'man' belongs to a *mægð* 'nation'; an *æðeling* 'nobleman' to an *eðel* 'native land'; *dom* 'judgment' must be *gedemed* 'judged'; and *wyrd* 'fate' must *geworden* 'come to pass.'

An artful skald could thwart expectations, placing alliterating and rhyming cognates in different clauses as Hallfreðr does in this haunting couplet:

upp **sǫg**ðu **lǫg**—**lag**ðisk
líf skjótt firum . . .

[axes] proclaimed the laws—life was swiftly laid aside for men.[54]

Old Icelandic *lǫg* 'law' (plural < *log* 'layer, what was laid down') shares a root with ON *leggja* (*lagði*) as in the formula *leggja lǫg* 'to pass laws' (late OE *lecgan laga*).[55] Here Hallfreðr grimly announces the result of one fatal skirmish in which axes laid down the law—and men's lives. In Old English scriptural poetry, Lucifer specializes in inverting pseudo-etymological ties. Man (*hæleð*) may not be holy (*halig*) but, as he declares, "mid *hæleða* forlore . . . is min mod *gehæled*" (with the damnation of men . . . is my heart healed) (*GenB* 757–58). The forging of perverse linkages was a first step on his downward path. The downhearted speaker of *Wulf and Eadwacer*, her expections (***wen****um*, 9, 13) of joy (***wyn***, 12) thwarted, hints in a final chiming word pair that her relationship with her lover may have been broken from the start:

Þæt mon eaþe tosliteð   þætte næfre gesomnad wæs,
uncer **giedd** **gead**or.

(*Wulf* 18–19)

One easily separates what was never joined, our song together.[56]

Unlike *dróttkvætt*, Old English verse had no rhyme requirements. Nevertheless, half-rhymes sometimes bridge the caesura, linking a- and b-verses in catchy sound chains:

frumsceaft **fira**	**feor**ran reccan	*Beo* 91
leomum ond **leaf**um	**lif** eac gesceop	*Beo* 97
mære mearcstapa	se þe **mor**as heold	*Beo* 103
won*sæl*ig **wer**	**wear**dode *hwil*e	*Beo* 105
metod for þy **mane**	**man**cynne fram	*Beo* 110
wean on**wen**dan;	wæs þæt ge**win** to swyð	*Beo* 191
furþur **fer**an	nu ge **feor**buend	*Beo* 254
hringa **hyrd**e	**hord**wyrðne dæl	*Beo* 2245
þone **leofes**tan	**lifes** æt ende	*Beo* 2823
beorht hofu **bærn**an	**bryne**leoma stod[57]	*Beo* 2313
wyrda ne **word**a.	**Weorod** eall aras	*Beo* 3030
iu*mon*na **gold**	**gald**re be*wun*den	*Beo* 3052
hæle hildedior	**hæle**ða monegum	*Beo* 3111
hwæt, we ge**frun**an	on **fyrn**dagum	*And* 1
ðu scealt þa **fore** ge**fer**an	on þin **feorh** *ber*an	*And* 216
leofne leodfruman	mid **lof**e sinum	*And* 989
folc and **fol**dan.	**Feal**lan *sceol*on	*Mald* 54
feoll þa to **fol**dan	**feal**o*hil*te swurd	*Mald* 166
lid*men* to **land**e	**lind**e bæron	*Mald* 99
lif forlætan	oððe **leof**ne gewrecan	*Mald* 208
þær wearð **hream** ahafen,	**hremm**as wundon[58]	*Mald* 106
ongan **ceal**lian þa	ofer **cal**d wæter[59]	*Mald* 91
þa **stod** on **stæðe**,	**stið**lice clipode	*Mald* 25
fyr on feondas	for **fyren**dædum	*Dan* 344
liðe and **lof**sum,	þæt wæs **lif**es beam	*GenB* 468
leofes leodfruman	on **lu**fan swiðe	*GenA* 1246
nu þin **cun**node	**cyn**ing alwihta	*Ex* 421
wera wuldorgesteald.	**Wer**igend lagon	*Ex* 589
lufsom ond liþe	**leof**um monnum	*ChristC* 913
liþes **lif**es,	þæs þe **aly**fed biþ	*ChristC* 1637
ðær is **leofra lufu**	**lif** butan endedeaðe	*ChristC* 1652
lif*wear*de **leof**	his ge**leafa** *wear*ð	*El* 1035
leofe on **lif**e	**lof** wide sprang	*Fates* 6
lufast and ge**ly**fest	ond his **lof** rærest	*Jul* 48

leofne **lof**iað ic þæs **lif**es ne mæg	*Phoen* 561
lufedon **leof**wendum **lif**es agend	*ChristB* 471
lifgað bi þam lissum þe us se **leof**a cyning	*Az* 114
lifgen on ge**leaf**an ond a **lu**fan dryhtnes	*JgD1* 49
swylce **lof** and **lif** and **leof**lic geþærnes	*JgD2* 271
mine **man**sceaþan on **men**nisc hiw	*GuthB* 909
lufena ond lissa. Min þæt **leof**e bearn	*GuthB* 1076
hrofas sind ge**hror**ene, **hreor**ge *tor*ras	*Ruin* 3
scearde **scur***beor*ge **scor**ene ge*dror*ene	*Ruin* 5
ræd under **rode**rum ic þa **rode** ne þearf[60]	*El* 918
nolde **gæd** **gead**or in **god**es rice	*MSol* 451
hrið **hreos**ende **hrus***an* bindeð	*Wan* 102
hæleða **hel**pend and þec, **hal**ig gast	*Dan* 402
haligne **hæle** under **heol**storlocan	*And* 144
helpend ond **hæl**end wið **hell**esceaðan	*Jul* 157
hæleð **hil**dedeor him wæs **hal**ig gast	*Ele* 935
hæleðum to **hel**pe, þæt me **hal**ig god	*Ele* 679, 1011
a**syn**drod from **syn**num swa ðin **sun**u mære	*Gloria* 1, 10
Cumað of **Thar**sis **tir**es eadige	*PPs* 71.10.1
gifena drihten for**gif**en *hæf*de	*GenA* 2936
treo sceolon brædan ond **treow** weaxan	*Max1* 159
sweordum a**swef**ede, swelce **seof**one eac	*Brun* 30

The poet of *The Battle of Maldon* expertly joined cognate words through alliteration, from half-line matches such as *þa **stod** on **stæðe*** (25), ***wig**an **wig**heardne* (75), and ***wig**an to **wig**e* (235) to etymological echoes bridging the caesura, as in **wig**an on ge*win*ne, **wig**end cr*un*con (302), and in the following long lines:

brimmanna **bod**a, a**bead** eft ongean (49)
se **flod** ut gewat, þa **flot**an stodon gearowe (92)
þær com **flowende** **flod** æfter ebban (65)
hicgan to handum and to **hig**e godum (4)
ond þæt spere **spreng**de þæt hit **sprang** ongean (137)

Even when an alliterating and rhyming pair are not cognate, as in *þæm **bur**þene, þa he **byre** hæfde* (*Mald* 121), the effect upon the ears is just as powerful.

The swan of Old English Riddle 7 is identified through a series of half-rhyming verbs, one of which derives from the same Indo-European root as "swan" itself:[61]

Hrægl min swigað þonne ic hrusan trede,
oþþe þa wic buge, oþþe wado drefe.
Hwilum mec ahebbað ofer hæleþa byht
hyrste mine ond þeos hea lyft,
ond mec þonne wide wolcna strengu
ofer folc byreð. Frætwe mine
swogað hlude ond swinsiað,
torhte singað, þonne ic getenge ne beom
flode ond foldan, ferende gæst.

My garment is silent when I step on the earth, or inhabit my lodgings, or ruffle the sea. At times my trappings and this high air raise me over the dwellings of men, and the strength of the clouds [= wind] then carries me far and wide over the people. My adornments resound loudly and make melody, brightly sing, when I am not resting on water and land, a traveling spirit.

The first two slant-rhyming verbs, *swigað* 'is silent' (1a) and *swogað* 'make noise' (7a), so alike in sound, so contrary in meaning, underscore the central paradox of the riddle: the existence of a creature mute when tied to earth and water, *folde* and *flod* (9a), but melodious when aloft. The poet's focus on the brightness of the swan's music (*swogað*, *swinsiað*, and *singað*) gradually uncovers a correspondence between name and essence, word and thing: a swan (OE *swan*) is so called because it makes melody (OE *swinsiað*). The final word of the riddle, a traveling *gæst* 'spirit,' 'soul,' 'stranger' recalls the legend that a swan sings most radiantly at the moment of death.[62] The poet's mute "swan" follows a pattern long familiar to the imagination.

In other poems, triple paronomastic chimes herald the joys of an earthly paradise:

Ne **fea**llað þær on **fol**dan **fea**lwe blostman . . .[63]

Faded flowers do not fall to earth there . . .

(*Phoen* 74)

The first two half-rhymes below are true cognates; the third, like *fealwe* 'pale, dusky,' above, is a poignant reminder of change, of dissolution lying in ambush on the other side:

> **wuna**ð geond **wyn**lond—þæt on**wen**ded ne bið . . .

> [perfume] pervades the joyous land—this will not be changed [before . . .]
> (*Phoen* 82)

Final lines are rich sites for half-rhyme linkages, from the conclusions of individual Advent lyrics—*þurh* ***hor****scne had* ***her****gan willað* ("[they] through wisdom desire to praise") (*ChristA* 49); *hu se* ***ear****ma sceal* ***ar****e gebidan* ("how the wretched shall wait for grace") (*ChristA* 70)—down to the tautological end of *Judgment Day I*: ***wel****an ah in* ***wul****dre se nu* ***wel*** *þenceð* ("he will possess happiness in heaven who now considers well") (119). The courtier Wulfgar ends his interview with Beowulf with a promise consisting almost entirely of rhyming syllables: *Ic þæs* ***wine*** ***Den****iga /* ***frean*** ***Scil****dinga* ***frin****an* ***wil****le* ("I shall ask the friend of the Danes, lord of the Scyldings about this matter") (*Beo* 350b–351). "I like that," said the king; "sing it again."[64]

Those Noisy Beasts of Battle

No viking-age *dróttkvætt* praise poem was complete, it would seem, without at least a sideways glance at the beasts of battle: the triad of wolf, eagle, and raven. Two of these creatures have starring roles in the following half-stanza, each odd line of which is linked by half-rhyme to the following even. Spears ring out and the beasts emerge for their feast:

> **Fjall**vǫnðum gaf **fylli**
> (**full**r varð) en spjǫr **gull**u,
> her**stefn**andi **hrǫfn**um
> (**hrafn** á ylgjar **tafn**i).

Herstefnandi gaf fjallvǫnðum hrǫfnum fylli, en spjǫr gullu; hrafn varð fullr á tafni ylgjar.[65]

The army-leader gave the mountain-accustomed ravens their fill, and spears cried out; the raven became full on the bloody prey of the she-wolf [CORPSE].

The dark raven in *Beowulf* similarly boasts about making a meal of the battle-kill alongside the wolf (3024–27). The forest animal does the heavy slicing; the birds scavenge alongside. Another skald, Halldórr ókristni 'the Un-Christian,' depicts an eagle sharing companionably in the wolf's dinner:

sleit ǫrn Gera beitu.[66]

---

an eagle tore at Geri's [wolf's] forage.

Einarr's stanza, like Halldórr's, is unusual in referring to raven and eagle with an everyday prosaic word, not one of the many *dróttkvætt* kennings for those birds: "Óðinn's seagull," "Gautr's cuckoo," "hawk of Gunnr," "goose of Hangi," "war-hawk," "mew of wounds," "battle-crane," "wound-falcon," "battle-vulture," and scores more.[67] In an extended kenning, Hallfreðr hails his prince, lost overboard in a sea battle, as a feeder of carrion birds, nourisher of "seagulls of the noise of the gleam of the animal of the sea-king" [SHIP > SHIELD > BATTLE > EAGLES/RAVENS)]. The provisioner may now himself be food.[68]

The beasts-of-battle set piece emerges at least four dozen times in viking-age *dróttkvætt* stanzas and fourteen times in Old English verse.[69] In the latter corpus, the *hrafn* 'raven' is dark, the *earn* 'eagle,' dewy and hungry, and the gray *wulf* 'wolf' of the *weald* 'woods' focused on *wæl* 'slaughter.' *The Battle of Brunanburh* is exceptional in referring to the eagle, skaldic-style, in terms of another bird: *guðhafoc* 'war-hawk' (64a). The poet of *Exodus* seems to put on a northern accent in his contribution to the type-scene: the raven is a *wælceasega* 'chooser of the slain' (164a), a compound possibly formed in imitation of Old English *wælcyrige*, Old Norse *valkyrja, valkjósandi* 'chooser of the slain.' The same poet describes the wolf as *cwyldrof* (166b), a compound of uncertain meaning: perhaps "killing-bold," perhaps "evening-bold" (cf. ON *kveld* 'evening'), perhaps both. The troop-corpses (*drihtneas*, dat. *drihtneum*) over which the beasts in *Exodus* rejoice may also have a northern cast (cf. ON *nár* 'corpse,' dat. *nám*). None of these Old English compounds occurs again.

The *Beowulf* passage featuring the three boon companions takes the form of a reported conversation:

> . . . ac se wonna *hrefn*
> fus ofer fægum   fela reordian,
> earne secgan,   hu him æt æte speow,
> þenden he wið **wulf**   **wæl** *reaf*ode.
> (3024b–27)

. . . but the black raven eager over doomed men [will] speak much, say to the eagle how he fared at the feeding when he strove with the wolf to strip the slaughtered.

This is the sole occasion in Old English poetry in which the two birds converse. The image of a raven boasting to the eagle about a recent dining experience has skaldic parallels: a particularly garrulous raven, called *arnar eiðbróðir* 'sworn brother of the eagle,' does much of the talking in Þorbjǫrn hornklofi's *Haraldskvæði* (*Hrafnsmál*), a praise poem in eddic meters.[70] The *Beowulf* poet's anonymous messenger here predicts destruction for his people: exile, slavery, a morning-cold spear; no sound of harps will awaken warriors in this darkness, just the strident chatter of two carrion birds. The Old English poet's feat of compression—three interlaced beasts in seven half-lines—recalls a gambit of viking-age skalds, several of whom managed to fit raven, eagle, and wolf into a single stanza.[71] Þormóðr Trefilsson accomplished this feat in four half-lines of only five syllables each: "The feeder of the swan of battle-din's swell [BLOOD > RAVEN > WARRIOR] sated the eagle on the wolf's feast [CORPSES] in Alftafjord."[72] There may have been a competition around the North Sea to make the beasts of battle scene as crisp as possible.

Although normally part of a threesome, sometimes a single raven fills the bill (*Finn* 5–7). In the *Beowulf* excerpt above (3024b–27), the final verb *reafian* 'reave, strip' (put in the raven's mouth) is a self-characterizing *skothending*: stripping bones is that bird's professional specialty. When wolves are not mentioned as part of the trio (*Mald* 106–7,

GenA 1983–85, 2087–89), it is because human opponents have assumed their role: *wælwulfas* ‘slaughter-wolves, viking warriors’ (*Mald* 96a, *And* 149a); *herewulfas* ‘army-wolves’ (*GenA* 2015b); and *hildewulfas* ‘battle-wolves, the Elamites’ (*GenA* 2051a).

Descriptions of the eagle frequently employ half-rhymes in addition to alliteration: the Old English ***earn*** ‘eagle’ is ***æ****tes* ***georn*** ‘eager for a meal’ (*Jud* 210a) and ***æ****ses* ***georn*** ‘eager for carrion’ (*Mald* 107a); its typical epithet, ***ur****igfeðra* ‘dewy-winged’ (*El* 52a, 111a, *Ex* 163a, *GenA* 1984b, *Jud* 210b), nearly forms a *skothending* with its name (**ur-/ear-**). The *wulf* ‘wolf,’ inhabitor of woods (OE *weald*) and devourer of the slain (OE *wæl*), regularly attracts these semi-rhymes and more, many bridging the caesura:

wælhreowra wig.	**Wulf** sang ahof	(*El* 112)
ne huru **wæl** wepeð	**wulf** se græga	(*Max1* 150)
wonn **wæl**ceasega.	**Wulf**as sungon	(*Ex* 164)
þenden he wið **wulf**	**wæl** reafode.	(*Beo* 3027)
wulf on **wealde**,	**wæl**rune ne mað	(*Ele* 28)
wulf on **wealde**.	Ne wearð **wæl** mare	(*Brun* 68)
wulfum to **wil**lan	ond eac **wæl**gifrum	(*Jud* 295)

These repeated sounds are not mere counters in an arbitrary signifying system. A poet’s favored alliterative and rhyming pairs, like makeup and dress, invite a certain attitude, a particular sort of attention. The ***wæl****reowe* ‘slaughter-cruel’ men (6) on Wulf’s island in *Wulf and Eadwacer*, and the woods to which he drags his and the speaker’s mysterious *hwelp* ‘cub’ (17), may have called up a pattern long familiar to the memory. Whatever is going on in this poem, Wulf is living up to his name. The *Maldon* poet provides a snapshot of one Wulfmær’s willful heroism:

wund *wearð* **Wulf***mær*, **wæl**reste geceas (*Mald* 113)

(Wulfmær was wounded, chose a slaughter-bed)

The habitual association in Old English verse of *wulf* ‘wolf’ and *wæl* ‘slaughter’ may have activated the separate elements of Wulfmær’s dithematic name: onomastic determinism draws *Wulf-* to a *wælrest* 'slaughter-bed,' just as it makes Usain Bolt a sprinter, Dr. Frye a burn specialist, and Mr. Fillen a substitute teacher. His "choice" to fall in battle was preordained.

The Family That Rhymes Together

Einarr's kenning for his emergent poem in *Vellekla* 11/2–4—"því kom vǫxtr í **Vínu** **vín**heims **vin**ar Lopts" (therefore growth came to the river of the wine-world of Loptr's friend [=Óðinn])—begins with *vinr* 'friend,' a syllable that then attracts the river name *Vína,* which in turn joins forces with a second flowing stream, that of *vín-* 'wine.' A new poem is brought into being through associative rhetoric, by a fresh combination of separate entities (friend, river, wine), each noun beginning with a vibrating *v/w* and ending with a low, humming *n.* Einarr's *Vellekla* is *dróttkvætt* at its ornamental finest. Its probable composition just before 975 renders it contemporaneous with the four major manuscript collections of Old English poetry.

Similar multiline paronomasia characterizes Old English verse. The poetic word *wine* 'friend, lord, husband, lover, protector' (= ON *vinr,* the standard term for "friend" in Scandinavia and Iceland today) is cognate with OE *wynn* 'joy,' *wunian* 'to dwell,' *wenian* 'to accustom,' *wycsan* 'to wish,' *winnan* 'to strive,' *gewinn* 'strife,' *wenan* 'to believe, hope,' and *wen* 'hope, expectation.'[73] *Wine* frequently reunites with these relatives. No social distancing for them: they freely embrace, encouraged by the fact that all but *wyscan* have stems that form alliterating half-rhymes with the rest.

Wine, as a simplex and as part of a compound, occurs one hundred times in Old English verse; its absence from the three *Christ* poems and the *Paris Psalter,* the longest Old English verse composition extant, is notable. A warrior in *The Battle of Maldon* vows to "wrecan on ge**winne** [his] **wine**drihten" (avenge in the strife [his] friend and lord) (248). Earlier in the same poem, Ælf*wine* (209a, 231a) had exhorted his *winas* 'companions' (228b) to advance boldly; he lives up to his aristocratic name. Most alliterative *wine*-linkages involve only one cognate: Waldere addresses Guthhere: "Hwæt, ðu huru **wen**dest, **wine** Burgunda" (you indeed expected, lord of Burgundians) (*WaldB* 14); it is in a

***wyn**leas* 'joyless' (*Beo* 1416) grove that woe comes to Hrothgar's ***win**um* 'retainers' (1418). But the *Beowulf* poet scores a triple home run with "**wist**on ond ne **wen**don þæt hie heora **wine**dryhten" (they wished and did not expect that they [would see again] their friend and lord) (1604). And the speaker of *The Wanderer* recalls how in years past "his gold**wine** / **wen**ede [hine] to wiste; **wynn** eall gedreas" (his gold-friend accustomed [him] to the feast; joy has all departed) (35b–36).

Wine-family reunions sometimes signal the end of a sectional division or poem. The speaker of *The Wife's Lament* begins by recalling her friendless state (***wine**leas*, 10a), the joyless (***wynna** leas*, 32a) abode in which she was compelled to dwell (***wun**ian*, 27a), and the former ***wynn*** 'joy' (46a) of her weary ***wine*** 'friend, lover' (49a); she concludes her lament with a bitter and extended *w–n* run: "Dreogeð se *min* **wine** / *mic*le modceare; he ge*mon* to oft / **wyn**licran *wic*" (my friend endures great grief of heart; he remembers too often a more joyous dwelling) (50b–52a). Section closures in *Christ and Satan*, a poem not famed for originality, are signalled by the *w–n* formula *wunian in wynnum* 'dwell in joy' (209b–10a, 235a, 506a [fitt 9], 554 [fitt 10], 592a [fitt 11]). A lyrical outburst of *w–n* paronomasia marks the final moments of *Guthlac B*, as a chorus of rhyming *wine-*, *wyn-*, and *wun-* stems escorts the saint to heaven (***wyn**sum*, 1321a; ***wine***, 1339; ***wyn**mæg*, 1345; ***wine**þearfende*, 1347). His disciple takes the hint and announces Guthlac's death by employing a-lines with double alliteration in the key of *w–n*:

> *wer*igra wraþu, *woruld**dream**um* of,
> **wine**mæga **wyn**, in *wuldres þrym*,
> gewiten, **winiga** hleo . . .
> (1363–65a)
> . . . .
> **wunað** *wæl*reste . . . (1368a)
>
> ———
>
> The support of weary ones, joy of beloved kinsmen, protector of friends [has] departed from worldly joys into the glory of heaven. . . . He inhabits a death-bed.

The poet's insistent drumming on *w–n* suggests that closure is imminent. Half-rhymes link *wine*, *wyn*, *winiga*, and *wunað*, as well as *wer-* and *wor-*, *dream* and *þrym*, and *wul-* and *wæl-*; the homophonic attraction of the anagrams *woruld* and *wuldor* imitates the final movement described, the saint's exchange of earth for heaven.

EXTRA ALLITERATION

Mapping the Terrain

Single, double, crossed (AB AB), or transverse (AB BA), cluster, continued, interlaced, enjambed, or strong-linked, weak-linked, end-linked, back-linked—these alliterative techniques are differently wily and form patterns that only rarely seem random.[74] Each type has the potential to surprise, uncover hidden relationships, and enhance recall. Structural alliteration—described in chapter 1—is the backbone of early northern verse. Yet vernacular poets, in full compliance with the regulations, also employed extra or secondary alliteration as aural punctuation and ornamentation, sophisticated signals caught by receptive ears.[75]

Not everyone agrees. Most nineteenth-century scholars of Old English scoffed at the possibility of deliberate sound effects involving the final stressed syllable of a long line: if perceived, such a pattern was the result of chance.[76] John Lawrence in 1893 was almost alone in recognizing conscious design in crossed alliteration.[77] Klaeber's third edition of *Beowulf* had expressed polite doubt about the prevalence of extra alliteration: "The so-called enjambment of alliteration, i.e. the carrying over of a non-alliterating stressed letter of a *b*-line as the alliterating letter to the following line, is to be considered rather accidental. . . . Regarding the much discussed phenomenon of transverse alliteration [here he lumps together crossed and transverse alliteration] . . . no consensus of opinion has been reached, but it seems not unlikely that it was occasionally recognized as a special artistic form" (lxx). Others expressed similar unease. Accidents happen. The editor of *The Riming Poem* even hesitates to attribute purpose to word pairs such as reader/rider and fearer/farer: "Given the limited number of different consonants or consonant groups which can end syllables, quite frequent consonant identities will automatically occur unless a poet specially avoids them."[78] As for extra alliteration, Donka Minkova seems doubtful about the possibility of deliberate design: "In rare alliterative sequences of the type ab/ab, called *cross(ed) alliteration*, the b-alliteration is assumed to be outside the metrical scheme, and is most likely fortuitous."[79]

Between 1950 and 2008, when the fourth edition of *Klaeber's Beowulf* arrived, several studies appeared that explored the alliterative art of that poem.[80] Nevertheless, *Klaeber* 4 seems more skeptical about intentional sound play than its predecessor was. The editors refer to the existence of "persuasive statistics" and conclude: "Occasionally there is alliteration that appears to be supplementary to the primary alliteration in a verse pair, in a pattern of cross-alliteration (. . . some 80 exx.) or transverse alliteration . . . (some 30 exx.). Such patterns, however, are almost certainly fortuitous . . ., as they occur irregularly and at a rate consonant with happenstance. . . . Probably accidental, as well, is so-called enjambment of alliteration, i.e., the matching of a non-alliterating stave in the off-verse with the alliterating staves in the following verse pair. It occurs some 200 times" (clxi).[81] Skaldicists as a group also tend to ignore the supererogatory sounds of their poets. Hans Kuhn accepted the presence of extra alliteration in eddic verse, but not in *dróttkvætt*.[82] The new (in-progress) edition of the skaldic corpus has so far avoided the issue in its commentaries and notes. Even the multiple crossed alliterations in Eyvindr skáldaspillir Finnsson's praise-poem *Hákonarmál* (ca. 961)—for example, "**sk**írar **sk**jald-**b**orgir í **sk**atna **b**lóði" ([kings reddened] shining shield-fortresses in the blood of men) and "**b**runnu **b**enj-**e**ldar í **b**lóðgum **u**ndum" (wound-fires [= swords] burned in bloody wounds)—are left unremarked.[83] We have come a long way since 1935 when Adeline Courtney Bartlett wrote concerning Old English verse: "I believe that poetic detail is almost never accidental and that Anglo-Saxon verse is genuine poetry, written by men who knew what they were doing."[84] Auden, her contemporary, was also suspicious of probability studies applied to poetry, advising in his Phi Beta Kappa poem of 1946: "Thou shalt not sit / With statisticians nor commit / A social science."[85]

Crossed Alliteration

Like his near-contemporary Eyvindr skáldaspillir, Guthormr sindri composed a *dróttkvætt* eulogy for Hákon the Good.[86] Its eight extant stanzas are rich in extra alliteration. In the three excerpts from his praise poem that follow, the "regular" alliteration is marked in bold, the extra or crossed alliteration is underlined:

Bif-rauknum trað **b**ekkjar
blá-rǫst konungr ǫ́rum.
(1/1–2)

The king trod the blue road [sea] on shuddering oxen of the rowing-bench [SHIPS] with oars.

Other early skalds repeat Guthormr's vertical placement of the two compounds forming crossed alliteration.[87] The alliterative scheme of the couplet above was probably as audible to the poet's audience as "**p**ar-**t**ridge in a **p**urple **p**ear-**t**ree" is to our ears.

Patterns of crossed alliteration vary widely within the same skald's poem:

Skatt-gilda vann **sk**yldir
skaut-jalfaðar Gauta.
(4/1–2)

The controller of the sail-bear [SHIP > SEA WARRIOR] made the Gautar tribute-paying.

Ónars **ei**ki grónu
austr geð-bœti hraustan
(5/3–4)

[Hákon set] the bold attitude-improver [RULER] over the woman of Ónarr [*Jǫrð* = *jǫrð* 'land'], grown with oak, in the east.

Guthormr's crossed alliteration in these three stanzas links the sea with its ships, a sea-ruler with his latest tributary, and a ruler with his forested land.

Crossed alliteration courses through the stanzas of Bragi inn gamli Boddason, the first named skald whose works have survived.[88] The extracts that follow illustrate a few of his aural designs:

með **d**reyr-fáar **d**róttir
draum í sverða flaumi.
(3/3–4)

[awoke to a bad] dream among blood-stained troops in the eddy of swords [BATTLE].

The identical sound pattern occurs in the final couplet of the same stanza:

þás **h**rafn-bláir **h**efndu
harma Erps of barmar.
(3/7–8)

then when Erpr's raven-black brothers avenged their injuries.

Crossed alliteration again marks the final couplet of each helming in stanza 8:

til **f**ár-huga **f**œra
feðr veðr boga hugði . . .
(8/3–4)

[she] thought to bring the storm of bows [BATTLE] with hostile intent to her father . . .

bar til **b**yrjar drǫsla
baug ørlygis draugi.
(8/7–8)

[she] carried a ring for the tree-trunk of battle [WARRIOR] to the horses of the fair wind [SHIPS].

This last couplet has the same alliterative design as the skald Þormóðr Kolbrúnarskáld's supposed final words after the battle at Stiklastaðir (1030), but with the rhymes differently arranged:[89]

fár verðr **f**agr af sǫ́rum,

fann'k ǫrva drif, svanni.
(25/3–4)

few become handsome from wounds; I found a shower of arrows, lady.

Crossed alliteration was a "thing" for the court poets of Knútr inn ríki 'the Great' Sveinsson (r. 1018–35). Hallvarðr háreksblesi's *Knútsdrápa* (poem about Knútr), composed in the *dróttkvætt* variant *skjálfhent* 'trembling rhymed,' contains almost as many occurrences of the technique as there are extant stanzas.[90] Stanza 6 provides two models of crossed alliteration:

bǫð-rakkr **b**œnar nǫkkva
bark-rjóðr ok Danmǫrku.
(6/3–4)

the battle-bold reddener of the bark of the ship of prayer [BREAST > BYRNIE > WARRIOR] [rules England] and Denmark.

(**h**jaldr-ǫrr **h**aukum þverrir
hungr) Nóregi þrungit.
(6/7–8)

the battle-ready one diminishes the hunger of [the valkyrie's] hawks [RAVENS/EAGLES] . . . [and] has forced [under him] Norway.

The *Knútsdrápa* of Óttarr svarti is another rich source of crossed alliteration:[91]

Hilmir, bjótt ok **h**ættir
harð-brynjuð skip kynjum;
(1/5–6)

Prince, you readied hard-armored ships and ventured remarkably.

Viking-age skalds had a style. The nine full and partial stanzas of Þorbjǫrn hornklofi's *Glymdrápa* (ca. 890) include at least two examples of transverse alliteration (ABB BA), each couplet opening with a finite verb that alliterates with the third syllable of the second line:[92]

> Háði **g**ramr, þars **g**núðu,
> **g**eira hregg við seggi . . .
> (5/1–2)

> The king held a storm of spears [BATTLE] against men, where [arrows] roared . . .

> Kømrat **y**ðr né **œ**ðri
> **a**nnarr konungmanna . . .
> (9/1–2)

> No other of kingly lineage will come more excellent than you . . .

The "illegal" transverse-alliteration patterns observed in *Beowulf*, especially those in lines beginning with a finite verb, may share, like that poem's heroes, a northern accent:

> cwædon þæt he **w**ære **w**yruldcyning[a] . . . (3180)

> they said that he was of earthly kings [the most generous of men][93]

Extra alliteration in Old English poetry has until recently gone relatively unnoticed. Cuthbert touted Bede's proficiency in composing vernacular verse; he cites as an example *Bede's Death Song*, a poem extant in more medieval manuscripts than any other surviving Old English verse:[94]

> Fore them neidfaerae naenig uuiurthit
> **th**oncsnotturra, than him **th**arf **s**ie
> to ymb**h**ycggannae aer his **hini**ongae
> huaet his **g**astae **g**odaes aettha yflaes
> aefter deothdaege doemid uueorthae.[95]

> Before that inevitable journey, no one turns out to be wiser in thought than that it is needful for him to consider before his going hence what may be the judgment, good or bad, upon his soul after his death-day.

Despite its opening understatement (= "many are more neglectful than they should be"), Alois Brandl complained about the failure of this verse to exploit vernacular style.[96] Eric Stanley, a fine reader of Old English poetry, observed that "Bede uses no ornament to express the single idea that a man will need such wisdom as has been granted to him to prepare for death and the terrible judgement that is to come."[97] Although the variation expected of vernacular verse is largely missing from these lines, other "extras" are present: line 2 boasts crossed alliteration; enjambed alliteration on *g* links line 3 to line 4; the final verb in the last line echoes the last verb in the first. Supererogatory sound effects characteristic of vernacular composition pervade even these grim lines.

Both the first and final fitts of *Guthlac B* open with dramatic crossed alliterations: *Đæt is* ***wide cuð*** ***wera cneorissum*** (819); *Đa wæs* ***Guðlaces*** ***gæst*** *gelæded* (1305). *The Whale* begins with crossed alliteration enhanced by a half-rhyme reuniting syllables across the caesura: *wille* ***woðcræfte*** ***wordum cyþan*** (2).[98] Crossed alliteration in *Genesis B* immediately precedes one illustration (*ðenden heo his* ***halige word*** ***healdan woldon***; 245) and follows another (*Ac* ***ðoliaþ*** *we nu* ***þrea*** *on* ***helle***, *þæt syndon* ***þystro*** *and* ***hæto***; 389). Riddle 76 in the Exeter Book begins (and ends) with a solitary cross-alliterating line: *Ic* ***ane geseah*** ***idese sittan*** ("I saw a woman sitting alone"). (The identification of the lady and what she is up to remain controversial.[99]) Crossed alliteration in *The Battle of Maldon* works to demarcate successive stages in the English defense:

> þæt hi on þam **ea-steðe** **ealle stodon**. (63)
>
> so that they should all stand on that river-bank.
>
> Hi þær **Pantan stream** mid **prasse bestodon** . . . (68)
>
> There they stood in their array around the river Pante . . .

The second sentence, echoing the first, begins a new verse paragraph.

Crossed alliterations in proverbial expressions such as "tempest in a teapot" or in the titles of popular songs ("love me or leave me") remain audible.[100] Extended patterns in Old English verse, such as "þæs þe **þ**incean **m**æg **þ**egne **m**onegum, / se þe æfter **s**inc**g**yfan on **s**efan **g**reoteþ" (as it might seem to many a thane who weeps in his heart for his treasure-giver) (*Beo* 1341–42), "on **m**orgen**t**id, **m**ære **t**ungol" (in morningtide, the illustrious star) (*Brun* 14), or the punning "embe **f**eower **n**iht, **f**olce ge**n**ihtsum" (in four nights, abundant for people) (*Men* 194), would have been relatively easy for ears to process and minds to record.[101] Catchy sound effects were sometimes repeated. The *Paris Psalter* twice uses one and the same crossed alliteration to imagine a homeland: "þær ic beo **f**ægere be**þ**eaht **f**iðerum **ð**inum" (where I shall be beautifully protected by your wings) (*PPs* 60.3.3, 62.8.1).

Additional forms of verbal ornamentation, such as enjambed and continued alliteration, were exploited in both corpora. Like crossed alliteration, such sound effects sometimes highlight key moments in a narrative, or embed a key image or idea in memory, functions difficult to prove statistically. Philology is largely evidential and conjectural, with interpretations based on individual cases and clues. Even if a stylistic feature turns out to be less frequent than statistically expected, the possibility that the poet has employed it for a particular effect at a particular moment is real. A five-line verse paragraph invoking the dawn (or morning star) in *Christ A* is rich in sound correspondences of many kinds, from half-rhyme to enjambed alliteration; it concludes with two verses a line apart: "ond **s**oð**f**æsta **s**unnan **l**eoma" (and truth-fast light of the sun) (106) and "of **s**yl**f**um þe **s**ym**l**e in**l**ihtes" (you from yourself illuminate always) (108). Listeners' radar probably caught the balanced **s**, **f**, **l** sound sequences in these parallel lines.

The Battle of Maldon, while indulging in a three-line flurry of *fl*-cluster alliteration (*flan*, *flyht*, *fyl*, *flod*, *flota*, *fela*), rings changes on other sound patterns:

Se *flod* ut ge**w**at; þa flotan *stod*on **g**e*ar*owe,
wicinga fela, **w**iges **g**e*or*ne.

(72–73)

———

The flood-tide departed; the sailors stood ready, a multitude of vikings eager for battle.

Tide goes out, vikings flood in. Trained ears would have heard, if only subliminally, the full rhyme of *flod/stod-*, the half-rhyme of *gear-/geor-*, and the subdued echo of *gewat* in *gearowe*, reinforced by *w*-alliteration (**w**icinga, **w**iges) in the following line. The examples gathered in the pages that follow tend to support the notion that extra alliteration, especially crossed alliteration, is a staple of Old English poetry, an ornamental technique that functioned rather like the extra rhymes in *dróttkvætt* compositions to tie words and history together.

Famously, in the first line of *Beowulf*, both a- and b-verses not only exhibit crossed alliteration (*g–d/g–d)* and half-rhyme (*gar-/gear-*), but they are of the same metrical type (taking *hwæt* as extrametrical), a symmetry across the caesura never again heard in the poem:

Hwæt, we **Gar-D**ena in **gear-d**agum . . .

———

Indeed, we of the Spear-Danes in days of yore . . .[102]

An almost identical pattern, crossed alliteration with exact repetition of the same metrical type across the caesura, appears in the first line of a couplet adjacent to Psalm 17:51, on fol. 25r in the mid-tenth-century Royal Psalter (London, British Library, Royal 2. B. v), a poetic pen-trial that paraphrases the marginal Latin prose commentary to that verse:[103]

Wæs mid **Iud**eum on **g**ear**d**agum
ealra cyninga gehwelc Cristus nemned

———

Among the Jews in ancient days, every single king was called "Christus."

Unlike *Gar-Dena*, *Iudeum* is not a nominal compound; nevertheless, the initial *iu-* of its first syllable alliterates with the *g-* of *gear-* in the b-verse, while the stressed *de-* of its second links up with *dag-*.[104] Perhaps the glossator was recalling a metrical version of Psalm 17 now lost; perhaps he decided to compose a new couplet of his own. The same double spondees and *iu-*(*g-*) and *d* crossed alliterations appear in the Old English *Descent into Hell*:

Eala **Iord**ane in **Iud**eum (103)
Ond for **Iord**ane in **Iud**eum (131)

The poet liked this pairing enough to use it twice; its employment does not seem random.

The opening section of *Beowulf* is unusually rich in double alliteration. On one occasion, the poet stacks consecutive a-verses and b-verses of identical metrical type vertically, culminating in sound effects more audible than a scribal "pointing" could be:

wuldres **w**ealdend **w**oroldare forgeaf:
Beo*w* wæs **b**reme —**b**læd wide sprang—
Scyldes **ea**fera **Sc**edelandum **i**n.
(17–19)

———

. . . the ruler of glory gave worldly honor: Beow was famed—his vigor sprang wide—the heir of Scyld in Scandinavia.

The a-verses above are all Sievers's type A; the b-verses, type E.[105] Paronomasia on *wuldres wealdend* and *worold* (*w–ld*) link the three alliterating words in line 17. There may be wordplay in line 18 (*beow* 'barley,' *blæd* 'prosperity, growth,' *bled* 'crops'). Crossed alliteration marks the triumphant finale, which links *Scyld* to *Scedeland* (*scld/scdl*), and his "heir" to an elegantly postposited preposition. This concluding drumroll is no more "by chance" than Housman's "**Malt** does **m**ore than **Mil**-**t**on can." Thomas Bredehoft conceded that such alliterative patterning "might best be considered as a useful (and usable) secondary poetic effect."[106] It is that, and perhaps something more.

The concentration of crossed alliteration in the first fifty-two lines of *Beowulf* appears unmatched, and includes verses such as *aledon **þ**a leofne **þ**eoden* (34), ***h**ildewæpnum ond **h**eaðowædum* (39),[107] and ***g**eafon on **g**ar**s**ecg; him wæs **g**eomor **s**efa* (49). Sometimes such sound patterns help to clarify the *Beowulf* poet's syntax:

Þær æt **h**yðe **st**od, **h**ringed**st**efna
isig ond **ut**fus, **æ**þelinges **f**ær.
(32–33)

———

There at the harbor stood a ring-prowed ship, ice-glittering and set to depart, the prince's vessel.

The crossed alliteration linking the halves of both long-lines ties ***æ****þelinges* ***f****ær* (33b) to ***i****sig ond* ***u****t****f****us* (33a), a binding that may suggest that the vessel in 33b is attached to these adjectives and not anchored to the previous sentence by a long parenthetical rope.[108]

One elegant alliterative pattern in *Beowulf* involves using the initial letter of the nonalliterating fourth position in a long line to foretell the alliteration of the next verse (= enjambed alliteration). It was a particularly noisy party that provoked Grendel:

þæt he **d**ogora ge**h**wam **d**ream ge**h**yrde
hludne in **h**ealle. Þær wæs **h**earpan **sw**eg,
swutol **s**ang scopes.
(88–90)

---

that he heard each day loud revelry in the hall. The sound of the harp was there, the clear voice of the poet.

Two consecutive enjambed alliterations, two double alliterations, and one crossed alliteration (88) are more than any lonely fen-dweller should be asked to endure. The ensuing performance in the Danish high hall (lines 90–98) might also have struck Grendel's ears as excruciatingly over the top:

Sægde se þe cuþe
frumsceaft **fira** **feor**ran reccan,
cwæð þæt se ælmihtiga eorðan **w**orhte,
wlite**b**eorhtne **w**ang, swa **w**æter be**b**ugeð,
gesette sigehreþig sunnan ond monan,
leoman to leohte landbuendum
ond ge**fræt**wade foldan **sceat**as
leomum ond **lea**fum, **lif** eac gesceop
cynna ge**h**wylcum þara ðe **c**wice **h**wyrfaþ.

The one who knew how to relate from far back the first-creation of men spoke, said that the almighty created the earth, the bright-in-beauty plain surrounded by water, set, triumphant, the sun and the moon, lamps as light for earth-dwellers, and ornamented the corners of the earth with branches and leaves, created life also for each of the kinds that move about alive.

Of the nine lines in this excerpt, two have crossed alliteration (93, 98), six have double alliteration (90–91, 93–95, 97), and one has enjambed alliteration (92–93). Wordplay is present (*leoman/leomum*, 95a, 97a), along with three *dróttkvætt*-style half-rhymes: *fira/feorran* (91); *fræt-/sceat-* (96); *leafum/lif* (97). Alliteration in the b-verse (with the exception of the two crossed alliterations) falls on the first position, as required in classical *dróttkvætt*; in the hymn itself, all but one b-verse (97) end in the falling cadence demanded by *dróttkvætt*. The sound effects are not regularized, but then neither are they in the earliest skaldic stanzas extant, in which some odd lines lack rhyme, in which many even lines have half-rhyme rather than full, and in which a light syllable (or two) sometimes precedes the alliterating stave in even verses. The range and arrangement of sound effects in this song sung in Danish Heorot bear a family resemblance to the subverbal sonic noise of the first Norwegian skalds.

The northern wall of sound holds strong in the early scenes of *Beowulf*. A famous set piece in Norse poetry is the encounter between a quarrelsome coast guard and a hero arriving at the shore, uninvited.[109] In *Beowulf*, the Danish officer questioning the new arrivals brandishes both a ***m**ægenwudu* 'mighty wooden-spear' and ***m**eþelword* 'formal words' (*Beo* 236), crossed alliteration that marks him prepared for whatever comes. His polite response to Beowulf's opening statement is rich in enjambed alliteration:

                    Æghwæþres **sc**eal
scearp **sc**yld**w**iga   ge**sc**ad **w**itan,
worda ond **w**orca,   se þe **w**el þenceð.
(*Beo* 287–89)

A sharp shield-warrior who thinks properly must recognize the difference between the two—words and deeds.

As in the previous passage (*Beo* 88–90), the final (nonalliterating) stressed word of the first line "establishes" the alliterative stave of the following line (here *sc*-), whose final word in turn sets the alliteration for the next line (here *w*-). This trick is employed about 200 times in *Beowulf* and 1,700 times in the corpus as a whole; students using alphabetized glossaries quickly learn that the first letter of the last word in a line is frequently the same as that of the key words in the next half-line. In line 288, the second element of the compound *scyldwiga* forms a crossed alliteration with *witan*. Insistent double alliteration marks the response of this Danish *ombeht unforht* 'dauntless official,' along with a dash of slant-rhymes in each line: *sceal*, *scyl-*, *wel*.

The Danish coast guard escorts the newcomers to a spot from which they can see Heorot, then returns to his post, bidding the group farewell. His is the shortest speech in the poem, brief and civil, consisting of two couplets. It is also aurally eloquent, with enjambed alliteration and slant rhymes as intricate as those in viking-age court poetry, if more loosely placed. The passage concludes a manuscript section:

Mæl is me to feran;   fæder **a**lwalda
mid **a**rstafum   **eo**wic gehealde
siða gesunde.   Ic to sæ **w**ille,
wið **w**rað **w**erod   **w**earde healdan.
(316–19)

Time for me to go; may the all-ruling father in his kindness keep you safe in your ventures. I'm off to sea, to keep guard against hostile bands.

The final two a-verses before the section break have double alliteration; the four penultimate syllables of this quatrain (*wal-*, *heal-*, *wil-*, *heal-*) form slant-rhymes with each other and with *mæl* (and *–al*) in line one, allowing the speaker's last word to circle back and chime with his first. In the final line, *wrað* forms a slant-rhyme with the preceding *sið-* (and unstressed *wið*), while *werod* shakes hands with *weard* across the caesura, joined by half-rhyme and by alliteration. As in the previous passage (*Beo* 287–89), the final (nonalliterating) stressed word of a preceding b-verse "establishes" the alliterative stave of the following line: enjambed alliteration on vowels links lines 316–17, on *–w*, lines 318–19. The anonymous coast guard's skill with words may hint at the traditional role of this figure in northern story, somewhat sanitized here. Two of the half-lines above seem, like a magnet, to point north and back. *Mæl* *is me to feran* has a distinguished pedigree;[110] so does *wearde healdan* (ON *vǫrð halda* 'hold watch'). This officer is no tongue-tied rustic: an artful symphony of sounds marks the end of his speech and his return to shore duty. The poet, an arch ventriloquist, sets characters on the stage and watches them act out their part.

Sounds reinforce structure. When two consecutive long lines in *Beowulf* share the same alliteration, they seem often to do so on purpose, pointing to the end of a conversation, verse paragraph, or fitt. Hrothgar's first speech to Beowulf concludes:

> **S**ite nu to **s**ymle ond on**s**æl meoto,
> sige**h**reð **s**ecgum, swa þin **s**efa **h**wette.
> (489–90)

> Sit now to the banquet and unwrap your thoughts, victory-glory for men, as your mind urges.

The poet's twofold consecutive triple alliterations on *s* (the consonant that begins more words in modern English than any other) may hint that closure is approaching; this aural punctuation is reinforced by slant-rhyme in 489 (*sit-/meot-*) and crossed alliteration (*s/h*) in 490. A few lines later (497b–98), the fitt culminates with a vision of happiness, illuminated by a final enjambed alliteration:

> Þær wæs hæleða **d**ream,
> **d**uguð unlytel **D**ena ond Wedera.

> The joy of heroes was there, a not-little body of Danes and Weders.

Similar anticipatory alliteration is frequent in Old English verse; its use across three lines in Beowulf's highly rhetorical rebuttal to Unferth (536–38; also 533–34, 568–69, 570–71) is particularly apropos.[111] Occasionally enjambment distributes a rhyming formula over two verses: compare *Beo* 896 (***bær** on **bear**me scipes* ***beor**hte frætwa*, "bore into the bosom of the ship bright trappings") with *Beo* 213b–14 (*Secgas* ***bær**on / on **bear**m nacan* ***beor**hte frætwe*, "men bore into the bosom of the ship bright trappings"); in each, the suite of threefold half-rhymes is kept intact. Mark Griffith has located the winner of the enjambed alliteration competition: six consecutive lines employing this device ornament Meter 29 in the Old English translation of Boethius's verses.[112] Curiously, the final six lines of the fragmentary Old High German *Lay of Hildebrand* almost match this record:

Do lettun se ærist asckim **sc**ritan
scarpen **sc**urun, dat in dem **sc**iltim **st**ont.
Do **st**opun tosamane **st**aimbort **ch**ludun,
heuwun **h**armlicco **h**witte scilti,
unti im iro lintun luttilo **w**urtun,
gi**w**igan miti **w**abnum. . . .[113]
(61–66a)

Then they first let ash spears rush in sharp showers, so that they stuck in the shields. Then they advanced to meet, shattered the battle-boards, hewed fiercely the white shields, until their linden shields grew little, struck by weapons.

The enjambed alliteration missing from lines 64b–65 marks the opening of a subordinate clause.

Beowulf is not particularly rich in consecutive alliteration.[114] When continued alliteration does occur, its presence tends to mark the end of one scene and the beginning of another. Just before the dragon awakens, the thief hands over the precious cup to his lord. Crossed alliteration on *f* and *sc* is followed by a backward-looking *f–r* sequence, recalling days long gone:

feasceaftum men; **frea sc**eawode
fira fyrngeweorc **for**man siðe.
(2285–86)

. . . for the miserable man; his lord viewed the ancient work of men for the first time.

The sole occasion on which three adjacent long lines in *Beowulf* share the same alliteration marks the notoriously abrupt transition from Sigemund's molten dragon to Heremod's meltdown. The first line (897) of this triple run ends with the aside *wyrm hat gemealt* 'the dragon, hot, melted' and completes the Sigemund section; the next two, slowly leaving the Volsung hero behind, open a new story, that of Heremod:[115]

Bær on bearm scipes   beorhte frætwa
Wæls eafera;   **w**yrm hat gemealt.
  Se wæs **w**reccena   **w**ide mærost
ofer **w**erþeode,   **w**igendra hleo . . .
(896–99)

He, the son of Wæls, bore bright ornaments into the ship's hold; the worm melted in its own heat. He was the most famous of exiles far and wide over the nations, protector of warriors . . .

The Battle of Maldon also manipulates consecutive alliteration to signal a change of scene. Byrhtnoth concludes his message to the vikings with enjambed alliteration on *w*:

God ana **w**at
hwa þære **wæl**stowe   **weal**dan mote.
(*Mald* 94b–95)

God alone knows who will be permitted to control the battlefield.

The narrator's move to the next event employs two more lines alliterating on *w*, followed by a third in which *w* supports a crossed alliteration:

Wodon þa **w**æl**w**ulfas,   for **w**ætere ne murnon,
wicinga **w**erod,   **w**est ofer Pantan,
ofer **sc**ir **w**æter.   **sc**yldas **w**egon . . .
(*Mald* 96–98)

The slaughter-wolves advanced, did not hesitate in the face of the water, the host of vikings, west over the Pante, over the gleaming water, they bore shields . . .

W has to be the most frequent alliterating consonant in the Old English poetic corpus. Still, the *Maldon* poet's run is sufficiently over the top to be considered an example of deliberate artistry.

The *Beowulf* poet's alliteration sometimes acts as a leitmotif, heralding the arrival of an important object or marking a particular theme, as in the *f–r* chimes surrounding a precious cup (2285–86). So, too, *b* and *h* alliteration repeatedly announce the appearance onstage of the hero's *byrne* 'byrnie':

> þær me wið laðum   licsyrce min
> **h**eard **h**ondlocen   **h**elpe gefremede;
> **b**eado**h**rægl **br**oden   on **br**eostum læg
> golde gegyrwed.
>
> (550–53a)

There my body-sark, strong, hand-locked, performed help for me against hostile ones; the woven war-garment lay on my breast, adorned with gold.

The hero has just explained to a challenger how his mail-shirt protected him on a long swim. Alliteration on *l* lightly links verse 550 to 551 (*-locen*) and 552 (*læg*), just as alliteration on *h* links verse 551 to 552 (*-hrægl*).

In Beowulf's next aquatic adventure, the same braided byrnie protects his *breost* 'breast,' enclosing it round, while the final *sc* (1447) circles back, skaldic style, to where it began:

> **Sc**olde **h**ere**b**yrne   **h**ondum ge**b**roden,
> sid ond searofah,   sund **c**unnian,
> seo ðe **b**an**c**ofan   **b**eorgan **c**uþe,
> þæt him **h**ildegrap   **h**reþre ne mihte
> eorres inwitfeng,   aldre ge**sc**eþðan.
>
> (1443–47)

The battle-byrnie braided by hands, broad and skillfully ornamented, had to make trial of the sea, the one that knew how to protect the bone-enclosure, so that a hostile-grip, the malicious grasp of an angry one, could not injure his breast, his life.

Here crossed alliteration—**h**ere**b**yrne **h**ondum ge**b**roden (1443); **b**an**c**ofan **b**eorgan **c**uþe (1445)—is buttressed by consonance on *b–r* stem-syllables (*byrn-*, *-brod-*, *beorg-*); the repeated chords affirm beyond doubt that a braided byrnie binds Beowulf's breast.[116]

When Wiglaf's father strips from a slain Swedish prince a ***b**run-fagne **h**elm **h**ringde **b**yrnan* 'shining helmet [and] ringed byrnie' (2615), *b* and *h* alliterations rush to describe the spolia. The two consonants form a transverse or chiastic pattern (ABBA), with *brun-* and *byrn-* guarding the perimeter.[117] Later, after young Wiglaf inherits the mail-coat, the poet once again accessorizes the garment with *h* and *b* alliterations:

hyran **h**eaðosiocum, **h**ringnet **b**eran,
brogdne **b**eaduser**c**ean, under **b**eorges **h**rof.
(2754–55)

[He] obeyed the battle-wounded one, bore the ring-net, the woven battle-sark, under the barrow's roof.

The second line inverts the pattern of the first: *h h–s h b* becomes *b b–s b h*,[118] as the young hero enters the dragon's cave. An unexpressed word—*herebyrne* 'battle byrnie'—lies underneath the sounds associated with it, "le mot sous les mots."[119]

The stylistic ploys of Old English poets are as various as their subjects: *Guthlac A* has a marked preference for *g*-alliteration, its saint's initial;[120] *The Battle of Maldon* favors *b* and *Beowulf* the cluster *gr-*, on comparable onomastic grounds. As a group, Cynewulf's signed works produce more alliterative fireworks than *Beowulf*;[121] verse on scriptural subjects and poems translating a Latin text boast a higher proportion of sparklers than *Widsith* or *The Battle of Maldon*.[122] *The Meters of Boethius* contain more vowel alliteration than any other Old English poetic text.[123] In *Genesis A*, a high concentration of enjambed alliteration differentiates God's addresses from those of mortals.[124] In *Christ C*, "God's great speech to the damned in lines 1379–1514 contains the great majority of the poem's hypermetric verses and a density of consecutive alliteration unparalleled in the poetic corpus."[125] In *Beowulf*, the lament of the Last Survivor (2247–66) contains more double alliteration than any other outburst in the poem; Wealhtheow's austere but intense speech to Beowulf about her sons (1216–31) comes in second.[126] An old man and a woman emerge as victors in this particular competition.

Female speakers weave words at least as ably as their menfolk. The Trinitarian prayer spoken by the eponymous heroine in *Judith* represents ornamental alliteration at its finest:[127]

Ic ðe, **fr**ymða **g**od, ond **fr**ofre **g**æst,
bearn *al***w***al*dan, **b**iddan **wy***l*le,
miltse **þ**inre, **m**e **þ**earfendre,
þrynesse **þ**rym. **Þ**earle ys me nu ða . . .
(83–86)

I want to request of thee, God of beginnings, and Spirit of consolation, Son of the all-ruler, majesty of the Trinity, thy mercy upon me in my need. Violently now is my [heart inflamed] . . .

In naming the Trinity, she invokes each person in succession (Father, Son, Holy Ghost), joining the three into one by sound associations. (The underlying unity of the three is demonstrated by her use of the singular pronoun "thou.") Each of the first three lines features crossed alliteration (with cluster alliteration in lines 83 and 86); there is half-rhyme in line 84. As for the culminating ***þrynesse þrym*** (86), seven of the eight instances of *þrynes* 'threeness, Trinity' in the verse corpus alliterate and collocate with *þrym* 'majesty,' a verbal coincidence suggestive of doctrinal inevitability.[128] Even adverbial *nu ða* seems to echo the sounds of the previous half-line.

Another woman, Juliana, encircles with serpentine half-lines a frightened devil not quite up to the job at hand:

Þa gen se **hal**ge ongon **hæl**eþa ge**w**innan,
wrohtes **wyr**htan, **wor**dum **fr**ignan,
fyrnsynna **fru**man: "Þu me **fur**þor scealt
secgan, **s**awla **f**eond, hu þu **s**oð**f**æstum
þurh **s**ynna **s**lide **s**wiþast **sc**eþþe,
facne bi**f**ongen."
(*Jul* 345–50a)

> Then again the saint began to question with words the enemy of men, the worker of strife, the originator of ancient sins: "You must further tell me, enemy of souls, enveloped by evil, how you injure the righteous most grievously through a falling into sins."

Hissing sounds—*s*, *sc*, and *f*—dominate her short speech. Enjambed alliteration links lines 345–47; crossed alliteration in line 348 and continued alliteration in 348–49 provide further containment. The *s*-alliteration in line 349 culminates in the nonalliterating cluster *sc-*, while *w–r* and *f–r* alliterating slant-rhymes and artful metathesis in 346–47 associate the demon's present threat (worker of slander) with his age-old function (originator of ancient sins).[129] The sounds of *synna slide* 'a sliding (or slipping) into sins,' along with ***s**awol*, ***s**wiþ*, ***sc**eþþan*, and ***sc**ealt **s**ecgan*, paint this devil in the sinister key of *s*, a cluster that includes serpentine, slither, slink, slight, cylinder, slick, sleek, slender, slake, slough, sly, sloth, subtle, seduce, sleuth, sleight, slaughter, and swerve—demonic attributes all. Stéphane Mallarmé, writing of sound correspondences and focusing on the slitheriness of snakes, observed how, when a phoneme moves from a set of referents to latent meaning, "the skeletons of etymology begin to rattle in their closet."[130]

The poet depicts Judith's decapitation of Holofernes, that scene beloved of painters, with special alliterative effects:

Næs ða dead þa gyt
ealles **o**rsawle; sloh ða **eo**rnoste
ides **e**llenrof **o**ðre siðe
þone **h**æðenan ***h**und*, þæt him þæt **h**eafod *wand*
forð on ða **f**lore. **L**æg se **f**ula **l**eap
gesne be**æ**ftan, **g**æst **e**llor hwearf
under **n**eowelne ***n**æs* ond ðær ge**n**yðerad *wæs*
susle ge**s**æled **s**yððan æfre,
wyrmum be***w**unden*, **w**itum ge*bunden*,
hearde ge**h**æfted in **h**elle bryne
æfter **h**insiðe.

(*Jud* 107b–17a)

———

> He was not yet dead, completely soulless; the valorous woman then resolutely struck the heathen dog for the second time, so that his head rolled away onto the floor. The foul trunk lay lifeless behind; his soul turned elsewhere under a steep headland and was there brought low, tied to misery ever after, wound about by serpents, bound by torments, imprisoned painfully in the fire of hell after the journey hence.

Two consecutive lines with double alliteration (108–9) alliterate on unlike vowels; consecutive alliteration occurs again in the final lines (116–17). Crossed alliteration raises its head in line 112 (and perhaps transverse, in 108); so does end-rhyme in 113 and 115, and end half-rhyme in 110. Double alliteration dominates a-verses. Consecutive a- and b-verses (114–116a) employ the same metrical type, a lineup suggesting that the end of both Holofernes and the fitt is near.

Every now and then, extra alliteration and/or half-rhyme highlight a rare or exotic-seeming poetic word. The first two times that *fengel* 'prince, lord' appears in *Beowulf*, the only poem in which the noun features, it supports a crossed alliteration:

> **w**icg **w**unden**f**eax, **w**isa **f**engel (1400)
> **s**nottra **f**engel, nu ic eom **s**iðes **f**us (1475)

On its one appearance in *Exodus*, OE *þengel* 'lord' (cf. ON *þengill*) stands tall in a setting that also implicates it in crossed alliteration:

> **M***an*na ***þ**en*gel **m**earc**þ**reate rad (173)

The *Beowulf* poet later joins both terms to "rings" through half-rhyme: *hringa þengel* (1507a) and *hringa fengel* (2345b), 'lord of rings.' An allusion to the famed *Brosinga mene* 'necklace of the Brosings' (Old Norse *Brísinga men*) is followed by two lines of crossed alliteration, inscribing through sound the circuitous movements of this mythological ornament (1200–1201). The section of *Genesis A* treating Noah's ark and the Flood is particularly rich in crossed alliteration (1291, 1298, 1307, 1321, 1331, 1346, 1350, 1354, 1413, 1445, 1456, 1484). The one person in *The Creed* whose person is singled out for ornamental crossed alliteration is Mary, at the precise moment of Christ's conception: *under*

***b**reost**c**ofan* ***b**earn a**c**ende* (16); *ac þær **h**alig **g**ast* ***h**and**g**yft sealde* (18); *þære **f**æmnan **b**osm* ***f**ylde mid **b**lisse* (19). The poet employs extra artfulness to emphasize the theological centrality of this scene.

Crossed alliteration as a stylistic device in Old English poetry is sufficiently frequent to take seriously. There are more than 1,500 occurrences across the corpus with 120 examples in *Beowulf* alone. Verses with crossed alliteration are sometimes accessorized with half-rhyme, cluster alliteration, and enjambed alliteration. The selected examples that follow include several subtypes of crossed alliteration, including two bilingual examples. Letters forming the crossed alliteration are set out in bold; additional sound effects have not been marked.

frea **æ**lmihtig. Næs him **fr**uma **æ**fre	*GenA* 5
gasta **w**eardas, þa he hit **g**eare **w**iste	*GenA* 41
nacod **n**ied**w**ædla **n**eorxna**w**anges	*GenA* 929
reðe **w**æstme. **R**æhton **w**ide	*GenA* 990
for **w**era **s**ynnum **w**ylme ge**s**ealde	*GenA* 1925
swa him **s**ægde **æ**r **s**wegles **a**ldor.	*GenA* 2879
gramum **a**mbyhtsecg, nales **g**odes **e**ngel.	*GenB* 582
þæt wæs **d**eaðes **b**eam þe him **d**rihten for**b**ead.	*GenB* 646
willan **b**ræcon. Stod se **w**raða **b**oda	*GenB* 686
spelbodan **ea**c. Se ðe **sp**ed **a**hte	*Ex* 514
burgum **w**ealdan, wæs him **b**eorht **w**ela	*Dan* 9
þæt sie **an** **m**etod **ea**llum **m**annum	*Dan* 578
scypend **s**eolfa. Nu earttu **sc**eaðana **s**um	*Sat* 57
drihten **h**ælend, in ðæm **d**eoran **h**am	*Sat* 218
hleoleasan **w**ic **h**wile **w**unedon	*And* 131
wuldor**c**yninges, swa ðu **w**orde be**c**wist	*And* 418
on **m**od**s**efan **m**aran **s**nyttro.	*And* 554
þurh **s**nyttra **c**ræft **s**oð on**c**nawest.	*And* 631
dreor to **f**oldan. Ic a**dr**eah **f**eala	*And* 969
on **f**yrhð**s**efan, þurh þa **f**ægeran ge**s**yhð	*El* 98
in**br**yrded **br**eost-**s**efa syððan **b**eacen ge**s**eh	*El* 841
ræd**þ**eahtende, ymb þa **r**ode **þ**reo	*El* 868
deopra **f**irena, þurh þæs **d**omes **f**yr.	*El* 1314
ond þæt **t**ydre ge**w**itt **t**ire be**w**inde	*ChristA* 29
þæt nu **b**letsung **m**ot **b**æm ge**m**æne	*ChristA* 100

þonne **m**ægne **c**yning	on ge**m**ot **c**ymeð	*ChristB* 832
se **m**icla **d**æg	**m**eahtan **d**ryhtnes	*ChristC* 868
þær se **l**eohta **b**eam	**l**eodum **b**yrhteð	*ChristC* 1089
scyld**w**yrcende	**sc**ondum ge**w**emdest	*ChristC* 1486
womma **c**læne	in ge**w**eald **c**uman.	*GuthA* 29
swa **w**aroþa **s**ond	ymb **s**ealt **w**ater	*Az* 39
swa se **h**alga **w**er	**h**ergende **w**æs	*Az* 49
moncynnes ge**f**ea,	**m**eþra **f**refrend	*Phoen* 422
ge**s**eon **s**igora **f**rean	**s**ine **f**ine	*Phoen* 675
in þam **r**eongan **h**am.	Ða se ge**r**efa **h**et	*Jul* 530
ond on his **d**æg**r**ime	**d**runcen to **r**ice	*Vain* 12
grund**f**usne **g**æst	**g**ode or**f**eormne	*Vain* 49
searo**h**wit **s**olaþ,	**s**umur**h**at colað,	*Rim* 67
fold**w**ela **f**ealleð,	**f**eondscipe **w**ealleð	*Rim* 68
ofer **h**arne **st**an	**h**ate **st**reamas	*Ruin* 43
mærne **þ**eoden,	þa him wæs **m**anna **þ**earf	*Beo* 201
lætað **h**ilde**b**ord	**h**er on**b**idan	*Beo* 397
be **y**ð**l**afe	**u**ppe **l**ægon	*Beo* 566
werhðo **d**reogan,	þeah þin **w**it **d**uge.	*Beo* 589
magorinca **h**eap.	Þa his **m**od a**h**log;	*Beo* 730
swylce **o**ft be**m**earn	**æ**rran **m**ælum	*Beo* 907
sigor**ea**dig **s**ecg.	**S**amod **æ**rdæge	*Beo* 1311
eald **e**þel**w**eard,	þæt ðes **eo**rl **w**ære	*Beo* 1702
gumena **d**ryhten,	ðonne ic **g**yt **d**yde	*Beo* 1824
æfter **w**ig**f**ruman	**w**ide **f**eran	*Beo* 2261
fæted **w**æge,	**f**rioðo**w**ære bæd	*Beo* 2282
on þam **f**eorh**b**onan	**f**æghðe ge**b**etan	*Beo* 2465
winia **b**ealdor,	ða se **w**yrm ge**b**eah	*Beo* 2567
syððan **ð**eod**c**yning	**þ**yder on**c**irde	*Beo* 2970
scyppendes **m**ægð	**sc**earpne **m**ece	*Jud* 78
þære **w**litegan **b**yrig	**w**eallas **b**lican	*Jud* 137
cyninga **w**uldor;	þæt ge**c**yðed **w**earð	*Jud* 155
el**ð**eodigra	**e**dwit **þ**oledon.	*Jud* 215
þær he his **h**eorð**w**eorod	**h**oldost **w**isse.	*Mald* 24
ofer **sc**ir **w**æter	**sc**yldas **w**ægon	*Mald* 98
wyrcan þone **w**ig**h**agen	and þæt **w**erod **h**ealdan	*Mald* 102
bæd **g**angan **f**orþ	**g**ode ge**f**eran	*Mald* 170

heowan **h**eaðo**l**inde	**h**amora **l**afan	*Brun* 6
on **m**orgen**t**id,	**m**ære **t**ungol	*Brun* 14
gar**m**ittinge,	**g**umena ge**m**otes	*Brun* 50
and ic **ea**lne **d**æg	**e**cne **d**rihten	*PPs* 55.9.3
Min **s**awl on **ð**e	**s**wyðe **þ**yrsteð	*PPs* 62.2.1
and **s**ymbel**d**agas	**s**wylce **d**rihtnes	*PPs* 73.7.3
on **eo**rð**w**ege	**ea**lle to**w**urpan	*PPs* 73.7.4
Mildheortnesse and **d**om	**m**ihtigan **d**rihtnes	*PPs* 100.1.1
Glæd **m**an **g**leaw**h**ydig,	**g**od and **m**ild**h**eort	*PPs* 111.5.1
rihtes **w**isran,	**r**ices **w**yrðran	*Met* 4.45
of **c**life **h**arum	**c**ol and **h**lutor	*Met* 5.13
ne huru ymbe **sc**ip**h**ergas	**sc**ealcas ne **h**erdon	*Met* 8.31
ealla ge**sc**eafta	**æ**rest ge**sc**eope	*Met* 20.53
gylleð **g**ræ**h**ama,	**g**uðwudu **h**lyneð	*Finn* 6
deormod **h**æleþ,	hwa ða **d**uru **h**eolde	*Finn* 23
git his **sw**eord **sc**ineð	**sw**iðe ge**sc**æned	*MSol* 223
Se **f**ugel **h**afað	**iiii** **h**eafdu	*MSol* 263
Geowes he hafað **f**iðeru	and **g**riffus **f**et	*MSol* 265
forma **m**onað;	hine **f**olc **m**ycel	*Men* 9
embe **f**eower **n**iht,	**f**olce ge**n**ihtsum	*Men* 194
ðinne **b**yrn**h**omon	**b**illum **h**eowun	*WaldA* 17
sitt þonne **s**igel**b**eorht	**s**wegles **b**rytta	*JDay II* 117
heora **s**innigan **b**reost	**s**wiðlice **b**eatað	*JDay II* 160
his **s**unu **b**liðe,	**s**igores **b**rytta	*JDay II* 279
blissiendum **m**odum,	**b**yrgum to**m**iddes	*JDay II* 286
rice **r**æd**w**itan,	**r**odera **w**eardas	*JDay II* 300
sitest **s**ige**h**ræmig	on ða **s**wiðran **h**and	*KtHy* 30
þæt þu þæt **e**ce **l**eoht	**ea**l ne for**l**eose	*Exhort* 19
and se **s**oð**f**æsta	**s**ummi **f**ilius	*Summons* 8
leofum **l**eod**sc**ipe	**l**æran **sc**eolde	*Seasons* 8
þætte **g**od**f**erhte	**g**ylt ge**f**ræmmað	*KtPs* 14
ymb his **w**om**d**eda	**w**aldendes **d**oom	*KtPs* 19
stune hætte þeos **w**yrt,	heo on **st**ane ge**w**eox	*MCharm* 2.14

Some of these verses end speeches; others are uttered by royalty or divinity; some draw attention to syntactic parallelism or variation; others underline a narrative tit-for-tat, such as the exchange of a precious cup for a peace contract. The final citation above, from *MCharm* 2.14, explores the ontological affinity between a plant and a rock. Other crossed alliterations underline key dramatic moments or begin and/or end sections of a poem.

The *Beowulf* poet appears partial to a form of crossed alliteration in which the final stressed position of the b-verse chimes with the second element of a nominal compound in a double-alliterating a-verse (e.g., *Beo* 33, 49, 57, 93, 288, 1065, 1311, 1400, 1702, 2108, 2285), a stylistic taste apparently shared by the poet of *Guthlac B*.[131] The first *Beowulf* verse cited below ends a speech, the second, a fitt:

sige**h**reð **s**ecgum,	swa þin **s**efa **h**wette.	*Beo* 490
wlite**s**eon **w**rætlic;	**w**eras on **s**awon.	*Beo* 1650

These lines have a distinctive rhythm and may have conveyed a sense of closure. Similar crossed alliterations in *Guthlac B* focus on a soul's final release from its body:

lic**h**ord on**l**ocen.	**L**eomu **h**efegedon	*GuthB* 956, 1029
sige**l**eoð **s**ungon,	**s**weg wæs on **l**yfte	*GuthB* 1315

Like the poet of *Guthlac B* (if not the same individual), Cynewulf seems sufficiently proud of his crossed alliterations and half-rhymes to repeat them more than once in the same poem:

acenned **w**earð,	**c**yninga **w**uldor	*El* 5, 178
ahangen **w**æs	**h**eofenrices **w**eard	*El* 445, 718
collen**f**erhðe,	**c**wen siðes ge**f**eah	*El* 247, 848[132]
godes **g**æst**s**unu,	ond us **g**iefe **s**ealde	*ChristB* 660, 860

Cynewulf sometimes repeats crossed alliterations with minor variations:

ecra **ead**gifa	ða cwom **e**ngel **g**odes	*Jul* 563
eorla **ead**giefan	**e**nglas to**g**eanes	*ChristB* 546

The poet of *The Phoenix* appears to imitate the crossed alliterations of *Guthlac B*, the poem preceding it in the Exeter Book:

on **n**eorxna**w**ang, þær him **n**ænges **w**æs *GuthB* 827
nemnað **n**eorxna**w**ang, þær him **n**ænges **w**æs *Phoen* 397

Guthlac B similarly hijacks the crossed alliterations of the preceding *Guthlac A*:

Ða wæs **G**uð**l**aces **g**æst ge**l**æded *GuthB* 1305
ac to **G**uð**l**aces **g**æste ge**l**æddun *GuthA* 188
Swa wæs **G**uð**l**aces **g**æst ge**l**æded *GuthA* 781

The *Beowulf* poet, too, had few qualms about repeating his own crossed alliterations:

ond þa **c**ear**w**ylmas **c**olran **w**urðaþ (282)
æfter **c**ear**w**ælmum **c**olran **w**eorðað (2066)

swið**h**icgende to **s**ele þam **h**ean (919)
swið**h**icgende on **s**ele þam **h**ean (1016)

gomen**w**udu **g**reted **g**id oft **w**recen (1065)
gome*n***w**udu **g**rette, hwilum **g**yd a**w**ræc (2108)

In general, crossed alliteration is most frequent in poems traditionally regarded as late, such as *Vainglory*, *Judith*, *The Battle of Brunanburh*, and the *Paris Psalter*, which boasts more than one hundred occurrences. The paratext to the *Kentish Psalm* opens with David "the harper" encased in crossed alliteration: ***D**auid wæs **h**aten **d**iormod **h**æleð* ("the courageous man was called David") (1). Two lines with crossed alliterations, both on the same secondary sound, introduce Dunnere, the penultimate doomed speaker in *The Battle of Maldon* (255–56):

Dunnere þa **c**wæð, **d**aroð a**c**wehte,
unorne **c**eorl, ofer **ea**ll **c**lypode.

Dunnere then spoke, shook his spear, a humble man, called out above everything.

The word *ceorl* governs both verbs, *clypode* and *acwehte*, with the rare double crossed alliterations marking a kind of syntactical reversal. As Eric Weiskott has pointed out, the syntax demands sequential reanalysis as the half-lines unroll in time, a movement mirrored by the crisscrossing sounds.[133] A similar double crossed alliteration with a repeated secondary consonant marks the opening of Gerard Manley Hopkins's "As **k**ing**f**ishers **c**atch **f**ire, **d**ragon**f**lies **d**raw **f**lame." Dense sound-patterning in introductory lines serve as stylistic bowwows, alerting listeners to the approach of a messenger.

The Play of *Sc-/Sk-* Clusters

Ther shyveren shaftes upon sheeldes thikke.

—Chaucer, *The Knight's Tale* (line 2605)[134]

A peculiarity of alliterative verse is the behavior of cluster alliterations, specifically the rule that initial consonant clusters consisting of *s* plus voiceless stop (*p*, *t*, *c*/*k*) are to be treated as distinct units: *sp-* alliterates only with itself, so, too, *st-* only with *st-*, and *sc-/sk-* only with *sc-/sk-*. Aldhelm followed this vernacular practice in his Latin verse.[135] Skalds in the age of Cnut were keen on *sk-* sound effects. Here is Þórðr Kolbeinsson noting in a first-person aside that Cnut himself asked Eiríkr jarl to join the campaign in England:

at **sk**yldligast **sk**yldi—
skilk, hvat gramr lézk vilja—

---

that [Eiríkr] should most obligingly—I understand what the ruler declared he wanted.[136]

Hallfreðr in his memorial poem for Óláfr Tryggvason had used similar *sk*-chimes in a first-person aside following a run of *s*-alliterations:

Hann lét of **s**ǫk **s**anna
(**s**verðjalmr óx þar) verða—
skilit frá ek—(fyr **sk**ylja)
skóð mǫrg roðin blóði.

He caused many damagers (weapons) to become reddened with blood in a true action; battle grew there before the king; I learned this clearly.[137]

Sk-alliterations in the poetry of Cnut's skalds are sometimes accompanied (in nonalliterating positions) by one of the remaining two *s*-clusters, as if to illustrate the rule. Here Óttarr addresses his newly victorious patron, highlighting the occasion with a *figura etymologica* (*Skjǫld-/skild-*), crossed alliteration (*vannt/verk*), and a constrasting *st*-cluster:

Skjǫldungr, vannt und **sk**ildi
skœru verk, inn **st**erki.

———

Strong Skjǫldungr, under shield you achieved a battle-deed.[138]

The aural patterning of each *dróttkvætt* stanza was unique, like a designer costume; workmanship and distinctiveness were richly rewarded.[139] So, apparently, was phonic play based on the name of the individual eulogized.[140] Arnórr Þórðarson, recording raids in mainland Scotland in the late 1020s, deployed alliterating and rhyming syllables as required: vowel alliteration (on three different vowels) in the first couplet, *þ*-alliteration in the next two, and *s*-alliteration in the final couplet. The order of the skald's alliterations follows the initials of the patron he was honoring: **J**arl **Þ**orfinnr **S**igurðar**s**on:

Ulfs *tugg*u rauð ***e**ggj*ar,
***e**itt* þars Torfnes *heit*ir,
—*ungr* olli **þ**ví ***þ**eng*ill—
(**þ**at vas *mán*adag) *frán*ar.
*Sung*u **þ**ar, til ***þ**ing*a,
***þ**unn* fyr Ekkjal *sunn*an
***s**verð*, es **s**iklingr *barð*isk
***s**narr* við Skotlands *harr*a.

Fránar eggjar rauð tuggu ulfs, þars eitt heitir Torfnes; ungr þengill olli því; þat var mánadag. Þunn sverð sungu þar til þinga fyr sunnan Ekkjal, es snarr siklingr barðisk við harra Skotlands.[141]

———

> Bright blades grew red on the wolf's chaw [CORPSE] at a place called Tarbatness (Torfnes). The young ruler caused that. It was a Monday. Slender swords sang there at the encounter south of the (river) Oykel (Ekkjall), as the bold prince fought against Scotland's ruler.

The skald's "official" alliterations (in bold) are shadowed by a large cast of extras and understudies. Alliterative concatenations bind each couplet internally and tie each couplet to the next. Extra vowel alliteration (*ungr*) joins lines 1–2 to line 3, *þ*-alliteration joins lines 3–4 to lines 5–6, linking the two half-stanzas; the final word of line 6 establishes the *s*-alliteration of lines 7–8, while *harra*, the last word in line 8, predicts the *h*-alliteration opening the next stanza. Crossed alliteration binds the first couplet, and transverse alliteration binds the third. The poet's alliterative carapace, like a whalebone corset, stands firm and shapely on its own. His rhymes, too, are overachievers: the *skothendingar* in line 3 form loose half-rhymes with *mán*- and *frán*- in line 4; those in line 5, with ***þ**un*- and *sun*- in line 6; and those in line 7, ***s**ver*- and *bar*-, chime with ***s**nar*- and *har*- in the final line. In his concluding couplet, the skald inserts a final *sk*-place-name (*Skotland*, 8) at the end of his *s*-alliterations, like a cat among the pigeons.[142]

The pointed nonalliteration between *s*- and *sc*-, *sp*-, and *st*-clusters in the verse of tenth- and eleventh-century skalds recalls lines of Old English verse such as ***sc**ealcas of **sc**eaðum **sc**irmæled **s**wyrd* (*Jud* 230), ***sc**ingelacum, þæt se **sc**yna **st**an* (*And* 766) (note the three half-rhymes), ***s**wæf **s**ymbelwerig, and him **s**elfa **sc**eaf* (*GenA* 1564), *þurh **s**ynna **s**lide **s**wiþast **sc**eþþe* (*Jul* 349), ***s**nel under **s**orgum, **s**wegl hate **sc**an* (*GuthB* 1330), *his **s**unu **s**ende on þas **s**idan ge**sc**eaft* (*Men* 227), *ofer **sc**ildhreadan **sc**eotend **s**endað* (*ChristB* 675), and the crossed-alliterating and rhyming *git his **s**weord **sc**ineð **s**wiðe ge**sc**æned* (*MSol* 223). Edwin Morgan in "A Song of the Petrel" ("He **sc**reams **sk**imming the **sc**attered **s**urf") and William Meredith in "A Kodiak Poem" ("Pre**c**ipitous is the **sh**ape and **st**ance of the **sp**ruce")[143] seem to imitate this northern predilection. Maria Dahvana Headley decorates Beowulf's boast about slaying a sea-monster with *sk*-, *sp*, and *st*- clusters fore and aft: "I made it a **sl**eeper as it *leap*t, **s**evered its **sp**ine, **sp**iked its **sk**ull, and **sp**lit it into **sm**ithereens."[144] A few tongue-twisting Old English *sc*/*s* combinations seem particularly beloved:

scan **sc**ir-wered **sc**adu **s**weþredon (*GuthB* 1288)
scire **sc**inan **sc**eadu **s**weðerodon (*And* 836)
scire leoman;
scinon **sc**yldhreoðan, **sc**eado **s**wiðredon (*Ex* 112b–113)[145]

The *Beowulf* poet had a trained ear. Following a succession of Latin poets from Catullus to Aldhelm and beyond, he avoided suffix rhyme on hissing sibilants in adjacent noun-adjective combinations by pairing, in the genitive case, weak adjective declensions with strong nouns, creating half-lines such as *widan rices* (1859b) instead of *wides rices* (cf. *sciran goldes*, 1694b; *wergan gastes*, 133a, 1747b; *hean huses*, 116a; *laðan liges*, 83a; *lænan lifes*, 2845a; *miclan domes*, 978b; *fættan goldes*, 1093a, 2246a).[146] Yet like the skalds, the *Beowulf* poet does not hesitate to insert a (nonalliterating) *s*-word into an *sc*- alliterative chain, and vice versa:[147]

swutol **s**ang **sc**opes. **S**ægde se þe cuþe (90)
þurh **s**liðne nið **s**awle be**sc**ufan (184)
seomode on **s***a*le **s**idfæþmed **sc**ip (302)
setton **s**æmeþe **s**ide **sc**yldas (325)
þæt ic **s**weord bere oþðe **s**idne **sc**yld (437)
scencte **sc**ir wered. **Sc**op hwilum **s**ang (496)
swiðe on**s**ittan, **S**ige-**Sc**yldinga (597)
sunne **s**weglwered **s**uþan **sc**ineð (606)
scriðan **sc**eadugenga. **Sc**eotend **s**wæfon (703)
sawle **s**ecan: þone **s**yn**sc**aðan (801)
þonne hit **s**wordes ecg **s**yððan **sc***e*de (1106)
sælde to **s**ande **s**idfæþme **sc**ip (1917)
Sige-**Sc**yldingum **s**orge gefremede (2004)
Þæt se **s**ecg wære **s**ynnum **sc**ildig (3071)

The *s/sc* sequences in *Beowulf* burnish a variety of actions: a ship sitting at anchor; shields checked at the door; a scop's song; the conclusion of a speech; an ancient curse. Gatherings of initial sibilants as in "she sells seashells on the seashore" seem welcomed.[148] The poet's nonalliterative association of *s/sc* largely peters out after the one-quarter mark of the poem; the figure of the *scop* with his *swutol sang* 'clear song' prophetically melts away after line 1066.

Both *dróttkvætt* and Old English verse followed etiquette in the placement of their cluster alliterations. The skald's clashing *s*-clusters adorn his most violent tableaux: ***sk**aut á **sk**jaldrim sveita; / **sk**okkr vas blóði **st**okkinn* ("gore spurted on the shield-rail; deck-planks were spattered with blood").[149] Battle scenes between the *Pater Noster* and the devil in *Solomon and Saturn* include tongue-twisters such as ***sc**yldigra **sc**yld, **sc**yppendes **s**eld* ("guilt of criminals, hall of the creator") (79) (note the three half-rhymes) and ***sc**yldigne **sc**eaðan, habbað **sc**earp **sp**eru* ("the sinful warrior; they have sharp spears") (128). In *Beowulf*, Grendel's shoulder is torn, *syndolh **sw**eotol; seonowe on**sp**rungon* ("a visible great wound; sinews sprang asunder") (817), and Wulf's sword strikes Ongentheow *þæt him for swenge swat ædrum sprong* ("so that blood sprang forth in streams because of that stroke") (2966) (both lines feature half-rhymes). *Christ B* freely alliterates *st*-clusters in the presence of other (nonalliterating) martial *s*-words: ***st**ælgne ge**st**igan. Sum mæg **st**yled **s**weord* (679); so, too, *Juliana*: ***st**rong wiþ**st**ondan **st**orma **sc**urum* (651) and *Riddle* 27: ***st**rengo bi**st**olen, **st**rong on **sp**ræce* (13).

The skald Sigvatr was at work when the *Beowulf* manuscript was new. *S/sk* sequences in his ten extant *dróttkvætt* poems and thirty *lausavísur* 'loose verses' are strikingly few. But several stanzas in his memorial ode for Erlingr Skjálgsson, ally of Cnut in the late 1020s, boast consecutive couplets with mirror-image *sk/s* sequences. The sharp hiss of sea, ship, and sword dominates, as the half-rhyme of the penultimate line below forms a half-rhyme with the final line:

> **Sk**eið hans lá **s**vá **s**íðan
> **s**iklings í her miklum
> (**s**narir bǫrðusk þar **s**verðum)
> **s**íbyrð við **sk**ip (fyrðar).

Skeið hans lá svá síðan í miklum her siklings, síbyrð við skip; snarir fyrðar bǫrðusk þar sverðum.[150]

His warship lay thus afterward in the great army of the ruler [= Óláfr], alongside the ship; bold men fought there with swords.

skeið vann **sk**jǫldungr auða—
skipsókn við þrǫm Bóknar.
Einn stóð **s**onr á **s**ínu
snarr **Sk**jalgs vinum fjarri.

. . . skipsókn við þrǫm Bóknar . . . skjǫldungr vann skeið auða . . . Snarr sonr Skjalgs stóð einn, fjarri vinum, á sínu . . .[151]

———

All Erlingr's ship-crew fell by the coast of Bokn; the prince [= Óláfr] emptied the warship. The bold son of Skjálgr [= Erlingr] stood alone, far from friends, on his . . .

In the first couplet above, three alliterating *sk*-clusters lead into the full rhyme ***sókn/Bókn-***; in the second, three alliterating *s*-words are preceded by an *st*-cluster and followed by the name Skjálgr; in the couplet below, *sk-* resumes command and overwhelms the minor *s*-key:

skers þótt **sk**úrir þyrrit,
Skjalgs hefnir **s**ér nefna.

hefnir Skjalgs . . . nefna sér, þótt skúrir skers . . . þyrrit.[152]

———

The avenger of Skjálgr [= Erlingr] [did not] ask [safety] for himself, though the showers of the skerry [of the axe] [> BATTLE] did not let up.

One robin does not make a spring; a single patterned *s/sk* alliteration might be a fluke; four in swift succession suggests purposefulness. The name of Erlingr, who died in battle against the forces of Óláfr Haraldsson, occurs seven times in the ten stanzas of Sigvatr's eulogy; the jarl's patronymic, son of Skjálgr 'the squinting,' twice, and only in the sequences mapped above. *Sk*jálgr + *s*on and the *s/sk* words attracted to them ("ship," "ruler," "bold," "ship-crew," "showers," "skerry," "sword") gradually form a leitmotif accompanying mention of this soon-to-fall ruler. So, too, hip-hop artists immortalize their names in song by rhyming them loosely with the symbols of rock star glory: Jay-Z with Mercedes and ladies. Yeats did something similar when he eulogized Robert Gregory, not by naming him but, instead, devising refrains that chimed discreetly with his last name: "Soldier, scholar, horseman, he, / As 'twere all life's epitome." A viking-age skald probably could count on some in his audience admiring his aural wit and informing the addressee or his heirs accordingly.

The Secret Celibacy of Vowels

Early graphic systems—Vedic Sanskrit, Egyptian hieroglyphs, Ancient Hebrew, Classical Arabic—did without vowels altogether, a sign perhaps of the restriction of early script to commercial transactions. Once the desire for temporal exactitude arose, vowels discreetly entered the system. Northern poets treated vowels and consonants differently: a consonant was companionable and sought its like across the caesura; vowels seem to have avoided such a restriction, not only in initial alliterative positions but also, to greater and lesser extents, when embedded in stressed syllables within the verse line. Monogamy for the single vowel was out, heterophony, at least within the class of vowels, was in. This behavior remains standard in Icelandic verse today.

Our ears have little difficulty hearing consonantal alliteration—"rum, ram, ruf"[153] or "Scania scorned Skjálgr's son"—but vowels can sneak by undetected. (For some reason, the *Beowulf* poet, unlike the *Judith* poet, went to some effort to avoid placing two alliterating vowels in the first half of his long lines: only 30 to 35 percent of his lines with vowel alliteration have double alliteration in the a-verse, compared to 55 percent of his lines with consonant alliteration.)[154] Snorri Sturluson, Icelandic skald, historian, and poet, advised that the chiming of different vowels was more elegant than that of identical ones, an opinion apparently shared by many (if not all) early poets in the North.[155] The *Beowulf* poet normally chose different vowels to link two half-lines: of the 493 examples of vowel alliteration in the 3,182 lines of that poem, only 35 alliterate twice on the same vowel and, in all these instances but one, one of the two identical vowels is followed by a nasal or liquid consonant.[156] Only once, in line 835, does the poet *seem* to alliterate three times on the same vowel (the short diphthong *ea*)—with the fourth and final stressed syllable of that line embracing the identical sound. In the aftermath of Beowulf's hall-struggle with Grendel, the warriors display the latter's severed arm for all to see:

earm ond **ea**xle þær wæs **eal** **gea**dor
Grendles *grap*e under *geap*ne hr[*of*].
(835–36)

The monster's torn-off hand, "arm and shoulder—all of Grendel's grip was together there—under the vaulted roof," is a Goya-esque or butcher-shop image of a carcass hanging from a hook. *Earm* and *eaxl*, "arm" and "shoulder," are joined by sound as well as by anatomy; the two alliterate twice more in *Beowulf* (972a, perhaps also 1117a) and once in the *Riddles* (86/6a).[157] It is not at all certain that speakers pronounced the vowel in *eal* the same as that in *earm* and *eaxl*.[158] But even if the poet were not standing hallowed convention on its head in lines 835–36, it seems significant that the repeated vowel sounds in this couplet mark both the end of a manuscript section and of Grendel himself.

Editors of *Beowulf* dutifully explain the grammar and narrative context of these lines by saying that 835b (*þær wæs eal geador*) may be a complete clause, that *grape* 'grip' is a genitive dependent on *eal* 'all,' and that the identity of the interior or exterior hall decorator is uncertain.[159] Literary commentary focuses on the legal meaning of this public exposure of Grendel's arm severed at the shoulder.[160] The poet's audience probably heard the alliterative enjambment of *geador* to the first stressed syllable of the following line,[161] the slant- (or half-rhyme) formed by *grap*- and *geap*- in line 836, and the frequency of one and the same diphthong in the couplet (repeated in *gead*- and, lengthened, *geap*-). The alliterating and rhyming pair *grap* and *geap* hints at openness and space: the *hrof* 'roof' of Heorot 'hart' is high and hollow, *geap* 'vaulted, curved' like a hart's horns or a pair of hands clasped bowl-like together (ON *gaupr*). Somewhere in our minds, front vowels suggest proximity, simultaneity, and similarity. The *Beowulf* poet's multiple plays on *ea* mirror the renewed community now gazing as one at Grendel's disarticulated limb. Alliteration is essential in early northern verse, like the rivets fastening a ship's boards together. One fracture or faulty joint, one loose tongue, and the poem sank along with your reputation as a craftsman.[162] But skilled poets do not just obey laws; they don the basic uniform, and then add color and luster. Their contemporaries would have been alert at least some of the time to these finishing touches.

Minding your *P*s and Cues

And then there was *p*. A letter—a written sign of speech—can grow strange over time, eventually vanishing, like the semiconsonantal *digamma* of Greek, or the runic *wynn* of Old English. Sometimes, like an aged actor, a sound makes a comeback, invigorated by foreign contact. Sigvatr is the first skald to wield *p*-alliteration, an initial sound largely foreign to Old Norse and Old English. (Indo-European *p* switches allegiance in Germanic—hence Modern English "*p*aternal grand*f*ather," "*f*ive-beat *p*entameter," even "*f*irst *p*rinciples" or "*f*irst *p*rimadonna.") Twice Sigvatr houses his collection of Old English and Continental *p*-loanwords—*páskar* 'Easter,' *palmsunnudagr* 'Palm-Sunday,' *prúðr* 'proud, attractive,' *peitneskr* 'from Poitou,' *Partar* (English name), *portgreifar* 'town reeves'—in the final couplet of a stanza, trumpeting their alliterative patter.[163] In stanza 14 of *Víkingavísur*, a *dróttkvætt* sequence in honor of King Óláfr Haraldsson, later a saint, the skald's *p*-words coordinate gracefully with the Canterbury milieu of the battle. In stanza 15 of *Nesjavísur*, Sigvatr observes that the sea-battle commemorated took place at the start of Holy Week—"on Palm Sunday and so I had to await Easter; I put on a Poitou-made helmet."[164] *Dróttkvætt*, like rap, is an aggressive medium, a contact sport, a competition, a combat of wit. Sigvatr's wry intimation of an iron Easter bonnet is up-to-date, rad, cool, and cosmopolitan. His concluding *p*-alliterations announce a sea change both in art and in society.

Seventh-century Anglo-Latin writers wielded *p*-alliterations like a club, as if making up for the near absence of this letter in their vernacular. Fifteen of the first sixteen words in the much quoted opening of Aldhelm's letter to Heahfrith (ca. 675) begin with *p*: *Primitus pantorum procerum praetorumque pio potissimum paternoque praesertim privilegio panagericum poemataque passim prosatori sub polo promulgantes* ("Principally, with particularly pious and paternal privilege, publicly proferring beneath the pole panegyric and poems promiscuously to the Procreator of all princes and praetors").[165] Less obtrusive alliteration on *p* could be found in the south of the country. Hæddi, bishop of the West Saxons, was the recipient of a *p*-rich trochaic octosyllabic poem from Archbishop Theodore himself, probably the earliest surviving Latin verse written in England:[166]

Te nunc, sancte speculator,
uerbi Dei digne dator,
Hæddi, pie presul, precor
pontificum ditum decor:
pro me tuo peregrine
preces funde Theodoro.

Holy bishop, gracious giver of the word of God, Hæddi, pious prelate, pearl of honored pontiffs, I pray you now: pour out prayers for me, your peregrinus, Theodore.

Seven *p*'s are embedded in this verse, which contains the same number of syllables as a *dróttkvætt* stanza; enjambed alliteration on *p* links lines in two couplets. Theodore's insistent alliteration and rhyme are regular until the final line: perhaps he had a familiar nickname, lost in transmission, that began in *f* and ended in *–inus*. The Greek-speaking archbishop from Tarsus flatters his English-speaking subordinate with courteous apostrophes, while playfully piling *p*-word upon *p*-word.[167]

Old English poets avoided primary alliteration on the occasional native *p*-word such as *pæð* 'path,' *pad* 'coat,' or *plegan* 'to play,' either placing the term in final position in the half-line (*Ex* 488b, *Rid* 58.9b) or as the second element in a compound (*an-*, *flett-*, *here-*, *mearc-*, *mil-*, *seolhpæð*, etc.).[168] In Old English verse, *p* is the least frequent word-initial sound in fully stressed (Sievers's) positions: none of the 3182 lines of *Beowulf* alliterates on *p*. This letter had to work hard to earn a place at the poets' table.

Riddle 72 in the Exeter Book depicts an ox, once a well-fed calf, now an enslaved draft animal, fetter around its neck, wooden beam on its back, repeatedly stabbed on its sides by a plowman's iron goads:

***m**earc**p**aþas* [. . .] *træd,* ***m**oras* ***p**æðde* (12)

I trod the boundary-paths, traversed the moors.[169]

The alliteration on *m* is primary, but the poet has used both *p*-options described above, creating a *dróttkvætt*-style etymological half-rhyme (*paþ-/pæð-*), one embedded in crossed alliteration (*m/p m/p*). Parallel sounds across the caesura imitate the movement of the ox's boustrophedon tracks over the fields. Its tread marks the passing of time, history as duration: "The tock, tock of my cane striking ice is like the noise that beads make as they click together on a string."[170] The animal's repetitive steps are the sound of memory at work, creating a necklace of narrative. Its tread also recapitulates Isidore's etymology for "oxen": "Latin speakers call them *triones* [i.e., plowing oxen] because they 'bruise, wear away' [*terere*] the earth" (*Etym* 12.1.30). The listener follows the sound chain to see where it leads,[171] from surface sense to something deeper. Decoding the answer, the identity of the speaking "I," is not the end of the story but the beginning of another.[172]

The Exeter Book collection includes three ox/bull riddles: numbers 12, 38, and 72. The first two have a long Anglo-Latin tradition behind them;[173] the third, largely unparalleled, is a sidelong glance at one of history's losers. The ox's space remains one of captive servitude, of exile and endurance: "I was silent," says the speaker, "never complained to any man about the pain of the pointed goad." The mood is nostalgic, retrospective: a prisoner looking far back to a former, tender-green freedom, images flashing up at every turn; a toiling ox recalling its carefree youth. The unknown creature—a model of zoological interiority—elicits something knowable in its viewers.[174]

In a letter Rosa Luxemburg wrote the year before she was killed and her corpse thrown into a canal, she described what she glimpsed from the window of her Breslau prison cell: wild Romanian water buffaloes, unaccustomed to working as draft animals, drawing military supply wagons. One army cart got stuck at the prison entrance gate; she described how a soldier whipped one animal until blood ran from its wounds: "Oh, my poor buffalo, my poor, beloved brother. We both stand here so powerless and mute, and are as one in our pain, impotence, and yearning."[175] The Old English ox-riddle does not envisage positive change for its speaker; nevertheless, its obliqueness sets up "an act of attention—pulled out of oblivion—that moves there and back, and leaves some residue of greater life."[176] Crossed alliterations reinforced by twin half-rhymes support an image of doubling, of significance above and beyond the literal meaning.

We Need to Talk about Names

Alliteration and rhyme offered poets a way to flatter patrons indirectly. Toward the end of *Knútsdrápa* (ca. 1027), Sigvatr skald recorded the pilgrimage to Rome of Cnut the Great. He describes that king as *kærr keisara, klúss Pétrúsi* ("dear to the emperor, close to Peter [i.e., the pope]"). All three words alliterating on *k* (Cnut's initial) are loanwords, occurring here in Old Norse verse for the first time; the fourth word, *Pétrús*, is the biblical name in Latin dress, installed at line's end, where *p* needed no partner.[177] Linked by alliteration and rhyme, all four words reenact, recapitulate Cnut's successful "networking" with the two great political powers of Western Europe, the emperor and the pope. A universal type of narcissism encourages people to prefer letters from their own names.[178] Baden-Powell, founder of the Boy Scouts, based the scouts' motto "**B**e **P**repared" on his own initials.[179] Wagner opened the *Ring* with a chant calling up part of his name: "Weia! Waga! / Woge, du Welle! / Walle zur Wiege! / Wagala weia!" Sigvatr's inclusion of four of the five letters of *Knútr* in the stanza's final four syllables (*klúss Pétrúsi*) might have pleased this English king of mixed Danish/Polish ancestry.

Northern poets were quick to note if a man's behavior reflected the meaning of his name. When the *Maldon* poet calls Wulfstan ('wolfstone') *wig-heardne* 'war-hard' (75), the pairing suggested, as William Camden surmised, that "fatal necessity concurred herein with voluntary motion in giving the name."[180] Transverse alliteration (***w**ig-**h**eardne/ **h**aten **W**ulfstan*) and a deliberately prosaic syntax may have drawn contemporary attention to this wordplay. A monumental series of onomastic "stone" puns stretches from Matthew 16:18 ("tu es *Petrus* et super hanc *petram*") down to twelfth-century England and William of Malmesbury's description of Dun*stan* as a man who "possessed that firmness which his name implied."[181] When the *Beowulf* poet says of young Wiglaf ('battle-heirloom') that *his mæges **laf*** 'his kinsman's heirloom' [= sword] did not *gewac æt **wige*** 'fail at battle' (2628b–29a), he, too, is hinting that *nomen est omen*.[182] "Deep in humankind," Nietzsche suspected, "is the horror of apparent meaninglessness."[183]

Both Norse skalds and Old English poets devised strategems to draw attention to the proper names starring in their verse. Sometimes simple paronomasia sufficed. In Old English verse, Sarah is sad (OE *sar*, *GenA* 2216), Nero causes distress (OE *nearu*, *Jul* 302, *Fates* 13), Eve behaves evilly (OE *yfele*, *GenB* 790), Pharaoh is guilty (OE *fah*, *GenA* 1860), and Deor, *dyre* 'dear' (*Deor* 37). Daniel, as befits the Hebrew meaning of his name, regularly comes to "judgment" (OE *dom*, *Dan* 150), Adam similarly reunites with *eorðe* 'earth' (*GenB* 365), Noah, with "rest" (OE *rest*, *GenA* 1304a), Seth, with "seed" (OE *sæd*, *GenA* 1145), and Jerusalem with "vision of peace" (OE *sibbe gesihð*, *ChristA* 50).[184] Saturn, following Isidore (*Etym* 8.9.29), must be "sated" or "satisfied" (*MSol* 18, 252). The poet of *Judith* created a complex setting for his heroine's Hebrew name: ***Iud****ith æt* ***guðe****,   swa hyre* ***god uðe*** (123): **Iud-** and **god** alliterate and form a half-rhyme; full rhyme links ***guð-*** and ***uð-***. The villain of the piece, Holofernes, is not handled so tenderly: only one adjective, ***egesful*** 'terrible,' picks up both the initial vowel of his name and the *f* of its penultimate syllable (21).

Certain Old English and Old Norse names were given royal treatment. A viking spear flies *þurh ðone* ***æþel****an* ***Æþel****redes þegen* ("through the noble retainer of Æthelred") (*Mald* 151), accompanied by a chorus of *þ*'s. A second warrior, **Æþel**ric, is called an ***æþele*** *gefera* 'noble retainer' (*Mald* 280). *The Battle of Brunanburh* similarly praises **Æthel**stan (1) and his brother, the ***æðel****ing* 'prince' (3), through crossed alliteration: ***ea****foran* ***Ead****weardes,   swa him ge****æðele*** ***w****æs* ("the heirs of Edward, as was befitting their noble descent") (7). Conversely, the *Maldon* poet, by alliterating the name of treacherous **God**ric 'good might' with **god** 'good' underlines the inappropriateness of that appellation.[185] As Mark Griffith first pointed out, the two warriors in the poem whose names contain elements meaning "spear" (*æsc* and *gar*) hurl darts and javelins at the vikings (lines 269, 321b–22a).[186] Their names shape their public behavior.

A century ago, Rudolf Meissner noted the skaldic predilection for torturing proper names.[187] Einarr skálaglamm, employing a device known as *ofljóst* 'too clear,' demonstrates his onomastic wit:

Búinn lézk **valdr,** ef **vildi**
valmey konungr heyja,
haulda morðs at *halda*
—herr fell of gram—velli.

Valdr morðs haulda lézk búinn at halda velli, ef konungr vildi heyja valmey; herr fell of gram.[188]

The controller of the death of men [BATTLE > RULER] declared himself prepared to keep the field, if the king wanted to hold the slaughter-maiden [VALKYRIE = Hildr 'battle']; the army fell around the prince.

Hildr, the name of a famed *valmey* 'slaughter-maiden,' or valkyrie, is also a common noun meaning "battle." When Hákon's opponent desires *at heyja valmey* 'to hold a valkyrie,' he has opted to wage war, not embrace a woman.

The kennings of *dróttkvætt* verse sometimes express one or both elements of a compound name. Personal names based on *arinn* 'stone hearth,' *áss* 'rocky, stony ridge,' *bjarg* 'rocks, sea-cliffs,' *hallr* 'large stone, rock,' or *steinn* 'stone' were targeted for such treatment. The rather repetitious nature of Kormakr's kennings for his beloved Steingerðr 'Stone-Goddess' derives from his plays on "stone" whenever she appears in person or in his thoughts. According to the saga preserving the skald's stanzas, he dies with her name on his lips: *greipa glóðar Gerðr* 'Goddess of the fire of the grasp [GOLD]' = Stone-Gerðr/Steingerðr.[189]

Dithematic names that did not fit into the confines of *dróttkvætt* were avoided or split in two, each part inserted separately in the half-stanza. The place-name Stiklastaðir, famed in northern history as the site of St. Óláfr Haraldsson's fall in 1016, is treated to tmesis whenever mentioned in the poetry, often emerging as *Stiklar* (genitive of a conjectured river name) plus *stǫðum* (the dative plural of *staðr* 'place').[190] Since the dative case of viking-age royal names such as Haraldr and Hákon was metrically unsuitable, their bearers had to be content with appearing in *dróttkvætt* either as subjects or direct objects.

Skalds whose patron's compound name called up a royal ideology made the most of their good luck. In tenth-century England, Latin and Norse poets visiting Æthelstan played on both elements of that king's name: *Æthel-* 'chief, preeminent, noble, glorious' and *–stan* 'stone, rock.' One cleric addressed the prince in biblically flavored Latin as *archale saxum* 'chief stone,' *augusta rupis* 'majestic cliff,' and *petrinum agmen* 'stone army.'[191] And one skald, Egill Skallagrímsson, played variations on the same royal name, Aðalsteinn, the 'chief rock':

Nú hefr foldgnárr fellda
—fellr jǫrð und nið Ellu—
hjaldrsnerrandi, harra
hǫfuðbað*mr*, þría jǫfra.
Aðalsteinn of vann annat,
allts lægra kynfræg*jum*
—hér s*v*erjum þess, hyrjar
h*r*annbrjótr—konungmanni.

Nú hefr hjaldrsnerrandi, foldgnárr, hǫfuðbað*mr* harra, fellda þría jǫfra; jǫrð fellr und nið Ellu. Aðalsteinn of vann annat; allts lægra kynfræg*jum* konungmanni; hér s*v*erjum þess, hyrjar h*r*annbrjótr.

Now has the battle-sharpener [WARRIOR = Aðalsteinn], towering over the land, chief descendant of kings, felled three princes; the land comes under the descendant of Ella [ENGLISH KING = Aðalsteinn]. Aðalsteinn has done more; all is lower than the kin-famous royal person; here we [I] swear to this, distributor of the fire of the wave [lit. "wave-breaker of fire"] [GOLD > GENEROUS MAN].

Nú liggr hæst und hraustum
hreinbraut Aðalsteini.
Nú liggr hæst hreinbraut und hraustum Aðalsteini.[192]

Now the highest reindeer path [MOUNTAIN] lies under bold
Aðalsteinn.

Egill stresses verticality: Aðalsteinn is the top, the Napoleon Brandy of royals; everyone and everything else is beneath him. Old Norse *aðal-*, the first element in the king's dithematic name, means "chief, head, legitimate": the English ruler is the chief-descendant (*hǫfuðbaðmr*) of kings. (The Old English poem *The Battle of Brunanburh* famously plays on *æþel-* 'noble' when praising the same ruler.) The second element of the king's name, Old Norse *-steinn* 'stone, rock,' evokes both hardness and highness: this king towers over the land like a cliff (the adjective *foldgnárr* occurs nowhere else); earth falls under the prince (a play on the homonymy of the common feminine noun "earth" and the giantess-name Jörð, Óðinn's much put-upon consort).[193] The refrain asserts that even the highest mountain, over which reindeer move, silently and very fast, now lies under Æthelstan, the biggest thing on the horizon. Toward the end of the stanza, the skald makes his presence known—"I swear to this"—before addressing the king directly as "breaker of the fire of the wave [= gold]," a distributor of underwater gleams—a subtle hint that wealth is to be put into circulation, even onto a poet's arms.[194] Æthelstan's reign represents what Matthew Townend has called a "high point of Anglo-Scandinavian interaction."[195]

No one called Æthelred II of England *unræd* 'redeless, bad counsel, unready' during his lifetime, at least openly.[196] Life at court was safer that way. Norse skalds sensibly stressed the positive in his name. Óttarr svarti's *Hǫfuðlausn* 'Head-ransom,' composed for Óláfr Haraldsson of Norway, tells of that king's assistance to the exiled Æthelred (Old Norse Aðalráðr) in 1014. In the following stanza, Óttarr seems to explore both elements of that English royal name:

> Komt í land ok lendir,
> láðvǫrðr, Aðalráði;
> þín naut rekka rúni
> ríki efldr at slíku.
> Harðr vas fundr, sás fœrðuð
> friðlands á vit niðja
> (réð áttstuðill áðan)
> Játmundar (þar grundu).

Láðvǫrðr, komt Aðalráði í land ok lendir; efldr ríki, naut rúni rekka þín at slíku. Fundr vas harðr, sás fœrðuð niðja Játmundar á vit friðlands; áttstuðill réð grundu þar áðan.[197]

Land-guardian [KING], you brought Æthelred ['noble/chief counsel'] into the land and secured [him]; strengthened with power, the counsellor of warriors [KING = Æthelred] had help from you in this. Hard was the fighting, by which you brought the kinsman of Eadmund [= Æthelred] into a friendly country; the prop of the family ruled the land there previously.

The second element of Aðalráðr's name means "counsel." Óttarr calls the English king a *rúni rekka* 'counselor of warriors,' noting that Æthelred previously *réð* 'ruled' (past tense of *ráða* 'to counsel, advise') the kingdom. In Old Norse, the words *rún-* and *ráð-* collocate, as do Old English *run* 'consultation' and *ræd* 'counsel, good advice'; Old Norse *ríki* 'power, kingdom' and *rekkr* 'man, warrior' also belong to this set or chain.[198] Óttarr's focus in the stanza on land and realm may relate to the first element of the royal name: *aðal* 'nature, inherited quality,' also 'chief-, head-.' Aðalráðr is the *áttstuðill* 'prop of the family/lineage,' a poeticism echoing Old English *eðelstæf* 'prop of the homeland'; 'kinsman of Eadmund,' he upholds the West Saxon royal dynasty. Óttarr's onomastic play confirms that his royal patron, brought back to England and the throne, is more than ready to rule. Even an unflattering royal nickname, such as *inn digri* 'the stout, fat,' might be durable (and endurable) if it evoked, through rhyme, key praise words (e.g., *sigr* 'victory'). The predictive power of a king's name mattered.

Saints' names also received careful attention. If French farmers invoked England's St. Boni*face* for curing facial ailments, their German counterparts looked to him for help in cultivating beans (*Bohnen*).[199] The meaning of the name Guthlac 'reward of battle' probably shaped the structure of that saint's life in *Guthlac A*, which describes his tribulations in warlike terms.[200] In *Andreas*, as Fred Robinson observed, the Mermedonians pledge their obedience to that apostle not by name but by the epithet *gumcyst* 'the virtuous one' (1606), Jerome's preferred etymology.[201] Isidore provides several onomastic glosses: Andrew, he proposes, can also mean "the one who answers" (*Etym.* 7.9.11). Beginning in line 189 of *Andreas*, the saint's presence is ushered in by a repeated b-verse:

Ædre him **And**reas   agef **and**sware

———

Swiftly Andrew gave answer to him

The formula, irregular meter and all, recurs with minor variations in lines 285b, 572b, 617b, 643b, 1184b, 1345b, and 1375b, and, transposed, as *ondsware agef* (*And* 628)—a frequency accounting for nearly half the occurrences of this half-line in the poetic corpus.[202] The productivity of this b-verse in *Andreas* and its insistent attachment to the saint's name seems pointed.[203] Stephanus is "stoned" (*El* 492b, 509b, 823b), and

Mattheus is "granted" (*And* 97b). Given that early northern poets did their best to tease latent sense out of the names bequeathed to them, an Old English maker might, encouraged by Isidore, have conceived of Andrew as the apostle "who answers."

Monosyllabic foreign names in Old English verse occasionally give rise to crossed alliterations: ***S**ethes **b**earn* 'the sons of Seth' get God ***s**are a**b**olgen* 'seriously enraged' (*GenA* 1257); so, too, the Israelites ***m**od**h**wate* ***M**oyses **h**yrde* 'boldspirited, obeyed Moses' (*Ex* 124).[204] Multisyllabic foreign names might be similarly framed: ***Ph**ilippus and* ***I**acob,* ***f**eorh a**g**efan* ("Philip and Jacob gave [their] lives") (*Men* 81). Alliterative patterns in Old English verse involving monosyllabic secondary elements of disyllabic Germanic names such as Guthlac, Hrothgar, Alfred, or Beowulf suggest that these elements maintained their semantic force and prosodic weight even when not inflected. More often than in any other poem, crossed alliteration in *Beowulf* highlights one or both elements of dithematic proper names, along with a few noncompound names, such as Scyld and Grendel:[205]

1 Hwæt, we **Gar-D**ena in **gear-d**agum
18 **B**eow[*ulf*] wæs **b**reme **b**læd **w**ide sprang[206]
19 **Sc**yldes **ea**fera **Sc**edelandum **in**.
64 Þa wæs **H**roð**g**are **h**ereswped **g**yfen
343 **b**eodge**n**eatas; **B**eowulf is min **n**ama
374 ðæm to **h**am for**g**eaf **H**reþel **G**eata
396 under **h**ere**g**riman **H**roð**g**ar geseon
506 Eart þu se **B**eo**w**ulf, se þe wið **B**recan **w**unne
530 Hwæt, þu **w**orn **f**ela, **w**ine min *U*n**f**erð
591 þæt næfre **Gr**e[n]del swa **f**ela **gr**yra ge**f**remede
653 **H**roðgar **B**eowulf, and him **h**æl a**b**ead
829 **G**eatmecga **l**eod **g**ilp ge**l**æsted
925 **H**roð**g**ar maþelode he to **h**ealle **g**eong
1017 **Hr**oðgar ond **Hr**oð**u**lf. **H**eo**r**ot innan **w**æs
1044 **eo**dor **I**ng**w**ina **on**weald geteah
1066 ðonne **h**eal**g**amen, **H**roþ**g**ares scop
1128 **w**æl**f**agne **w**inter **w**unode mid **F**inne
1143 þonne him **H**un**l**afing **h**ilde**l**eoman
1162 **w**in of **w**under**f**atum. Þa cwom **W**ealhþeo **f**orð
1181 **g**lædne Hroþ**u**lf, þæt he þa **g**eogoðe **w**ile

1201 **Eo**rmen**r**ices, geceas **e**cne **r**æd
1203 **n**efa **S**wertinges **n**yhstan **s**iðe
1301 æfter **m**aþðum**g**ife **m**ærum **G**eate
1319 **f**rean Ing**w**ina, **f**rægn gif him **w**ære
1420 oncyð **eo**rla ge**h**wæm, syðþan *Æ*sc**h**eres
1483 **H**roðgar **l**eofa, **H**ige**l**ace onsend
1488 Ond þu ***U***nferð **l**æt **ea**lde **l**afe
1854 licað **l**eng swa **w**el, **l**eofa Beo**w**ulf.
1968 **b**onan **O**ngenþeoes **b**urgum in **i**nnan
2120 **w**ig**h**ete **W**edra. **W**if un**h**yre
2147 **s**unu Healf**d**enes on *min*e **s**ylfes **d**om·
2161 **h**watum **H**eoro**w**earde, þeah he him **h**old **w**ære
2186 (**dr***y*)hten **We***d*e*r*a ge**d**on **w**olde
2482 **h**eardan **c**eape; **H**æð**c**ynne wearð
2510 **B**eo**w**ulf maðelode, **b**eot**w**ordum spræc
2745 **W**iglaf **l**eofa, nu se **w**yrm **l**igeð
2907 ofer **B**io**w**ulfe, **b**yre **W**ihstanes
2958 **S**weona **l**eodum, **s**egn Hige**l**ace*s*
2965 **W**ulf **W**on**r**e*d*ing **w**æpne ge**r**æhte
3066 Swa wæs **B**io**w**ulfe, þa he **b**iorges **w**eard

The association between Beo**w**ulf's name and *b–w* crossed alliteration (*Beo* 506, 2510, 2907, 3066) is such that, when the hero dives into the mere, unique compounds such as ***b**rim**w**ylm* 'sea-surge' (1494) and ***b**rim**w**ylf* 'she-wolf of the sea' (1506, 1599) gather round him, suggesting the rightness or at least inevitability of his quest: *similia similibus*. When, late in the poem, the narrator refers to him as ***w**inia **b**ealdor, ða se **w**yrm ge**b**eah* ("lord of friends, when the dragon coiled") (2567), with *b* and *w* both times in reverse sequence, the epithet still seems to call up, as in a library catalogue, his name.

Sometimes echoes appear where officially outlawed. The *Beowulf* poet introduces two characters in a-verses that foreshadow through alliteration the name and/or rank given in the b-verse:

Hwilum for (**d**)uguðe **d**ohtor **H**roðgares (2020)

At times, before the retainers, Hrothgar's daughter

cwæð þæt hit **h**æfde **H**iorogar **c**yning (2158)

---

he said that King Heorogar owned it

Hwilum and *cwæð* do not normally possess sufficient metrical weight to alliterate, let alone transversely. Nevertheless, the initial sounds of the unstressed adverb and verb chime with a noun in the b-verse and lend special prominence to the names mentioned.[207] Hrothgar in his so-called sermon employs two transverse alliterations within five lines (1728, 1732), the first marked by cluster alliteration ("**Hw**ilum he on **l**ufan **l**æteð **hw**orfan"), the second ("ge**d**eð him swa ge**w**ealdene **w**orolde **d**ælas"), both lines surrounded by verses rich in multiple full and half-rhymes. The final three verses of *Beowulf,* relating what the riders circling the hero's tomb recite in his praise, begin, as noted earlier in this chapter, with a similarly "illegal" transverse-alliteration pattern (bA Ab), enhanced by half-rhyme. This verse (3180) deviates conspicuously from the two-word norm in the half-lines that bring the poem to a close:[208]

cwædon þæt he **w***ær*e **w***or*uld**c**yning[a]
manna mildest ond mon(*ðw*)ærust,
leodum liðost ond lofgeornost.
(3180–82)

---

they said that he was of worldly kings the kindest of men and the gentlest, the most generous to his people and most intent on honor.

The riders' final word of praise, the compound *lofgeornost*, reverberates in endless notes and an endless silence.[209]

Outside *Beowulf,* only rarely do both elements of an Old English dithematic personal name participate in crossed alliteration. The first line of the verse proem to the *Meters of Boethius* may provide one instance: *Đus* ***Æ****lfred* ***us*** ***ea****ldspell* ***r****eahte* ("Thus Alf-red related old stories to us"); another occurs when the hero at Maldon, ***B****yrht[****h****]elmes* ***b****earn* 'son of Byrht[h]elm' calls out, and ***b****eornas ge****h****lyston* 'men listened' (*Mald* 92). More often only one element of a compound name contributes to the crossed alliteration: *Her* ***E****adgar* ***w****æs,* ***E****ngla* ***w****aldend* ("Here Edgar, ruler of the Angles, was . . .") (*CEdg* 1).

Crossed alliteration sometimes serves as a guide to the pronunciation of foreign names. Abraham 'High Father (of many nations)' (*Etym.* 7.7.2) occurs around eighty-five times in the Old English *Genesis*; its uninflected base, on rare occasions trisyllabic (A-bra-ham), normally occupies only two metrical positions (A-bram), rendering the *h* added by God to the patriarch's name to alter its meaning (Gen. 17:5) inaudible.[210] Crossed alliteration and a groan-inducing onomastic pun result when the trisyllabic Abraham meets and marries Sarah:

þæt him **Abraham** **i**dese **br**ohte
wif, to **ham**e . . .
(*GenA* 1720)

———

that Abraham brought a woman to his home . . .

Crossed alliteration based on the disyllabic version of Abraham's name marks key moments in the narrative, such as the barrenness of Sarah and the births of Ismael and Isaac:

Þa wearð **un**b**l**iðe **Ab**rahames cwen *GenA* 2261

———

Then Abraham's wife became unhappy

Þa wearð **Ab**rahame **I**smael ge**b**oren *GenA* 2299

———

Then Ishmael was born to Abraham

þin **a**gen **b**earn **Ab**raham leofa *GenA* 2398[211]

———

[you will soon look upon] your own son, dear Abraham.

Similar crossed alliterations involving the disyllabic name Abraham surface in the final scene of *Genesis A* as the patriarch prepares to sacrifice young Isaac, an episode prefiguring the central drama of Christian story:

Þa **Ab**rahame spræc to his **om**b**i**htum *GenA* 2880

———

Then Abraham spoke to his servants

An angel interrupts:

Abraham leofa, ne sleah þin **a**gen **b**earn *GenA* 2914

dear Abraham, do not slay your own son

The Old English *Exodus* calls up crossed alliteration when invoking the patriarch's disyllabic name, and ends the episode by employing the same angelic chimes as in *Genesis A*:

***A**b**raham Isaac, ***a**dfyr on**b**ran* *Ex* 398

Abraham [led] Isaac, kindled the funeral fire.

*ne sleh þu, **A**b**raham, þin **a**gen **b**earn* *Ex* 419

Do not, Abraham, slay your own son

In the Vulgate account (Gen. 22:12), God's angel conveys his message without notable sound effects: "Non extendas manum tuam super puerum neque facias illi quicquam" (Lay not your hand upon the boy, nor do anything to him). Old English poets did it differently, adding extra alliteration to draw attention to this particularly significant event. Paired sounds such as ***A-bra**(ha)m/**agen** **b**earn* were easy to remember and could do duty as discreet typological punctuation. The repetition of similar sounds linking related things turns a style associated with pagan sympathetic magic into a tool of Christian supernaturalism.[212] The alliterative line was a smooth, supple instrument, more like a wand than a hammer. Northern poetic etiquette preferred hints to exposition, indirection to straightforward exegesis.

Meter is a mighty force and pressures words to conform to its ways. Crossed alliteration can sometimes moderate such despotism, at least when foreign loanwords are involved. Three times in the Old English *Menologium*, a trisyllabic Latin name fills the a-verse, a lightness that alarms:[213]

Nouem**b**ris **n**iða **b**earnum (196)

November to the children of men

Decem**b**ris **d**rihta **b**earnum (220)

December to the children of princes

Agus**t**us yrmen**þ**eodum (139)

August to the mighty nations

Three learned Latin names have here succeeded in wriggling out of meter's grasp. The a-verses they fill are catalectic, consisting of three rather than four metrical positions, as in the odd lines of the Old Norse meter known as *kviðuháttr* 'poem's form.' Scribal error, a missing monosyllabic or disyllabic *monað* 'month' after these names, is sometimes invoked to explain this lightness; but the word *monað* already occurs in 138a, 195a, and 219b, lines immediately preceding the three in question. Crossed alliteration anglicizes the pronunciation of these three Latin month names, lending them the initial stress typical of Old English, perhaps casting the shadow of a smile at the Latin/Romance enunciation of Old English *þ/th* as *t*.[214] *The Menologium*, usually dated to ca. 1000, is a poem about the calendar, reconciling different ways of looking at time. From the vantage point of the caesura, these three-position a-verses point backward to a learned foreign heritage, the four-square b-verses, to vernacular expectations and politesse. Perhaps the Red Queen was too quick to tell Alice that it was never etiquette to cut someone she had just been introduced to.

CHAPTER 3

Accentuating the Negative

We are the Knights who say . . . Ni!

—*Monty Python and the Holy Grail* (film)

SAYING NO

The secret to success in almost any relationship is knowing what not to say. Speaking to anyone not yourself is always problematic, but, then, so is talking to yourself. A shared sense of wit or style is often the spark for a friendship. Intimacy is the thing with feathers that makes your interlocutor either respond quickly with an appreciative "I get it; I know just what you mean," or send you to a specialist. Both *dróttkvætt* verse and Old English poetry have a knack for wryness and obliqueness, for systematic withholding, for turning hearers into accomplices. In both corpora, evaluations of events, individuals, and things are kept inexplicit, cunningly camouflaged within a flow of compliments, negations, weasel words, and litotic politesse. Northern poets talk the talk, and it is a refined, circumspect, and statesmanlike idiom. Relevancy, openness, frankness, logical fullness, staid clarity, the need to be informative—these cherished modern conversational and compositional principles are rarely in sight. But lies, too, are missing. The speaker's laconic insouciance is a vehicle for complex social messaging, for highlighting the unstable and tentative, for forcing hearers to read between half-lines.

Poetry tattles on society. What does it mean to say "no" incessantly, to posit something only in order to deny it? A flood of negations in both corpora evokes the absent, people who are not present, events and emotions not told. Episodic legendary material had to conform to some extent to what the poet's listeners already knew. The ruler of Babylon wakes up after a bad dream: "His mind was not joyous" (*Dan* 117b). Was Nebuchadnezzar terrified, hungover, or mildly troubled? "That was not a sluggish king" (*Wid* 67b), observes another poet with reference to Burgundian Guðhere (Gunnarr), a ruler prominent in legend over a wide area and for a long time. Was he heroic, heavily caffeinated, or just doing his job? The same poet praises the celebrated Lombard king Alboin for his "most unstingy heart" (*Wid* 73a), referring to his generous payouts, not his spiritual qualities. He declares Widia and Hama, Ermanaric's fabled companions, "not the worst" of heroes (*Wid* 125b), even if he names these international celebrities last.

Evaluative language using incomplete negation is frequent. Noah, unconscious in a drunken stupor, "little [= not at all] recognized" that he was naked (*GenA* 1566b). The narrator of *Andreas* observes that the saint's tormenters "little [= not at all] cared" what their retribution afterward would be (1227b). Speakers wield down-toners on all sorts of occasions and with varying degrees of irony. A wretched soul returning to its body castigates its dust: "Little [= not at all] did you consider" (*Soul II* 19b, 23a) that your earthly sins meant hell for me. An anthropomorphized bagpipe with webbed hands and feet cannot "fly or walk much" (*Rid* 31/8) = at all. The *Beowulf* poet is peculiarly fond of constructions involving the verb *lean* 'to blame, find fault with,' a term used in poetry only here: the horse-riders "not at all blamed" the Danish king (862b) = they praised him to the skies; wise counselors "little [= not at all] blamed Beowulf for that undertaking" (202–3a); indeed, they urged him on. The magnificence of the gifted gold treasures was such that "no one might find fault with them" (1048b). A gentleman to the end, Beowulf "did not at all blame in words" the useless sword lent to him (1811b–12a). The young Geat handles courtly etiquette like a pro.

The skald's inner ironist goes into overdrive when reporting famous incidents of mythological and legendary story. Þórr's fishing trip to catch the world serpent ended inconclusively: hooked, the monster gave such a tug on the line that the god's foot went through the bottom of the boat.[1] One *dróttkvætt* stanza devoted to the incident comments urbanely that the fishing line lay "not at all slack" on the vessel (Bragi *Þórr* 2/2). "Not slack," a shadow of the real situation, encompasses all semantic gradations from "extremely taut" to "somewhat tense," with a range of senses in between. Another early Norwegian skald, Þjóðólfr ór Hvini, tells of a life-bestowing goddess whom the giants abducted and brought to their home: they "were not upset at that" (*Haustl* 10/1–2) = they were deliriously happy. The frequent translation "joyful were the giants" is not wrong, but it wipes out the smile of recognition exchanged between skald and recipient, erasing the speaker's wink and voice. The perpetrator "was not to be accused of cowardice" (*Haustl* 2/7–8) = far from it; it was a bold act, indeed, to snatch that lady from under the gods' noses. As for the thief, Loki "was not gracious to him" (*Haustl* 3/7–8) = not a surprise; no one did rudeness better than Loki. When the gods incinerate an eagle-costumed giant, the poet mildly observes: "There was a swerve in his course" (*Haustl* 13/4) = the fellow's air-joys were over for good. The skald Illugi uses an emphatic negative to pinpoint the moment in northern story when a mounted Sigurðr managed to penetrate the wall of flame surrounding Brynhildr's hall: "It was not a speedy ride for the valiant prince to the woman's dwelling" (*Har* 3/2–3). Why not? Did his horse take a tumble or were local environmental conditions unfavorable? In the *Þórsdrápa* of Eilífr Goðrúnarson, as the god and the giant Geirrøðr fight to the death in the latter's hall, its residents "did not suppress ale-cheer [*ǫlteiti*]" (*Þdr* 16/3–4). This is the ultimate in northern cool: nothing was going to disturb their partying.[2] The same skald's refrain expresses a positive negatively: "The heart of neither Þórr nor Þjálfi trembled with terror" (*Þdr* 11/7–8, 22/3–4); brave heroes keep emotions under check. Poet after poet in the viking-age North practiced ostentatious verbal restraint, counting on listeners to fill in the gaps according to taste and knowledge. There is an aching incompleteness and indeterminacy to such verse, a sense of something not quite said.

The behavior of "nothing," "no," "not," and "non-" leads to scary wordplay, and has been a subject of concern to Western logicians, metaphysicians, linguists, philosophers, lawyers, and poets from Simonides and Aristotle down to the present day. Homer was an early player: "No one . . . is altogether nameless," notes an island king to Odysseus, punning on "No One," his new guest's acquired name, while hinting broadly that he desires to learn the still-secret one.[3] Highly literate wordplay undergirds the title of Samuel Butler's *Erewhon* (1872), an inverted "Nowhere." Dylan Thomas's Llareggub in *Under Milk Wood* (1954) names a small Welsh fishing village; reversed it is a rude English phrase for "Nothingness." The most frequent type of understatement in modern English, classical Latin epic, and Norse prose—the denied negative—is avoided in northern verse.[4] Quintilian had recommended double negation as a form of ornamentation or elegant variation: "Instead of 'I know,' we say 'I am not ignorant.'"[5] Erasmus, too, favored the trope, approving the modesty of "not ungrateful" as an improvement over "very grateful."[6] Fowler declared that "the very popularity of the [not un-Adj] idiom in English is proof enough that there is something in it congenial to the English temperament, and it is pleasant to believe that it owes its success with us to a stubborn national dislike of putting things too strongly."[7] But early northern poets reject out of hand constructions such as *vir non indoctus* 'a not unlearned man' or *sectator non incelebris* 'a not undistinguished adherent.'[8] Such fastidiousness might have pleased George Orwell, who condemned double negation as affecting "an appearance of profundity" and famously recommended as cure for this verbal disease memorizing the sentence: "A not unblack dog was chasing a not unsmall rabbit across a not ungreen field."[9] Yet Orwell's own prose includes references to people who are *not unhappy*, grins that are *not unfriendly*, and songs sung *not untunefully*.[10] Philip Larkin's poem "Talking in Bed" in *The Whitsun Weddings* closes with a double "not-un" iteration:

At this unique distance from isolation
It becomes still more difficult to find
Words at once true and kind,
Or not untrue and not unkind.

Negativity can reduce friction and promote modesty, as Erasmus pointed out under the slogan-like heading *Commuta in Negationem* (Change it into a negative).[11] Incomplete negation takes more time but is equally effective. Edward Gibbon confides in a footnote: "The portrait of Athanasius is one of the passages of my history with which I am the least dissatisfied" = I'm rather partial to that section. Let Horace boast about the immortality of his poetry: "I have executed a memorial longer lasting than bronze" (*Odes* 3.30). The northern poet proceeds cautiously and modestly: a *dróttkvætt* ode is "a not eager-to-be-broken [= strong, enduring] praise-pile"; verses built to cross the sea of centuries are "slow-to-grow old [= unforgettable, lasting] ships of the dwarves [= poems]."[12]

These negations reflect social virtues such as self-restraint, self-discipline, and discretion in the face of power. Someone has suggested that a plausible title for a recent 448-page investigative report should have been "We Didn't Not Find Anything."[13] A praise poet's roundaboutness, his excruciatingly careful good manners, amplifies the virtues of his subject, whether animal, vegetable, or mineral. Compare "I like champagne" with the slightly more circumspect "champagne pleases me not a little." One early eleventh-century skald whose patron survived a perilous storm at sea reported the event with exquisite indirection: "The strong current would have been able to *trouble* [= sink] the merchant ships on the waves if a crew *worse* in vigor [= not as experienced or excellent] had been on board" (Ótt *Hfl* 14/5–8). The tough take life-threatening tempests in stride. The same skald extols his lord northern style: "I do not think, prince, you cared much for sitting in peace" (Ótt *Knútdr* 3/3–4).[14] This negative evaluation conveys a strong positive: "Cnut, you were a tiger in battle." Another skald, addressing his prince intimately in the second person, does so in sentences larded with hedges and negations: "Magnús, you caused no small defense of territory to issue from you" (ÞjóðA *Magnfl* 15/3–4) = you protected your nation with exceptional vigor. "That day [your army] would not be the first to let up with their spears" (ÞjóðA *Magnfl* 10/3–4) = your forces stood and fought heroically. The Norwegian king's victories in battle are manna to his womenfolk: "[They] will not receive such news with sorrow" (ÞjóðA *Magn* 1/3–4); the skald assumes that wives prefer their husbands alive. Sigvatr opens a battle-stanza modestly: "and next I shall recount not the smallest storms of barbs" = now, folks, let me tell you about a really impressive battle.[15] In the Old English *Waldere*, the hero's betrothed takes time out to encourage him with an extended negation of the opposite: "Not at all, my friend, do I taunt you with my words that I saw you at swordplay disgracefully give way before the onslaught of any man or flee behind walls, protect your life" (12–16a). This long-winded Burgundian princess stands by her man—physically and with litotic eloquence. She, too, is gripped by a rhythm, that of northern politesse.

SAYING LESS AND MEANING MORE

The famous
Northern reticence, the tight gag of place
and times: yes, yes.

—Seamus Heaney, "Whatever You Say, Say Nothing"

Students of Old English quickly encounter the word *litotes*, a device "not uncommon in Anglo-Saxon poetry," as one critic litotically notes.[16] Cicero, with reference to an intestinal ailment, used the Greek word to mean "simplicity, plain living."[17] Litotes as a Latin rhetorical term emerged three centuries later, referring to a kind of understatement in which something is affirmed by denying its opposite.[18] When in an Old English poem a soul released from hell to visit his decayed body sums things up: *nis nu se ende to god* ("the end is not now too good") (*Soul II* 35b), the speaker's self-control recalls the stiff-upper-lip stoicism routine in *Monty Python* comedies. "Such is not a beautiful joy," says another poet, evaluating the suffering in hell at a safe distance (*Sat* 79b); "that is no splendid mansion . . . nor a hopeful home at all" echoes a third with reference to the same dwelling (*JDay I* 23a–24a). The sardonic observations continue: Grendel's "parting from life did not seem painful to any warrior" (*Beo* 841b–42). "Nor did his life-days seem useful to anyone" (793–94a). The giant blade used to slay Grendel's mother "was not useless" (1575b). "My sword will not play false with me" (*WaldB* 22), correctly predicts another hero. When Eofor kills Ongentheow, "he did not hold back the deadly blow" (*Beo* 2489b) but at once felled the Swedish king. "It was not a one-day hostility" (*Max I* 193b), a poet says with reference to Cain's slaying of Abel, the murder that marked the entrance of death and fratricidal war into the world. "That will not be a small convocation to hold" (*JDay I* 8b–9a), says another with reference to the inaugural Doomsday crowd, the biggest ever.

Litotes courses through current, past, and future news reports. At Maldon, defecting English troops do not flee the field; it seems that they just "don't care for battle" (*Mald* 192b). Doomed men in the same poem boast that the folks back home "will not be able to reproach [them] for retreating from the fray" (220, 249–52)—a modest way of saying that their glorious defense in the marshes of Essex will live forever in the minds of their countrymen. "They did not wish to take flight at that ford" (81) = they fought and died to a man. Because an English warrior "did not hold back the stroke" (118b), one more viking bit the dust. Indeterminacy rules. King Harald, says his skald, "did not soften his treatment of the Raumar" (Arn *Hardr* 6/1). Did he increase their taxes or burn them alive? Óláfr Tryggvason, says another, "did not ask his men to think of flight" (Hfr *ErfÓl* 3/5–8). Was his order to rush the enemy, stand their ground, or take a coffee break? Outcomes are consistently understated: "I do not believe that there was mercy during the onslaught" (*Eirfl* 5/1), reports Halldórr ókristni of a bloodbath, adding that the attendant wolf was "little hungry" (5/7–8). "The lips of the wound-gull [raven or eagle] were not lacking in blood" (Egill *Hfl* 11/3) = Eric Bloodaxe had lived up to his name. "The breaker of rings [generous man] will not praise hoard-torpor [stinginess]" (*Hfl* 17/3–4), announces the same skald. Great kings give good gifts. In early northern verse, as in conversation today, context and intonation are all-important. "Not bad" can signal "middling, adequate" or "not bad at all," "stunningly superior," depending on when and how you say it and to whom. Negations intimate without being specific, imparting an inherent fuzziness or imprecision to evaluations. Positive assessments such as "your mother was a hamster and your father smelt of elderberry" were infrequent in northern verse.[19] Viking-age audiences preferred, with Puttenham, "the privy nippe."[20]

Diminution (*meiosis*) or incomplete negation (not "negating the contrary" but "understating the contrary") substitutes for "not," a minimalizing adjective or adverb, such as "little" = not at all, "few" = none, "much" = at all, "often" = always, "most" = all, "enough" = abundant, "long" = never. This code, in which adverbs such as "least," "slow," "poorly," "little," "middling," "shortly," "scarcely," and "reluctantly" all mean "not at all," is deeply embedded in vernacular verse. In the Old English *Andreas*, a killing flood supplies "drink enough" (1534b–35); the number of liters swallowed is left to the imagination. Aggressors everywhere "worry little" (= not at all) about their victims' welfare (*GuthA* 238b). A messenger conveying grim news is "little [= not at all] silent" (*Beo* 2897b). "Too few [= no] defenders" supported their lord in his final fight (*Beo* 2882b). Did these "battle-slow" retainers (*Beo* 2846a) just need a pick-me-up or are they lily-livered cowards? Deor in the Old English poem bearing his name uses a minimalizing adverb to underscore the plight of Widia's illustrious father, Weland the smith, now captive and hamstrung: "[he] often [= continually] endured misery" (*Deor* 4b). This is like saying that Sisyphus was frequently frustrated. In *Exodus*, a lamenting nation experiences "few worldly joys" (42): one deadly plague was bad; ten seemed over the top. Minimalizing adjectives and adverbs, where context might call for a maximum, are staples of early northern poetics.

General guides to English literature affirm that litotes is one of the "characteristic figures of speech of Old English poetry."[21] In their *Guide to Old English*, Bruce Mitchell and Fred Robinson speak of "the Anglo-Saxons' predilection for understatement."[22] Eric Stanley refers to "litotes, common in Old English," and to "a tone of grim jesting about horrible things."[23] Beowulf observes that the man-eating sea-monsters he had just served with his sword got no joy in feasting (*Beo* 562). How could they? He dispatched them before the first course. If Grendel devours me, says Beowulf to the Danish king, "you won't have to worry overlong about feeding me" (450b–51). The lad has a sense of humor. So does the narrator. After Beowulf's victory, Unferth, shamed into silence, was "quieter in boasting of his war-deeds" (980–81). Grendel's mother drags Beowulf to her underwater den: "He was not at all enthusiastic about that" (1508b).[24] "It was not decided by lot," says the narrator, who would plunder the unguarded hoard (3126) = the rush to loot was something to see. The coast guard did not greet the departing hero "with insults" (1892a): hugs and kisses were more like it. Young Beowulf was not more hated by his grandfather than any of the latter's sons were (2432–33) = the king loved him as his own child. Hygelac did not give booty to his troops (2919b–20a) = he fell in battle. The hero reports with well-bred reserve that his first venture inside a treasure mound had been granted "not at all pleasantly" (3089) = a fire-breathing dragon was lying in ambush. The *Beowulf* poet describes his hero's swift journey home under sail: "Not at all there did the fair wind hinder the ship in its journey" (1907–8a) = a tailwind got him back in record time. An eleventh-century Norse skald comments similarly on a sea-journey under a favorable breeze: "The raging wind did not spare the swayed mast" (ÞjóðA *Magnfl* 2).

Skalds shed crocodile tears for a fallen enemy: "Sveinn's comrades have clearly lost out on their homecoming" (ÞjóðA *Magn* 2/1–4) = they won't be seeing their wives any time soon. "Roofs and shingles endure distress" (ÞjóðA *Magn* 6/7) is a reticent way of reporting that the king had incinerated every thatched dwelling in his path. Litotic postbellum gloating about widow-making and the horrors of war surfaces in *dróttkvætt* verse into the eleventh century. Even a doomed giant comes in for scorn: "The rock-gentleman [= the giant Hrungnir] was not desirous of waiting long after that for Þórr's much-battering blow" (Þjóð *Haustl*

17/5–8) = the wretched creature's protective shield had somehow got stuck to his feet. Skalds evoke abstractions by eliminating their opposites: the "bane of greed" is "satiety" (Egill *Hfl* 12/1); a "breach of silence" is "hearing" (Egill *Hfl* 20/2). Grief, too, is expressed obliquely. After the king's death, his skald understates a situation for the last time: "Eager men did not carry the glorious Magnús into the grave" (ÞjóðA Lv 1/3–4) = weeping and wailing were general. This polite style is easy to master and parody, as when A. E. Housman has a Greek chorus chant to a stranger: "To learn your name would not displease me much."[25]

Readers have long marveled at the nonheroic contemplative tone of *Beowulf.* Although the 3,182 lines of the poem represent about one-tenth of the Old English verse corpus, they contain almost a third of its "na's," "no's," "and "nealles's," along with sixty-four examples of *ne* plus a verb, either contracted or uncontracted. Terse negative evaluations surface every thirty lines or so. The narrator and his characters practice ostentatious self-restraint. Hrothgar did not fail to carry out his vow (*Beo* 80a) = he said he would build a hall and he did. Cain did not rejoice in that crime (109a) = God sent him packing east of Eden, trembling and groaning. Grendel mourned not at all for his crimes (136b–37a); suing for peace or paying wergild was not his way (154b–56). He was more of an eat-and-run kind of guy, with the result that "none of the wise men there had need to expect bright compensation at the hands of the slayer" (157–58).[26] His death did not seem painful to those tracking his bloody footprints (841b–43). The monster's ravaging of the hall entailed rental losses for the king: "It was easy to find those who arranged for beds elsewhere, farther away in the district" (138–39). Litotes in *Beowulf* attaches itself to the economics of buying and selling. The narrator notes that Grendel could by no means buy his life by leaving his arm behind (972b–73), that Beowulf did not tally up Grendel's life as being of benefit to anyone (793–94b). Grendel's mother seized the king's favorite: "That was not a good exchange" (1304b), observes the speaker—and more than a few poets since.[27] "That was not an easy purchase" (2415b), says the narrator with reference to the dragon's gold. "Little did any regret that they hastily brought out precious treasures" (3129b–31a). (The bearers must have been grinning obscenely. Something to tell the grandchildren about.) A queen is introduced: "She was not stingy, however, nor too sparing of gifts" (1929b–30a) = although young, she already conducted business like a grown-up. Onela "did not reproach him for that hostile act" (2618b) = he rewarded the killer handsomely.

When Beowulf sailed off to free Heorot from its ravager, "wise men dispraised him little for that undertaking" (*Beo* 202–3b): Go, kid, go. "Do not refuse my request," says the youthful hero to the king (429a): this new Ajax had come a long way to cleanse the royal seat. "That is not the undertaking of a coward" (2541b) is how the narrator cautiously evaluates Beowulf's dragon-fight. In *Beowulf* as elsewhere, litotes favors particular verbs: "Indeed Hildeburh had no need [*ne þorfte*] to praise the good faith of the Jutes" (1071–72a) = they destroyed all her joy in the world. "The Hetware," says Beowulf, "had no need at all [*nealles . . . þorfton*] to exult" (2363), for "few [= none?] returned home from that battle" (2365b–66). Beowulf observes that with him in the troop, his lord had no need (*þearf, þurfe*) to search far afield for an inferior warrior (2493b–96a); he already had the best. "Not at all did the nation's king need [*nealles . . . þorfte*] to boast of his army-comrades" (2873–74a) = they ran to the woods like rabbits. The negations roll on. The king's men "did not at all find fault with him" (862) = they praised him to the skies. The sword Hrunting, famed for its excellence, was not "the most insignificant of powerful helps" (1455). (Some might have put it lower on the usefulness spectrum.) "The people of the Geats then prepared a not-mean [= impressive] pyre on the earth" (3137–38). *Nis þæt heoru stow* ("that is not a pleasant place") (1372b), says the Danish king of Grendel's mere, a verdict encompassing a spectrum of possibilities from "a trifle shabby" to "utterly hellish" (cf. English "not pretty"). Hrothgar reveals the truth while hiding it, thereby demonstrating an ability to see reality whole and, legally speaking, unimpeachably. Whatever the conditions on the ground when he gets to the mere, whatever subterranean terrors lurk within its waters, Beowulf will not be able to sue the Danish king for misrepresentation.

Beowulf contains more than a hundred examples of litotes along with a supporting cast of negations. As the poem draws to a close, the incessant "no's" of its narrator and characters evoke a sense of loss or absence, as noun after noun, adjective after adjective is snatched away by a negative particle or litotic adverb.[28] The narrator of *Beowulf* bestows praise not by adding up virtues but by subtracting faults: "By no means did Beowulf slay his closest companions at their drink—his heart was not savage" (2179b–80). The poet notes with reference to his hero's slaying of a poison-spewing dragon: "Indeed, few of men [= no one] on earth . . . succeeded at that, to my knowledge" (2836–37). Beowulf at the end of his life is silent about his own good deeds.[29] With death drawing near, he recites a do-it-yourself obituary loaded with negations: "There was not [*næs*] any king who dared threaten me . . . I did not go looking [*ne sohte*] for trouble . . . I did not swear [*ne me swor*] many oaths wrongfully" (2733b–39a): "A conspicuous example of litotes," comment the editors (*Kl* 4, 256). This distinctive style is absent from Old English prose. The presence in a homily of a negative observation such as "that plan *did not profit* them" (= it was a disaster) is a clue that the speaker is here quoting vernacular poetry.[30] Old English prose and poetry followed different drummers.

Vernacular poets occasionally added a litotic tag or two when translating from Latin, as if domesticating an imported dessert by adding locally crafted candles. Having accused the Arian Theodoric of beheading Pope John, the poet of *The Meters of Boethius* asserts: *Næs ðæt herlic dæd* ("that was not a noble deed") (1.43b), a half-line repeated when Nero sets Rome afire for his amusement (9.18b). But how bad was it? The speaker leaves the degree of depravity open—anything in the range from "rather" wicked to "exceedingly" so. When the text points out that men, unlike animals, possess the faculty of reason, the poet enthusiastically interjects: *Nis ðæt scandlic cræft* ("that is not a shameful power") (20.188b). Denials win out over affirmations. And when the philosopher proposes that men do not fish for salmon on mountains or hunt for deer in the sea, the Old English poet uses a minimalizing adverb to give this argument more bite: "You might think that you will seek them [the deer] far more often [= always] in the woods than out at sea" (19.17b–19). This sardonic observation, an exception to the tendency in Old English for litotes to be associated with the historical past, is not found in Boethius's Latin or in the Old English prose translation from which the verse was derived; nor are any other litotic expressions in the *Meters* (or in the Old English *Genesis A* for that matter) copied from the source text. Wry understatement is a vernacular habit whose distribution within the poetic corpus is uneven and illuminating: *The Wanderer* is litotes-rich; *The Seafarer*, not at all. Battle-poetry revels in understatement as do saints' lives and poems dealing with secular legend. *Genesis A* and *B*, *Exodus*,

Daniel, and *Christ and Satan* are relatively resistant to litotes; so, too, more surprisingly given its militant heroine, is *Judith*. *The Gifts of Men* lacks litotes; *The Fortunes of Men*, in the same manuscript and of similar length, boasts four examples. Hell attracts more litotes than heaven does.

The *Guthlac* poems tower, with *Beowulf*, atop the litotes chart. The demonic tribe attacking that saint *lyt sorgedon* 'little sorrowed' (= had no concern) for his life (*GuthA* 238b). Like *þurfan* 'to need,' verbs such as (*be*)*murnan* 'to mourn, bewail' and (*be*)*sorgian* 'to regret, shrink from' are prolific breeders of litotes, especially when accompanied by the adverbs *lyt* 'little,' *swiðe* 'greatly,' or the emphatic *no* 'not at all.' "Not at all did the fiends have need to rejoice there" (*GuthA* 421), reports the narrator. Guthlac's weeping servant announces the holy man's death with exquisite reticence: "Indeed, I have no need to rejoice greatly in his journey hence" (*GuthB* 1356b–57a); the devil in *Juliana* uses the same formula with regard to his own misery (526b). The dying Guthlac reveals that "he does not greatly dread the hordes of hell's retainers" (1069–70a). In *Judith*, the evil Holofernes lodged in hell "has no need to hope" for relief (117b). God tells Abraham that he will have a son, an heir about whom he will "not need to feel shame" (*GenA* 2329b): Isaac will prove a good boy. A sinful soul will "not at all need to boast of being heaven-bound" (*JDay I* 68b–69). The poet describes Juliana's tormenters on their way to hell: "The warriors in that dark house, the band of comrades in that low pit, had no need to expect appointed treasures from that lord, that they, on the ale-bench of a wine-hall, might receive rings, burnished gold" (683–88). To describe indescribable suffering, the poet calls a more pleasant situation to mind and then cancels it through negation, leaving all other possibilities weakly asserted.

The verb *þurfan* 'to need' is still hard at work in tenth-century *Chronicle* verse, where defeated foes are given no cause to exult, boast, or laugh. "The old warrior had no need to rejoice at the intercourse of swords" (*Brun* 39–40a) = he lost his son and companions at the battle. "The old evil one had no need to boast of the swordplay" (*Brun* 44b–46a). Opponents of the English "had no need to exult" (*Brun* 47b) that they came out better in the battle. Throughout the corpus, the speech of the best and the worst crackle with rhetorical reserve. The Danish king tells Beowulf that, if he rids the land of Grendel, *ne bið þe wilna gad* ("there will not be a lack of good things for you") (*Beo* 660b). God in *Genesis B* pleads with the first couple to behave; his opening words promise them a reward for obedience: *Ne wyrð inc wilna gæd* ("there will not be a lack of good things for you two") (236b). Four hundred lines later, Satan is tempting Eve, humankind is about to fall, but the poet keeps his perspective: *nalles he hie freme lærde* ("not at all did [the devil] preach to her advantage") (610b).[31] Christ in the Old Saxon *Heliand* takes a similar line when he rebukes the Pharisees: "That will not turn out to your benefit" (3818b). When a pagan judge sentences Juliana to be beheaded, the poet quickly assures hearers: "That death did not profit him" (*Jul* 605b). Just so, Cain "did not rejoice in his crime" (*Beo* 109a). All those years in the desert took their toll. A speaker who discourses negatively gives the appearance of possessing a fuller, more complete awareness of reality than one who makes positive assertions. The former's statements are also less likely to prove false.

Old English negations convey contempt with a light touch. "The Mercians did not refuse battle to the Northmen" (*Brun* 24b–28) = they jumped at the chance. The commander of the English forces at Maldon set the tone when he told the viking messenger: "We'll give you payment in war-gear that will not benefit you in battle" (*Mald* 48) = it will cost you your lives. Sardonic asides confirm and ruin reputations. The Egyptian army received such a "deep reward" in the Red Sea that not one warrior was left to tell the news to his womenfolk (*Ex* 506b–12). A soldier in Beowulf's troop pierces a sea-beast with an arrow: "It was slower at swimming in the waves, when death took it" (*Beo* 1435b–36), observes the narrator, like a mobster reporting success to his boss. A wolf in *Maxims I* "does not weep over the slaughtered" (150): no, indeed; the prospect of dining outdoors makes this carrion beast deliriously happy. A saint unleashes a saltwater flood on a city of cannibals, and the mass drowning that results is imagined as an outpouring of free liquor: "The cupbearers, the serving-men, did not delay—there was drink enough immediately ready for all" (*And* 1533b–35). When Andreas himself is slain, listeners are quickly assured that the killer "did not end up surrounded by laughter" (*And* 1702b–3a) = hell is no fun house. In *Juliana*, the saint refuses to marry her passionately pagan suitor "unless," she says sardonically, "he more eagerly worships the god of hosts than he has yet done" (109b–10). This dark style occasionally surfaces in Anglo-Latin texts of the period. In his prose *Life of Saint Oswald*, Byrhtferth, monk at

Ramsey Abbey (ca. 970–1020), reports the hearsay that Oda, sometime archbishop of Canterbury (941–58), was the son of a Dane who came over with the great heathen army of 865–66. He concludes dryly: *ideo pater non penitus Christo seruire studuit* ("for that reason, his father did not wholly seek to serve Christ").[32] Centuries earlier, a Merovingian bishop, in receipt of a spoiled grain shipment, noted tactfully that the produce was *non bella* 'far from attractive' = totally inedible and disgusting.[33] Juliana's father, fed up with her recalcitrance, *nales frætwe onheht* ("did not promise her adornments") (*Jul* 118b); no, he vowed to have her torn by wild animals for her stubbornness.

Characters in Old English verse frequently say "never" or "always" via down-toners. Beowulf speaking of an early exploit boasts that he does not brag about it *much* = not at all (*Beo* 586b). A truth-speaking messenger does not lie *much* (= not at all) in words or facts (3029b–30a). Those entering the dragon's cave will see *enough* (= a great many) treasures there (3104). The hero praises his sword, which early and late *often* (= always) stood by him (2499b–2500). Fate *often* (= always) protects the undoomed man (572b–73a). It was the habit of the Geats that they were *often* (= always) ready for action (1247). An adverbial down-toner appears in what may be the earliest surviving Old English poem, the two-line *Proverb from Winfrid's Time*, embedded in an early eighth-century Latin letter. It is introduced with the words: "Remember the Saxon saying: the man who is *dædlata* [slow in action] [= lacking in courage] often [= always] puts off glory." In Old English poetry, the massing of such hedges quickly colors a character aristocratic. The reticent speaker in *The Wanderer* has few (= no) dear companions (31); he must long (= forever) do without his beloved lord's counsels (38). In his dreams remembered kinsmen often (= always) drift away (53), having exchanged not many (= no) known utterances (55). "Sorrow is renewed for the one who must very frequently [= always] send his exhausted mind over the binding of the waves" (55–57). The speaker's insistent down-toners, about one every five lines, embody a vision of life as bounded and needy. So, too, the sad woman in *The Wife's Lament*, abandoned in a cave under an oak tree in a foreign land, keeps a sense of proportion as her world collapses: "I have few [= no] friends, beloved ones, in this place" (16). Down-toners, like bandages, add a protective padding to things, as if letting in too much air and sunlight would be painful.

The good, the bad, and the ugly sound a lot alike in northern verse. Juliana's devil boasts of the evil deeds he did *nalæs feam siðum* 'not at all a few times' (354b) = over and over again; the same half-line is used of the multiple miracles worked by Christ (*And* 605b) and the multiple offenses committed by Judas before he became a bishop (*Ele* 817b). A poet who hits upon a pleasing b-verse litotic formulation is likely to repeat it. At least two of Cynewulf's "denials of the opposite" are unique to his signed poems and to *Guthlac B*. In *Elene*, a wolf *wælrune ne mað* ("did not hide his murderous intent") (28b) and a praying bishop *hygerune ne mað* ("did not hide his heart's intent") (1098b); so, too, when Guthlac's disciple reports that saint's death, *he þa wyrd ne mað* ("he did not hide that event") (*GuthB* 1345b). (The formulaic *ic ne þearf behlyhhan* 'I do not need to rejoice' has the same distribution.) The litotic half-line *nis seo tid latu* 'the time is not slow' (= it is at hand) occurs three times (*And* 1210b, *GuthB* 903b, 1265a). A demonic tribe of Mermedonians quickly attacks Matthew: *nalas late wæron* 'not at all were they slow' (*And* 46b), reports the poet. More complex is Saturn's complaint in *Solomon and Saturn II* that fate "will be slow (*late*) to tire [= never tire] of engendering enmity" (449–50). Old Saturn knows of what he speaks.

English polite conversation is still rich in indirections that puzzle outsiders: "He's had a bit to drink" (= he's soused); "I wouldn't mind a lift" (= get me out of here). Some understatements are more subtle than others, requiring hearers to make a mental leap. The *Beowulf* poet depicts water monsters sunning themselves on headland-slopes "such as those who in the morning often [= always?] observe a sorrowful [ship-] journey on the sail-road" (1427–30). Why "sorrowful"? Perhaps because when these amphibians sight ships, they sink same. A laconic, understated style allows for urbane self-promotion that on occasion evokes a teasing response. In *Andreas*, the apostle asks a conveniently stationed helmsman (Christ in disguise) for ship-passage, adding grandly that he can repay this kindness with *beaga lyt, sincweorðunga* 'few rings, treasures' (271b–72a) = no fare-money at all. The holy skipper, an apparent foreigner, pretends to take the apostle's face-saving politesse literally, and begins to negotiate for the appropriate sum (296–98). Inexperience with heroic indirection can be seriously discommoding, as witnessed by the recognition scene in the *Hildebrandslied*. When old Hildebrand realizes that the young man challenging him to single combat is his son, he warns Hadubrand in vain to withdraw, stating the reason negatively and reticently: "you never yet sought a meeting with so closely related a man" (29–30) = I'm your daddy, Haddi. The son remains tragically uncomprehending. Nothing short of DNA testing will convince him that his father is not dead but standing right there before him. Even wily Odysseus was clearer, telling his doubting son that no other Odysseus than the one he sees before him will be arriving in Ithaca.

Words formed with negative affixes are frequent in both Old English and *dróttkvætt* verse, forming a relentless drumbeat. There are seventy *un*-adjectives in *Beowulf*, at least two-thirds of which alliterate on their opening syllable.[34] The prefix turns negative connotations positive (*untæle* 'unblameworthy' = praiseworthy), and vice versa (*unleofe* 'the not loved ones' or 'badly loved ones' = the scorned and despised). William Morris in his 1895 translation of *Beowulf* tried to convey the Old English poet's fondness for *un*-compounds, rendering *unforht* as 'unafeared,' *ungeara* as 'unyore,' *unfæge* as 'unfey'; so, too, *unrot* 'unglad,' *unfrod* 'unaged,' *unslaw* 'undull,' and *unwaclic* 'unweaklike.' Both Seamus Heaney (whose poetic coinages include *unstingable*, *unscarfing*, *unshiftably*, *un-get-roundable*, *unkindled*, *unbleeding*, *unhomesick*, and *undrowned*) and A. E. Housman (*strengthless*, *truceless*, *hueless*, *sumless*, *diamondless*, *unpearled*, and *undishonored*) milked this rhetorical device in their own verse.[35] Fritzner's *Ordbog* records more than a thousand Norse *ó*-words (along with a battalion of deprivative *ør-*, *mis-*, *van-*, and *var-* prefixed compounds); most appear only in prose. Thirty or so of the approximately 200 *ó*-compounds listed in the *Lexicon Poeticum* occur in *dróttkvætt* verse of the Viking Age. Examples collected from the poems of one early eleventh-century skald, the cosmopolitan Sigvatr, include *ófár* 'not a few, many' (*Nesv* 8/8), *ótrauðr* 'unreluctant' (*Víkv* 9/2), *ókunnr* 'unknown' (*Austv* 15/6), *órýrr* 'not decreasing'? (*Berv* 16/2), *ólítill* 'unlittle' (*Víkv* 4/5), *ómjúkr* 'unyielding' (*ErfÓl* 19/4), *ófalr* 'not for sale' (Lv 13/4), *óframr* 'uncourageous' (*Berv* 15/3), *ókristinn* 'unchristian' (*Austv* 8/4), *óskeggjaðr* 'unbearded' (*Berv* 16/2), *ótvinn* 'unwavering' (*Austv* 5/8), *óþekkr* 'disagreeable' (*Austv* 5/6), and *óblíðari* '(much) more unagreeable' (Lv 24/8); the first two of these *un*-compounds, referring to numberless corpses floating in the sea and to the battle-eagerness of a young king, seem certifiably litotic.

The term "litotes," mentioned briefly in the general introduction to *Skaldic Poetry of the Scandinavian Middle Ages*, appears dozens of times in editorial notes within the published volumes. Its frequency in the commentaries to *dróttkvætt* court poetry with English associations is striking.[36] Some early skaldic sequences are litotes-free. The nine complete or partial stanzas of the Norwegian skald Þorbjǫrn hornklofi's *Glymdrápa* 'Resounding-poem' (ca. 890) furnish no examples of the figure; nor do the surviving eight stanzas of Guthormr sindri's *Hákonardrápa* (ca. 960). A few *lausavísur* 'loose verses,' not securely dated, make limited use of litotic expressions: Torf-Einarr announces *þeygi dylk* . . . ("I do not hide at all that . . .") (Lv 3/5) = I tell you openly. The sole *dróttkvætt* stanza attributed to Hildr Hrólfsdóttir (ca. 900), Norwegian mother of the alleged founder of the duchy of Normandy, threatens the king with harsh retribution if he doesn't pardon her son—but does so indirectly: if outlawed, her boy *muna við hilmis hjarðir / hægr* ("will not be gentle with the ruler's herds") (Lv 1/7-8) = he will destroy the king's men.

Beginning in the last quarter of the tenth century, *dróttkvætt* stanzas seem increasingly open to litotic politesse. The fourteen "loose" stanzas of Norway's Eyvindr skáldaspillir Finnsson (ca. 961–90) contain a number of such expressions, including *oss gerask hneppt . . . setuefni* ("the possibility of sitting in peace is becoming scant for us") (Lv 1/3–4) = battle is imminent; *meðaldyggr* 'middling-brave' (Lv 5/2) = lacking all prowess; "king, they said you little let your spirits falter" (Lv 7/1–4) = Haraldr, you fought with pizzazz. Swords clashing in battle are *ófolginn* 'unconcealed' (Lv 7/5) = drawn. Another skald assures a victorious patron, not completely selflessly: "I do not think that the stones of the Rhine [gold] are diminishing for the chieftain's warriors" (Eskál *Hardr* 1/3–4) = you are such a winner that your supporters are smiling all the way to the bank. The *Gráfeldardrápa* (ca. 975) of Glúmr Geirason provides at least one example of litotes. The skald laments that *Haralds dauði réðat oss til auðar* ("Haraldr's death did not bring about riches for us [me]") (12/3–4); this unemployed Icelander must now seek another patron. Einarr skálaglamm Helgason's *Vellekla*, composed for Earl Hákon of Lade (r. ca. 970–995), perhaps the most powerful pre-Christian ruler of late tenth-century Norway, contains relatively few understatements and those are brief. Its thirty-seven extant stanzas and half-stanzas include *né hlítik frýju of þat* ("I shall not get a reproach for that") (5/1–2) = the prince is certain to like my praise; *gramr svafði bil* ("the prince ended delay") (6/4) = the battle began; *vasat at frýja* ("one did not have to provoke [that warrior into battle]") (7/1–4) = he dove right in; *gnótt flaut nás fyr nesjum* ("a sufficiency of corpses floated off the headlands") (22/7) = huge numbers were killed in that sea-battle; *vasat gengiligt at ganga í gǫgn her þeira* ("it was not easy to go against their army" (27/1–4) = the battle against Emperor Otto II and his troops at the Danevirke was no push-over. Litotic styles take off in the first half of the eleventh century. The skalds of this period seem particularly addicted to the ironic and negatively put, as if such language had become required or at least approved etiquette at northern royal courts.

READING RETICENCE IN THE AGE OF CNUT

The examples of skaldic litotes given below are extracts from praise-poems and "loose verses" attributed to Icelandic skalds who were in residence at foreign courts between about 1000 and 1035. The list, incomplete as it is, illustrates verbal politesse at various centers in Scandinavia and England at a time when relations between the two regions were especially close. Three generations of Danish kings sat on the English throne between 1013 and 1042, a period that saw a substantial Scandinavian settlement of landowners in the south and west of the country and the movement of English clergy into Scandinavia.[37] Some of the citations below take the form of parenthetical asides, comparable to the occasional b-verses of Old English poetry ("that was not a pleasant place"; "that was not a sluggish king"). Others color heroic a king's leadership on the battlefield, assigning praise to his troops and heaping scorn upon his enemies. Still others, opening with the skald's personal and subjective "I think that" (or "do not think that") or "I'd say that" (or "I wouldn't say that"), give the appearance of innocent diffidence where neither innocence nor diffidence is felt, and where the speaker assumes his listeners will recognize this. The poems from which these examples are taken record contemporary events; a few were probably composed for delivery in England, even in London or Winchester.

1. Hallfreðr vandræðaskáld Óttarsson

Erfidrápa Óláfs Tryggvasonar, ca. 1000[38]

St. 2
Frægr flugþverrir nam aldrigi vægja fyrri
"The famed flight-diminisher never yielded first" = the king always fought until the bitter end

St. 3
Baðat rekka sína hyggja á flótta
"[He] did not ask his men to think of flight" = he told them to stand firm

St. 4
Flaug brodda vas lítt hept
"The flight of pikes was little hindered" = arrows and spears flew thickly

St. 8
Gnóg til gumna feigðar
"Enough for the doom of men" = more than enough, abundant

St. 22
Kannka mart við veifanarorði manna
"I don't care much for the vacillating accounts of men" = I hate pettifoggery

St. 23
Dauði góðs grams brá gœði ófárar þjóðar
"The death of the good prince snatched away well-being from not a few nations" = everybody lost when Óláfr died

Hákonardrápa, ca. 995[39]

St. 2
Ólítit hryngráp vápna Egils brestr hart á skyrtum Hamðis

"Not a little ringing hail of Egill's weapons [ARROWS] falls fiercely upon Hamðir's shirts [BYRNIES]" = an intense storm of arrows noisily assails the warriors

St. 6
Því hykk frægjan fleygjanda [auðs] mjǫk trauðan at láta systur Auðs eina
"For that reason I think the famed flinger of riches [PRINCE] is very reluctant to desert Auðr's sister [Jǫrð 'earth' > LAND]" = the king will never give up his newly acquired territory

2. Halldórr ókristni, *Eiríksflokkr*, ca. 1001[40]

St. 3
Fjǫrð kom Ormr inn langi í heldr harða
"Last year the Long Serpent [ship] endured a rather harsh [trial]" = it was an extremely fierce sea-battle

St. 5
Hykkat vægð at vígi, ógnharðan spǫrðu sik
"I don't think there was mercy during the fight, [or that] the battle-fierce one spared himself" = the engagement was brutal and the leader outdid himself

Sóti Sifjar vas lítt svangr
"The horse of the goddess [WOLF] was little hungry" = piled-up corpses were made available for its dining pleasure

3. Þórðr Kolbeinsson, *Eiríksdrápa*, ca. 1020[41]

St. 3
[The ruler directed ships] *hót at móti Sigvalda*
"somewhat against Sigvaldi" = at full force

St. 10
Fár flestra ýta bilar fátt
"Misfortune little fails most men" = grief comes to all

St. 15
. . . *sás né sjaldan gaf hrafni sollit hold*
"The one who not seldom gave swollen flesh to the raven" = he slaughtered men exceedingly often

4. Þórðr Særeksson, *Róðudrápa*, ca. 1026[42]

St. 1
[Knútr] *skaut nær skarpt at móti hǫnum; sonr Sveins vasa slær at reyna*
"[Cnut] shot rather sharply against him; the son of Sveinn [Cnut] was not weak to test" = the Danish king fought back ferociously; he was one tough guy

5. Sigvatr Þórðarson

Víkingarvísur, ca. 1015[43]

St. 2
Né svik fǫlusk
"Treachery was not hidden" = the schemers' duplicity was out in the open

Fár beið sára ór stað
"Few stood waiting (in that place) for wounds" = all his opponents ran away in terror

St. 10
Þeir bǫðut sér síðan slíks skotnaðar
"They did not ask for such luck for themselves after that" = their battle-lust decreased after their homesteads were destroyed

Nesjavísur, ca. 1016[44]

St. 8
Ófár nár flaut ǫrt við eyri

"Not a few corpses floated swiftly by the gravel-bank" = a huge naval force perished in that sea-battle

St. 13
Né hykk . . . dróttinssvik þóttu hœfilig
"I do not think . . . betrayal of the ruler seemed becoming" = their treachery was a disgrace

Fragments[45]

St. 1
En telk næst eigi in smæstu él nadda
"And next I shall relate not the smallest storms of arrows" = don't go away; big bloody battles will be my next topic

Austrfararvísur, ca. 1019[46]

St. 6
Þeygi bella . . . tíri
"Not at all do [men] display praiseworthiness" = they behave like thugs

St. 7
Þó reiðik lítt lǫst lýða
"Yet I little broadcast people's faults" = clearly (if you've been listening) I do so a lot

St. 13
Spǫrðumk fæst
"I pampered myself very little" = the bags they made me carry weighed a ton

Flokkr about Erlingr Skjálgsson, ca. 1027[47]

St. 5
Né lamðisk landvǫrn

"His defense of territory did not fail" = he fully protected his land

St. 8
Ek drakk eigi drykkju allglaðr þann dag
"I did not drink a drink very happily [lit. happy] that day" = I was miserable when I learned of my friend's murder

Knútsdrápa, ca. 1027[48]

St. 9
[Knútr] *vildi hafa fæst rǫ́n foldar*
"Cnut allowed the least plundering of the land" = he allowed none at all

St. 11
Fár hringdrífr mun hafa svá metinn fetum . . .
"Few ring-distributors will have thus measured with their feet" [the path to Rome] = no prince had made this pilgrimage on foot before

Erfidrápa Óláfs helga, ca. 1035[49]

St. 10
Friðbann vas þar
"A ban on peace was there" = fierce battles raged

St. 12
Gnógr styrr vas þar
"Enough fighting was there" = as I just said, the battle was exceptionally fierce

St. 16
Slœtt réð sízt at bíta
"The blunt [sword] succeeded least in biting" = the king's sword, dulled by magic, did not cut at all

Lausavísur (before 1036)[50]

St. 3
Né lastak síðan
"Nor will I find fault [with the sword] later" = it was a superb gift, now and forever

St. 9
Munk snytrask at hróðri heldr síð
"I am likely to make myself wise in praise poetry rather late" = King, no more eloquent odes for you if nuts are to be my sole reward

St. 11
. . . þykki mér seinn sunnan
"[The king] seems to me late (in coming) from the south" = the king is dead

St. 16
Lítt sék lofðung óttask
"Little do I see the prince show fear" = No one has ever seen him quail

St. 25
Lof opt byrjuð austan . . . erut of spǫrð
"The praises often originating from the east are not too sparing" = reports concerning his valor are constant and exorbitant

St. 27
[Those who know verse-craft best] *síðr finna braglǫstu at hróðri svinns Sighvats*
"will less find verse-flaws in the odes of wise Sigvatr" = experts will not fault my poetry in any way; those who do are ignoramuses

Bersǫglisvísur, ca. 1038[51]

St. 3
Vasat hlið á her, þars stóðk
"There was no gap in the ranks where I stood" = I did not turn and run

St. 5
Enn eru búendr seinir af, þvís minnir
"The farmers still are slow to give up what they remember" = shape up, king; those who overthrew your father will come for you if you're not careful

6. Óttarr svarti

Hǫfuðlausn, ca. 1025[52]

St. 11
Gumnar guldut sjaldan hollum dǫglingi goll
"Men not seldom paid gold to the gracious prince" = you forced the English to pay enormous sums as tribute

Frák stundum stór þing fóru ofan til strandar
"I heard that at times large things went down to the shore" = cartloads of tribute were regularly loaded onto your ships

St. 17
[You let your enemies] *hafa laun mundangs*
"have a payment of appropriateness" = the plotters were all banished or mutilated; well played, king

Knútsdrápa, ca. 1027[53]

St. 3
Hykkat, þengill, þik þekkðusk mikla kyrrsetu
"I do not think, prince, you cared much for sitting in peace" = you engaged in battle after battle

St. 8
Sverð knǫttut verða slæ, þars sóttuð kastala
"Swords did not become blunt where you attacked the fortified settlement" = your army did serious damage during the assault

St. 10
Jǫfurr, vátt gnógt nafn
"Prince, you won a great enough name by fighting" = your name is now exceedingly famous throughout the North

7. Þórarinn loftunga

Tøgdrápa, ca. 1029[54]

St. 1
Ólítinn flota
"no small fleet" = a very great force

St. 4
Vasa fǫr ǫrbeiðis eyðilig
"The journey of the warrior was not lacking in splendor" = the sailing of your armada was a sight to remember

8. Anon, *Liðsmannaflokkr*, ca. 1015–16[55]

St. 3; also st. 9/5–6.
[The man] *mun gjarn síðarla arna*
"will gladly rush late [to battle]" = this draft-dodger is happy to sit it out

[The warrior] *berr eigi rǫnd upp á Englandi í ári*
"does not carry a shield up into England in a hurry" = the coward won't even leave his warm bed

St. 4
Liðar Þorkels þóttut mér dvelja at ganga í folk

"Thorkell's men did not seem to me to delay in joining the fray" = they rushed helter-skelter to battle

The wryness and reserve of these evaluations, their speakers' refusal to indulge in unwarranted enthusiasm, are coded signals. They suggest intimacy and informality. Precise denotation is unnecessary. Notions widely shared do not need to be fully articulated. In a landscape bristling with armed coherent packs, watchfulness and verbal agility were essential skills. The skalds' cool shorthand messaging is the dialect of an in-group. The examples listed above concern battle-readiness and aggression, gift-exchange and tribute-taking, an ethic of self-sacrifice, an emotional attachment to one's leader and cohort, along with distaste, bordering on scorn, for those outside the group and those rejecting its ethos. In some instances, greater explicitness might have put the speaker's life and position in danger; the vaguer and more imprecise the formulation, the safer the witness. The skald's terse concision seems at times to mask (or at least imply) an excess of feeling: "Late will grief lift from me" (= never) is how one early eleventh-century skald, Arnórr jarlaskáld Þórðarson, described the loss of his beloved kinsman and patron.[56] Like the rulers whose warlike deeds they publicized, the skalds had a taste for flash-forwards and strategic withdrawals; unexpectedness was an artistic as well as a military principle. Their verse documented mores but also modeled them, remaking history in the image of poetic language.

Jonathan Swift defined verbal etiquette briskly as "proper words in proper places,"[57] that is, acceptable expressions set out according to established formal requirements. In the two northern corpora examined here, terse evaluative comments and adverbial down-toners are anchors of subjectivity in a turbulent sea. The poets' elliptical asides and tight-lipped understatements are northernisms for which there is no northern name. They share a characteristic tonal delicacy and a respect for the hearer's intelligence. When the narrator of *Guthlac B* observes of Adam and Eve that "they wearied too soon of performing the will of God" (844), he was not suggesting that the couple should have waited another hour or two before their fatal *déjeuner sur l'herbe*; the poet was composing for connoisseurs who knew their biblical stories and who prized vernacular urbanity. Before describing Þórr's misadventures at the hands of two giantesses, the skald Eilífr Goðrúnarson observed *friðsein vas þat* 'that was a peace-delay'; he, too, counted on his listeners' cultural competence, their readiness to convert the irony-laden litotes of "there was some slowness in making nice-nice" into the closed-captioned summary: "Þórr at once swung his hammer."[58] There are things the line knows but does not tell.

DIETROLOGIA

Time will say nothing but I told you so.

—W. H. Auden

Dietrologia 'behind-looking,' an Italian term only a few decades old, refers to the conviction that something unpleasant is lurking beneath the surface of things. It is a form of controlled paranoia or justifiable suspicion, a sense that somewhere, not far off, storm clouds are gathering. The tales lightly told in northern verse can seem warped in a way that suggests the pull of a hidden backstory, a black hole distorting the shapes of objects around it.[59] Places and people vibrate with anxiety. In *Beowulf*, three Scandinavian dynasties are fated to fall, but these catastrophes are sensed only indirectly, by the shadows they cast and by their gravitational force. History hangs heavy over the actors. Familiar stories emerge as shards, as a series of fragments whose links are unspoken. The poet zooms in on an ominous scene, takes a quick snapshot, and then departs, trailing atoms of dread behind. To be effective, the dark matter alluded to had to be so well known that it did not have to be spelled out. Poets counted on an audience's instinct to construct a story out of the briefest of hints. The *Beowulf* poet, observing that Cain's descendants were a bad lot, asserts sardonically: "[God] gave them a reward for that" (114b). He trusted at least some of his listeners to "get it," to look back and remember the deluge, the environmental catastrophe that wiped out almost all the earth's population, leaving behind only Noah and his sketchy family.[60] Similar stand-alone allusions to legendary history, isolated and hemmed in, emerge here and there in *Beowulf*, gradually providing the "sense of an ending."[61] The poet acknowledges the reality of a horrendous history without staring at it directly.

Submerged narrative awakens, Kraken-like, in the opening lines of the poem. We get a snapshot of the dynasty's founder, young Scyld, tugging at mead-benches, disturbing furniture, grabbing shiny objects with his little fists. The light will be brighter once he reaches the top. He begets an heir; then shoves off. That's life for you. The poem has barely begun when we are told of the future destruction by fire of Heorot, Hrothgar's newly erected hall, that golden-roofed mansion-*sur-mere*, and of in-law trouble waiting impatiently in its wings. These two brief allusions to Danish story serve as a table of contents, a weather report warning of storms ahead:

Sele hlifade
heah ond horngeap; heaðowylma bad,
laðan liges— ne wæs hit lenge þa gen
þæt se ecghete aþumsweoran
æfter wælniðe wæcnan scolde.
(*Beo* 81b–85)

The hall towered, high and wide-gabled; it awaited deadly surges, hostile flame—nor was it longer from then that sword-hatred would awaken between son-in-law and father-in-law after deadly enmity.

The first indication that something is rotten in Denmark is the narrator's matter-of-fact statement that Heorot is destined to go up in flames (81b–83a). The timing of this burning is left open, perhaps to accommodate different versions of the story in circulation. In Saxo's *Gesta Danorum* (2.7.11–12), fire imagery illuminates Heoroweard's night attack on Hrothulf, whose last stand at the royal hall was widely celebrated in the poetry of the North.[62] Correspondences between fleeting allusions in *Beowulf* and much later Danish/Icelandic Scylding materials have haunted our handbooks since 1852.[63] Three decades earlier, the scholar and poet N. F. S. Grundtvig recognized the Scyldings of *Beowulf* as the Skjöldung rulers of early Danish story and their legends as behind the entire first part of the poem.[64] In 1875, another Dane, Ludvig Schrøder, explicated certain scenes as foretelling the fall of the house of the Scyldings, the poem's ominous backdrop.[65] Subsequent discussions by Axel Olrik, R. W. Chambers, Dorothy Whitelock, Arthur Gilchrist Brodeur, and Marijane Osborn deepened the link, confirming that the *Beowulf* poet alluded to the fall of the Danish dynasty in a way that encouraged listeners to fill in the gaps.[66]

Following the principle that the first shall be last, the final allusion in *Beowulf* to Danish Scylding legend, a passage dispatching one Heoroweard in two and a half brisk lines, begins to fill in the legendary backdrop to the conflagration mentioned in verse 83a. Beowulf, having arrived home, presents Hrothgar's gifts to his lord and uncle, saying that the Danish king wanted it known that the mail-coat in the collection was a royal heirloom, that before coming into his possession it had belonged to Heorogar, his older brother and predecessor on the throne. The latter for some unstated reason refused to give this armor to his own (and loyal) son Heoroweard. As for Heoroweard, "there he is," observes Marijane Osborn, "in the shadows of the story, waiting for the twelfth-century *Lejre Chronicle* to develop him into a nemesis."[67] Before handing over this battle-gear to the king, Beowulf recites its genealogy in a short passage rich in extra alliterations and half-rhymes:

Me ðis hildesceorp   Hroðgar sealde
snotra fengel.   Sume worde het
þæt ic his ærest ðe   est gesægde.
Cwæð þæt hyt hæfde   Hiorogar cyning
leod Scyldunga   lange hwile.
No ðy ær suna sinum   syllan wolde
hwatum Heorowearde   þeah he him hold wære
breostgewædu.   Bruc ealles well.
(2155–62)

Hrothgar, the wise prince, gave me this battle-gear. He commanded that I should first tell you in certain words his good will. He said that King Heorogar owned it, man of the Scyldings, for a long time. Not at all the sooner did he wish to give the breast-garment to his son, bold Heoroweard, although he was loyal to him. Enjoy all well.

This presentation speech ends abruptly, concluding with two attention-grabbing crossed alliterations (2161–62). Why mention Heoroweard at all? The information provided about the armor seems supererogatory and raises questions. Was this prince initially passed over because he was too young? If so, why didn't Hrothgar give him his father's armor when he came of age? The gifted mail-coat marks a royal succession that did not go from father to son but from one brother to another, casting if not a shadow at least some uncertainty concerning future accessions to the Danish throne. A single piece of hardware is made so conspicuously absent that the cause and result of its denial demand to be recalled. The later fiery night attack on the Danish royal hall by the disinherited prince, a catastrophe famed in song throughout the North, brought the glory of the Scylding dynasty to an end. The speaker's awareness of this tragic family drama, here represented by a single mail-coat, is expressed obliquely if at all. Beowulf hands over the armor, saying: "Enjoy all well."

Exquisite verbal etiquette is not a rarity in court culture. Ānandavardhana, a ninth-century literary theorist from Kashmir, cited a two-line enigmatic Prākrit poem composed eight centuries earlier, a couplet spoken by a woman trying, the Sanskrit commentator says, to lure a mendicant away from the garden where she had arranged to meet her lover:

> Enjoy your visit without fear, pious monk,
> That dog is gone.
> Just today, from the grove by the Godā river,
> Came a fierce lion and killed him.[68]

The speaker tells the monk that he may wander through the garden without a care—but does so in a way that suggests that the stroll might turn out badly. As in the *Beowulf* passage, a causal connection between what is spoken and what is hinted at is not spelled out. Still, whenever a character in an Old English poem says "enjoy," the wish seems seriously time-limited.

The next allusion in *Beowulf* to Scylding dynastic history, here an in-law feud, comes fast behind the first (83b–85), and is given complex litotic expression: *ne wæs hit lenge þa gen* ("it was not longer from then"

(= sooner); that is, the discord between father- and son-in-law arose before the previously mentioned burning of the hall.[69] The penultimate reference to Danish legend in *Beowulf* picks up this second thread and draws it out, introducing the chief protagonists in a feud that ended in battle at Heorot: one Ingeld and his father-in-law, Hrothgar (2024–69a).[70] On the basis of a piece of information picked up at the Danish court, Beowulf supplies the Geatish king with an astute political forecast. Hrothgar has pledged his daughter to Ingeld, here prince of the Heathobards, in the hope of settling past discord. Beowulf assesses the chances for success as nil, underlining the limited capacity of the Scyldings for action as they tread their predestined paths, fate stacking the odds against human aspirations, against any attempts to circumscribe the inevitable. Beowulf, foreseeing the outcome as told in a widely known legend, predicts a wedding party from hell, and imagines a scene in which an unnamed old warrior (a placeholder for the famous Starkaðr/Starcatherus of Danish legend) incites Ingeld's troops to vengeance. A plundered ancestral Heathobard sword spotted in the possession of a young Danish retainer will ensure that all bets are off:

> Þonne bioð (a*b*)rocene   on ba healfe
> aðsweord eorla;   (syð)ðan Ingelde
> weallað wælniðas,   ond him wiflufan
> æfter cearwælmum   colran weorðað.
> (2063–66)

> Then on both sides the oaths of men will be broken; then deadly hostility will boil up in Ingeld, and his love for the woman will become cooler after the seething of sorrow.

The disaster predicted is expressed with restraint. The compounds *wælnið* 'deadly violence' and *aðsweord* 'oaths' repeat the very terms used by the poet in his opening allusion (83b–85), the second and rare one, *aðsweord* 'oath,' echoing the unique copulative (or 'dvandva') compound *aðumsweoras* 'son-in-law and father-in-law' (84), perhaps "oath-swearers."[71] The precise details of this in-law feud remain elusive. As the groom's rage boils over, Beowulf distills Ingeld's change of heart into a single comparative adjective: his love for the woman will become "cooler." The final crossed alliteration (æfter **c**earw**æ**lmum **c**olran **w**eorðað) (2066) alarms. Beowulf's reserve leaves it to others to supply what remains unsaid, indeterminate. Will Ingeld send his bride away? Kill her? Or will he just lose that special feeling? All semantic gradations from somewhat chilly to fatally cold are available. Hearers fill in the blanks according to taste and previous knowledge. Beowulf ends his diplomatic report with a convoluted diagnosis rich in negations and legal terminology: "For that reason, I do not consider the Heathobards' loyalty, their part in the alliance, to be without deceit [*unfæcne*] to the Danes, nor their friendship firm" (2067–69).[72] His hedged conclusion places the loyalty of the Heathobards somewhere on a sliding scale from shaky to nonexistent. The diagnosis is grim. In the poetry of northern legend the faintest trace of narrative smoke sets off an alarm. The poet's contemporaries presumably knew what is not stated, that the feud would culminate with Ingeld's defeat at Heorot, a downfall confirmed by the Old English poem *Widsith* (45–49). More than 2,000 lines separate the *Beowulf* poet's initial telegraphic fragments of Scylding history (the hall-burning and the in-law feud) from the later, still partial allusions (a royal byrnie with a history and Ingeld's melt down). The gap is wide, requiring hearers to pay attention, to step in, to recall or invent what happened between the two sets of snapshots chiastically deployed: the destruction of Heorot and its cause occupies the outer circle; the son-in-law and father-in-law conflict and its instigator, the inner. Hearers have to take possession of each story backward: first the result, then the motivation, a familiar syntactic move in early northern verse. The poet's third and final pairing of scenes from Scylding legend, nesting within this outer perimeter, performs a similar act of foreboding.

This doubled tableau comes immediately before and after the telling of a famous Danish victory at Finnsburg. In each scene, the narrator zooms in on two relatives, Hrothgar and Hrothulf, uncle and nephew, sitting at drink. Both pictures are close-ups frozen in time, images caught and made to stand still. A contemporary audience, aware of what subsequently happened, might have "read" these feasting scenes as ominous, as we would a painting of Judith beguiling Holofernes at a banquet, or of Judas nodding at the Last Supper. The narrator's first look at the two relatives seems positive, but things quickly go downhill. The two

Scylding kinsmen, embraced by crossed and enjambed alliteration, sit at their drink:

> **s**wiðo**h**ycgende on **s**ele þam **h**ean,
> **H**roðgar ond **H**roðo**u**lf. **H**eorot innan **w**æs
> freondum afylled; nalles facenstafas
> Þeod-Scyldingas þenden fremedon.
> (1016–19)

. . . strong-minded ones in the high hall, Hroðgar ond Hroðulf. Heorot inside was filled with friends; *at that time* the Nation-Scyldings did *not at all* practice deceit.

"Not at that time" does not fully reassure. As many have observed, the stressed and alliterating adverb *þenden* seems to project the end of the very concord that the poet is advertising. The *facenstafas* 'treachery, deceit' (ON *feikenstafr* 'baleful rune') that the Scyldings did not *then* practice does double duty as a magnetic "ye olde" sign, pointing to a distant time and place. According to several versions of the legend, at some interval after Hrothgar's death, Hrothulf (Hrólfr kraki) is attacked and slain by his cousin Heoroweard (Hjǫrvarðr), the culminating act of the Scylding dynastic drama.

The song of victory sung, the same ambiguously joyous feast and the same two kinsmen stagger again into view. This time the two are identified by the rare copulative compound *suhtergefæderan* 'nephew (brother's son) and (paternal) uncle' (1164). This compound occurs in *Widsith* 46, with reference to the same two men and alliterating with the same word, *sibb* 'kinship, concord, relationship' (ON Sif, *sifjar*). This is their word and theirs alone, trumpeting the tie of avuncularity and perhaps saying something specific about their extra-close relationship. The narrator then introduces a third man into the portrait, embedding him in hypermetric lines that stand out from their surroundings. Each a- and b-verse, beginning in line 1163, ends in an unstressed, falling syllable, resembling the trochaic cadence of *dróttkvætt* odd and even lines:

> Leoð wæs asungen,
> gleomannes gyd. Gamen eft astah,
> **b**eorhtode **b**enc**s**weg; **b**yrelas **s**ealdon

win of wunderfatum. Þa cwom Wealhþeo forð
gan under gyldnum beage þær þa godan twegen
sæton suhtergefæderan; þa gyt wæs hiera sib ætgædere,
æghwylc oðrum trywe. Swylce þær *U*nferþ þyle
æt fotum sæt frean Scyldinga; gehwylc hiora his ferhþe treowde,
þæt he hæfde mod micel, þeah þe he his magum nære
arfæst æt ecga gelacum.

The song was sung, the entertainer's lay. Joy again arose, bench-noise brightened, cup-servers poured wine from wondrous vessels. Then Wealhtheow came forward, walking under a golden torque to where the two good ones sat, brother's son and paternal uncle; then yet was their friendship joined, each true to the other. Likewise the spokesman Unferth sat there at the feet of the lord of the Scyldings; each of them trusted his spirit, that he had great courage, even though he had not been honorable to his kinsmen at the play of swords.

Unferth attracts grim litotes: this brother-slayer "had not been honorable to his kinsmen in battle." Nor is the narrator's "then yet" comforting: it hints rather firmly at trouble down the line. In both *Beowulf* passages, and in the allusion to Hrothgar and Hrothulf in *Widsith*, the ominous hint about the future comes in the form of a temporal adverb: *þenden* 'then,' *þa gyt* 'still,' *lengest* 'for the longest time.'[73] The poet counts on his hearers' acquaintance with Scylding legend to recognize when he means more than he says. Like distant trumpets, crossed alliterations in the two verses introducing the hypermetric passage prepare audiences to hear what the poet refuses to state directly, that future discord between these relatives will end in the fiery annihilation of the Danish royal line. The *Beowulf* poet flies under the radar and quietly drops a little bomb. This form of narrative shorthand, this technique of decipherable concealment, was also favored by the *dróttkvætt* poets of the early North.

MORE THAN KIN

The designation of someone or something through a statement of family relationship is a frequent type of periphrasis. Aristotle reports that when Simonides was asked to compose a poem celebrating the victor in a mule race, he refused on the grounds that he could not compose about mules. But when his fee was raised, he wrote: "Hail daughters of storm-footed horses."[74] The Norwegian and Icelandic skalds who alluded in shorthand to northern legend also took this genealogical route. They sprinkled their stanzas with kinship circumlocutions that warned of big trouble below the waterline.

The first named skald to whom *dróttkvætt* stanzas are attributed, Bragi *inn gamli* 'the old' Boddason, is thought to have worked in Norway in the second half of the ninth century. The opening sequence of his poem *Ragnarsdrápa* describes mythological and legendary scenes on an ornamented shield, beginning with the slaying of the legendary heroes Hamðir and Sǫrli in the hall of Ermanaric, historical ruler of the Goths (d. 375 CE). Their story, told in eddic verse and in Old Norse and Latin prose, is somber, punctuated by denunciations, kin murders, amputation of limbs, a stoning, a hanging, and a brutal trampling by horses. But Bragi tells it light. The opening of his narrative, which begins *in medias res*, presents an image, a single frame, pretending to tell only what the skald can see painted on a shield. The bloody result comes first, followed by a subordinate clause of time slipping into one of cause:

Knátti eðr við illan
Jǫrmunrekkr at vakna
með dreyrfáar dróttir
draum í sverða flaumi.
Rósta varð í ranni
Randvés hǫfuðniðja,
þás hrafnbláir hefndu
harma Erps of barmar.

Jǫrmunrekkr knátti eðr at vakna við illan draum með dreyrfáar dróttir í sverða flaumi. Rósta varð í ranni Randvés hǫfuðniðja, þás hrafnbláir of barmar Erps hefndu harma.[75]

Jǫrmunrekkr then awakened to a nightmarish scene among blood-stained troops in a torrent of swords [BATTLE]. There was uproar in the hall of Randvér's chief-kinsman [= Jǫrmunrekkr][76] when Erpr's raven-black bosom-brothers [= Hamðir and Sǫrli] avenged their injuries.

The two brothers have attacked the Gothic king in his palace, in revenge for his execution of their sister and his wife, Svanhildr, along with Randvér, his son, on false suspicion of adultery.

On the journey to Ermanaric's court, the two raven-black brothers slay, with disastrous consequences, their half-brother Erpr 'the dark one.' The major protagonists in the second half-stanza are identified solely by circumlocutions detailing their kinship relations. The first, "Randvér's chief-kinsman," names Ermanaric by referring to the son he cruelly hanged on the gallows; the second, "Erpr's bosom-brothers," designates Hamðir and Sörli through the brother, their mother's son (*barmi* 'a child fed at the same breast'), whom they wrongheadedly and self-destructively slew. This allusiveness is *dietrologia* 'backward looking' with a vengeance. When Pindar chose not to provide details about another famous kin-killing, that of Phocus by his half brothers Peleus and Telamon, he announced his decision openly: "I will stop: it is not always beneficial for the precise truth to show her face, and silence is often the wisest thing for a man to heed."[77] Northern audiences needed no such warning: they were trained to draw inferences from the slightest hints, to retrieve the unsaid in the said.

A subsequent half-stanza completes Ermanaric's family album:

> Mjǫk lét stála støkkvir
> styðja Gjúka niðja
> flaums, þás fjǫrvi næma
> Foglhildar mun vildu.
>
> Støkkvir flaums stála mjǫk lét styðja Gjúka niðja, þás vildu næma Foglhildar mun fjǫrvi.[78]
>
> ———
>
> The impeller of the torrent of steels [Jǫrmunrekkr] caused the descendants of Gjúki [Hamðir and Sǫrli] to be greatly propped up [by spears?], when they wanted to take the "delight of Bird-hildr" [=Svanhildr > Jǫrmunrekkr] from life.

Gjúki, a legendary king, is the maternal grandfather of the two brothers, a designation that evokes the image of Guðrún, the mother who instigated their fatal journey. The skald refers to Jǫrmunrekkr as "the joy [or lover] of Bird-*hildr*" (cf. *svanr* 'swan'), a kinship epithet naming the young wife whom the king cruelly executed. The poet's pointed circumlocution, a reminder of what might have been, opens cracks in the frame surrounding the immediate action, letting past and future in. Bragi's epithets are condensed allusions to a history everyone knew. Read innocently, they describe the Gothic king as a devoted husband and father, and Hamðir and Sǫrli as deeply attached to their younger sibling and famous mother; treated suspiciously, these kinship kennings are mocking reminders of the disintegration of two aristocratic families and the subsequent fall of Jǫrmunrekkr and his nation.

The Old English poem *Widsith* opens with its long-lived and far-traveled fictional poet escorting a bride-to-be, a "peace-weaver" named Ealhhild (*Wid* 5b–6a) to the land of the Goths, to the home of Ermanaric (Jǫrmunrekkr). The narrator calls the latter a *wraþ wærloga* 'cruel traitor' (*Wid* 9), a strangely harsh epithet for a famed historical king.[79] It seems likely, as R. W. Chambers concluded, that some specific evil deed, an outrage such as the slaying of his young bride, accounted for this characterization: "That Ealhhild is Eormanric's wife appears to me to be demonstrable: that legend attributed to her the same tragic story as to Swanhild is probable enough, but not equally demonstrable."[80] Kemp Malone disagreed, he refused to see any allusion here to Ermanaric's future slaying of his wife, declaring that as far as we can tell the Ealhhild of the Old English poem was on the best of terms with her husband.[81] Such optimism, endearing as it is, might not hold up in court. For it ignores the deceptiveness of early northern poetry, its habits of indeterminacy, its fluidity on many levels. The poets seldom tell the stories they allude to, and their allusions are often elliptical to the point of obscurity. They set kinship epithets free to evoke stories lurking outside the frame of the narrative, tales of sibling rivalry, kin murder, shaky marriages, incest, theft, and treachery; here, an underdog's defiant resistance, there, the fall of a leader, and everywhere the automaticity of revenge. When toward the end of *Widsith* the speaker reports that he sang the praises of Ealhhild throughout many lands (97–102), he seems to be boasting that he alone, our self-regarding scop, is responsible for her fame in Germanic legend.

At the end of *Deor*, the anonymous speaker reveals his name and misfortune: he is none other than Heoden's spurned court poet, the scop cast aside for the golden-voiced Heorrenda (ON Hjarrandi). Deor is a new figure injected into a famous legend, a poet forced into early retirement by a minstrel whose artistry so captivated one Hild that she consented to elope with Heoden. In multiple retellings of this popular legend, the result is an everlasting battle between father-in-law and son-in-law, over which Hild 'battle,' true to her name, presides.[82] Bragi's stanzas on this Hjaðningavíg 'battle of the Heodenings' focus on the events leading up to the clash. But the kennings he employs for Hild reveal her true role as the force motivating men to fight one other until the end of time. In these signifying circumlocutions, she is the *ósk-Rán ofþerris æða* 'goddess wishing for an over-drying of veins' (= a bleeder of men) and the *hristi-Sif hringa* 'the shaking-goddess of rings' (Bragi *Rdr* 8), a kenning in which the use of the goddess-name *Sif* 'kinship' ironically underscores the determination of Hild to break family bonds. The skald's next kenning for Hild, *bœti-Þrúðr dreyrugra benja* 'the curing-goddess of bloody wounds' (9), alludes to a time fast approaching in which each evening this valkyrie will revive the dead so that they might fight again in the morning. Bragi's earlier reference to Hǫgni as *draugr ørlygis* 'tree-trunk of battle' = warrior (8/8) probably plays on the dual sense of *draugr* 'tree-trunk' but also 'ghost, revenant,' alluding to his everlasting postmortem returns. But the consequences of an act are only hinted at, not hammered home.

The skald Þjóðólfr ór Hvini, Bragi's countryman and near-contemporary, employed kinship-kennings that similarly hinted at serious trouble down the road. In the poem *Haustlǫng* 'Autumn-long,' Þjóðólfr refers to Loki, carried aloft by a giant in eagle-costume, as *farmr arma Sigvinjar* 'cargo of the arms of Sigyn,' naming this half-god's wife:

Þá varð fastr við fóstra
farmr Sigvinjar arma,
sás ǫll regin eygja,
ǫndurgoðs, í bǫndum.

Þá varð farmr Sigvinjar arma, sás ǫll regin eygja í bǫndum, fastr við fóstra ǫndurgoðs.[83]

> Then the cargo of the arms [LOVER] of Sigyn [= Loki], the one whom all the gods eye in bonds, was [stuck] fast to the fosterer of the ski-deity [= the giant Þjazi]

But Sigyn is nowhere in sight. This kenning for Loki, followed by the relative clause "whom all the gods eye in bonds," is a flash-forward to the eve of the destruction of the world, when the gods bind Loki to stone slabs deep in a cave; writhing beneath a serpent's dripping venom, he is cradled by his unhappy wife who holds a vessel to catch some of the poison.[84] Whenever she turns to empty the basin, drops of poison fall on Loki's face, his shudders causing earthquakes. Here an innocent-seeming, domestic circumlocution for a cherished husband foretells the northern holocaust, at which time Loki's bonds will break and fire engulf the world. Once again, a skald's kinship reference opens cracks in the frame surrounding the immediate action, letting the future seep in.

Living memory is of short duration, with an upper limit of approximately eighty years and a standard life span of about forty. Inherited memory is dependent on a culture's will to keep certain stories alive, the *ealfela ealdgesegena* 'many multitudes of ancient tales' alluded to in *Beowulf* (869). One precision-crafted tool in the vernacular poets' compositional kit involves "losing it," that is, carefully not mentioning something (preferably unspeakable) in order to activate an audience's recall. Early northern poets sometimes forgot so that others might remember.

The morning after Beowulf's victory over Grendel, as the company is riding back from the monster-mere, a royal retainer sings of Sigemund, famed Vǫlsungr exile (Old English *Wælsing*). This presumably traditional set-piece is ornamented by *dróttkvætt*-type half-rhymes and other special sound effects.[85] The Danish oral poet relates that Sigemund would speak of his exploits to one Fitela (Old Norse Sinfjǫtli), *eam to nefan*, 'mother's brother to nephew' (*Beo* 881a).[86] This may have been a raising-of-eyebrows moment for those listening. For in the opening chapters of the much later *Vǫlsunga saga*, Sigemund is indeed, as in *Beowulf*, "mother's brother" [= uncle] to young Sinfjǫtli, but he is also, unwittingly, the boy's father. The saga tells how Sigmundr's disguised twin sister, Signý, slept with him in order to bear a hero with Vǫlsungr genes on both sides, a thoroughbred capable of killing her husband. More than a century ago, Levin L. Schücking declared the *Beowulf* poet's "discreet mention of Fitela . . . striking."[87] The third edition of Klaeber's *Beowulf* (1950, 159) reviewed various scenarios: early medieval England may not have known the incest story; references to Fitela as Sigemund's *nefa* accurately reflects Sigemund's ignorance of their true relationship; the kinship term *nefa* 'nephew' (but also, ambiguously, 'grandson' or 'illegitimate son') may have been used euphemistically. Dorothy Whitelock considered it "possible that both [poet and audience] were fully aware of this feature and that the poet's 'uncle to his nephew' is a deliberate use of understatement—*nepos, vel plus quam nepos* 'nephew and more than nephew,' a later age might have expressed it—employed for ironic effect."[88] James W. Earl detected a skeleton or two rattling in the characters' family closet and surmised that the Old English poet suppressed the incest story as too hot to handle, a kind of self-censorship.[89] Ovid's Juno cracked jokes about being both sister and consort of Jove, wondering which gave her higher status in society. Northern poetic etiquette was more discreet.

Beowulf is identified over and over again as the son of Ecgtheow and follower of Hygelac, his maternal uncle (*Beo* 371–75). Patronymics reassure. Grendel has a genealogy of sorts, even if his mother doesn't. But Fitela's parents are never identified. Why not? Could an incestuous backstory account for why Fitela, like the mute Hrothulf, remains without patronymic or matronymic? (Hrothulf, known throughout the North as "Yrsa's son and brother," had complications of his own to contend with.)[90] Fitela is named twice, the same number of times as his famed "uncle." On his second mention, the information provided is distinctly minimal: *ne wæs him Fitela mid* ("Fitela was not with him") (889b), a parenthetical aside that serves chiefly to remind hearers of his existence—or disappearance. Also puzzling is the fact that the metrical structure of the half-line establishing Fitela's relationship to Sigemund is (to understate the situation) "somewhat anomalous."[91] The oddly flexible half-line *eam to nefan* (881a), a rabbit-duck metrical puzzle, is almost unparalleled in the corpus: *eam*, if uncontracted, represents two short syllables, while *nefan*, with its two short syllables resolved, counts as one. Each of the two words oscillates imperceptibly between one metrical position and two, like the "qubits" of quantum computers, as if shadowing the indeterminate relationship between Sigemund and Fitela. A skillful poet who plays with or thwarts the strict formal demands of alliterative verse usually has good reason for doing so. The opening consonant of *nefa* lingers by virtue of continued alliteration on *n* in the next line.[92] Attentive ears may have sensed that something important, some half-said thing was hanging ominously in the air. Perhaps young Fitela trailed more than clouds of glory.

The Old English poet steps with extreme delicacy; he does not stare directly upon the face of incest but gestures toward it, a reticent sideways look. For such indirection to be effective, his audience—like that of the early skalds—had to be able to respond to a storytelling technique so economical and so skilled in implication that the slightest hedge might be deeply meaningful. The poet hovers above things, transforming the distinctly earthbound into an image as light and transient as a raised eyebrow. He proceeds like the jazz vocalist who, with full orchestral backup, sings the lyrics of the song "April in Paris"—but never the three words in everyone's head: "April in Paris."[93] The half-line *eam to nefan* is a narrative precipitate, a condensed allusion to a violent story that everyone (except perhaps the pair in question) knew, its incompleteness, drawing the viewer, willy-nilly, into the memory game. The horror is kept under wraps, half-hidden in the swamp, "like something almost being said."[94]

Material objects in northern legend arrive preloaded with pasts of their own, items, like Heorogar's mail-coat, whose transmission from one individual to another speaks ominously for the future. A gifted necklace experiences a similar downward trajectory in *Beowulf*.[95] Boar-helmets accompany the cremations, pagan sacrifices, drinking rituals, and other late fifth- and early sixth-century activities described in that poem.[96] One seems especially mobile. Scandinavian prose texts from the late twelfth and early thirteenth centuries associate a peripatetic boar-helmet with at least three characters named in *Beowulf*: the Swedish king Onela (son of Ongentheow, who was apparently its original owner), Onela's estranged nephew Eadgils, and—in an event that takes place after the poem ends—the Danish king Hrothulf.[97] The Old English poet explores through eponymy the *enfance* of this helmet, seemingly confident that at least some in his audience were aware of its later movements. A warrior named Eofor 'boar' fatally attacks Ongentheow, causing his helmet to slide off (2487, 2979). Along with other military paraphernalia, Eofor presents this *entisc helm* 'giant-helm' (2987), by now mentioned twice, to Hygelac, whose only daughter is then given in marriage to the slayer (2997–98). The narrated adventures of the helmet stop here. But it seems likely that after Hygelac's death and Beowulf's recovery of his uncle's battle-gear (2362), Heardred inherits both throne and helmet; and that after Heardred's death in battle (2388), his slayer Onela retrieves this ancestral Swedish armor. The boar-helmet is his in several viking-age *dróttkvætt* stanzas. Two helmet-kennings in these verses use the name Áli (= Onela) as a definer: *gǫltr Ála* 'boar of Áli' = helmet (Eyv Lv 5) and *hǫttr Ála* 'hood of Áli' = helmet (Egill Lv 28 [Eg 57]). The legendary boar-helmets of the Old English poem gain depth and perhaps a fraught future by reuniting with their northern cousins in tenth-century skaldic verse. "Singularity," Sir Arthur Conan Doyle advised (not necessarily thinking of late Latin *singularis* 'wild boar') "is almost invariably a clue."[98]

Swords handed down or looted also serve as markers of kin-strife. In the midst of the dragon-fight, at the moment when Wiglaf is feeling his blood relationship and loyalty to Beowulf most keenly, the narrator provides a brief history of Wiglaf's sword. Weohstan, Wiglaf's father, had killed Eanmund, Onela's nephew, apparently on that Swedish king's instigation. Onela's pleasure upon receiving his slain kinsman's war-garments is conveyed by a decorous understatement:

no ymbe ða fæhðe spræc,
þeah ðe he his broðor bearn abredwade.
(*Beo* 2618b–19)

Not at all did he [Onela] speak about that hostile act, although he [Weohstan] had butchered his brother's son.

Not only did Onela not reproach Weohstan for the killing, but he rewarded him with the victim's battle-gear. Years later, Weohstan bequeaths these gifted royal heirlooms, sword included, to his own son, a *damnosa hereditas* if there ever was one. For Eanmund's brother Eadgils is now sitting on the Swedish throne, obligated to avenge his brother's death on the slayer's son, the "last of the Wægmundings," the family tie that Wiglaf shares with Beowulf and the latter's father (2813–14a). The genealogy of Wiglaf's sword (2611–25a) is of more than antiquarian interest; it predicts the end of the Geatish king's paternal and maternal family lines.[99]

In *Beowulf*, mail-coat, necklace, boar-helmet, and sword have ominous backstories. In *dróttkvætt* verse praising Cnut the Great (r. 1016–35), shields seem to have had comparable dynastic significance, as in this stanza from the *Knútsdrápa* composed by the skald Hallvarðr háreksblesi:

> Knútr, lézt framm til Fljóta
> —frægr leið vǫrðr of ægi
> heiptsnarr hildar leiptra—
> harðbrynjuð skip dynja.
> Ullar lézt við Ellu
> ættleifð ok mǫ́ reifðir
> sverðmans snyrti*h*erð*ir*
> sundviggs flota bundit.

> Knútr, lézt harðbrynjuð skip dynja framm til Fljóta; frægr, heiptsnarr vǫrðr leiptra hildar leið of ægi. Snyrtiherðir Ullar sundviggs, lézt flota bundit við ættleifð Ellu ok reifðir mǫ́ sverðmans.[100]

———

> Knútr, you caused your hard-byrnied ships to rush forward to Fljót; the famous, battle-bold guardian of the lightnings of battle [SWORDS > WARRIOR] glided across the sea. Splendid strengthener of Ullr's sea-horse [SHIP > SHIELD > WARRIOR], you had your fleet moored in the patrimony of Ælla [= England], and you gladdened the gull of the sword-girl [VALKYRIE > RAVEN/EAGLE].

This skald depicts Knútr's voyage west to England and his swift conquest of its land and people. In the first half-stanza, the king's ships are *harðbrynjuð* 'hard-armored' (4), presumably referring to the shields hung along the gunwale.[101] The allusion to Ælla in the second half-stanza is probably to the king of Northumbria killed by Ívarr the Boneless during his conquest of York in 867.[102] By having Knútr, the "shield-strengthener" (7–8) moor his ships in "Ælla's family inheritance," the skald reminds his audience that the Danish king is heir to Ívarr's conquests, that in possessing England the king has only reclaimed what was his by ancestral right.

Ívarr and his brothers seem to have gone under the name of Scyldings (lit. "shield-men") in the conquered territories; and by 1030 at the latest, Knútr's descent from Ívarr and his ninth-century settlers appears to have been the official party line.[103] Saxo's *Gesta Danorum* envisaged a Danish royal line running from the eponymous Skjǫldr 'shield' through Ívarr to the historical dynasty of Gormr the Old, Knútr's pagan great-grandfather buried circa 958 in the north mound at Jelling.[104]

Sometimes a shield is not just a shield but an oblique claim to stolen family property, a justification for harassing a relative or invading a neighbor. Hallvarðr, by stating his political message obliquely, keeps things light. He says things that northern poets say in the slant ways that northern poets say them. The art of implication was central to northern verse etiquette: you don't insult people by telling them what they already know. Like Perseus, who refused to stare directly at the face and snaky locks of Medusa but only upon her image as mirrored in his bronze shield, both skald and Old English poet worked hard to filter the horror of history and keep it at a safe distance. By drawing words through a tight mesh of meter, alliteration, and rhyme, early northern poets stitched together a poetics of indirection, an art form that enticed audiences to hear between the lines.

TO THE EGRESS

> *Poetical feelings are a peril to scholarship. There are always poetical people ready to protest that a corrupt line is exquisite. Exquisite to whom? The Romans were foreigners writing for foreigners two millenniums ago; and for people whose gods we find quaint, whose savagery we abominate, whose private habits we don't like to talk about, but whose idea of what is exquisite is, we flatter ourselves, mysteriously identical with ours.*
>
> —Tom Stoppard, *The Invention of Love*

A. E. Housman, aged seventy-seven, here addressing his younger self, casts a cold eye on "poetical people" who praise the exquisiteness of verse from an imperfect past. The task of the philologist, as he sees it, is to diagnose, to weigh data and empirical evidence, "to strike a finger on the page and say, 'Thou ailest here, and here.'"[105] The scholar cuts away diseased parts, thereby restoring health to an abused corpus. In 1785, Yuan Mei wrote these lines in praise of the philologist Lu Wenchao:

> You tell me that collating texts is the great passion of your life—
> To sort them out with as fine precision as a sieve sifts rice;
> That to get a single right meaning is better than a ship-load of pearls,
> To resolve a single doubt is like the bottom falling off the bucket.[106]

His allusion is to the Zen Buddhist monk Zhenxie Qingliao (d. 1151) who was watching meal being cooked in a bucket when the bottom of the bucket fell out. Onlookers observed: "What a sad waste!" But the Zen master said: "On the contrary, the shock was well worth the loss." The removal of dross, of excess weight, brings pleasure.

The preceding pages have sought to read the past through language, to draw an evocative sketch from evidence that is always insufficient. Each chapter placed two vernacular poetries of the long Viking Age into conversation, an interchange that seemed at moments to suggest their membership in a single community of taste, a federation linked by a traditional stylistic ecology that did serious political and historical work. Their makers possessed a strong sense of propriety, an etiquette prized and understood by their audiences, a verse form that was open to cultural influences of many kinds. The art of the northern poet was a carefully constructed, highly ornamented craft, whose sails were set to catch prevailing winds.

This book began on a blue note, pondering broken structures, chipped sentences, lonesome roads, and the charge, variously expressed, that extant northern alliterative verse was a "belated aesthetic." The central chapter examined the architecture of this poetry, the tools and materials used by its makers, its structural and stylistic peculiarities, its rhymes and consonances, its tight verbal detail work. M. Valerius Probus's teachings on euphony, recorded by Aulus Gellius in the second century CE, stressed the importance of thinking with ears, of catching auditory memories and unexpected meanings by attending to the sonic qualities of language.[107] Neither Wallace Stevens's modernist dictum that "poetry is words; and . . . words, above everything else, are, in poetry, sounds" or Basil Bunting's pronouncement that "poetry . . . deals in sound—long sounds and short sounds, heavy beats and light beats, the tone relations of vowels, the relations of consonants to one another" would have shocked the early poets of the North.[108] This third chapter has surveyed the codes of reticence held in common by both skald and Old English poet, a shared etiquette of negation, indirection, and understatement, a laconic insouciance that encouraged audiences to read between half-lines, to hear what was not said.

Poets have designs on particular groups or communities.[109] The alliterative verse of the long Viking Age depicts a seesawing world of instability and recurrence; it glamorizes this terrain and reflects it slant. Poets snatch away expectations with a down-toner here, a negative particle there. Sometimes they model transience through aural and rhythmical correspondences: *wea bið wundrum clibbor*; *wolcnu scriðað* ("sorrow is wondrously clinging; clouds glide by") (*Max II* 13).[110] Through negation, they evoke and magnify the absent.[111] Subjects and objects, transformed, metamorphosed, repeat and repeat: the good leader and the bad, the generous act and the cowardly, youth and age, the saved and the damned, sunrise and sunset, gold and the grave. Like grim editors, the sequences go round and round, pleading and pleading, revising and revising, slip-sliding from *æfter wiste, wop* 'after prosperity, lamentation' (*Beo* 128) to *gyrn æfter gomene* 'sorrow after pleasure' (*Beo* 1775a).

Ends have a habit of returning to beginnings. The last three lines of *Beowulf* wrap things up by hearkening back to the poet's opening chords: the unusual transverse alliteration of 3180 competes with the crossed alliteration of line 1; the metrical pattern of 3181b and 3182b replicates that of 1a and 1b. The final stressed syllable of the poem, *-georn* (3182b), echoes the alliterating half-rhymes (*gar-*, *gear-*) of the first line of the poem, while the joining of *leod-* and *lof-* in 3182a-b repeats that of 24a-b, the only other *lof*-compound in *Beowulf*.[112] So, too, the earliest intact *dróttkvætt* encomium echoes in its concluding lines three of the four half-rhymes of its first stanza, an aural signal to those still listening that it is closing time.[113]

The typical inclination of sound, stress, and pitch within the northern alliterative line is downward, a final trochaic beat signaling a finish, a sinking back. W. H. Auden exploited this chord to sustain pessimism: "Many have perished; more will."[114] G. P. Marsh's *dróttkvætt* imitation, reproduced by Gerard Hopkins, begins and ends with falling snow.[115] The cadence of J. R. R. Tolkien's unpublished *dróttkvætt* poem, "The

Derelicts," is distinctly downbeat.[116] Philip Larkin employed both alliteration and half-rhyme—"a wrangle for a ring"—to dissect with economy the underpinnings of twentieth-century wedlock.[117] Robert Rendall's *dróttkvætt* poem, composed in an Orcadian Scots rich in half- and full-rhymes, records the forced separation of Norse sea-raiders and local crofters, of "**vikings**" who never came "**seek**an **back** tae **Rackwick**."[118] In Seamus Heaney's "A **l**ost **syn**tax of **l**ooms and **spin**dles," a "flash of **conson**ants / **c**leaving the **lin**e," alliteration and half-rhyme underscore a cutting off, an unbridgeable historical divide.[119]

As I write these last sentences, epidemiologists are analyzing a virus in terms applicable to literary systems: a silent incubative period; an opportunistic hijacking and replication; the role of asymptomatic cases in transmission; and a variable person-to-person infectivity rate dependent on individual susceptibility and exposure. Early northern verse was a communicative medium transmitted from person to person and subject to constant mutation. Its stylistic good manners, whether floating on the breeze or circulating in feedback loops within the courts and minsters of the North, appear to have been highly contagious. We can track the movements of this vanished poetics, its public relations savvy and aural signals, even if we no longer catch breath at the places where breath used to be caught.

Scientists in Siberia have recently brought back to life frozen, long-buried 32,000-year-old flowering plants, making the old new again.[120] Sir Thomas Browne in *Religio Medici* (1643) alluded to a similar process, one involving fire rather than ice: "But to a sensible artist the forms are not perished, but withdrawn into their incombustible part, where they lie secure from the action of that devouring element. This is made good by experience, which can from the ashes of a plant revive the plant, and from its cinders recall it into its stalk and leaves again."[121] To restore an alien poetry to a state even partially resembling its former self, to recall it into its stalk and leaves once more, has been the goal of these chapters.

ABBREVIATIONS

ASPR — *The Anglo-Saxon Poetic Records*. 6 vols. Edited by George Philip Krapp and Elliott Van Kirk Dobbie. New York: Columbia University Press, 1931–53.

BT — Toller, Thomas Northcote, ed. *An Anglo-Saxon Dictionary Based on the Manuscript Collections of the Late Joseph Bosworth*. Oxford: Clarendon, 1898. *Supplement* by Thomas Northcote Toller. Oxford: Clarendon, 1921. *Enlarged Addenda and Corrigenda* by Alistair Campbell. Oxford: Oxford University Press, 1972.

CV — Cleasby, Richard, Gudbrand Vigfusson (Guðbrandur Vigfússon), and W. A. Craigie. *An Icelandic–English Dictionary*. 2nd ed. Oxford: Clarendon, 1957.

DOE — *Dictionary of Old English, A to I Online*. Edited by Angus Cameron, Ashley Crandell Amos, Antonette diPaolo Healey, et al. Toronto: Dictionary of Old English Project, 2019. https://tapor.library.utoronto.ca/doe/.

DOEC — *Dictionary of Old English Web Corpus*. Edited by Antonette diPaolo Healey, with John Price Wilkin and Xin Xiang. Toronto: Dictionary of Old English Project, 2009. https://tapor.library.utoronto.ca/doecorpus/.

Fritzner — Fritzner, Johan. *Ordbog over det gamle norske sprog*. Vols. 1–3. Kristiania (Oslo): Den norske forlagsforening, 1883–96; Vol. 4, *Rettelser og tillegg ved Finn Hødnebø*. Oslo: Universitetsforlaget, 1972.

Kl 4 — *Klaeber's Beowulf and the Fight at Finnsburg*. 4th ed. Edited by R. D. Fulk, Robert E. Bjork, and John D. Niles. Foreword by Helen Damico. Toronto: University of Toronto Press, 2008.

LP Finnur Jónsson. *Lexicon poeticum antiquae linguae septentrionalis: Ordbog over det norsk-islandske skjaldesprog, oprindelig forfattet af Sveinbjörn Egilsson.* 2nd ed. Copenhagen: Møller, 1931.

Skjd *Den norsk-islandske skjaldedigtning,* A1-2: *Tekst efter håndskrifterne*; B1-2: *Rettet tekst.* 4 vols. Edited by Finnur Jónsson. Copenhagen: Villadsen & Christensen, 1912–15. Reprint, Copenhagen: Rosenkilde & Bagger, 1967–73.

SkP *Skaldic Poetry of the Scandinavian Middle Ages.* Turnhout: Brepols. In progress. https://skaldic.abdn.ac.uk/db.php. Available volumes: *Poetry from the Kings' Sagas: From Mythical Times to c. 1035* (*SkP* 1), 2 vols., edited by Diana Whaley (2012); *Poetry from the Kings' Sagas: From c. 1035 to c. 1300* (*SkP* 2), 2 vols., edited by Kari Ellen Gade (2009); *Poetry from Treatises on Poetics* (*SkP* 3), 2 vols., edited by Kari Ellen Gade, in collaboration with Edith Marold (2017); *Poetry on Christian Subjects* (*SkP* 7), 2 vols, edited by Margaret Clunies Ross (2007); *Poetry in fornaldarsögur* (*SkP* 8), 2 vols., edited by Margaret Clunies Ross (2017).

NOTES

MAKING AN ENTRANCE

1. Howe, "New Millennium," 497. The epigraph, from Heaney's collection *The Spirit Level*, is carved on the poet's gravestone.

2. Ker, *Epic and Romance*, 324, 349; Ker, *Dark Ages*, 1–23.

3. Wellek, *Rise of English Literary History*, 25.

4. Wallace, ed., *Cambridge History of Medieval English Literature*; Simpson and Cummings, eds., *Cultural Reformations*; Ashe, *Oxford English Literary History*, 13. On literary periodization and its discontents, see Weiskott, *Meter and Modernity in English Verse*, esp. xiii–xviii; also Underwood, *Why Literary Periods Mattered*, and Davis, "Periodization and the Matter of Precedent." Current convulsions in the OE field are described in Ellard, *Anglo-Saxon(ist) Pasts*, esp. 254n31, and 338n3. On the applications of the term "Anglo-Saxon" over the centuries, see Wilton, "What Do We Mean by *Anglo-Saxon*?"

5. Moretti, *Distant Reading*; also Moretti, *Graphs, Maps, Trees*, 1.

6. See Johnson, *Practicing Literary Theory in the Middle Ages*, 14–15, on New Formalism. Also Cannon, *Grounds of English Literature*, 1–15; Lerer, "Endurance of Formalism in Middle English Studies"; Liu "Power of Formalism"; for OE poetry, see Trilling, *Aesthetics of Nostalgia*, 6–27.

7. Foucault, *Archaeology of Knowledge*, 109.

8. On the arrival of the word "style" in Middle English, see Nolan, "Invention of Style." Also Gauger, "Zur Frage des Stils"; J. Hillis Miller, "Poetics Today"; de Man, "Task of the Translator."

9. For the transformation of *stilus* into a literary term, see Sauerländer, "From Stilus to Style."

10. Extracted from Sutherland, "Newly Unoriginal," 36.

11. Calvino, *Six Memos*, 16.

12. Vogrin, "Unceasing Call of Style," 111, citing *Oeuvres posthumes de Victor Hugo: Post-scriptum de ma vie* (Paris: Calmann-Lévy, 1901), 53: "Le style, c'est le fond du sujet sans cesse appelé à la surface."

13. On the Latin word *alliteratio* in classical rhetoric and in English historical poetics, see Cornelius, *Reconstructing Alliterative Verse*, 28–37. On the durability of the vernacular alliterative tradition, see Weiskott, *English Alliterative Verse*.

14. Watkins, *Dictionary of Indo-European Roots*, s.v. **steig*-. Also Dumitrescu and Weiskott, *Shapes of Early English Poetry*, 1–12. The word "character" similarly connects with an instrument: its Indo-European root **gher*[5] has the sense "tool for branding, pointed stake."

15. Lewis Carroll (Charles Lutwidge Dodgson), *Through the Looking Glass*, chap. 9 (Gray, *Alice's Adventures in Wonderland*, 201). Carroll early parodied Victorian etiquette guides: "Hints for Etiquette; Or, Dining Out Made Easy" (1849); reprinted in Carroll, *Refectory Umbrella*.

16. Brown and Levinson, *Politeness*, 36.

17. Gregory the Great, *Moralia in Iob*, vol. 143, bk. IV, praef., 158, lines 19–21: "Sicut enim ignotorum hominum facies cernimus et corda nescimus, sed si familiari eis locutione coniungimur, usu colloquii eorum etiam cogitationes indagamus." On close reading versus surface reading, see Best and Marcus, "Surface Reading."

18. Stanley, "OE Poetic Diction," 414.

19. Abram, "Object-Oriented Skaldic Poetics"; Abram, *Evergreen Ash*.

20. Metrical studies over the last thirty-five years, published at a rate unrivaled even by late nineteenth-century standards, include in rough chronological order: Kuhn, *Dróttkvætt*; Hoover, *Theory of OE Meter*; Donoghue, *Style in OE Poetry*; Russom, *OE Meter*; Obst, *Rhythmus des Beowulf*; Creed, *Reconstructing the Rhythm of Beowulf*; Cable, *English Alliterative Tradition*; Kendall, *Metrical Grammar*; Kristján Árnason, *Rhythms of Dróttkvætt*; Hofmann, *Versstrukturen der altsächsischen Stabreimgedichte*; Fulk, *History of OE Meter*; Whitman, *Comparative Study of OE Metre*; Hutcheson, *OE Poetic Meter*; Gade, *Structure of ON Dróttkvætt*; Suzuki, *Metrical Organization*; Momma, *Composition of OE Poetry*; Russom, *Beowulf and Old Germanic Metre*; Blockley, *OE Poetic Syntax*; Getty, *Metre of Beowulf*; Minkova, *Alliteration and Sound Change*; Bredehoft, *Early English Metre*; Yakovlev, "Alliterative Metre"; Terasawa, *OE Metre*; Suzuki, *Meters of ON Poetry*; Myrvoll, "Constitutive Features"; Weiskott, *English Alliterative Verse*; Russom, *Evolution of Verse Structure*; Cornelius, *Reconstructing Alliterative Verse*; Hartman, *Poetic Style and Innovation*; Cable, "Progress in OE Metrics." Mark Griffith's magisterial essay "Extra Alliteration" appeared after this manuscript was submitted; references have been subsequently incorporated.

21. Hfr *ErfÓl* 15/7, ed. Heslop; *SkP* 1.1:421. The metaphor became general in the twelfth century.

22. See Watkins, *Dictionary of Indo-European Roots*, s.v. *(*s*)*lei*-. Words under the *sl*-phonestheme include not only "slow," "sluggard," and "sloth," authorial sins already confessed, but also (reviewers please ignore) "sloppy," "slick," and "slipshod." The term *phonestheme* was coined ca. 1930 by Firth, *Tongues of Men*, 211.

23. Cf. George Eliot, *Mill on the Floss* (1860), 5.4: "It is mere cowardice to seek safety in negations." For Pope, Swift, and Arbuthnot ("Martinus Scriblerus," *Art of Sinking*, 115), litotes was "the peculiar talent of Ladies, Whisperers, and Backbiters"; for Orwell, "Politics and the English Language," in *Collected Essays* (London, 1961), 131, it was the affecting of "an appearance of profundity." See Horn, "Lie-toe-tease."

24. The first stanza of Lewis Carroll's "Jabberwocky" was privately published (1855) as "Stanza of Anglo-Saxon Poetry," subsequently, with six additional stanzas, in *Through the Looking Glass* (1871). This is the ultimate origin of Tolkien's famous reference to "the jabberwocks of historical and antiquarian research" who "burble in the tulgy wood of conjecture, flitting from one tum-tum tree to another" (Tolkien, "*Beowulf*: Monsters," 253). See Jones, *Fossil Poetry*, 130–35.

25. When a poet departs from his normal practice, the possibility that he is doing so on purpose should be explored; see Griffith, "Alliterating Finite Verbs," 111.

26. Stoppard, *Invention of Love*, 37.

27. See Plumer, "Construction of Structure."

28. Miner, *Comparative Poetics*; Strohm, "Middle English Narrative Genres"; Zumthor, *Toward a Medieval Poetics*, 118; Butterfield, "Medieval Genres"; Jauss, "Theory of Genres"; Hiatt, "Genre without System"; Grønlie, *Saint and Saga Hero*, 257–58. Bampi et al., *ON Literary Genres*.

29. The following section could be headed "Introduction," but nobody reads an introduction, and I wanted these pages to be read. I admit this in an endnote, because no one reads endnotes either.

30. Gombrich, *Art and Illusion*, 304–5, and index s.v. "Constable, *Wivenhoe Park*."

31. The six named individuals to whom extant OE verse has been attributed with varying degrees of plausibility are Cædmon (9 lines), Bede (5 lines), Cynewulf (4 poems and counting), Alfred, Byrhtferth of Ramsey, and Owun. For a list of named authors of Latin or OE verse in pre-1100 England, see Thornbury, *Becoming a Poet*, 243–47; also O'Donnell, *Cædmon's Hymn*, 13–14. For a proposed chronology of OE poems, see Fulk, *History of OE Meter*, esp. 348–418.

32. See Ghosh, *Kings' Sagas and Norwegian History*, 25–100. Gade, "Dating and Attribution of Verses," 50–74, employs linguistic and stylistic criteria to argue that many *dróttkvætt* stanzas conventionally given a viking-age date are indeed what they claim to be. On weak, strong, and absolute dating criteria, see Males, *Poetic Genesis*, 60–61, 72–75, 166–68, 263–65.

33. *The Battle of Maldon* survives only in an early modern transcript; *The Finnsburh Fragment* was transcribed before 1705 from a now lost manuscript.

34. Theodoricus, *Historia* 1.7–13; Saxo, *Gesta Danorum*, Pr. 1.6, 7.

35. The bibliography is extensive: see Ellen C. Garland et al., "Dynamic Horizontal Cultural Transmission of Humpback Whale Song at the Ocean Basin Scale," *Current Biology* 21, no. 8 (April 26, 2011), https://doi.org/10.1016/j.cub.2011.05.019;

Clare Owen et al., "Migrating Convergence Facilitates Cultural Transmission of Humpback Whale Song," *Royal Society Open Science* 6, no. 9 (2019), https://doi.org/10.1098/rsos.190337.

36. Gullbekk, "Coins and Epigraphy," 43. On literary activity in the viking colonies, see Jesch, *Viking Diaspora*.

37. Page, review of *The Vikings*, 309. Hunts for nonvernacular echoes in northern verse range from Andersson, *Early Epic Scenery*, to Johnston, "*Beowulf* as Anti-Virgilian," 40–42. On the *Aeneid* in early England, see Lapidge, *Anglo-Saxon Library*, 325–26. Thornbury, *Becoming a Poet*, 49, notes that much-read texts are likely to be underrepresented in surviving manuscripts.

38. See, e.g., Hadley, "In Search of the Vikings," 19.

39. Cameron and Mould, "Saxon Shoes," 465.

40. Bailey, *Viking Age Sculpture*; Kershaw, "Culture and Gender in the Danelaw"; Kopár, *Gods and Settlers*, esp. 181–208; Itó, "Gosforth Fishing Stone." Parallels between northern graphic art (including metalwork) and poetry, both possessing unnatural "highly stylized, formulaic vocabularies, . . . elaborate frameworks, and an abiding fondness for tricks and puzzles," are frequent; see Webster, "Style: Influences," 461; also Orton, "Rethinking the Ruthwell and Bewcastle Monuments." See Leyerle, "Interlace Structure"; Bloomfield, "Interlace," early demurred.

41. OE poetic *eorl* 'man' appears to have the sense of ON *jarl* in *Brun* 31 (translated by Æthelweard ealdorman as *consul*) and in *Mald* 203. Hofmann, *Lehnbeziehungen*, 161, 167, 197; Peters, "Lehngut," 94; Dance, *Words Derived from ON*, 419; Townend, *Language and History*, 11; Pons-Sanz, *Norse-Derived Vocabulary*, 176–81; Pons-Sanz, *Anglo-Scandinavian Linguistic Contact*, 80–81; Syrett, *Vikings in England*, 47–48. On *metan* 'to traverse,' see Hofmann, *Lehnbeziehungen*, 92–93. Cf. Sigv *Knútdr* 11/2, ed. Townend; *SkP* 1.2:663, and *Beo* 514, 917, 924, 1633.

42. On the backdrop of early Anglo-Latin and Hiberno-Latin verse, see Orchard, *Poetic Art of Aldhelm*, 43–54, with extensive bibliography. On Alcuin's berating of his countrymen for adopting the hairstyle of pagan Northmen, see Chase, *Two Alcuin Letter-Books*, 55; on Ælfric's similar rebuke two centuries later, see Clayton, "Ælfric's *Letter*." Also Ælfric, *Homilies of Ælfric: A Supplementary Collection*, 1:56. Hairstyles similarly changed in a Zambian wildlife sanctuary when one trendsetting chimpanzee placed long, stiff blades of grass in and around her ears; her children and entire social network rapidly adopted this new look: see Natalie Angier, "Social Influencers of the Animal Kingdom," *New York Times*, May 11, 2021, D8.

43. Bjork, "Scandinavian Relations"; Frank, "Anglo-Scandinavian Poetic Relations," and Frank, "Skaldic Tooth"; Bouman, *Patterns*. On Norse coloration in OE royal eulogy, see Opland, *Anglo-Saxon Oral Poetry*; Harris, "*Brunanburh* 12b–13a"; Niles, "Skaldic Technique in *Brunanburh*." Griffith, "Convention and Originality," 194, makes a good case for ON literary influence on *Exodus* and *Brunanburh*. Also Niles and Amodio, eds., *Anglo-Scandinavian England*; Rowe, "Irony"; Hall, "OE *sæbeorg*: *Exodus* 442a, *Andreas* 308a," and Hall, "*Exodus* 166b, *cwyldrof*; 162–67";

Niles, "Danish Origins"; Harris, "Elegy in OE and ON"; Magnús Fjalldal, *Anglo-Saxon England in Icelandic Medieval Texts*; Clark, "Dying with One's Lord." Neidorf and Pascual, "ON Influence on the Language of *Beowulf*," on the grounds that the poem "in all likelihood" was composed ca. 700, treat OE/ON lexical and syntactical similarities as archaisms. On the label archaic, see Weiskott, *English Alliterative Verse*, 36–37. On evidence in viking-age *dróttkvætt* for ON–OE poetic contact, see Hofmann, *Lehnbeziehungen*; also Townend, *English Place-Names in Skaldic Verse*, Townend, *Language and History*, and Townend, *Antiquity of Diction in OE and ON Poetry*; Poole, "Crossing the Language Divide"; Bibire, "North Sea Language Contacts"; Dance, "OE-ON Relations."

44. See Even-Zohar, "Polysystem Theory" and Even-Zohar, "Laws of Literary Interference." Also Tynjanov, "Literary Fact."

45. Cicero, *De oratore* 1.5.18; 1.25.114; 1.27.128.

46. Ibrahim ibn Yaqub al-Tartushi's original account, which does not survive, is cited by a thirteenth-century cosmographer said to have followed his sources faithfully; see Jacob, *Arabische Berichte*, 29n10. See Gade, "Recitation of ON Skaldic Poetry," 130–31; Würth, "Skaldic Poetry and Performance." Gade, *Structure of ON Dróttkvætt*, 224–26, notes that the skald's delivery would have clarified his syntax. Foote, "Beginnings and Endings," stresses the rocklike reliability of the stanza's trochaic cadence.

47. Studies include See, "Skop und Skáld"; Frank, "Search for the Anglo-Saxon Oral Poet;" Faulkes, *Poetical Inspiration*; Thornbury, *Becoming a Poet*; Guðrún Nordal, *Tools of Literacy*, 117–95.

48. On these flare-ups, see Suzuki, "In Defense of Resolution"; Fulk, "Inductive Methods," 6–7; Fulk, *A History of OE Meter*, 332; Pascual, "Bliss's Rule"; Minkova, "Prosody-Meter Correspondences," 122–27. See now Cable, "Progress."

49. Griffith, "Alliterating Finite Verbs."

50. Russom, "A Bard's-eye View."

51. Weiskott, "Three-Position Verses."

52. Le Page, "Alliterative Patterns," 439, regards the absence of verbal ornamentation as a plus: "apart from double alliteration, extra-alliteration has no stylistic significance in Old English poetry: . . . lack of it indicates a high degree of conscious artistry." See Fulk, "On Argumentation in OE Philology"; also *Kl* 4, clxi.

53. Recent studies of skaldic intertextuality include Patria, "Quotations," and Nyquist, "Compositional Techniques." On the *Andreas* poet's recycling of other OE poems, see Orchard, "Originality."

54. Dodwell, *Anglo-Saxon Art*, 15–16; Farr, "Style in Late Anglo-Saxon England"; Karkov, *Art of Anglo-Saxon England*; Webster, "Style: Influences, Chronology, and Meaning."

55. Hreinn Benediktsson, *First Grammatical Treatise*; Haugen, *First Grammatical Treatise*; Björn Magnússon Ólsen, *Den tredje og fjærde grammatiske*

avhandling; Krömmelbein, *Die Dritte Grammatische Abhandlung*; Clunies Ross and Wellendorf, *Fourth Grammatical Treatise*. All four Icelandic treatises, along with Snorri Sturluson's *Edda*, are preserved in Codex Wormianus (AM 242 fol.), ca. 1350. See Guðrún Nordal, *Tools of Literacy*; Quinn, "Emergence of Skaldic Pedagogy"; Tranter, "Medieval Icelandic *artes poeticae*"; Gade, "Ælfric in Iceland"; Copeland, "Grammar, Rhetoric, and Figurative Language"; Males, "Applied *Grammatica*," and Males, *Poetic Genesis*. Major works from England and the Continent during the same period include Matthew of Vendôme, *Ars versificatoria* (ca. 1175); Geoffrey of Vinsauf, *Poetria nova* (ca. 1210); Gervase of Melkley, *Ars versificaria* (ca. 1215); and John of Garland, *Parisiana poetria* (ca. 1230).

56. Óláfr Þórðarson, author of the *Third Grammatical Treatise* (ca. 1250), cites the first two words of Eyv Lv 8/1, ed. Poole; *SkP* 1.1:226–27 (*Bǫrum Ullr*) to illustrate the Latin poetic vice of *collisio*, where a consonant stands between the two vowels—not a blemish in ON. See Björn Magnússon Ólsen, *Den tredje og fjærde grammatiske avhandling*, 16, 71. Óláfr, like Snorri, accepts deviations by the oldest skalds but warns younger poets against imitating them. See Krause, *Die Dichtung des Eyvindr skáldaspillir*, 243–49.

57. As described in *SkP* 1.1:lx–lxi; Gade, *Structure of ON Dróttkvætt*, 7–12, 226–38. Poole, "Metre and Metrics," 278, suggests a relationship between *dróttkvætt* meter and OE hypermetric half-lines, which typically possess three primary stresses and a final trochaic cadence.

58. See, for example, McKinnell, "Eddic Poetry in Anglo-Scandinavian Northern England" and McKinnell, "*Vǫlundarkviða*."

59. This corpus is examined in Campbell, *Skaldic Verse*; Poole, "Skaldic Verse and Anglo-Saxon History," Poole, "*Liðsmannaflokkr*," Poole, "Cyningas sigefæste," and Poole, "Crossing the Language Divide"; Frank, "King Cnut in the Verse of his Skalds," and Frank, "Taste for Knottiness." Relevant publications by Townend include "Ella," Townend, *English Place-Names in Skaldic Verse*, Townend, "Contextualizing the *Knútsdrápur*," Townend, *Language and History*, Townend, "Knútr and the Cult of St Óláfr," Townend, "Cnut's Poets," Townend, "Pre-Cnut Praise-Poetry," Townend, "Norse Poets and English Kings," and Townend, with O'Donnell and Tyler, "European Literature and Eleventh-Century England." Also Jesch, "Knútr in Poetry and History," Jesch, "Scandinavians and 'Cultural Paganism,'" Jesch, "Norse Gods in Scotland," Jesch, "Norse Gods in England and the Isle of Man," and Jesch, "Skaldic Verse in Scandinavian England."

60. See Abrams, "Anglo-Saxons and the Christianization of Scandinavia." On insular secular material culture (e.g., drinking horns, swords) in viking-age Norwegian graves, see Mikkelsen, *Looting or Missioning*, 57–61.

61. On Northwest Germanic during this period, see Nielsen, *OE and the Continental Germanic Languages*, 187–204.

62. Townend, "Viking Age England," and Townend, *Language and History*, 110–38. Campbell, *Chronicle*, xxxvi, lix–lx, 9, 37, 40; Ælfric, *Homilies: Supple-*

mentary Collection, 2:683–85. See Abram, "Anglo-Saxon Influence in the Old Norwegian Homily Book." On Æthelweard's efforts to connect his family history to Danes in England, see Cross, *Heirs of the Vikings*.

63. Haugen, *The First Grammatical Treatise*, 12–13; Hreinn Benediktsson, *The First Grammatical Treatise*, 209 (84.14). See Harris, *Linguistic Past*, and Harris, "*Tam Anglis quam Danis*."

64. Viðar Hreinsson, *Complete Sagas*, 1, 315.

65. Hofmann, *Lehnbeziehungen*, 21–110; Fischer, *Die Lehnwörter*, supplemented by Simensen, "Nordic Lexicon," in Bandle, *The Nordic Languages*. The introduction to de Vries, *Altnordische etymologische Wörterbuch*, lists OE loanwords in ON. Also Naumann, "English Keywords in ON Literature."

66. Kubouchi, "Wulfstan's Scandinavian Loanword Usage"; also Pons-Sanz, *Norse-Derived Vocabulary*.

67. Smith, "Early Literary Relations of England and Scandinavia."

68. See Seaton, *Literary Relations*; Omberg, *Scandinavian Themes in English Poetry, 1760–1800*. Denmark's Ole Worm had given Icelandic scholarship on Norse vernacular verse wide circulation. Warton's (unpaginated) preface to his *History of English Poetry* cites Worm to the effect that the skalds made "the Scandinavian tongue" familiar in Britain—"unless it be rather presumed, that a previous knowledge of that tongue in Britain was the means of facilitating the admission of these poets"; cited in Jones, *Fossil Poetry*, 55. See Quinn and Clunies Ross, "Image of Norse Poetry and Myth in Seventeenth-Century England."

69. Temple, "Of Poetry," in *Miscellanea*, blamed medieval Scandinavia for introducing rhyme to English and European literature. Both Conybeares concurred (lxvi, xvi–xvii), pointing to the influence of skalds on OE poets in the age of Cnut; cited in Jones, *Fossil Poetry*, 88. Also Niles, *Idea of Anglo-Saxon England*, 200–201; O'Donoghue, *English Poetry and ON Myth*, 32–33, 41, 45, and 48–49. Weiskott, *English Alliterative Verse*, 13, observes that "the appearance around 1100 of internal rhyme in English alliterative verse has traditionally been referred to Anglo-Norman precedents, but ON *aðalhending* is another possibility." On the history and function of rhyme in English verse, see Harmon, "Rhyme." For anyone still curious about blood-eagling, see Frank, "Viking Atrocity"; Ellard, *Anglo-Saxon(ist) Pasts*, 61–100.

70. See Percy, "Essay on the Ancient English Minstrels," in *Reliques*, 1:xv–xvii, 2:260–61. The third edition (1775) of this prefatory essay identifies the Danes as proto-English. See, too, Percy, *Five Pieces*; Clunies Ross, *ON Poetic Translations of Thomas Percy*.

71. Morris, *Time's Anvil*, 52.

72. Ellis, *Specimens*. See, esp., Jones, *Fossil Poetry*, chap. 1. Also Quinn and Clunies Ross, "Image of Norse Poetry and Myth in Seventeenth-Century England"; Clunies Ross, *Norse Muse in Britain* and *ON Translations of Thomas Percy*.

73. Cornelius, *Reconstructing Alliterative Verse*, 28–29.

74. Hickes, *Linguarum veterum septentrionalium thesaurus*, 1:177–221. Sharon McCabe's translation of the *Thesaurus*, chap. 23 ("Poetic Art of the Anglo-Saxons") is housed at digitalrepository.unm.edu/engl_etds/8.

75. Recent studies distinguish the metrical, lexical, and structural innovations of the "southern mode" of late OE poetry from the "northern" or "classical" styles of *Beowulf, Exodus, Genesis A*, and Cynewulf; see Thornbury, *Becoming a Poet*, 223–37, and Weiskott, "*Paris Psalter* and English Literary History." Also Bredehoft, *Authors, Audiences*, 11–13, 61–63.

76. Rühs, *Über den Ursprung*. See further Fidjestøl, *Dating of Eddic Poetry*, 30–33.

77. Scott, *Ivanhoe*, chaps. 1 and 25.

78. Conybeare, *Illustrations of Anglo-Saxon Poetry*, xli–xlvii, xxxvi.

79. See Bjork, "Grímur Jónsson Thorkelin's Preface," 303–5. On contemporary reactions, see Shippey and Haarder, *Beowulf: Critical Heritage*; Craigie, *Northern Element*, 7. Gräslund, *Beowulfkvädet*, contending that the poem derives from an ON text, locates its place of origin in Gotland.

80. Wright, "On Anglo-Saxon Poetry," 87–88.

81 Wawn, *Anglo Man: Þorleifur Repp*; on Eiríkur Magnússon, see Wawn, "Cult of 'Stalwart Frith-thjof'"; on *Brunanburh*, see Wawn, "Anglo-Saxon Poetry in Iceland."

82. Hammerich, *De episk-kristelige oldkvad*, 3; Metcalfe, *The Englishman and the Scandinavian*, 175.

83. Craigie, *Northern Element*, 7; Chambers, *Beowulf*, 102.

84. Fourteenth-century skalds repudiated the *hulin fornyrðin* 'obscure archaisms' of *dróttkvætt*; see *Lilja* 98, ed. Martin Chase; *SkP* 7.2:673–75. For appreciative comments, Wawn, "Post-medieval Reception"; also Clark and Phelpstead, *ON Made New*; O'Donoghue, *English Poetry and ON Myth*; Larrington, *Winter Is Coming*. For OE, see Clark and Perkins, *Anglo-Saxon Culture*; Jones, *Strange Likeness*, and Jones, *Fossil Poetry*.

85. Henry of Huntingdon, *Historia Anglorum*, 310–11: "extraneis tam uerbis quam figuris." See Rigg, "Henry of Huntingdon's Metrical Experiments"; Tiller, "Anglo-Norman Historiography"; and Harris, *Linguistic Past*, 71.

86. Milton, *The History of Britain*, in *Complete Prose Works*, 5:308–9.

87. Bosworth, *Elements of Anglo-Saxon Grammar*, 210–12.

88. Turner, *History of the Anglo-Saxons*, 345 (book ix, chap. 1).

89. Taine, *Histoire*, 41.

90. Cunningham, "Dead (and Live) Poets' Society," 25. Also Larkin, *Selected Letters*, 39.

91. Ker, *Dark Ages*, 256.

92. Brooks, ed., *Andreas*, xxi–xxvii.

93. See remarks collected by Weiskott, "*Paris Psalter*," 107–8; Macrae-Gibson has harsh words for the *OE Riming Poem*, 12. Cædmon is scolded by Alexander, "OE Literature," 52.

94. Liberman, review of *The Verse and Language of Old Germanic Poetry* by O. A. Smirnitskaia, 105.

95. Peacock, *Complete Novels*, 1:305.

96. Ker, *Epic and Romance*, 157.

97. Hopkins to poet Robert Bridges, Letter of November 26, 1882, in Hopkins, *Collected Works of Gerard Manley Hopkins*, Vol. 2, *Correspondence 1882–1889*, 551.

98. Marsh, *Lectures on the English Language*, 2nd ed. (London: Samson Low, 1860), 553–57; Humpfry House and Graham Storey, eds., *The Journal and Papers of Gerard Manley Hopkins* (London: Oxford University Press, 1959), 284; for text and discussion, see Jones, *Fossil Poetry*, 203–4.

99. Auden, *Dyer's Hand*, 41–42. See Remein, "Auden, Translation, Betrayal."

100. Auden, *Collected Poems*, 516.

101. Frank, "Dróttkvætt," 393.

102. Belitt, *Poet's Other Voice: Conversations*, 62.

103. Puttenham, *The Arte of English Poesie*, 68, speaks of the monosyllables of "our natural & primitive language of the *Saxon English*." (To be fair, many OE-derived words in current English are monosyllabic [cf. 'lord' < OE *hlaford*; 'king' < OE *cyning*], having been contracted and/or shorn of inflectional endings.) Franciscus Irenicus (Franz Friedlieb) said of German in 1518: "et pene quicquid monosyllabam excedit, peregrinum ac non germanicum est" (and almost everything longer than a syllable is foreign and not German); cited by Jellinek, "Geschichte der deutschen Grammatik," 60. In her preface to *Rudiments of Grammar*, Elizabeth Elstob correctly disputed the notion that OE was predominantly monosyllabic.

104. The reference to noise and the first section heading in the next chapter are indebted to Howe, "What We Talk about When We Talk about Style." His title alludes to a painful story by the late Raymond Carver called "What We Talk about When We Talk about Love."

CHAPTER 1

1. Studies of OE poetic style over the past century include Schücking, *Untersuchungen*; Wyld, "Diction and Imagery"; Bartlett, *Larger Rhetorical Patterns*; Andrew, *Syntax and Style*, and Andrew, *Postscript*; Storms, "Subjectivity"; Brodeur, *Art of Beowulf*; Clemoes, *Rhythm and Cosmic Order*; Shippey, *OE Verse*; Greenfield, *Interpretation of OE Poems*; Calder, "Study of Style," Calder, *Cynewulf*, and Calder, "Histories and Surveys"; Anderson, *Cynewulf*; Niles, *Beowulf*, chap. 6; Grinda, "Pigeonholing Poetry"; Olsen, *Speech, Song, and Poetic Craft*; Robinson, *Appositive Style*; Godden, "Literary Language"; Wine, *Figurative Language*, 29–73; Stanley, *In the Foreground*; Pasternack, *Textuality of OE Poetry*; Orchard, "Artful Alliteration," Orchard, *Critical Companion*, 57–97, and Orchard, "Both Style and Substance"; Schaefer, "Rhetoric and Style"; Crépin, *OE Poetics*; Tyler, *OE Poetics*; Steen, *Verse and Vertuosity*; Trilling, *Aesthetics of Nostalgia*; Hill, *Aesthetics*;

Beechy, *Poetics of OE*; Davies, "Literary Languages"; Momma, "OE Poetic Form"; Mize, *Traditional Subjectivities*; Cavell, *Weaving Words*; Louviot, *Direct Speech*; Maring, *Signs That Sing*. Studies of *dróttkvætt* style include Falk, "Med hvilken ret"; Reichardt, *Studien*; Lie, "Skaldestil-studier," and Lie, *"Natur" og "unatur"*; Hollander, *Skalds*; Turville-Petre, *Scaldic Poetry*; Kreutzer, *Dichtungslehre*; Frank, *ON Court Poetry*; Clover, "Skaldic Sensibility"; Clunies Ross, "Style and Authorial Presence," and Clunies Ross, "Stylistic and Generic Definers"; See, *Skaldendichtung*; Fidjestøl, *Det norrøne fyrstediktet*, and Fidjestøl, *Selected Papers*; Lindow, "Narrative"; Kuhn, *Das Dróttkvætt*; Engster, *Poesie einer Achsenzeit*; Poole, *Viking Poems*, and Poole, *Skaldsagas*; O'Donoghue, *Poetics of Saga Narrative*; Clunies Ross, *History of ON Poetry and Poetics*; Bergsveinn Birgisson, *Inn i skaldens sinn*; Goeres, *Poetics of Commemoration*.

2. On the influence of vernacular poetics on Anglo-Latin verse, see Lapidge, "Aldhelm's Latin and OE Verse"; Orchard, *Poetic Art of Aldhelm*, 49–54. On complex OE/Latin interlingualism, see Orchard, "Alcuin and Cynewulf"; Lapidge, "The School of Hadrian and Theodore," Lapidge, "Some Latin Poems," and Lapidge, "Anglo-Latin Octosyllabic Verse"; Townsend, "Latinities, 893–1143"; Thornbury, *Becoming a Poet*, and Thornbury, "Æthilwulf poeta."

3. Lapidge, "Postpositioning of Prepositions," and Lapidge, "OE Poetic Compounds"; Steen, *Verse and Vertuosity*, 62–64, 136–37. Godden, "Literary Language," observed that "if Old English poetic diction had a basis in Common Germanic culture, as the evidence suggests, it would seem that Anglo-Saxon poets expanded it prodigiously" (500).

4. Poole, "Ekphrasis," and Poole, "Scholars and Skalds"; Amory, "Tmesis."

5. Early comparative studies include Heinzel, "Über den Stil der altgermanischen Poesie"; Meyer, *Die altgermanische Poesie*; Bugge, *Bidrag til den ældste skaldedigtnings historie*; Paetzel, *Die Variationen in der altgermanischen Alliterationspoesie*; Wolff, "Über den Stil der altgermanischen Poesie"; Heusler, *Deutsche Versgeschichte*, and Heusler, *Die altgermanische Dichtung*; Scholtz, *Kenning in Anglo-Saxon and ON Poetry*; Storch, *Angelsächsische Nominalcomposita*; Carr, *Nominal Compounds in Germanic*.

6. A division between eddic and skaldic verse still structures ON scholarship; see Chase, "Introduction," *Eddic, Skaldic, and Beyond*.

7. Grice, "Logic and Conversation."

8. *Mei-shan hsä-k'ao*, trans. Susan Bush, in *Chinese Literati on Painting: Su Shih (1037–1101) to Tung Ch'i-Ch'ang (1555–1636)* (Cambridge, MA: Harvard University Press, 1971), 110.

9. Shippey, *OE Verse*, 36–38.

10. Turner, *History of the Anglo-Saxons*, 2:278.

11. Ellis, *Specimens*, 3rd ed., 1:12–13.

12. On syntactical reversals, half-lines that glance over their shoulders while marching forward, see Weiskott, "OE Poetry." On labile half-lines in *The Wife's Lament*, see O'Brien O'Keeffe, "The Poetics of Affect," 45–46.

13. Mone, "Zur Kritik," 130.

14. Brandl, "Die angelsächsische Literatur," 1005.

15. Berendsohn, "Altgermanische Heldendichtung," 640.

16. Heinzel, "Über den Stil," 4.

17. Gummere, *Handbook of Poetics*, 176.

18. Klaeber, *Beowulf*, lvii. *Kl* 4, xcv, substitutes the heading "Non-Linear Narration."

19. Carroll, *Through the Looking Glass*, 170.

20. Brodeur, *Art of Beowulf*, 39.

21. Alexander, *First Poems in English*, xxi.

22. O'Brien O'Keeffe, "Diction, Variation, the Formula," 95.

23. Lanham, *Analyzing Prose*, 48; cited by Vogrin, *On Style*, 119.

24. On shared poetic simplices, see Cronan, "Alliterative Rank," 148. On shared compounds, see Niles, "Compound Diction," 496–97. For a full list of OE poetic words, see Griffith, "Poetic Language and the Paris Psalter," 183–85.

25. See Robinson, "Significance of Names"; Frank, "Onomastic Play," Frank, "Some Uses of Paronomasia," and Frank, "Taste for Knottiness"; Hall, "*Mansceaðan*"; Allen, "Name-Play"; Stanley, "*Geoweorþa*"; Thornbury, "*Đa Gregorius gamenode*"; Novacich, "OE *Exodus* and the Read Sea."

26. The sheen of fire, gold, and swords illuminates many OE poems, while "fire of the water" is a productive gold-kenning type in *dróttkvætt*. In theory, a skald could create 2,496 different kennings on this model, using attested synonyms for the two (antithetical) elements; see Fidjestøl, "Kenningsystemet," in *Selected Papers*, 31.

27. In OE, *Beo* 342a, 396a, 404a, 2049a, 2539a, 2605a; *Jud* 203a; in eddic meters, *HHj* 28/3, *Helr* 7/3; *HHund I* 15/5, *HHund II* 7/7, 14/6; *Hamð* 19/4, *Fáfn* 44/2; in skaldic, Glúmr *Gráf* 5/1, VGl Lv 2/1, StjOdd, *Geirdr* 4/7, Eyv *Hák* 3/8, 4/8. See Mastrelli, "Sotto l'Helmo." Orchard, *Critical Companion*, 65–66, notes that *Beo* 403a/404a and 2539a/2540a are the only line pairs in the poem in which "under" appears in consecutive lines: the hero "under helmet" goes "under Heorot's roof" and "under the dragon's stone-cliff."

28. *Mæl* fails to alliterate as expected in initial a-verse position in the Danish coast guard's speech (*Beo* 316) and in initial position in several ON stanzas: Anon *Bjark* 1/3; Egill, *Skjalddr* 1/1; *HHund II* 21/5, 49/1; *Hávm* 111/1; *Vsp* 14/1; *Innkv* (*Hálf*) 9/5 (29); in the same half-line, the infinitive *feran* after *to* is uninflected; cf. ON: *mál er mér at ríða* 'time for me to ride' (*HHund II*, 49/1). See Suzuki, *Metre of Old Saxon Poetry*, 263; *Kl* 4, 137.

29. Hofmann, *Lehnbeziehungen*, 77.

30. Ibid., 83; see Townend, "Antiquity of Diction," 2–5.

31. The compound also occurs in Þorbjǫrn hornklofi's tenth-century *Glymdrápa*, st. 7/4, ed. Marold, *SkP* 1.1:87, with reference to Haraldr Fair-hair.

32. Poole, "Crossing the Language Divide," 597; Kuhn, "Westgermanisches," 212–13, regards ON *þjóðkonungr* as a Continental borrowing. Neidorf and

Pascual, "ON Influence," minimize the likelihood of postmigration cross-cultural reinforcement.

33. On the emendation *eorlas* (MS *eorl*) and reservations about nominative *eorl*, see *Kl* 4, 112. Also Weiskott, "OE Poetry," 116–17. For the reading Heruli, see Shippey, "Names," 59; Drout and Goering, "Terrified."

34. For a different interpretation of the syntax, see Fulk, "Six Cruces in *Beowulf*," 351–53, and *Kl* 4, 115.

35. Frank, "North-Sea Soundings."

36. Frank, "Skaldic Tooth," 340–42.

37. See Robinson, "Aspects of the *Maldon* Poet's Artistry," and Robinson, "God, Death, and Loyalty in *The Battle of Maldon*." Among the lexical items in *Maldon* suggestive of Norse–English contact are *ceallian, dreng, eorl, grið, hilde dælan*, and *snell* (ON *snjallr*).

38. Hall, "*Exodus* 166b, *cwyldrof*." The three OE compounds listed (*guðhafoc, hasupada*, and *wælceasega*) are, like *cwyldrof, hapax legomena*.

39. Robinson, "Lexicography and Literary Criticism," 107.

40. Woolf, "Ideal of Men Dying with Their Lord"; See, "Hastings, Stiklastaðir und Langemarck," and See, "*Húskarla hvǫt*"; Frank, "Ideal of Men Dying with Their Lord"; Clark, "Dying with One's Lord." Many of the gold-kennings in stanzas 4, 5, and 6 of *Bjarkamál* occur only in verse from the mid-twelfth century onward: Nordal, *Tools of Literacy*, 329–30; the style of the first three stanzas is thought to resemble that of poems composed in the tenth century: Anon *Bjark*, ed. Clunies Ross; *SkP* 3.1:496.

41. On Bragi, see Kuhn, *Das Dróttkvætt*, 275. Kershaw, *Anglo-Saxon and Norse Poems*, 167; the echo of *Hávamál* was pointed out by Meyer, *Die altgermanische Poesie*, 321. See de Vries, *Altnordische Literaturgeschichte*, 1:145n83; Marold, "Das Walhallbild," 24; Frank, "ON Memorial Eulogies." On legendary material shared by tenth-century ON skaldic verse and OE poetry, see Lendinara, "L'Episodio di Sigemund."

42. Boar-helmets: *Beo* 303b–305, 1110–12a, 1285–87, 1327–28a, 1451–54; Eyv Lv 5/5–7, Glúmr *Gráf* 7/5, ÞTref *Hrafn* 1/3, SnSt *Ht* 2/5, Þul *Hjálms* 2/1. See Frank, "Boar on the Helmet." On arm-ornaments, cf. OE *earmhread* (*Beo* 1194b) and ON *armhrauð* (Arn Frag 4/3; *SkP* 3.1:6).

43. Klaeber, *Beowulf*, 146 (note to line 480).

44. For Árni's comment and its context, see Jón Helgason, *Handritaspjall*, 113, cited from AM 436 4to ff. 30v–31r; Eiríkur Benedikz, "Árni Magnússon," *Saga-Book of the Viking Society for Northern Research* 16 (1962–65): 92, lightly modernized Árni's spellings: "Svo gengur það til í heiminum, að sumir hjálpa erroribus á gang og aðrit leitast síðan við að útryðja aptur þeim sömu erroribus. Hafa svo hverir tveggju nockuð að iðja" (It is the way of the world that some people put errors into circulation while others then try to eradicate these same errors. This keep everyone busy.) My gratitude to Guðvarður Már Gunnlaugsson of the Stofnun Árna Magnússonar í íslenskum fræðum in Reykjavík for confirming the accuracy of this account.

45. John Leland, *Hip: The History* (New York: Ecco, 2004), 32–33.

46. On skalds knowing and using each other's works, see Townend, "Norse Poets and English Kings," and Townend, "Cnut's Poets"; Grove, "Recreating Tradition"; Poole, "Some Examples of the Adverbial Genitive." On OE poets imitating one another, see Mize, *Traditional Subjectivities*, 26–28; Riedinger, "Formulaic Relationship."

47. This *ars longa* tag, associated with Horace, derives from the *Aphorismi* of the Greek physician Hippocrates of Kos. Longfellow, "Psalm of Life," line 13 (orig. pub. October 1838 in *The Knickerbocker* and frequently reprinted); see *inter alia* Thomas R. Lounsbury, ed., *Yale Book of American Verse* (New Haven, CT: Yale University Press, 1912), no. 55. The words in the poem come from a speaker who wants the "dead Past [to] bury its dead"; the northern poets were more attune to Seamus Heaney's prayer: "Old fathers, be with us / Old cunning assessors / of feuds and of sites / for ambush or town"; see Heaney, "Viking Dublin, Trial Pieces," in *North* (London: Faber, 1975).

48. Cf. the viking-age warrior-kenning *hjǫrva gnýstafir* 'roaring staves of swords' (ÞjóðA *Magnfl* 14/6; *SkP* 2.1:81). In Icelandic poetry after ca. 1400, the clusters *sl-*, *sm-*, and *sn-* count as *gnýstuðlar.* The early eleventh-century skald Sigvatr seems alone in using *sm-* in the three alliterative positions of a *dróttkvætt* couplet; see Ragnar Ingi Aðalsteinsson, "Ljóðstafurinn s."

49. See Nielsen, "Linguistic Status," 549; also Losquino, *Early Runic Inscriptions.*

50. On the dithematic name Hlewagastir, see Jackson, "Det urnordiska namnelementet *-gastiz*," 10–13; also Grønvik, "Runeinnskriften på gullhornet fra Gallehus." The translation of *tawido* as "made" is challenged by Markey, "HlewagastiR Exposed."

51. Ten are included in Robinson and Stanley, *OE Verse Texts*; for others, Bredehoft, *Authors, Audiences*, 49–61. For a recently discovered object from Lincolnshire with a few fragmentary lines of OE verse inscribed in runes, see Hines, "*Benedicite* Canticle."

52. On a Danish crofter's discovery of the horn in 1734 and its subsequent role in the rise of Romanticism in the North, see Spurkland, *Norwegian Runes*, 21–25. Klingenberg, *Runenschrift*, 17–27, discerned a Fibonacci sequence, or golden section, in the inscription (13:8:5:3). See Naumann, *Metrische Runeninschriften*; also Mees, "Style, Manner and Formula." On distinguishing metrical from nonmetrical inscriptions in the older runic alphabet, see Marold, "Vers oder nicht Vers?"

53. Longfellow, "Anglo-Saxon Literature," 100n154. Bosworth, *Elements of Anglo-Saxon Grammar*, 221: "When smiths are hammering with their sledges a certain regular return in their strokes produces rhythm." Also Green, *Short History*, 27. Longfellow's description is echoed in Tennyson, *Harold: A Drama* (London: Henry King, 1877), 120: "iron on iron clang / hammer on anvil bang." See Irving, "Charge of the Saxon Brigade," 180–81; Stanley, "Aesthetic Evaluations of the Sound of OE."

54. Alexander, *Earliest English Poems*, 18.

55. Skeat, "Essay on Alliterative Poetry," xxxiv–xxxv.

56. Gummere, *Handbook*, 176; and Gummere, *Germanic Origins*: "The very meter of their poetry is the clash of battle, and knows scarcely any other note" (232).

57. Tolman, "Style of Anglo-Saxon Poetry," 22: "the blows of the sturdy syllables." Spaeth, *OE Poetry*, 228, refers to the "hammer-blow style of the Anglo-Saxon."

58. See, e.g., Fulk, *History of OE Meter*, 233–34.

59. The ad was subsequently changed to "Safe, Supportive, Scottish."

60. On the requirement of double alliteration in specific Sievers's metrical types, see Bliss, *Metre of Beowulf*, 26, 36–38, and appendix C, table 1, 122–23; Kendall, *Metrical Grammar*, 100–110; Terasawa, *OE Metre*, 37, 42, 59; Bredehoft, *Early English Metre*, 19–20, 30–34, 126–27; Orton, *Transmission*, 160. Hutcheson, *OE Poetic Meter*, 271, charted the percentages of double alliteration in the a-verses of thirty-three OE poems. See now Griffith, "Extra Alliteration," 76–86.

61. Rubin, *Memory in Oral Traditions*, 74.

62. Masonry comparison from Tolkien, "Monsters," 273; Coltrane, from Golston, *Versatility*, 106. On the combination of OE verse-types into lines, see Hutcheson, *OE Poetic Metre*, 297–99.

63. Griffith, "On the Lexical Property Termed 'Rank,'" 3n28, reports that approximately half the lines in the OE verse corpus have a verb in final position. (*Taw-* by chance forms a half-rhyme with *Hlew-* in the first half-line.) By altering this traditional Proto-Germanic SOV (subject/object/verb) order (also typical of Sanskrit, Homeric Greek, and Latin), OE poets establish their relative modernity. See Griffith, ed. *Judith*, 37–42; also Toswell, "Translation Techniques of the OE Metrical Psalter."

64. Naumann, *Metrische Runeninschriften*, 151–52, provides bibliographical guidance; also Harris, "Rök Stone," an introduction in English to the Rök industry, along with photos (16–20). For recent meter-marring attempts to remove Theodoric from the inscription and to read the stone as a response to climate change, see Holmberg et al., "Rök Runestone."

65. Wessén, "Theoderikmyt"; See, *Germanische Verskunst*, 47–49; Vogt, "Binnenreime," 229; Gade, *Structure of ON Dróttkvætt*, 234–35; Naumann, *Metrische Runeninschriften*, 143–52.

66. Agnellus, *Book of the Pontiffs*, 206. The identity of the equestrian figure and the fate of the statue after Charlemagne's reign remain unresolved. Bullough, *Carolingian Renewal*, 47, rejects the notion that the statue represented Zeno, emperor at Ravenna (r. 474–91).

67. Poole, "Scholars and Skalds."

68. *Annales Regni Francorum*, 1:106.

69. Most scholars place Bragi's verses in the ninth century; for a tenth-century dating (and an association of the poem with the reconquest of Northumbria by the Danes), see Marold, "*Ragnarsdrápa*."

70. *Rdr* 3/1-4, ed. Clunies Ross; *SkP* 3.1:31–32. The referent of the kenning (a periphrastic expression consisting of two or more parts) is given in capital letters inside square brackets.

71. Terasawa, *OE Metre*, 63.

72. The basic Sievers's A-type half-line (*mærðo mæned*, 857a) is here joined to the rarer E-type (*monig oft gecwæð*, 857b); line 858 links a B and C type, while each of the remaining three A-type b-verses (*oþer nænig, selra nære, rices wyrðra*) is attached to a different, more complex a-verse. *Judith*, in the same manuscript as *Beowulf* but arguably a later poem, generally combines, like *Beowulf*, different metrical subtypes to form the long line; see Griffith, *Judith*, 34.

73. On full rhyme in "classical" OE poetry, see Bredehoft, *Early English Metre*, 57–68, 79–80. For discussions of rhyme and further references, see Kluge, "Zur Geschichte des Reimes im Altgermanischen"; Stanley, "Rhymes in English Medieval Verse"; Bredehoft, "OE and Old Saxon Formulaic Rhyme"; Griffith, "Extra Alliteration," 79.

74. Hickes, *Thesaurus*, 177, acknowledged this split. Cf. Kemble, *Codex Vercellensis*, ix: "The language of poetry is as distinct from that of prose among the Anglo-Saxons as any two dialects."

75. Zipf, *Human Behavior*, 19–20.

76. Borges, "Pierre Menard," 37.

77. *Rand* (*rond-*) in poetry means "shield" (17x) or "shield-boss" (3x); in prose, "rim, edge." See Brady, "Weapons in *Beowulf*." On compounding, see Brodeur, *Art of Beowulf*, 7–38, 254–71; Krackow, *Nominalkomposita*. Cronan, "Poetics of Poetic Words," 265, counts 2,549 OE compounds that occur only in a single poem, including the two in this passage.

78. The first element, *eormen-* 'powerful, vast,' forms compounds in both corpora and in proper names (cf. Jǫrmunrekkr/Eormenric); in ON, it is an Óðinn-name, cognate with Old Saxon and Old High German *irmin-* 'powerful.' See Davis-Secord, *Joinings*; Chapman, "Composing and Joining." Two poems signed by Cynewulf contain the inflected adjectival form *yrmen* 'huge': *geond / ofer ealne yrmenne grund* 'over all the vast earth' (*ChristB* 481; *Jul* 10).

79. See Griffith, "OE Poetic Diction," 120. The simplex occurs nine times in *Beowulf* alone, whose poet shuns the compound-type "sea-horse"; cf. *yþmearh, lagumearh, sæmearh, brimhengest, fearoðhengest, merehengest, sæhengest, sundhengest, wæghengest*, each of which signifies "sea-horse" = ship in *Elene, ChristB, GuthB, Andreas, Meters, Whale, Riddle* 14, and the *Rune Poem*.

80. Meissner, *Kenningar*, 211.

81. Page, "*A Most Vile People*," 12–13, 26–27. The poem, composed before 1045, was first recognized as such by Bredehoft, "OE *yðhengest*." Text in Weiskott, *English Alliterative Verse*, 177.

82. Cf. the formulaic matrix *ofer rumne grund* (*GenA* 123a, 213a), *geond rumne grund* (*LPr II*, 38b), *geond sidne grund* (*GenA* 1388a, 1429b, *Jul* 332b, *ChristB* 785a,

Met 29, 59a), *geond ginne grund* (*And* 331a, *Wid* 51a), *under ginne grund* (*Beo* 1551a), *ofer grenne grund* (*Exo* 312a), *ofer sidne grund* (*El* 1289a, *Phoen* 118a), etc.

83. *Beo* 1297b, 1685b, 1956b; *Exo* 443b, 513b; *GuthA* 266b, *GuthB* 1367b; *PPs* 71.8a. The formula in *Beo* 1956b is followed in the next half-line by the poetic compound *eormencynn* 'immense race, humankind,' repeating the pairing in *Beo* 858–59.

84. According to Klaeber, *Beowulf*, lxv (also *Kl* 4, cxviii), variation is "the very soul of the Old English poetical style." See Robinson, *Appositive Style*; Brodeur, *Art of Beowulf*, 40. Paetzel, *Die Variationen*, treats the device as a feature common to all Germanic alliterative verse.

85. On the adverb *ne* used in poetry with other negatives, see Mitchell, *OE Syntax*, §§1608–13.

86. See Fidjestøl, *Det norrøne fyrstediktet*, 191–93, for *dróttkvætt* stanzas praising historical Norwegian kings by negating a comparative: "There is no one better."

87. On repetition as a "bracketing" device, see Orchard, *Critical Companion*, 78–85. On ring composition or envelope patterns, see Bartlett, *Larger Rhetorical Patterns*, 9–29; Hieatt, "Envelope Patterns"; Parks, "Ring Structure"; Tonsfeldt, "Ring Structure"; Dane, "Notion of Ring Composition"; Niles, "Ring Composition"; Niles, *Beowulf*, 152–62; Stévanovitch, "Envelope Patterns in *Genesis*"; Stévanovitch, "Envelope Patterns."

88. The existence of this runestone (Run Öl 1) with its boustrophedon ("as an ox turns in plowing") inscription was first recorded in 1634, at which time the monument stood at the foot of a gravemound. See Naumann, *Metrische Runeninschriften*, 101–5. Also Frank, "Like a Bridge of Stones"; Jesch, *Ships and Men*, 1–6; Marold, "Karlevi. §2: Runenkundliches."

89. Peterson, *Nordiskt runnamnslexikon*, 71.

90. Marold, "Karlevi. §2: Runenkundliches," 276–77.

91. In line 6, *stark-* makes a full rhyme with *mǫrk-* (*ǫ* being the reflex of the *u*-umlaut of *a*). Elsewhere in the skaldic corpus, Denmark (*Danmǫrku* in the cadence) rhymes with *bark-* (Hallv *Knútdr* 6/4, Hfr *Óldr* 2/6) or, as here, *-stark* (Þfagr *Sveinn* 10/8, ÞjóðA *Magn* 9/6). On half-rhymes, see See, "Skothending." The number of consonants following a vowel that count as part of the rhyme is controversial; see now Þorgeir Sigurðsson, "Rímstuðlar"; Myrvoll, *Kronologi*, 53–82; and Kristján Árnason, "On the Principal," 87–93, 97–107. In line 5, the finite verb *munat* (a sequence of one short plus one enclitic syllable) counts as one metrical position through resolution.

92. On suggested meanings for the name Grendel, including "grinder," see *Kl* 4, 467–68.

93. Addition restrictions apply: a monosyllabic noun or adjective in the fourth syllable of the line must be syllabically short; the two alliterations in an odd line cannot fall before both rhyming syllables. See Kuhn, *Das Dróttkvætt*, 89; Gade, *Structure*, 21, 52–54.

94. Sweet, "Sketch," 6.

95. Quoted by Becker, *Subtle Channels*, 13. Perec is echoing Queneau's reference to Oulipians as rats who construct the labyrinth from which they intend to escape.

96. Jakobson, "What Is Poetry?," 368.

97. ON *róg-* forms at least thirty-one different poetic compounds; the only other adjectival compound in the group, *rógǫrr* 'strife-bold,' occurs in a poem composed ca. 1047 by the skald Arnórr Þórðarson: *Magndr* 1/2; *SkP* 2.1:207.

98. The phrase is stolen from Paterson, *The Poem*, 11.

99. The OE chain for this "root" includes *rædan* 'to counsel, rule' and *rad* 'riding'/*ridan* 'to ride.' On the *ráða-* 'to rule'/*ríða* 'to ride' collocation group, see Ruggerini, "Alliterative Lexical Collocations," 317–21.

100. On the poetics of paronomasia, see, *inter alia*, Quirk, "Poetic Language"; Jakobson, "Linguistics and Poetics"; Frank, "Paronomasia"; Kintgen, "*Lif, Lof, Leof, Lufu*, and *Geleafa*."

101. The translation of *ørgrandari* 'more blameless, more without fault' has been queried on the basis of the compound *grandvarr* 'damage-wary, circumspect' (ESkál *Vell* 13/4). See Marold, "Runeninschriften," 671.

102. Page, *Chronicles of the Vikings*, 86; Naumann, "*Hann var manna mestr óníðingr*," 499–501. OE *unniðing* 'generous, honest man,' a term borrowed from ON, is recorded in the Peterborough Chronicle; see Irvine, *Chronicle E*, s.a. 1087.

103. Standard studies are Meissner, *Kenningar*; Krause, *Die Kenning*; Mohr, *Kenningstudien*; Lie, "Skaldestil-studier"; Marold, *Kenningkunst*; Krömmelbein, *Skaldische Metaphorik*; Fidjestøl, "Kenningsystemet"; and Amory, "Towards a Grammatical Classification," and Amory, "Kennings, Referentiality and Metaphors." Recent work includes Malm, "Two Cultures of Visual(ized) Cognition," and Malm, "Varför heter det kenning?"; Bergsveinn Birgisson, "Cognitive Archaism in Skaldic Poetry"; and Abram, "Towards an Object-Oriented Skaldic Poetics."

104. Borges, "Kenningar," 17: "Eine der unverfrorensten Verirrungen der Literaturgeschichte."

105. Machan, "Snorri's *Edda*."

106. Calvino, *Six Memos*, 4.

107. Cf. Pascal's definition of man as "a thinking reed." See Weber, "Of Trees and Men."

108. *Haugr* and *draugr* rhyme in other *dróttkvætt* stanzas while belonging, as here, to different phrases: cf. *éldraugr skarar hauga* (Eyv Lv 5/6; *SkP* 1.1:221). On the double sense of *draugr* in the Karlevi inscription, see Foote, "Skandinavische Dichtung der Wikingerzeit," 327. *Draugr* has the same dual sense ("tree-trunk, ghost") in Bragi *Rdr* 8/8; *SkP* 3.1:39–41.

109. Lindqvist, *Gotlands Bildsteine*. On the distribution of carved stones depicting ships, see Jesch, *Ships and Men*, 120n3.

110. See Egeler, *Avalon, 66° Nord*, 113–80. On the welcoming valkyrie on the eighth-century Tjängvide 1 stone from Gotland, see Hultgård, "Midgardbrinner."

111. Terrain-terms—*haugr*, *-mǫrk*, *-grund*, and *land*—course through the stanza; cf. *fold* 'land.' On Saussure's search for such name-anaphones in Saturnian verse epitaphs, see Starobinski, *Les mots sous les mots*. Saussure never published his notebooks, whose number varies from 99 to 134, depending on the investigator counting. See Heller-Roazen, *Dark Tongues*, 109–30, and 203n16.

112. Nabokov, "The Vane Sisters," in *American Fantastic Tales*, ed. Peter Straub (New York: Library of America, 2009), 146 (sonnets 88 and 131).

113. Albert Uderzo and René Goscinny, *Astérix et Cléopâtre*, first published in *Pilote* magazine, 1963, issues 215–57; album in French (Paris: Hachette Livre, 1965).

114. Fragment 2, section 2.5, in Carl Huffman, "Alcmaeon," *The Stanford Encyclopedia of Philosophy* (Summer 2021), ed. Edward N. Zalta, https://plato.stanford.edu/archives/sum2021/entries/alcmaeon.

115. On ring-composition and other mnemotechnic designs in OE verse, see note 87 above. On syntactical patterning in *dróttkvætt*, see Reichardt, *Studien*; Edwards, "Clause Arrangement"; Gade, *Structure of ON Dróttkvætt*.

116. Hallv, *Knútdr* 4, ed. Townend; *SkP* 3.1:235.

117. Eyv Lv 8, ed. Poole; *SkP* 1.1:226.

118. Saxo, *Gesta Danorum*, 2.7.15; 1:132–33. A verse attributed to Þjóðólfr Arnórsson in praise of another Haraldr (*harðráði* 'hard-ruler,' d. 1066 in England) appears to play upon Eyvindr's stanza, referring twice to the same Hrólfr kraki legend and using similar imagery and vocabulary: ÞjóðA *Sex* 27; *SkP* 2.1:140–42.

119. For the story of Fróði and the giantesses Fenja and Menja, see Snorri, *Edda: Skáldskaparmál*, 52; on its interpretations over the centuries, See et al., *Kommentar*, 3:837–57 (introduction to *Grottasǫngr*); also Jesch, *Viking Diaspora*, 146–47. On the continuation of the myth in later Orkney folklore, see Alfred W. Johnston, "Grotta söngr and the Orkney and Shetland Quern," *Saga-Book of the Viking Society* 6, no. 2 (1910): 296–304.

120. *Edda, Vafþrúðnismál* 21/1; *Grímnismál* 40/1.

121. Parody of *Time* magazine style in Wolcott Gibbs, "Time . . . Fortune . . . Life . . . Luce," *The New Yorker*, November 28, 1936, 20–25.

122. The sequence of alliterative staves in this stanza follows the initial sounds of the skald's name: **Ey**vindr **F(f)**innsson **m**ælti 'spoke.'

123. ESkál *Vell* 11, ed. Marold; *SkP* 1.1:297–98.

124. *Snorri Sturluson, Edda, Skáldskaparmál*, 1: for the story of the mead, 3–4, relevant stanzas from *Vellekla*, 12–13. See now Males, *Poetic Genesis*, 148–159.

125. Rainer Maria Rilke, "Schwerkraft," in *Sämtliche Werke* (Munich: Insel, 1956), 2:179–80, cited by Carson, *Economy of the Unlost*, 94.

126. W. H. Auden parodied this list of potential misfortunes (substituting largely psychological maladies) in Auden, *The Orators: An English Study* (1931), section II, 3rd part; cited by Jones, *Strange Likeness*, 105. Morgan, *Collected Poems*, 374, grimly updates the OE litany.

127. Commentary has been largely concerned with what the man was doing up a tree. Answers range from watching for enemies, carpentry, falconry, and collecting fodder to Christ ascending the cross and Germanic initiatory rites. See Howard, "OE Tree Climbing"; Cross, "On the Wanderer"; Isaacs, "Up a Tree"; Tripp, "Odin's Powers"; Swenson, "Death Appropriated"; and Brady, "Death and the Landscape." The ability to climb a tree is accounted a gift in *ChristB*, 678b–79a. Paul Muldoon's poem "Yggdrasill" (in *Quoof* 1983) opens with a speaker climbing a tree to gain wisdom. According to the anthropologist Frank W. Marlowe (*The Hazda*, 160), elderly men in that hunter-gatherer society "are the most likely to fall out of tall baobab trees to their deaths, since they continue to collect honey into old age."

128. On the possible confusion in line 26b of OE *feorh* 'life' and OE *ferhð* 'mind,' see Lockett, *Anglo-Saxon Psychologies*, 52. On OE *sið* in the Exeter Book poems, see Niles, *God's Exiles and English Verse*, 210–12. The intermingled *s*- and *f*- alliterations of this final couplet draw things to a close.

129. Thoreau, "Autumnal Tints," in *Collected Essays and Poems*, ed. Elizabeth Hall Witherall (New York: Library of America, 2001), 382.

130. Wallace Stevens, "An Ordinary Evening in New Haven," in *Auroras of Autumn* (New York: Knopf, 1950), 132–33.

131. Quintilian, *Orator's Education* 9.2.65–66.

132. On the alliteration of *eodur* and *ut*, see Liuzza, "Iron and Irony in *Beowulf*."

133. Morgan, *Beowulf: A Verse Translation.*

134. Raffel, *Beowulf: A New Translation.*

135. Alexander, *Beowulf: A Verse Translation.*

136. Donaldson, *Beowulf: A Prose Translation.*

137. Chickering, *Beowulf: A Dual Language Edition.*

138. Osborn, *Beowulf: A Verse Translation.*

139. Liuzza, *Beowulf.*

140. Clark Hall, *Beowulf and the Fight at Finnsburg: A Translation.*

141. Heaney, *Beowulf: A New Verse Translation.*

142. Tolkien, *Beowulf: A Translation and Commentary*, 32.

143. Headley, *Beowulf*, 31.

144. DiNapoli, *A Far Light*, 165.

145. Clover, "Regardless of Sex," esp. 381–85; Frank, "*Quid Hinieldus cum Feminis*"; Porck, *Old Age in Early Medieval England*, esp. chaps. 5 and 6.

146. E.g., Tindr *Hákdr* 1, *SkP* 1.1:338; Stefnir Lv 2, *SkP* 1.1:450; Vígf Lv, *SkP* 1.1:364. A fierce ship battle is said to be *not* at all like when a maiden brings mead to a retainer; Earl Hákon throws off his chain mail in the midst of a sea-battle and his skald notes: "It was *not* at all like when a woman prepares a bed for a warrior."

147. See Ziolkowski, "Obscenity in the Latin Grammatical and Rhetorical Tradition."

148. The *k*-spelling is rare, occurring in *Beowulf* only in the word *kyning* (4x, compared to more than 50x with the spelling *c*-). The half-line *cyninga wuldor*

'glory of kings' = Christ/God, occurs in the signed poems of Cynewulf (*El* 5b, 178b; *ChristB* 508a, *Jul* 279b) and in *And* 555b, 854b, 899a, *Res* 21a, *Jud* 155a, and *Men* 1b.

149. See Griffith, "Verses Quite Like *cwen to gebeddan*," esp. 157–60.

150. Kendall, *Metrical Grammar*, 108, 119.

151. *Cwen* signifies woman, but also wife, noble lady, and queen; Abraham's Sarah, like Wealhtheow, is both *gebedda* and *cwen* (*GenA* 2261b).

152. See Magennis, "'No Sex Please, We're Anglo-Saxons'"; Frank, "Sex in the *DOE*."

153. Karkov, "Hagar and Ishmael"; Anlezark, "An Ideal Marriage."

154. See *DOEC*, s.v. *gebedda, gebeddan*. Prose *gebedda* can designate "husband."

155. The phrase *to gebeddan* otherwise occurs in HomU 37 (Nap 46) 221, where a corpse is "as food and bedmate to worms."

156. Stafford, *Queen Emma*, 174.

157. On this queen's landed wealth, see Meyer, "Queen's Demesne," 81–83, 103–4.

158. Donoghue, *Lady Godiva*, 16.

159. Anon *Nkt* 8/2, 17/8; *SkP* 2.2:767, 773; Egill Lv 23/7; *SkP* 5.1; *Þul kvenna* 4; *SkP* 3.2:959; Qgm *Eyb* (Qrv 31), Lv 31/5; *SkP* 8.2:844.

160. Skúli Lv 1/1-2, ed. Heslop; *SkP* 3.1:367–68.

161. Doubled full-rhymes, in similar a/b a/b sequence, decorate each odd and even line of a *dróttkvætt* half-stanza from ca. 1030, which begins "*Þér eig*um *vér veig*ar" (we must [repay] you for drinks) (Refr *Giz* 3, ed. Marold et al.; *SkP* 3.1:256).

162. The royal couple's postsunrise emergence eliminates any suggestion of the twilight before dawn, a period associated in OE verse with misery; see Stanley, "OE Poetic Diction," 434–35; Lochrie, "Anglo-Saxon Morning Sickness."

163. On *brydbur*, see Fischer, *Engagement, Wedding and Marriage*, 51–55. The extant OE poetic corpus includes about 150 different self-alliterating compounds; 12, like *brydbur*, occur once in verse and numerous times in prose and glosses. See Griffith, "Extra Alliteration," 93n104. For a list of prose words in OE poetry, see Stanley, "Studies in the Prosaic Vocabulary." The relevant section of Vulgate Psalm 18:6 runs: "tamquam sponsus procedens de thalamo suo, exultavit." After the OE rendition of the psalm verse in Bl Hom 1 (HomU 18), the compound *wuldorcyning* (= Christ/God) follows: Morris, *Blickling Homilies*, p. 9, line 32. (*Brydbur* occurs three more times in the same homily: 7, 31; 9, 10; 9, 26). The figural layering at work in the *Beowulf* poet's choice of words is translucent, like that in *dróttkvætt* stanzas with mythological undercurrents.

164. Cf. *Beo* 665b: *kyningwuldor*. The compound *wuldorcyning* occurs about 42 times in verse and only once more in prose: LS 14 (Margaret CCCC 303). Morris, *Blickling Homilies*, p. vi, noted the resemblance between aspects of the description of Grendel's mere in *Beo* 1357–66, and that of hell in Blickling Homily 16 (LS 25

[MichaelMor], 209, 30–210, 1). Homiletic formulas in the poem such as *manað swa ond myndgað* 'thus admonishes and reminds' (2057a), *weaxe(ð) ond wrideð* (1741a), and *frofor ond fultum* 'consolation and help' (698a, 1273a), occur in the same homily (197, 3; 199, 2; 201, 28; 203, 21 and 26.) Another alliterative collocation, *mildust and mon(ðw)ærust* (*Beo* 3181), graces Blickling Homily 6 (71, 4), etc.; see Mary P. Richards, "A Re-examination of *Beowulf*, ll. 3180–3182," *English Language Notes* 10 (1973): 163–67.

165. Ted Hughes, "Hawk Roosting," in *Lupercal* (London: Faber & Faber, 1960), n.p.

166. Seamus Heaney, *The Cure at Troy: A Version of Sophocles' "Philoctetes"* (New York: Farrar, Straus, and Giroux, 1990).

167. For Gothic and Old High German cognates (*hansa* 'troop, cohort, crowd, company'), see Orel, *Handbook of Germanic Etymology*, s.v. *xansō; also Walde, *Vergleichendes Wörterbuch*, 1: 458–59; Helm, "Hansa," 194–96; Feist, *Etymologisches Wörterbuch*, 182; Damico, *Beowulf's Wealhtheow*, 72–74.

CHAPTER 2

1. Albert Einstein, *Autobiographical Notes*, trans. and ed. P. A. Schilpp (La Salle, IL: Open Court Press, 1979), 9.

2. Virginia Woolf, "A Sketch of the Past," in *Moments of Being: A Collection of Autobiographical Writings*, ed. J. Schulkind (New York: Harcourt, 1985), 72.

3. On roots and asterisks, see Heller-Roazen, *Echolalia*, 99–112; Zamboni, *L'etimologia*, 12–13. As for Chinook salmon, fewer and fewer are reaching their 112-mile-long mountain spawning area in the Columbia River basin; see Jim Robbins, "How Long Before These Salmon Are Gone?," *New York Times*, September 17, 2019, D1 and D6.

4. General works on early etymologizing include Sanders, "Grundzüge"; Opelt, "Etymologie"; Klinck, *Die lateinische Etymologie*; Amsler, *Etymology and Grammatical Discourse*. For the Babel story, see Borst, *Der Turmbau*; Major, *Undoing Babel*. Also Fear and Wood, eds., *Isidore of Seville and His Reception*; Males, *Etymology and Wordplay*; Carruthers, "Inventional Mnemonics and the Ornaments of Style."

5. See Tom Stoppard, *Arcadia*, 1.1.

6. See, e.g., Culler, *Theory of the Lyric*; Attridge, *Moving Words*; Tucker, "Unsettled Scores"; Noudelmann, *Penser avec les oreilles*; Perloff and Dworkin, eds., "Introduction," in *Sound of Poetry*, 1.

7. For this particular wordplay, see Frank, "Paronomasia," 209–15.

8. Frank, "Late OE *þrymnys* 'Trinity.'"

9. On the etiquette of initial light half-lines, see Stanley, "Oldest English Poetry," 128–29.

10. ÆCHom I, 31. In *Ælfric's Catholic Homilies, First Series*, 450, lines 323–24.

11. Isidore of Seville, *Etymologiarum libri*. Also *"Etymologies" of Isidore of Seville*, trans. Barney et al.

12. Metal mail-shirts developed from leather cuirasses: things change but names stay the same. Cf. "clothes-iron," "ice-box," "university." See Frank, "Reading *Beowulf* with Isidore's Etymologies."

13. On Isidore's *Etymologies* in Leofric's inventory of donations to Exeter, see Connor, *Anglo-Saxon Exeter*, 1–11.

14. See, e.g., Pfeifer, "Early Anglo-Saxon Glossaries"; Lapidge, "An Isidorian Epitome"; Porter, "Isidore's *Etymologiae* at the School of Canterbury"; Howe, "Aldhelm's *Enigmata* and Isidorian Etymology"; Salvador-Bello, *Isidorian Perceptions of Order*; Hawk, "Isidorian Influence in Ælfric's Preface to Genesis"; Hussey, "Dunstan, Æthelwold, and Isidorean Exegesis in OE Glosses," 682; O'Camb, "Isidorean Wolf Lore." Nineteen full or partial Anglo-Saxon manuscripts of the *Etymologies* survive, at least eleven of which were in England before the Norman Conquest; see Lapidge, *Anglo-Saxon Library*, 311. For knowledge of Isidore in Iceland, see the database at http://islandialatina.hum.ku.dk, s.v. "Etymologiarum libri XX." Large sections of the work are translated in the ON paraphrase of the Pentateuch known as *Stjórn*. On manuscripts of the *Etymologiae* in Norway, see Karlsen, "Fragments," 229–30.

15. Firth, *Papers in Linguistics*, 11.

16. See now Males, *Poetic Genesis*, esp. pp. 20–37, on the evolution of *dróttkvætt* internal rhymes from laxness and license to strictness and regularity by the turn of the millennium.

17. Snorri Sturluson, *Háttatal*. See Hollander, "Observations on Skaldic Rime Usage," 893–95. Kahle, *Die Sprache der Skalden*, offers a partial dictionary of *dróttkvætt* full and half-rhymes. For an overview, Kuhn, "Geschichte des skaldischen Innenreims."

18. *Skothending* (or half-, slant-, para-rhyme) involves two syllables participating in partial internal rhyme: the vowels are different but their postvocalic environments are similar: e.g., leader/header, kick/back, Howdy-Doody, struts/frets. Some *skothendingar* also alliterate: sing-song, ding-dong, pitter-patter, Auden's "midden . . . madden," "fearer to farer," and "hearer to horror" ("Epilogue" to *The Orators*; *English Auden*, 110).

19. ÚlfrU *Húsdr* 4/1–2, ed. Marold; *SkP* 3.1:413.

20. De Vries, *Altnordisches etymologisches Wörterbuch*, s.v. *stirðr, storð* (**ster*).

21. ÚlfrU *Húsdr* 5/1–2, ed. Marold; *SkP* 3.1:414.

22. Þjóð *Haustl* 12/7–8, ed. Clunies Ross; *SkP* 3.1:449.

23. Bragi *Rdr* 4/7–8, ed. Clunies Ross; *SkP* 3.1:33.

24. See Holtsmark, "Gevjons plog," 173.

25. Bragi Frag 1/3–4, ed. Clunies Ross; *SkP* 3.1:54.

26. Bragi *Þórr* 5/3–4, ed. Clunies Ross; *SkP* 3.1:51.

27. Further examples of Bragi's rhymes tying together couplets: *Rdr* 2/1–2, 4/5–6, 5/5–8, 9/7–8, 11/5–6, *Þórr* 2/3–4. Þjóðólfr ór Hvini's poem *Haustlǫng* (Norway, ca. 900) has a comparable supply of rhyming couplets: 2/3–4, 4/1–2, 4/7–8, 7/7–8, 9/1–2, 12/7–8, 15/3–4, 19/3–4. On the skald Gísli Súrsson's predilection for rhyme across the odd and even verses of a couplet, see Myrvoll, "Authenticity of Gísli's Verse," 229–37.

28. The OE cluster consists of *lif* 'life,' *leof* 'beloved,' *lof* 'praise,' *lufu* 'love,' *lufian* 'to love,' *geleafa* 'belief,' *geliefan* 'believe,' *leaf* 'permission,' *leaf* 'leaf,' and their relatives and satellites (e.g., *lofsum, liðe, lofian, lissum, libban, leod*). See Kintgen, "*Lif, Lof, Leof, Lufu,* and *Geleafa*"; Borroff, "Systematic Sound Symbolism"; Creed, "*Beowulf*-Poet: Master of Sound Patterning."

29. ÞKolb *Eirdr* 11/1–4, ed. Carroll; *SkP* 1.1:504.

30. Viking-age examples of the linkage include Anon *Liðs* 8/3, Arn *Hardr* 11/3, Arn *Magndr* 13/4–5 (linking two helmings), Arn *Þorfdr* 5/1, ESkál *Vell* 11/1, Glúmr *Gráf* 5/1, Hfr *ErfÓl* 5/3, *Hókr* Eirfl 8/1, Sigv *Austv* 14/7, Sigv *Víkv* 5/8, Steinn *Óldr* 15/1, ÞKolb *Eirdr* 13/7, Þhorn *Gldr* 6/5, ÞjóðA *Magn* 8/7.

31. For an overview, see Kuhn, *Das Dróttkvætt*, 272–311.

32. A skaldic half-stanza from ca. 1030 boasting two full rhyming pairs in every line further develops this scheme: Refr *Giz* 3, ed. Marold et al.; *SkP* 3:256.

33. Þhorn *Gldr* 6/1–4, ed. Marold et al.; *SkP* 1.1:85; also ibid., 8/1–2 and 3–4:88. Snorri Sturluson calls this rhyming technique *dunhent* 'echoing rhyme'; see *Háttatal* 'Enumeration of Verse Forms,' 24, ed. Gade; *SkP* 3.2:1130–31; also *Háttalykill inn forni* 'The Old Key to Verse Forms,' 65–66, ed. Gade; *SkP* 3.2:1073–75. On *Glymdrápa*, its stanzas and attribution, see Abram, "Scribal Authority."

34. Þhorn *Gldr* 6/5–8, ed. Marold et al.; *SkP* 1.1:85. *Prúðr* is a loanword, borrowed directly or indirectly from French; cf. late OE *prud/prut*.

35. The meaning of the byname *skálaglamm* is uncertain. Cf. OE *healgamen* 'hall-entertainment,' 'hall-sport' (*Beo* 1066): *Kl* 4 n; Weiskott, "Three *Beowulf* Cruces." For discussion of Einarr's rhymes, see Kuhn, "Vor tausend Jahren," 303–4.

36. ESkál *Vell* 1/1–4, ed. Marold et al.; *SkP* 1.1:283.

37. Ibid., st. 5/3–4, 289.

38. Ibid., st. 8/3–4, 292.

39. Ibid., st. 10/7–8, 295.

40. Wolfson, "Reading for Form," 6.

41. Gretsch, *Intellectual Foundations*, esp. 420–23. ON *prúðr* 'brave, magnificent' and the anagogical *prýði* 'bravery, ornament' enter *dróttkvætt* verse in the first half of the eleventh century.

42. D. R. Howlett, *British Books*, 268–69, locates a more complex series of rhymes in *Cædmon's Hymn*.

43. Bede, *Ecclesiastical History*, 4.24, 416.

44. Noted by Shippey, *OE Verse*, 120–21.

45. On phonesthemes (a sound sequence and its associated meaning), see Magnus, *Gods of the Word.* On phonosemantics, see Westcott, "Linguistic Iconism"; Firth, "Use and Distribution of Certain English Sounds"; Genette, *Mimologiques*; Hinton, *Sound Symbolism*; and Malkiel, *Diachronic Problems in Phonosymbolism.* For OE, see Reinhard, *Alliterative Collocations in "Beowulf"*; Griffith, "Extra Alliteration," 96–104. Self-rhyming compounds such as *sondlond* 'sandy shore' (or *waroþfaruþ* 'surf-strand,' *And* 197a) are rare in OE verse; most occur only once.

46. Tolkien, *OE Exodus*, 71, singled out the "noisy exaggeration" of this tripartite rhyme for condemnation. See Stanley, "Rhymes in English Medieval Verse," 19–38, 53–54.

47. Orchard, *Critical Companion*, 210–11.

48. On circumspect speech in OE verse, see Stanley, "Courtliness," esp. 82–96. The piling up of syntactically disrupted kenning-elements for royalty in viking-age *dróttkvætt* panegyrics is observable in Þorbjǫrn hornklofi's ninth-century *Glymdrápa* (*SkP* 1.1:73–91); on vertical placement of vocative epithets in *dróttkvætt*, see Óttarr svarti's eulogies for Óláfr Haraldsson of Norway and Knútr Sveinsson of Denmark and England (*SkP* 1.2:739–83). Reichardt, *Studien*, 72; Gade, *Structure*, 205.

49. The chimes of this final verse may have inspired Henry of Huntingdon to end his Latin translation of *Brunanburh* with penultimate-syllable half-rhymes and etymological paronomasia: "**reg**es fuga**ver**unt **reg**na susce**per**unt." See Rigg, "Henry of Huntingdon's Metrical Experiments," 69–70; also Weiskott, *English Alliterative Verse*, 183–86.

50. E. G. Stanley, "Notes on OE Poetry," 330–34, would connect all three *hwilum*'s (864, 867, 917), forming what he calls a "sentence-monster." See Kluge, "Zur Geschichte des Reimes im Altgermanischen," 429–31, for comments on OE rhyme and skaldic *skothending*; Bredehoft, "OE and Old Saxon Formulaic Rhyme."

51. The meaning of OE *fealu* 'dun' is difficult to pin down; so, too, Lat. *fulvus* 'brown, tawny, sandy,' a word with which, although etymologically unrelated, it half-rhymes. See Ruff, "Aldhelm's Jewel Tones," 230–31. On the Danes' dun steeds, see Neville, "Hrothgar's Horses." Cf. *Helgakviða Hundingsbana* II 49.1–2 (Neckel-Kuhn, 160), whose hero rides a *fealu* horse to Valhöll: "*Mál er mér at ríða roðnar brautir / láta* ***fǫlvan*** *ió flugstíg troða*" (It's time for me to ride the reddened roadways, let the pale horse tread the flight-path).

52. On the homophonic attraction of OE *mann* 'man' to *man* 'sin,' see *ChristC* 1094, 1416, 1600, *GenA* 1271, *GenB* 297–99, 451; *GuthB* 909, *El* 626, *Jul* 459, *Beo* 110, 712, *MSol* 327, *PPs* 61.3.1, 61.9.1, 63.8.2, 139.4.3, *Met* 4.48.

53. On this pairing, see Ruggerini, "Alliterative Lexical Collocations," 317–21.

54. Hfr *Erf Ól* 8/1–2, ed. Heslop; *SkP* 1.1:413.

55. On the OE loanword *lagu* 'law,' see Pons-Sanz, *Lexical Effects*, 84–87, 157–59.

56. Many commentators, and perhaps the speaker of this poem, associate OE *giedd* with a root meaning "join" or "unite" (cf. *geador* 'together'); others derive

the word from a stem meaning "prayer, emotional state." For references, see Gwara, "Paradigmatic Wisdom," 786–87, who argues for a derivation related to "prediction, prophecy."

57. OE metathesis involving a mobile *r* or *l* is a breeder of half-rhymes: e.g., **firum** . . . **frea** (*CH* 9), ***fyrn*** *ge**frun**an* (*Men* 190a), ***frod*** *wæs se **fyrd**rinc* (*Mald* 140a), **wroht**es **wyrht**an (*Jul* 346a), ***stream**as stodon* ***storm*** *up gewat* (*Ex* 460), *on þæm **glæd**stede* ***gild*** *onsægde* (*GenA* 2843), *ond þam **werode wrað** þe he ær **wurðode*** (*GenA* 35).

58. On this curious pair, see Dance, "*Þær wearð hream ahafen.*"

59. Dance, "*Battle of Maldon* line 91."

60. Cynewulf paired *rod* 'the rood, cross' and *rodor* 'the heavens' fifteen times: *El* 147, 206, 482, 624, 631, 855, 886, 1022, 1066, 1074, 1234; *Jul* 305, 447; *ChristB* 727; the poet of *Rid* 55/8 also joined the two nouns. See Frank, "Uses of Paronomasia," 10.

61. IE **swen-* 'to sound': Holthausen, *Altenglisches etymologisches Wörterbuch*, s.vv. *swan, swinn, swinsian.* On *swan/swinsian*, see Frank, "Unbearable Lightness," 493–94. On European swan species, see Bitterli, *Say What I Am Called*, 38–39.

62. On the swan that sings when about to die, see Lactantius, *De ave Phoenice* 138.49; Dietrich, "Die Räthsel," 462. A flute carved from a swan's wing bone nearly 42,000 years ago in the Swabian Jura is the oldest musical instrument so far unearthed. See Hahn et al.,"Knochenflöten."

63. Cf. *Mald* 166: "**feoll** þa to **fol**dan **feal**o*hil*te swurd" (the dusky-hilted sword fell then to earth).

64. Cribbed from Geoffrey Hill, *Mercian Hymns*, 1, in which Offa basks in the flood of epithets with which he is addressed.

65. ESkál *Vell* 35/1–4, ed. Marold et al.; *SkP* 1.1:327.

66. Hókr *Eirfl* 7/6, ed. Gade; *SkP* 1.1:482. The identical line occurs in ESk Frag 8/2, ed. Gade; *SkP* 3.1:159. Both half-stanzas are showcased as *dróttkvætt* variants, *áttmælt* and *dunhent*, respectively.

67. Meissner, *Kenningar*, 119–23. On this unholy trio, see Jesch, "Eagles, Ravens and Wolves," and Jesch, *Ships and Men*, 247–52; also Fidjestøl, *Den norrøne fyrstediktet*, 200–203.

68. *Heita dýrbliks dynsæðinga*, Hfr *ErfÓl* 18/1–4, ed. Heslop; *SkP* 1.1:425. Within the half-stanza, the parts of this extended kenning are joined by enjambment, alliteration, and vertical stacking. See Gade, *Structure*, 202–8, 216–17.

69. See Griffith, "Convention and Originality," 189; Honegger, "Form and Function." Magoun, "Theme of the Beasts of Battle," listed twelve occurrences of the motif. Stanley, "OE Poetic Diction," 259–60, added several more; Neckel, "Die kriegerische Kultur," has fewer.

70. Þhorn *Harkv* 4/3, ed. Fulk; *SkP* 1.1:97.

71. Grani *Har* 2, ed. Gade; *SkP* 2.1:298.

72. *Hrafn* [*Eb* 33] 3/1–4, *SkP* 5 (forthcoming); *Skjd* B1, 196, 3/1–4.

73. OE *wine* and ON *vinr* are derived from PIE **wen* 'to love, wish, desire,' proto-Germanic **weniz* 'friend.' The English word retired before the fourteenth century, taking a (prosaic) last bow in the fifteenth. See Frank, "To Commemorate Friendship," 5.

74. For examples of these techniques, see Orchard, "Artful Alliteration." On the difficulties of classification, see Stanley, *In the Foreground*, 134–38. For the subdivision into categories, see Ross, "Philological Probability Problems," 32. The terms "crossed alliteration" (sometimes "cross-alliteration") and "transverse alliteration" are frequently confused; for clarification, see Terasawa, *OE Metre*, 18n4. Early studies include Emerson, "Transverse Alliteration," and C. Lewis, "Notes on Transverse Alliteration." See also Hutcheson, "Accidental Alliteration"; Bredehoft, "Estimating Probabilities"; Hieatt, "Alliterative Patterns"; Stanley, "Alliterative Ornament"; and Scragg, "The Nature of OE Verse," 62. See now Griffith, "Extra Alliteration."

75. R. Lewis, "OE Poetry: Alliteration and Structural Interlace," 597, lists twenty-three examples in *Beowulf*; also Lewis, "Plurilinear Alliteration." See, too, Pasternack, *Textuality of OE Poetry*, esp. 37, 124–26. For the use of sound repetitions in *dróttkvaett* verse to clarify sectional divisions, see Chase, "*Concatenatio*"; Poole, *Viking Poems*, 69–72. About half the stanzas in Arnórr Þórðarson's *Þorfinnsdrápa* (ed. Whaley, *SkP* 2.1:229–69) link couplets by means of extra alliteration. In Iceland today, the ability to hear alliteration means possessing a *brageyra* 'poetic ear': Kristján Árnason, "Alliteration."

76. Skeptics include Emerson, "Transverse Alliteration"; Horn, "Metrik des Heliand," 165–66; Sievers, *Altgermanische Metrik*, 41, § 41(d); Suzuki, *Metrical Organization*, 314.

77. Lawrence, *Alliterative Verse*, chap. 2, "Crossed Alliteration in *Beowulf*": "Close examination would, I am convinced, reveal a far greater wealth of alliteration and assonance in the verse of *Beowulf* than we notice in casual reading" (50).

78. Macrae-Gibson, ed., *OE Riming Poem*, 22n2.

79. Donka Minkova, *Alliteration and Sound Change*, 38.

80. Orchard, *Critical Companion*, 61–69, with bibliography.

81. The statistics and probability figures relied on by *Kl 4* are reexamined by Griffith, "Extra Alliteration," 73–76, 122, 131, and found wanting; for a complete list of OE verses with crossed alliteration on fully stressed syllables and on syllables bearing secondary stress, see Griffith, appendix 5, 170–75.

82. Kuhn, *Das Dróttkvætt*, 73. On the rich crossed and transverse alliterative designs in eddic verse, see section 7 in the introductory commentaries to individual poems in See et al., *Kommentar*.

83. Eyv *Hák* 6/7–8 and 7/1–2, ed. Fulk; *SkP* 1.1:180–82; both citations are in the eddic meter *málaháttr*. The alliterative staves (here AAB AB) are indicated in bold. Hákon góði 'the Good' Haraldsson, the Norwegian king commemorated, had been raised at the English court of king Æthelstan.

84. Bartlett, *Larger Rhetorical Patterns*, 17–18.

85. Auden, "Under Which Lyre: A Reactionary Tract for the Times" (Phi Beta Kappa Poem, Harvard, 1946), in Auden, *Collected Poems*, 339.

86. Gsind *Hákdr*, ed. Poole; *SkP* 1.1:155–70.

87. See, e.g., Hallfreðr's memorial ode to Óláfr Tryggvason, ed. Heslop, 16/1–2; *SkP* 1.1:422–24: "**Ó**grœðir sá **au**ða / **a**rmgrjóts Trana fljóta" (The non-increaser of arm-gravel [GOLD > GENEROUS RULER] saw Trani [ship-name] floating empty), with the two vertically placed compounds linking through crossed alliteration "increase" and "wealth"—in contrast to the empty ship. The two cross-alliterating compounds in Þjóðólfr ór Hvini's *Haustlǫng* 15/5–6 are similarly placed (ed. Clunies Ross; *SkP* 3.1:455–56): "þás **h**ofregin **h**afrar / **h**ógreiðar framm drógu" (then when the goats drove forward the temple-god of the pleasant chariot).

88. Bragi, *Rdr*, ed. Clunies Ross; *SkP* 3.1:26–46.

89. Þorm Lv, ed. Fulk; *SkP* 1.2:843–44. As in the Bragi excerpts, syllables in positions 2, 3, and 4 of even lines do not participate in the crossed alliteration.

90. Hallv *Knútdr*, ed. Townend; *SkP* 3.1:230–40. Crossed alliteration: 1/1–2, 2/1–2, 3/5–6, 4/3–4, 6/3–4, 6/7–8.

91. Ótt *Knútdr*, ed. Townend; *SkP* 1/2:767–83. Further examples of crossed alliteration in the nine complete stanzas and two half-stanzas of the poem: 2/1–2; 5/1–2; 6/1–2; 6/5–6; 10/1–2; 11/3–4.

92. Þhorn *Gldr*, ed. Marold et al.; *SkP* 1.1:73–91.

93. Cf. *Heiland* 3827; *Sie **qu**aðun that it **uu**ari **uu**erold **k**esures* (they said it was of the world-emperor).

94. "Epistola de Obitu Bedae" in Bede, *Ecclesiastical History*, ed. Colgrave and Mynors, 582–83. These lines, attributed to Bede on his deathbed (735), were noted by Wilberct and recorded by Cuthbert in his letter to Cuthwin. See Bredehoft, *Authors, Audiences*, 20–26.

95. Text from MS St Gallen, Stiftsbibliothet, Cod. Sang. 254, p. 253. See *DOE*, s.v. *hingang, heonangang*; Northumbrian *hiniongae* = West Saxon ***h**eonengange*. Of the four compounds in these five lines, the first three are restricted to verse (*neidfaerae* is a *hapax legomenon*). See O'Donnell, "*Cædmon's Hymn*," 78–97.

96. Brandl, *Geschichte der altenglischen Literatur*, 1032.

97. Stanley, "Oldest English Poetry," 18.

98. Although edited as the second line of the poem, the first line concludes with a point, as if it were a heading: "and now for a fitt about fish."

99. Recent studies combine Riddle 76 with 75 (also set out in the MS as a one-liner); see Williamson, *OE Riddles*, 110 (no. 73); Wilcox, "Tell Me What I Am"; Niles, *OE Poems*, 96–100.

100. Song by Gus Kahn, memorably adapted by Dorothy Parker: "Take me or leave me; or, as is the usual order of things, both" (*New Yorker*, February 4, 1928).

101. The *Beo* citation includes the half-rhymes *þin-/mon-*, *mæg/þeg-*, ***g**yfan/**s**efan*; similarly, *mor-/mær-* in *Brun* 14.

102. Orchard, *Critical Companion*, 66–67, notes that the last two lines of *Beowulf* (3181–82) combine precisely repeated rhythms, stacked vertically.

103. Bergman, "Supplement," 13; Gretsch, *Intellectual Foundations*, 78–79, 129–30, 309–10. Also Bredehoft, *Authors, Audiences*, 114–15; Weiskott, *English Alliterative Verse*, 59–60; Toswell, *Anglo-Saxon Psalter*, 266–67. Cited also by Roberts, "Some Anglo-Saxon Psalters," 51; Leneghan, "Making the Psalter Sing," 175. The Latin gloss: "Omnis rex in antiquis diebus aput Iudeos nominabatur Christus." Ker, *A Catalogue*, no. 249; Gneuss and Lapidge, *Anglo-Saxon Manuscripts*, no. 451.

104. On *Iudeum* alliterating with *g*, cf. *And* 12, 966, 1408; *El* 216, 278, 288, 328, 976, 1202; *ChristB*, 637; *PPs* 75.1.1.

105. The MS reads "beowulf" (18a), not "Beow"; if unemended, the line would exhibit crossed alliteration (*b–w/b–w*). Line 18b toggles ambiguously between Sievers-Bliss Types D2 and E; Cable, "Metrical Simplicity," supported merging the two types. *Kl* 4, 113n, classifies 18b as D4; *Kl* 4, 336, as E. (Klaeber had "D4" in both places.) See Terasawa, *OE Metre*, 43–44; Weiskott, *English Alliterative Verse*, 25.

106. Bredehoft, "Estimating Probabilities," 21.

107. Crossed alliteration involving two compounds occurs again in *Beo* 236: ***m**ægen**w**udu **m**undum* *__m__eþel__w__ordum frægn.*

108. Two later crossed alliterations in *Beo* 1341–42 set off a parenthetical couplet from its surrounding matrix, as crossed alliteration appears to do here. Ships seem to attract extra alliteration: e.g., ***h**ilde**w**æpnum ond **h**eaðo**w**ædum* (*Beo* 39); ***b**unden**st**efna ofer **b**rim**st**reamas* (*Beo* 1910), and ***h**ringed**st**efnan, **h**olm **st**orme weol* (*Beo* 1131).

109. See Clover, "Germanic Context"; Parks, *Verbal Duelling*. Hostile coast guard dialogues include those between the well-born Guðmundr (on shore) and the ship-steering hero Sinfiǫtli in the eddic *Helgakviða Hundingsbana I*, sts. 32–44; also *Helgakviða Hundingsbana II*, sts. 19–24, and *Helgakviða Hiǫrvarðssonar*, sts. 12–30.

110. See Hofmann, *Lehnbeziehungen*, 142; Suzuki, *Metre of Old Saxon Poetry*, 263; *Kl* 4, 137; Frank, "Conversational Skills," 35–36.

111. For a complete list of enjambed alliteration, see Griffith, "Extra Alliteration," appendix 4, 166–170. Also Bjork, "Speech as Gift in *Beowulf*," 1012.

112. Griffith, "Extra Alliteration," 128.

113. The spelling *chludun* represents *hludon*. See Schlosser, *Althochdeutsche Literatur*; also *Kl* 4, 341.

114. See now Griffith, "Extra Alliteration," appendix 2, 161–65. Le Page, "Alliterative Patterns," 437, concluded that the *Beowulf* poet avoided having two consecutive lines with the same main alliteration.

115. The OE poetic corpus boasts several runs of continued *w*-alliteration over three lines: *GenA* 35–37, 1014–16; *Soul I* 82–84; *GuthB* 1363–65; *Rid* 40.47–9; *PPs* 85.7.3–8.2, 91.6.4–6, 101.23.2–4, 118.14.1–3, 151.1–152, 127.2.3–3.2. For a complete list of continued consonant alliteration in the corpus extending through three lines, see now Griffith, "Extra Alliteration," notes 192–93 and appendices 2 and 6.

116. *Byrne*, *beorgan*, and *breost*, apparent cognates, join a fourth, *beorh* 'barrow,' in Beowulf's command to his men: "Gebide ge on *beor*ge *byr*num *wer*ede" (Wait here, protected by byrnies, on the barrow) (*Beo* 2529).

117. Rieger, "Die alt- und angelsächsische Verskunst," 21, suggested reversing the order of the words in the second half-line. Also *Kl* 4, appendix C §41. This particular transverse alliteration in *Beowulf* is generally recognized by metrists; verses classified as Sievers's A3, such as ***Hw**ilum he on **l**ufan* *læteð **hw**orfen* (1728) and ***hw**earf þa be **w**ealle,* *wæpen **h**afenade* (1573), both of which exploit the *hw*-cluster phonestheme associated with whirling, winding, wheeling, and encircling, might be added to the list.

118. See Cavell, *Weaving Words*, 51. On verses apparently featuring both double and crossed alliteration (e.g., ***l**eoda **l**andgeweorc* *laþum beweredon*, "protected the people's stronghold from foes"; *Beo* 938), see Stanley, *In the Foreground*, 134–38.

119. Starobinski, *Les mots sous les mots.*

120. Thornbury, *Becoming a Poet*, 165–67.

121. Le Page, "Alliterative Patterns," 439, concludes on this evidence that the *Beowulf* poet was the more accomplished craftsman.

122. Orchard, "Artful Alliteration," 442–45.

123. Griffith, "Extra Alliteration," 119–20n235.

124. Griffith, "The Register of Divine Speech," 66–67.

125. Ibid., 78 and n46.

126. Reinhard, *Alliterative Collocations in Beowulf*, 237.

127. See esp. Griffith, *Judith*; also Bredehoft, *Early English Metre*, 63–66.

128. Frank, "Late OE *þrymnys* 'Trinity,'" 106n17. On the *lorica* form, Hill, "Invocation of the Trinity."

129. On *fyrn-/fyren*, see Robinson, "A Sub-Sense"; also Zacher, "Cynewulf at the Interface," 366–69. On the *w–r* and *f–r* transpositions in lines 346–47, see Robinson, "Metathesis in the Dictionaries."

130. Cited from Roger Pearson in Marina Warner, "Who Can Shave an Egg? Beckett, Mallarmé, and Foreign Tongues," *Raritan* 27, no. 4 (2008): 72–73.

131. See now Griffith, "Extra Alliteration," appendix 5c, 173.

132. *Weorces* replaces *siðes* in *El* 848. The signed poems as a group repeat favorite half-rhymes and alliterations, e.g., swa **lif** swa d*eað*, swa þe **leof**re b*ið* (*ChristB* 596, *El* 606).

133. Weiskott, "OE Poetry, Verse by Verse," 104–5.

134. Chaucer reserves alliteration for extended battles scenes, that of Actium in the *Legend of Good Women* (lines 629–52) and the tournament in the *Knight's Tale*, here and in 1:2612: "He thurgh the thikkeste of the throng gan threste" (*Riverside Chaucer*, ed. Benson, 60).

135. Orchard, *Poetic Art of Aldhelm*, 46.

136. ÞKolb *Eirdr* 11/5–6, ed. Carroll; *SkP* 1.1:504.

137. Hfr *ErfÓl* 12/5–8, ed. Heslop; *SkP* 1.1:417.

138. Ótt *Knútdr* 10/1–2, ed. Townend; *SkP* 1.2:779.

139. Cnut may have paid fifty marks for a poem, an amount equivalent to two hundred cows. For the calculation, see Fidjestøl, "Har du høyrt eit dyrare kvæde?," 62.

140. See Starobinski, "Lettres et syllabes mobiles," 8: To establish "the glory of a name," its elements can be "mobilized . . . as if the reordering of the letters and the phonemes in a name better twisted the branches of the crown belonging to the subject of praise."

141. Arn *Þorfdr* 9, ed. Whaley; *SkP* 2.1:240–41. The adverbial phrase *til þinga* 'to the meeting [battle]' can be taken with either sentence in the half-stanza or both. The reading here follows Kock, *Notationes Norrœnæ*, §830. This spelling out through alliterative staves of the honoree's name may be serendipitous, just as "typewriter" is the longest English word able to be written on the top row of a QWERTY keyboard. As someone in a Claude Chabrol film once said, "Chance exists—and it is fantastic" (stolen from Miller, *Hidden Hitchcock*, 17).

142. Arnórr elsewhere sprinkles *s* words among *sk-* and *st-*cluster alliterations and vice versa, esp. in his opening couplets: e.g., *Rǫgndr* 3/1-2: *s* [*st*] *s s*; *Þorfdr* 1/1–2: *s s s* [*st*]; 7/1–2: *sk sk sk*, 7/5–6: *st st st* [*s*]; 21/7–8: *sk sk* [s] *sk st*; *Hryn* 13/1–2: *sk sk sk* [*s*]; *Magndr* 15/1–2: *s s s* [*st*]; ed. Whaley, *SkP* 2.1:181, 231, 237, 254, 198, 225. His contemporary Þjóðólfr Arnórsson regularly exploits this device: cf. *Magnfl* 9/1–2; ed. Whaley, *SkP* 2.1:74: "**Sk**otit frák **sk**eptiflettum / **sk**jótt ok mǫrgu **sp**jóti (. . . á breiða **sk**jǫldu)" (I learned that shafted weapons and many a spear were shot sharply . . . onto broad shields).

143. Morgan, *A Vision of Cathkin Braes*, in *Collected Poems*; Meredith, *Partial Accounts*, 5.

144. Headley, trans., *Beowulf* (New York: Farrar, Strauss and Giroux, 2020), 26; the immediately preceding and following lines include *sk-* and *st-*clusters.

145. Cf. the *sc-/s-* chains in *Sat* 308, *Dan* 263, *ChristC* 1273.

146. Frank, "Discreet Charm," 249.

147. Nonalliterating *s*-clusters in lines alliterating on *s* (and vice versa) occur throughout the verse corpus. The *Beowulf* poet's lead-in to the Sigemund story includes *sp-* and *st-* patterns (*__s__weordum ge__s__æged.   __S__igemunde ge__sp__rong*, 884; *__s__ið Beowulfes   __s__nyttrum __st__yrian*, 872), and also the poem's sole alliteration on the *sp-*cluster (873). Similar *s-/st-* chains occur in adjoining poems in the Exeter Book: e.g., *__s__igora __s__ellend.   Þæt wæs __s__wete __st__enc* (*Pan* 64) and *__s__wimmað __s__undhwate   þær se __s__weta __st__enc* (*Whale* 57).

148. On the origin and author of this ditty, see Jones, *Fossil Poetry*, 271.

149. Arn *Þorfdr* 21/7–8, ed. Whaley; *SkP* 2.1:254.

150. Sigv *Erlfl* 1/5–8, ed. Jesch; *SkP* 1.2:631.

151. Ibid., 3/3–6; 633.

152. Ibid., 4/3–4; 634.

153. Chaucer, *Canterbury Tales*, "Parson's Prologue," 43; *Riverside Chaucer*, ed. Benson, 287.

154. Classen, *Vowel Alliteration*, 25, who observed that double alliteration tends to be rarer in a-verses with vowel alliteration. Also Salmon, "Anomalous Alliteration."

155. *Snorri Sturluson. Edda. Háttatal*, ed. Faulkes, 4. Pope, *Eight OE Poems*, 3rd ed., rev. Fulk, 133, and Terasawa, *OE Metre*, 16, observe that poets avoided alliteration on identical vowels. *Dróttkvætt* skalds support Snorri's preference. Only 9 of the 284 couplets in Einarr Skúlason's *Geisli* (ca. 1153) alliterate on the same vowel (sts. 5, 9, 37, 50, 54, 58, 63, 67), and in five of these occurrences the vowel is followed by a nasal. (The First Grammarian, working in the same decades, distinguished nasalized vowels from their nonnasalized counterparts.) In the 100 stanzas of Snorri's *Háttatal*, all three alliterating vowels in a couplet are dissimilar 85 percent of the time. See Hollmérus, *Studier över allitterationen*; Jakobson, "Vowel Alliteration in Germanic Verse." This contrasts with the situation in the Old Saxon *Heliand*, which repeats like vowels in lines with vocalic alliteration; see Mayer, "Die vokalische Allitteration im Heliand"; Lehmann, *Alliteration of Old Saxon Poetry*, 15.

156. Alliteration on same vowel twice: *Beo* 248, 421, 425, 637, 655, 732, 761, 835, 869, 928, 955, 1185, 1324, 1328, 1356, 1529, 1547, 1679, 1717, 1727, 1740, 1753, 1787, 2042, 2111, 2248, 2506, 2535, 2763, 2790, 2876, 2896, 3010, 3063, 3166. In *Deor*, *Brunanburh*, and *Waldere*, vowel alliteration always involves different vowels; in *Widsith*, twenty-eight examples of vowel alliteration link different vowels; three do not: the exceptions are lines 83 and 87, a section often declared interpolated, and line 35, where one of the two vowels was probably nasalized. The *Christ* and *Guthlac* poems alliterate across the caesura on the same vowel; so, too, *Elene* and *Dream of the Rood*.

157. *Eal* 'all' alliterates with *eald-* in *Beowulf* when a scop recalls ancient stories: *se ðe* ***eal****fela* ***eal****dgesegena . . .* (869); see, too, the pen-trial in the margin of London, BL, Harley 208, fol. 88: "hwæt ic eall feala ealde sæge." Ker, *Catalogue of Manuscripts*, item 229, 304; Opland, *Anglo-Saxon Oral Poetry*, 186; Orchard, "Word Made Flesh," 309; Weiskott, *English Alliterative Verse*, 208n11.

158. The other examples of (possible) triple *ea* alliteration all involve *eal*: *GenA* 1191: *eafora eahtahund* ***ealra*** *hæfde*; *PPs* 131.8.2: *þu earce eart* ***eall****haligra.*

159. Purvis's rendering of *Beowulf* places Grendel's arm indoors in a specified location: "The scraps of shoulder they placed under Heorot's vaulted roof, along a beam braced above the throne" (40). Others place the limb outside, within sight of the *stapol* (perhaps) 'stone pedestal.'

160. See Lockett, "Role of Grendel's Arm."

161. The phrase "enjambment of alliteration" is from Campbell, *Brunanburh*, 32. Orchard, "Artful Alliteration," 443, calls this feature "strong-linked alliteration"; Terasawa, *OE Metre*, 19, "linked alliteration"; others, "continued alliteration." For clarification of terminology, see now Griffith, "Extra Alliteration," 70–72.

162. Skalds likened alliteration to ship construction: Kreutzer, *Die Dichtungslehre*, 246–63; Sayers, "Scarfing the Yard with Words"; Clunies Ross, *History of*

ON Poetry, 87 and 201n11, translates the relevant section of chapter 15 of the second section of Óláfr Þórðarson's *Third Grammatical Treatise*. See Krömmelbein, *Dritte grammatische Abhandlung*, 186.

163. Sigvatr's two stanzas with *p*-alliteration are Sigv *Víkv* 8/7–8, ed. Jesch; *SkP* 1.2:546–47; and Sigv *Nesv* 15/7–8, ed. Poole; *SkP* 1.2:578. In Sigv *Víkv* 14/8, 554, the nonalliterating place-name *Peitu* 'Poitou' supports a full rhyme: "in the settled land—the town is so named [*heit-*]—of Poitou." The parenthetical insert supplying the rhyme seems comic in its desperation, but it resembles an OE naming construction with *hatan* (ON *heita*); see Mitchell, *OE Syntax*, I, 616–19, and Bately, "Place Which Is Called 'at X,'" 343–45. In Sigv *Austv* 12/2, ed. Fulk; *SkP* 1.2:600, and ÞjóðA *Har* 2/4, ed. Whaley; *SkP* 2.1:151, the (nonalliterating) loan-adjective *prúðar* 'elegant, proud' in final position supports a full rhyme; in contrast, the skald Arnórr places the ON place-name *Péttlandsfjǫrðr* 'Pentland Firth' (commemorating the Picts and recorded here for the first time) in the center of an even line, ensuring that the *p*-syllable neither alliterates nor rhymes (Arn *Þorfdr* 21/2, ed. Whaley, *SkP* 2.1:254).

164. On this Easter imagery, see Poole, "*Cyningas sigefæste þurh God*," 269–70.

165. Text from Gwara, "Record of Anglo-Saxon Pedagogy"; *Aldhelmi Opera Omnia*, ed. Ehwald, 488. Translation by Herren, *Aldhelm: Prose Works*, 160. Also Orchard, *Poetic Art of Aldhelm*, 36–37.

166. Lapidge, "Theodore and Anglo-Latin Octosyllabic Verse," 240; Lapidge, "School of Theodore and Hadrian," 46–47. Orchard, *Poetic Art of Aldhelm*, 30; additional examples of *p*-alliteration at 113–14.

167. The run of *p*-alliteration in the Latin analogue to *Andreas* has no counterpart in the OE poem; see Orchard, "Originality of *Andreas*," 343. My gratitude to Scott Barker for introducing me to the Renaissance Latin poem *Pugna porcorum* (1530), each word of whose 248 dactylic hexameter lines begins with the letter *p*. See John Placentius, *The Pig War*, ed. and trans. Michael Fontaine (New York: The Paideia Institute, 2019).

168. Skalds before Sigvatr placed *p*-words in nonalliterating positions; cf. *Svǫlnis sal-penningr* 'the penny of Óðinn's hall' = shield (Bragi *Rdr* 12/2, ed. Clunies Ross; *SkP* 3.1:46), with *penningr* perhaps ultimately from Latin. Two vernacular *p*-words are primary alliterative staves in *Mald* 68: the river name Pante and the noun *prass* 'pomp, array,' both probably Latin in origin but sometimes given Welsh ancestry; see Ekwall, *English River-Names*, 319–20; Breeze, "*Maldon* 68." *Prass* occurs four times in late homiletic prose: ÆLS (Maccabees) 302; ÆLS (Denis) 208; LS 34 (Seven-Sleepers) 23; HomU 27 (Nap 30) 181. See Kuhn, "Anlautend *p*-" [1961, 1969].

169. The ellipsis represents the word *walas*, whose presence disrupts the meter. A dark herdsman is mentioned earlier in the riddle, and dark-haired Celts/slaves (including one with restless hands) appear in an earlier ox-enigma (12/4, 8). On slavery in the OE riddles, see Pelteret, *Slavery in Early Mediaeval England*, 51–53; Wyatt, *Slaves and Warriors*, 240–41; Irving, "Heroic Experience," 207–8; Denno, "Oppression and Voice"; Cavell, *Weaving Words*, 157–91.

170. Urquhart, *Underpainter*, 9.

171. Overing, "*Beowulf*: A Poem in Our Time," 311–17.

172. Neville, "Fostering the Cuckoo," 434.

173. Cavell, *Weaving Words*, 159–63; Bitterli, *Say What I Am Called*, 26–34; Tupper, *Riddles of the Exeter Book*, 93. Latin ox-riddles occur in the *Enigmata* of Aldhelm and Eusebius, in the *Lorsch Riddles* and the *Collectanea* of Pseudo-Bede. See von Erhardt-Siebold, *Die lateinischen Rätsel der Angelsachsen*; also Orchard, "Enigma Variations," esp. 297–99.

174. Mize, *Traditional Subjectivities*, 12.

175. Letter from Breslau to Sophie Liebknecht before December 24, 1917, in *Letters of Rosa Luxemburg*, ed. Georg Adler, Peter Hudis, and Annelies Laschitza, trans. George Shriver (London and New York: Verso, 2011), 453.

176. Anne Carson, *Economy of the Unlost*, 99.

177. The word *kærr* 'dear' is from Old French; *keisari*, from Latin via OE or German; *klúss* 'close,' ultimately from Latin via OE, French, or German (Sigv *Knútdr* 10/7–8, ed. Townend; *SkP* 1.2:661–62). Nonalliterating *p* remains the rule in longer *dróttkvætt* poems. The anonymous twelfth-century *Plácitusdrápa* 'Poem about Plácitus' invariably places that saint's name in the third and fourth syllables of an even line, where it neither alliterates nor rhymes; see Anon *Pl*, ed. Louis-Jensen and Wills; *SkP* 7.1:182–220, sts. 11, 18, 25, 34, 35, 40, 42, 44, 47, 50, 59.

178. Nuttin, "Narcissism."

179. Baden-Powell confesses this in his awkwardly named *Scouting for Boys*, pt. 1 (London: H. Cox, 1908).

180. Cited by Griffith, "Alliterative Licence," 72. Camden, *Remaines*, 55. The skald Egill Skallagrímsson repeatedly plays on the name of his friend Arinbjǫrn 'stonehearth-bear,' calling him *grjótbjǫrn* 'gravel-bear,' *arnstalls sjǫtulbjǫrn* 'eagle's crag (stone-) abode-bear,' and *birkis ótta bjóð-bjǫrn* 'birch's terror (fire's) table (stone-hearth)-bear': *Skj* B1, 40 (sts 16, 17), *Skj* B1, 48, st. 27.

181. William of Malmesbury, *Gesta Regum Anglorum*, 1:238 (bk. 2, chap. 147).

182. The poet's much discussed reference to a wicked queen—*mod**þryðo** wæg / fremu folces **cwen***, (perhaps) "the bold queen of the nation acted arrogantly" (*Beo* 1931–32)—may similarly play on the elements of a name such as Cwenthryth.

183. Cited by Bloomfield, "Stylistics," 281.

184. Frank, "Uses of Paronomasia"; Orchard, "Artful Alliteration," and Orchard, *Critical Companion*, 61–69; Griffith, "Alliterative Licence," and Griffith, "Convention and Originality"; Robinson, "Sub-Sense of OE *fyrn*(-)"; Zacher, "Cynewulf at the Interface"; Stanley, "Playing upon Words, I and II"; Dance, "*Þær wearð hream ahafen*." On OE onomastic play, see Robinson, "Significance of Names," Robinson, "Personal Names," Robinson, "Anglo-Saxon Onomastics," and Robinson, "Uses of Name-Meanings." (The last four essays are also in Robinson, *Tomb of Beowulf*, 183–235.) Allen, "Name-Play and Structure"; Thornbury, "Ða Gregorius gamenode"; Whatley, "OE Onomastics"; Hill, "Ælfric's Use of Etymologies."

185. "Godric" was a Norman nickname for an Englishman; see Withycombe, *Oxford Dictionary*, 130–37.

186. "Alliterative Licence," 70.

187. Meissner, *Kenningar der Skalden*, 84; also Kuhn, *Das Dróttkvætt*, 111–13.

188. Eskál *Vell* 20/1–4, ed. Marold; *SkP* 1.1:307–8. The rhyming sequence *valdr* 'controller,' *vildi* 'wanted,' and *valmey* 'slaughter-maiden' culminates in line 4 with *velli* '(to hold the) field,' completing the circle of sound. The *h* of *heyja* (the initial of Einarr's patron Hákon) links the first couplet to the second through enjambed alliteration; the *valdr*, *vildi*, *val-* of the first couplet contribute by forming *skothendingar* with *haulda* and *halda* in line 3.

189. Korm Lv 64, *Skjd* B1, 85. See Bjarni Einarsson, *Skáldasögur*, 161.

190. E.g., ESk *Geisl* 17, 1–2; ed. Chase; *SkP* 7.1:21; Anon [TGT] 37, 1–2, ed. Wills; *SkP* 3.1:562; Sigv *ErfÓl* 10/7, ed. Jesch; *SkP* 1.2:677.

191. Lapidge, "Latin Poems as Evidence for the Reign of Athelstan," 72–73; Wieland, "New Look at the Poem 'Archalis clamare triumuir'"; Gallagher, "Latin Acrostic Poetry in Anglo-Saxon England." On the name-element *Æðel-*, see Colman, "Name-Element"; on the elements of OE dithematic names, see Colman, *Grammar of Names*, 105–25.

192. *Skjd* IB, 30; Sigurður Nordal, ed. *Egils saga*, 146–47, sts. 21–22. See Hofmann, *Lehnbeziehungen*, 24–25; Jesch, "Skaldic Verse in Scandinavian England," 316; Poole, "Anglo-Scandinavian Language and Literature," 582–84. Parsons, "Scandinavian Language," 307. Egill's stanza includes the first attestation of the ON word *harri* (OE *herra*).

193. Frank, "Lay of the Land," and Frank, "Marketing Odin's Mead," 251. On Ella/Ælle as the most frequently named Anglo-Saxon in skaldic court poetry, see Townend, "*Ella*."

194. Cf. Isidore, *Etym.* 16.18.1: "gold [*aurum*] is named from 'gleam' [*aura*], that is, from its luster."

195. Townend, "Pre-Cnut Praise Poetry," 356.

196. Keynes, "Declining Reputation," 240–41; Roach, *Æthelred the Unready*, 6–7. The nickname is first attested by Walter Map in the 1180s.

197. Ótt *Hfl* 13, ed. Townend; *SkP* 1.2:756–58. See Poole, "In Search of the Partar," 294.

198. A proximity search of the *DOE Corpus* finds more than a dozen such collocations, in poetry and prose. See Ruggerini, "Alliterative Lexical Collocations," 317–21. Hrothgar calls Æschere his *runwita* 'confidant' and *rædbora* 'counselor' (*Beo* 1325), while a *rædels* 'riddle' challenges *rynemenn* 'interpreters, those skilled in secrets' (*Rid* 42/13). See Paterson, "Phantom," in *Rain*, 55: "turn runic and unreadable again."

199. Robinson, "Significance of Names," 205.

200. On Guthlac, ibid., 206–12.

201. Robinson, "Uses of Name-Meanings," 229–30; Jerome, *Liber interpretationis hebraicorum nominum*, ed. P. de Lagarde, Corpus Christianorum, Series Latina 72 (Turnhout: Brepols, 1959), p. 142, lines 24–27.

202. The same formulaic half-line occurs in Cynewulfian saint's lives (*El* 455b, 462b, 662b; *Jul* 105b, 117b, 130b, 147b, 175b, 319b; *GuthB* 1163b, 1224b), but without a proper name in the a-verse; also *Mald* 44b. See Fulk, *History of OE Meter*, 208, who notes that this formula violates Kuhn's first law. Also Orton, "Anglo-Saxon Attitudes to Kuhn's Laws," 293.

203. Only lines 401 and 1345 do not name Andreas in the a-verse. God uses the past tense *ondswarode* 'answered' when replying to Andrew: 202, 260, 277, 290, 343, 510, 623, 925. The trisyllabic name "Andreas" occurs thirty-one times in the poem, twenty-five in the a-verse.

204. Possible crossed alliterations involving proper names include *GenA* 1114, 1257, 1423, 1914, 2008, 2407, 2491, 2905; *Ex* 124, 332, 352; *Dan* 167, 726, 735; *And* 691, 1513; *Fates* 51, 64; *El* 9, 21, 62, 250, 283, 492; *ChristA* 250; *GuthA* 188, 239, 449, 598, 781; *GuthB* 879, 1305; *Jul* 673; *Wid* 24, 26, 33, 44, 123; *Hell* 50, 103, 131; *Jud* 21, 253; *PPs* 86.1.2, 102.7.3, 105.15.2, 120.4.3, 124.5.4, 128.3.5, 131.1.1; *Met* 10.37; *Brun* 7, 20, 33; *Mald* 68, 255, 320; *Sat* 235; *MPrefPC* 9; *DEdg* 24; *Creed* 12, 23; *Men* 81; *KtPs* 1; *Dur* 13.

205. On the alliterating second elements of such proper names and the evidence of manuscript spacing, see Bredehoft, "Secondary Stress in Compound Names"; also Fulk, *History of OE Meter*, 191.

206. Both scribes separate the two elements of these dithematic names with a space, e.g., *hige lace* (2958); the (probably scribal) expansion *beowulf* (18) has no such space, but neither does *healfdenes* (2147).

207. "Illegitimate" transverse alliteration involving an (unstressed) verb, adverb, or pronoun in a Sievers's type A3 a-verse is rare—but audible when it occurs at the start of a sentence or fitt; see *Beo* 47, 535, 1184, 1482, 1573, 1728, 1732, 1892, 1933, 2020, 2053, 2158, 2377, 3058, 3164, and 3180. Cf. ***s****wilce þa ge****b****roþer* ***b****egen æt****s****amne* (*Brun* 57).

208. No a-verse in the corpus beginning with (*ge*)*cwæð* or (*ge*)*cwædon* forms transverse alliteration except *Beo* 2158 and 3180.

209. On last words, see Smith, *Poetic Closure*; Agamben, *End of the Poem*. On *lofgeornost*, see *Kl* 4, 271–72.

210. Ælfric notes the name change from *Abram* 'high father' to *Abraham* 'father of many nations,' and from *Sarai* 'my chief' to *Sarra* 'chief' (Ælfric, *Catholic Homilies, The First Series*, 1.6, "The Octaves and Circumcision of our Lord," 224–25). The OE *Exodus* poet alludes briefly to the patriarch's new name (381). Sulpicius Severus in his *Chronicon* ignores the name change, perhaps on the grounds that "Abraham" was most likely a dialectal variant of "Abram"; see Theo Vennemann, "Germania Semitica: **abr*- 'strong,'" *Sprachwissenschaft* 26 (2001): 85–92. Isidore,

noting the change, observes sagely that it is "not contained in the name, but understood" (*Etym.* 7.7.2). See Wright, "*Genesis A* ad litteram," 161. No comparable metrical cause for the *OE Genesis* poet's vagueness on Abraham's circumcision is discernible (*GenA* 2312–16). See Zacher, "Views on Circumcision in OE Literature," 110–11.

211. In addition to these citations, the (disyllabic) name Abraham attracts crossed alliteration in *GenA* 1891, 2751, and 2759; *GenA* 2261 and 2398, respectively, begin and end a fitt, settings in which extra ornamentation might be expected.

212. For background on the typology of Isaac's sacrifice, see, *inter alia*, Daniélou, *Sacramentum futuri*, 97–128. The Abraham of *GenA* is the only character in the poem associated through paronomasia with God the Father: *he is* ***god*** *and gleaw, mæg self wið* ***god*** *sprecan* ("he is good and wise, he can himself speak with God") (*GenA* 2658).

213. See Thornbury, "Light Verse," on the spirit of play and metrical inventiveness in OE and Anglo-Latin verse. For a recent edition and study of the *Menologium*, see Karasawa, *The OE Metrical Calendar.*

214. The poetic compound *yrmenþeod* is a *hapax legomenon* with relatives in *Beowulf* and in the inscription on the Karlevi Stone.

CHAPTER 3

1. This fishing expedition appears in multiple viking-age literary and visual sources. See Dronke, *Poetic Edda*, 94–100; Kopár, *Gods and Settlers*, 61–68; Jesch, *Viking Diaspora*, 142.

2. Cf. *ealuscerwen* 'ale-dispensing' (*Beo* 769), a compound that, as *Kl* 4 understatedly reports, "has provoked endless controversy" (161).

3. Homer, *Odyssey* 9.364–68 (Lattimore, trans., 135) ; Heller-Roazen, *No One's Ways*, chap. 1; Peradotto, *Man in the Middle Voice*; Dimrock, "Name of Odysseus"; Simpson, "*Odyssey* 9"; Horn, *Natural History of Negation.* Lewis Carroll plays with Alice's seeing nobody on the road: "I only wish I had such eyes," the king remarked in a fretful tone. "To be able to see Nobody! And at that distance too!" (*Alice's Adventures in Wonderland*, chap. 7).

4. Frequent use of "not-/un- + positive adjective" in modern translations of northern verse (e.g., "not unwilling" for OE/ON "unreluctant") obscures the absence of denied negatives in the original.

5. Quintilian, *Institutio oratoria* 10.1.12.

6. Erasmus, *Colloquia*, 617–18.

7. Fowler, *Dictionary*, 383.

8. Beowulf twice uses a negative in conjunction with an *un*-word employed in OE law codes. The hero's cautious verdict "Þy ic Heaðo-Bear[d]na hyldo **ne** telge, / dryhtsibbe dæl Denum **un**fæcne, / freondscipe fæstne" ("for that reason,

I do **not** consider the loyalty of the Heathobards, their part in the peace-alliance, **un**-deceitful [= sincere] toward the Danes, their friendship firm") (*Beo* 2067–69) is the sole use of *unfæcne/unfacne* in verse; the term signals "clear, straightforward" in the OE laws of Æthelberht of Kent ca. 600 (nos. 30 and 76 in Liebermann, *Gesetze*) and of Hloþhere and Eadric (685–86) (no.11 in Liebermann, *Gesetze*); see Oliver, *Beginnings of English Law*, 68–69, 78–79, 132. The second *un*-word used by Beowulf in a negative construction is OE *unriht* 'a wrong, injustice,' a "positive" term (like "unhappy") occurring 2,458 times in the corpus (including suffixed forms). Beowulf says: "I did not swear [***ne** me swor*] many oaths **on unriht** [wrongfully]" (*Beo* 2738b–39a); cf. OE *unlagu*; see Pons-Sanz, *Lexical Effects*, 86, 448.

9. Orwell, "Politics and the English Language," 131.

10. See Horn, "Lie-toe-tease." The introduction and notes of *Kl* 4 include numerous denied negatives ("not unknown," xliii, xcix), sometimes reinforced by a qualifying adverb ("not entirely unknown," cxxxiii, cxlviii). Instances include "a ship funeral not wholly unlike Scyld's" (312); equestrian cheek-ornaments "not wholly unlike decorations still used at horse-shows today" (179); a "manner not wholly unlike . . ." (lxix), a passage "not indisputably defective" (175), and the "not unlikely evidence of an archaic exemplar" (174). The hero of the poem is "not unlikely of Scandinavian origin" (l), while the editors "in not entirely dissimilar fashion" (clxxii) use phrases such as "not wholly regrettable" (cxxii), "not wholly inseparable" (clxxiii), and "not entirely unsympathetic" (170). Some things are "not altogether improbable" (120), others "not inherently improbable" (163), and still others "probably not much more improbable" (clxx). Denied negatives sound a note of diffidence or hesitancy, both cautious and knowing at the same time. An adjective such as "probable" that can fight its way through two negatives and a tough multisyllabic adverb ("not altogether improbable") is muscular indeed. Frege's dictum that "wrapping up a thought in double negation does not alter its truth value" may not be entirely unproblematic; see Frege, "Negation," 361.

11. Erasmus, *Colloquia*, 617–18. See Horn, *Natural History of Negation*, Horn, "Uncovering the Un-word," and Horn, "Multiple Negation in English." See also the essays in part 1 of Turner and Horn, *Pragmatics, Truth.*

12. Egill Skallagrímsson, *Arkv* 25 (*Eg* 121), *Skjd* A1, 48; B1, 41; Anon (*SnE*) 1, ed. Gade et al.; *SkP* 3.1:512–13.

13. *The Mueller Report: Report on the Investigation into Russian Interference in the 2016 Presidential Election*, by Special Counsel Robert S. Mueller III (2019).

14. On the sometimes intimate "you" relationship between skald and patron, see Marold, "Der Skald," 467–68.

15. This half-stanza survives only in Snorri's *Skáldskaparmál*, 1, 80; see *Skjd* B1, 254; Sigv Frag 1, ed. Whaley; *SkP* 3.1:347–49.

16. Liuzza, *Beowulf*, 54; see also Chickering, *Beowulf*, 9–10. Early studies of OE negation and understatement include Knörk, *Die Negation*; Schuchardt, *Die Negation*; Haber, *Comparative Study*, 34–36; Wärtli, *Stilistische Dämpfung*;

Bracher, "Understatement"; Shuman and Hutchins, "The *un*-Prefix"; Storms, "Subjectivity"; Liggins, "Irony and Understatement"; Harris, "Litotes and Superlative"; Schaefer, "Rhetoric and Style." Recent work includes Patterson, "Heroic Laconic Style"; Frank, "Incomparable Wryness," and Frank, "Conversational Skills"; Graham, "Emotion and Litotes." For Latin litotes, see Weyman, "Studien über die Figur der Litotes"; Hoffmann, *Negatio contrarii*. For medieval German, see Krause, *Litotes und ähnliche Figuren*; Hübner, *Die mhd. Ironie*.

17. Cicero to M. Fabius Gallus, *Epistulae ad familiares* 7.26.2; letter 210 in *Cicero's Letters to His Friends*, 1, 363–64.

18. Jesperson, *Negation in English*, 22.

19. Spoken by a French soldier in *Monty Python and the Holy Grail* (1975), and translated into Low Valyrian in *Game of Thrones* (Season 4, episode 3). On the conventionality of OE insults, see Chapman, "'You Belly-Guilty Bag.'"

20. Puttenham, *Arte of English Poesie*, 201.

21. Harmon and Holman, *Handbook to Literature*, 293.

22. Mitchell and Robinson, *Guide to Old English*, 8th ed., 269.

23. Stanley, *In the Foreground*, 195, and Stanley, "Narrative Art," 78.

24. The meaning of this half-line is disputed; see *Kl* 4, 206, and Mitchell, *OE Syntax*, 2, §3474.

25. Housman, *Collected Poems*, 236.

26. On metaphors that allude to violence in terms of a financial transaction (= making someone pay), see Frotscher, "Treasure and Violence."

27. O'Donoghue, "Owed to Both Sides." Mendelson, *Early Auden*, 42.

28. Use of the noun and adverb *lyt* 'little' (= 'no') increases in the course of the poem.

29. See Saltzman, *Bonds of Secrecy*, 154–58, on the efforts of early English saints to remove themselves from social media in order to keep the specifics of their holiness secret.

30. Wright, "More OE Poetry."

31. *Genesis B* fills a lacuna (lines 235–851) in *Genesis A*. The overlapping lines (791–817a) reveal a close verse-to-verse correspondence between the OE translation and its Old Saxon source.

32. *Byrhtferth, Lives of St Oswald and St Ecgwine*, 17.

33. Shanzer, "Frodebert's Tail," 397.

34. Kendall, "The Prefix *Un-*." Around 1,250 OE words have *un*-prefixes.

35. See Donoghue, "Seamus Heaney"; the Housman examples are extracted from *Collected Poems*.

36. E.g., Anon *Liðs* 3, Hfr *ErfÓl* 2, Sigv *Erlfl* 10, *ErfÓl* 16, *Knútdr* 9, 11, *Vestv* 3, Frag 1, 3–4, ÞKolb *Eirdr* 3. See Hollander, "Litotes in ON."

37. Jesch, "Skaldic Verse in Scandinavian England," 318; Poole, "Anglo-Scandinavian Language and Literature," 591–96. The so-called Copenhagen Wulfstan manuscript of Latin homilies (with annotations in the Archbishop's

hands) was sent to Denmark around 1020, shortly after its compilation. See Cross and Tunberg, *Copenhagen Wulfstan.*

38. Ed. Heslop, *SkP* 1.1:400–441.
39. Ed. Heslop, *SkP* 3.1:212–25.
40. Ed. Gade, *SkP* 1.1:469–85.
41. Ed. Carroll, *SkP* 1.1:486–513.
42. Ed. Gade, *SkP* 1.1:242–44.
43. Ed. Jesch, *SkP* 1.2:533–56.
44. Ed. Poole, *SkP* 1.2:556–78.
45. Ed. Whaley, *SkP* 3.1:347–50.
46. Ed. Fulk, *SkP* 1.2:578–614.
47. Ed. Jesch, *SkP* 1.2:629–43.
48. Ed. Townend, *SkP* 1.2:649–63.
49. Ed. Jesch, *SkP* 1.2:663–98.
50. Ed. Fulk, *SkP* 1.2:698–737.
51. Ed. Gade, *SkP* 2.1:11–30.
52. Ed. Townend, *SkP* 1.2:738–67.
53. Ibid., 767–83.
54. Ibid., 851–63.
55. Ed. Poole, *SkP* 1.2:1014–28.
56. *Þorfinnsdrápa* 1/2, ed. Whaley; *SkP* 2.1:231. On emotional responses to the death of kings, see Goeres, *Poetics of Commemoration.*
57. Swift, *Letter to a Young Gentleman*, 6.
58. Eil *Þdr* 14/6, ed. Marold et al.; *SkP* 3.1:105.
59. Earl, "Forbidden *Beowulf*."
60. See *Kl* 4, 291, for the *Chronicle* genealogy sub anno 856 identifying Bedwig (Beowi, MS D), "son of Sceaf [that is, son of Noah] who was born on Noah's ark." Also Hill, "Myth of the Ark-born Son of Noe"; Anlezark, "Sceaf, Japheth."
61. Kermode, *Sense of an Ending.* Also Saussy, "Jueju."
62. Commentators sometimes take these lines as a reference to a Danish vs. Heathobard feud, either Ingeld's assault on Heorot or his father's in the previous generation. Osborn notes that "three different occasions for such a fire are available in the traditions" ("Legends of Lejre," 252). Chambers, in his revision of Wyatt's *Beowulf*, took lines 82b–83a as an allusion to the burning of Hrothulf's hall in the course of Heoroweard's attack. For translations of the Scylding material, see Niles and Osborn, *Beowulf and Lejre*, 297–387; also Anon *Bjark*, ed. Clunies Ross; *SkP* 3.1:495–506. On the conflagration, see Saxo Grammaticus (*Gesta Danorum*, 1.2.7, lines 4–28, 122–41), who notes that he has "particularly composed this set of admonitory speeches in metre because the same thoughts and arguments, arranged within the compass of a Danish poem, are frequently recited from memory by many who are conversant with ancient deeds" (140–41).

63. Gísli Brynjúlfsson, "Oldengelsk og oldnordisk," 130; cited by Andersson, "Sources and Analogues," 130.

64. Grundtvig, "Et par ord"; cited by Shippey and Haarder, *Beowulf: Critical Heritage*, 108–13; Osborn, "Lejre Connection," 287–88.

65. Schrøder, *Om Bjovulfsdrapen*.

66. Olrik, *Danmarks heltedigtning: ein oldtidsstudie*; Chambers, *Beowulf*; Whitelock, *Audience of Beowulf*, 34–35; Brodeur, *Art of Beowulf*, 77n5; Osborn, "Legends of Lejre," 235. On narrative indirection in the retelling of these legends, see Frank, "*Beowulf* and the Intimacy of Large Parties."

67. "Legends of Lejre," 253. *Kl* 4 unaccountably omits Heoroweard from its Danish genealogical chart (lii).

68. Ollett, *Language of the Snake*, 7–8; Ingalls et al., *Dhvanyāloka of Ānandavardhana*, 83–92. See Martha Ann Selby, "Desire for Meaning: Providing Contexts for the Prākrit *Gāthās*," *Journal of Asian Studies* 55 (1996): 81–93. For implicature and verbal etiquette in classical Indian aesthetics, see Pollock, *A Rasa Reader*. I am indebted to Ross G. Arthur for these references.

69. I here follow the reading in Fulk, "Six Cruces," 353–54.

70. Ingeld (Hinieldus) is named in the "pagan song" to which the English poet and scholar Alcuin objected in his much-cited letter of 797; Dümmler, ed. MGH Ep. 4, 181–84, epist. 124. For context, Garrison, "Quid Hinieldus cum Christo?"; Poole, "Southern Perspectives on Starcatherus."

71. See Weber, "Sworn Swords."

72. On *unfæcne* 'clear, unblemished' as a legal term, see Oliver, *Beginnings of English Law*, 68–69, 78–79, 132. In *Beowulf*, the anonymous spear-warrior who does the inciting is *eald* 'old' (2042) with a *grim (se)fa* 'fierce mind' (2043); Starkaðr 'fierce battler' in *HHund I* 27 is *grimmúðgastr* 'most savage minded'; in *Málsháttakvæði* (ca. 1200) he is "not gentle in repose" (= savage): *Máls* 7/3, ed. Frank; *SkP* 3.2:1221. Perhaps hearers were to detect a suppressed name from its bearer's attributes; see O'Hara, *True Names*, 79–82.

73. See Chickering, *Beowulf*, 321–22. On rhetorical uses of OE hypermetric verse, see Hartman, *Poetic Style and Innovation*, 38–51.

74. Aristotle, *Rhetoric* 1405b 24–28 = Simonides, fragment, in Page, *Poetae Melici Graeci*, 515; Lefkowitz, *Lives of the Greek Poets*, 57.

75. Bragi *Rdr* 3, ed. Clunies Ross; *SkP* 3.1:31. Note that odd lines 1, 3, and 5 lack rhyme where classical *dróttkvætt* would have *skothending*, and line 2 has *skothending* instead of the full rhyme that by 1000 became the norm; only lines 4 and 8, each of which ends a half-stanza, have the expected full rhyme; line 7 has *skothending* along with a form of (secondary) crossed alliteration with line 8. Sound effects in both ON and OE often intensify as stanzas or verse paragraphs reach their end.

76. The compound translated "chief kinsman" is plural in the manuscripts; the reading "Randvér's chief kinsmen," referring to the dynastic line of the Goths, would be equally ominous. See Stavnem, "Kennings in *Ragnarsdrápa*," 169–74.

77. *Nemean Ode* 5, in *Pindar* 2.46–47.

78. Bragi *Rdr* 6, ed. Clunies Ross; *SkP* 3.1:36.

79. For discussion of the name Ealhhild, see Chambers, *Widsith*, 21–28; also Hill, *OE Minor Heroic Poems*, 64–65. Heinzel may have been the first to identify Widsith's princess with Svanhildr ("Über die Hervararsaga") and Boer, *Sagen von Ermanarich*, 16, to suggest that the name-element *ealh* designated some sort of bird.

80. Chambers, *Widsith*, 28.

81. Malone, *Widsith*, 140–41.

82. See the commentary by Clunies Ross in *SkP* 3.1:39–42. Multiple versions of the legend of Hildr and the Hjaðningar survive; the battle may or may not be portrayed on the Stora Hammar stone on Gotland. See Jesch, *Viking Diaspora*, 146–47.

83. Þjóð *Haustl* 7/2, ed. Clunies Ross; *SkP* 3.1:441–42. The poem includes at least seven references to Loki in terms of his relationships, along with an ironic description of him as "deep-minded" (6/5) and "stratagem-sparing" (= helpless, incompetent) (4/7–8).

84. This scene was carved at the bottom of the west side of the early to mid-tenth-century Gosforth Cross, Cumbria; see Bailey, *Viking Age Sculpture*, 125–32.

85. See Orchard, *Critical Companion*, 107. On the legendary background, see Griffith, "Difficulties in *Beowulf*," 25–28; Robinson, "Sigemund's *fæhðe ond fyrena*," 202; on Sigemund (ON Sigmundr) and Fitela (ON Sinfjötli) in *Eiríksmál*, a eulogy composed for the last Norse king of York (d. 954), see Lendinara, "L'Episodio di Sigemund," and bibliography therein.

86. On uncle–nephew relationships in the poem, see Bremmer, "Importance of Kinship."

87. Schücking, "Wann entstand der Beowulf?," 400.

88. Whitelock, *Audience of Beowulf*, 57.

89. Earl, "Forbidden *Beowulf*."

90. Various Scandinavian texts focus on Hroðulf's incestuous birth. See Niles and Osborn, *Beowulf and Lejre*, 297–387. Also Chambers, *Widsith*, 84. For translations of the later Scylding material, see *Kl* 4, 291–315, and Niles and Osborn, *Beowulf and Lejre*, 297–387.

91. Fulk, *History of OE Metre*, 97–98n6, adjudges the meter of *Beo* 881a "ambiguous and somewhat anomalous." See, too, Bredehoft, *Early English Metre*, 48; Weiskott, "Three-Position Verses." The only other time that the two words are conjoined (*eam ond nefan*; *Riddle* 46/6a) is in connection with Lot's incest. For a suggestion of the antiquity of *Beo* 881a, see Kendall, *Metrical Grammar*, 137–38.

92. On *nefa* and much else, see Griffith, "Some Difficulties in *Beowulf*, 25–28.

93. The composer, Vernon Duke (Vladimir Dukelsky), originally intended "May" but "the rhythm required two syllables." I owe this reference and the following URL address (at track 12) to Ross G. Arthur: https://www.allmusic.com/album/jazz-of-the 1950s-mw0000596204 .

94. Larkin, "The Trees," in *Collected Poems*, 166.

95. The "greatest of neck-rings" (1195b) bestowed on Beowulf will be worn by Hygelac on the day of his storied death (1202–5a). It appears to be one of the treasures that the dying Beowulf bequeaths to Wiglaf (2809).

96. Boar-helmets surface in *Beo* 303b–5, 1110–12a, 1285–87, 1327–28a, and 1451–54. Relevant studies include Stjerna, "Hjälmar och svärd"; Falk, *Altnordische Waffenkunde*, 157–60; Hatto, "Snake-swords and Boar-helms," 155–60; Beck, *Ebersignum*, 4–33; Glosecki, *Shamanism and OE Poetry*, 54–59, 192–97; Frank, "Boar on the Helmet."

97. For the legend, see Boer, "Studier over Skjoldungedigtningen"; Jakob Benediktsson, "Icelandic Traditions of the Scyldings"; Bjarni Guðnason, *Um Skjöldungasögu* and *Sǫgur Danakonunga.*

98. Doyle, "The Boscombe Valley Mystery," in *Adventures and Memoirs of Sherlock Holmes*, 70.

99. See *Kl* 4, 252–53, note to 2623, and Leneghan, *Dynastic Drama of Beowulf*, 98–102; for an overview, Earl, "The Swedish Wars."

100. Hallv *Knútdr* 3, ed. Townend; *SkP* 3.1:233.

101. Jesch, *Ships and Men*, 157–59; Townend, "Cnut's Poets," 203–4. The compound occurs in identical position in Óttarr's *Knútsdrápa* 1/6, with reference to the same king's ships, and nowhere else in the corpus.

102. See Townend, "Ella."

103. Frank, "King Cnut," 111–12. On Danish invaders = Scaldingi in an eleventh-century Northumbrian text, see Smith, *Historia de Sancti Cuthberti*, 48, 50, 52. On Scyld's tardy appearance in Scandinavia, see Anderson, "Scyld Scyldinga."

104. Bjarni Guðnason, *Um Skjöldungasögu*, 114–32.

105. Stoppard, *Invention of Love*, 37.

106. Arthur Waley, *Yuan Mei: Eighteenth Century Chinese Poet* (Stanford, CA: Stanford University Press, 1970), 163; cited by Benjamin Elman, *From Philosophy to Philology: Intellectual and Social Aspects of Change in Late Imperial China* (Cambridge, MA: Harvard University Press, 1984), 200.

107. Aulus Gellius, *Noctes Atticae*, ed. Leofranc Holford-Strevens (Oxford: Oxford University Press, 2020), 13.21.1–4.

108. Wallace Stevens, *The Necessary Angel: Essays on Reality and the Imagination* (New York: Vintage Books, 1951), 32. Bunting, "Poet's Point of View," in Bunting, *Complete Poems*, 11. See also Bunting, "Thumps," in *Basil Bunting on Poetry*, ed. Peter Makin (Baltimore: Johns Hopkins University Press, 1999), esp. 29–30.

109. See Allen, "01: Without Style," esp. 9–11.

110. William Nicolson in a 1699 letter to George Hickes declared that he could not follow the sense of this line (*sensum non assequor*), yet his tentative Latin translation (*luctus stupore magis est fixus*) was correct; see Harris, *A Chorus of Grammars*, 287. The manuscript reading *wea* 'sorrow' held until 1881 when Cosijn, "Anglo-

saxonica," tentatively proposed the emendation *weax* 'wax,' i.e., "wax is amazingly sticky." Dobbie, *Anglo-Saxon Minor Poems*, *ASPR* 6, 175, followed suit, deeming MS *wea* "hardly defensible." See Poole, *OE Wisdom Poetry*, 24–25.

111. On infinitization, see Heller-Roazen, *No One's Ways*, esp. 70–73. For "the idea of the object as 'not existing' as necessarily the idea of the object as 'existing' with, in addition, the representation of an exclusion of this very object by the actual reality taken *en bloc*," see Bergson, *Creative Evolution*, 302; cited in Carson, *Economy of the Unlost*, 102.

112. Kendall, *Metrical Grammar*, 9, early noted some of these aural echoes.

113. The poem is Einarr Skúlason's *Geisli* 'Light-beam' (1153), ed. Martin Chase, *SkP* 7.1:5–65. The rhymes of stanza 1 (lines 1, 4, and 7) are echoed in the final stanza 71 (lines 1, 4, and 5). Key words and one half-rhyme (*ágætr* 'excellent' and *ítr* 'glorious') are repeated.

114. Malin's final line in Auden's *The Age of Anxiety*, repeated by other characters; see Auden, *Collected Poems*, 456. See essays in Wehlau, ed., *Darkness, Depression, and Descent in Anglo-Saxon England.*

115. For text and discussion, see Chris Jones's exemplary detective work in Jones, *Fossil Poetry*, 203–204; Marsh, *Lectures on the English Language*, 2nd ed. (London: Low, 1860), 553–57.

116. Three stanzas of J. R. R. Tolkien's poem remain in a box file of his unpublished papers. Christopher Tolkien found these verses in his father's copy of *Heimskringla.* My gratitude to Dennis Wilson Wise, University of Arizona, for tracking their current location.

117. Larkin, "Annus Mirabilis," in *Collected Poems*, 167.

118. Rendall, "Shore Tollye" [*tollye* 'struggle'], in *Orkney Variants and Other Poems* (Kirkwall: Kirkwall Press, 1951); also John McQueen and Tom Scott, eds., *Oxford Book of Scottish Verse* (Oxford: Oxford University Press, 1966), 516–17.

119. Heaney, "The Wool Trae," in *Wintering Out* (1972); Heaney, "Bone Dreams," in *North* (1975). Note the wordplay on "cleave" at the caesura—both "to separate" and "to join."

120. S. Yashina et al., "Regeneration of Whole Fertile Plants from 30,000-year-old Fruit Tissue Buried in Siberian Permafrost," *Proceedings of the National Academy of Sciences of the United States of America* 109, no. 10 (2012): 4008–13; published online (February 21, 2012): doi:10.1073/pnas.1118386109.

121. Browne, *Religio Medici*, 48. In modern editions of the work, the passage cited is in either section 46 or 48.

BIBLIOGRAPHY

Abram, Christopher. "Anglo-Saxon Influence in the Old Norwegian Homily Book." *Mediaeval Scandinavia* 14 (2004): 1–35.

———. *Evergreen Ash: Ecology and Catastrophe in Old Norse Myth and Literature*. Charlottesville: University of Virginia Press, 2019.

———. "Scribal Authority in Skaldic Verse: Þorbjǫrn hornklofi's *Glymdrápa*." *Arkiv för nordisk filologi* 116 (2001): 5–19.

———. "Kennings and Things: Towards an Object-Oriented Skaldic Poetics." In Dumitrescu and Weiskott, eds., *The Shapes of Early English Poetry*, 161–88.

Abrams, Lesley. "The Anglo-Saxons and the Christianization of Scandinavia." *Anglo-Saxon England* 24 (1995): 213–50.

Ælfric of Eynsham. *Ælfric's Catholic Homilies: The First Series*. Edited by Peter Clemoes. Early English Text Society, supplementary series 17. Oxford: Oxford University Press, 1997.

———. *Ælfrics Grammatik und Glossar: Text und Varianten*. Edited by Julius Zupitza. Berlin: Weidmann, 1880. Reprinted with preface by Helmut Gneuss, Berlin, 1966; 2nd reprint with new introduction by Gneuss, Hildesheim: Weidmann, 2003.

———. *Homilies of Ælfric: A Supplementary Collection*. 2 vols. Edited by John C. Pope. Early English Text Society, original series 259–60. London: Oxford University Press, 1967–68.

Agamben, Giorgio. *The End of the Poem: Essays on Poetics*. Translated by Daniel Heller-Roazen. Stanford, CA: Stanford University Press, 1999.

Agnellus of Ravenna. *The Book of the Pontiffs of the Church of Ravenna*. Translated by Deborah Mauskopf Deliyannis. Washington, DC: Catholic University of America Press, 2009.

———. *Liber pontificalis, ecclesiae Ravennatis*. Edited by Deborah Mauskopf Deliyannis. Corpus Christianorum, Continuatio Mediaevalis 199. Turnhout: Brepols, 2006.

Alcuin of York. *Alcuini sive Albini Epistolae*. Edited by Ernst Dümmler. Monumenta Germaniae Historica, Epistulae Carolini Aevi 4:18–481. Berlin: Weidmann, 1895.

Aldhelm of Malmesbury. *Aldhelmi Opera Omnia.* Edited by Rudolf Ehwald, Monumenta Germaniae Historica, Auctores Antiquissimi, 15. Berlin: Weidmann, 1919.

———. *Aldhelm: The Prose Works.* Translated by Michael Lapidge and Michael Herren. Cambridge: D. S. Brewer, 1979.

Alexander, Michael. *Beowulf: A Verse Translation.* London: Penguin, 1973.

———. *The Earliest English Poems.* Berkeley: University of California Press, 1970.

———. *The First Poems in English.* London: Penguin, 2008.

———. *Old English Literature.* London: Macmillan, 1983.

Allen, Mark. "Name-Play and Structure in the Old English *Exodus.*" *Literary Onomastics Studies* 10 (1983): 301–13.

Allen, Valerie. "01: Without Style." In *On Style: An Atelier*, edited by Eileen A. Joy and Anna Klosowska, 1–14. New York: Punctum Books, 2013.

Amory, Frederic. "Kennings, Referentiality and Metaphors." *Arkiv för nordisk filologi* 103 (1988): 87–101.

———. "Tmesis in MLat., ON, and OIr. Poetry: An Unwritten *Notatio Norrœna.*" *Arkiv för nordisk filologi* 94 (1979): 42–49.

———. "Towards a Grammatical Classification of Kennings as Compounds." *Arkiv för nordisk filologi* 97 (1982): 67–80.

Amsler, Mark E. *Etymology and Grammatical Discourse in Late Antiquity and the Early Middle Ages.* Amsterdam: Benjamin, 1989.

Anderson, Carl Edlund. "Scyld Scyldinga: Intercultural Innovation at the Interface of West and North Germanic." *Neophilologus* 100 (2016): 461–76.

Anderson, Earl R. *Cynewulf: Structure, Style, and Theme in His Poetry.* Rutherford, NJ: Fairleigh Dickinson University Press, 1983.

Andersson, Theodore M. *Early Epic Scenery: Homer, Virgil, and the Medieval Legacy.* Ithaca, NY: Cornell University Press, 1976.

———. "Sources and Analogues." In Bjork and Niles, eds., *A Beowulf Handbook*, 125–48.

Andrew, Samuel O. *Postscript on Beowulf.* Cambridge: Cambridge University Press, 1948; 2nd ed., New York: Russell and Russell, 1969.

———. *Syntax and Style in Old English.* Cambridge: Cambridge University Press, 1940.

Anlezark, Daniel. "An Ideal Marriage: Abraham and Sarah in Old English Literature." *Medium Ævum* 69 (2000): 187–210.

———. "Sceaf, Japheth and the Origins of the Anglo-Saxons." *Anglo-Saxon England* 31 (2002): 13–46.

Annales Regni Francorum. 3 vols. Edited by Reinhold Rau. Quellen zur karolingischen Reichsgeschichte. Darmstadt: Wissenschaftliche Buchgesellschaft, 1955.

Ashe, Laura. *Oxford English Literary History: Conquest and Transformation.* Oxford: Oxford University Press, 2017.

Attridge, Derek. *Moving Words: Forms of English Poetry*. Oxford: Oxford University Press, 2013.

Auden, W. H. *Collected Poems*. Edited by Edward Mendelson. London: Faber & Faber, 1994.

———. *The Dyer's Hand and Other Essays*. London: Faber & Faber, 1963.

———. The *English Auden: Poems, Essays and Dramatic Writings, 1927–1939*. Edited by Edward Mendelson. London: Faber & Faber, 1977.

———. *The Orators: An English Study* (1932). 3rd ed. London: Faber & Faber, 1966.

Bailey, Richard N. *Viking Age Sculpture in Northern England*. London: Collins, 1980.

Bampi, Massimiliano, Carolyne Larrington, and Sif Rikhardsdóttir, eds. *A Critical Companion to Old Norse Literary Genre*. Woodbridge: Boydell & Brewer, 2020.

Bandle, Oskar et al. *The Nordic Languages: An International Handbook of the History of the North Germanic Languages*. 2 vols. Berlin: De Gruyter, 2002.

Bartlett, Adeline Courtney. *The Larger Rhetorical Patterns in Anglo-Saxon Poetry*. New York: Columbia University Press, 1935.

Bately, Janet. "The Place Which Is Called 'at X': A New Look at Old Evidence." In *Essays for Joyce Hill on Her Sixtieth Birthday*, edited by Mary Swan. Special issue, *Leeds Studies in English*, n.s., 37 (2006): 343–63.

Beck, Heinrich. *Das Ebersignum im Germanischen: Ein Beitrag zur germanischen Tier-Symbolik*. Berlin: De Gruyter, 1965.

Becker, Daniel Levin. *Many Subtle Channels: In Praise of Potential Literature*. Cambridge, MA: Harvard University Press, 2012.

Bede. *Bede's Ecclesiastical History of the English People*. Edited and translated by Bertram Colgrave and R. A. B. Mynors. Oxford: Clarendon, 1969.

Beechy, Tiffany. *The Poetics of Old English*. Burlington, VT: Ashgate, 2010.

Belitt, Ben. *The Poet's Other Voice: Conversations on Literary Translation*. Edited by Edwin Honig. Amherst: University of Massachusetts Press, 1985.

Berendsohn, Walter A. "Altgermanische Heldendichtung." *Neue Jahrbücher* 18 (1915): 633–48.

Bergman, Madeleine M. "Supplement to *A Concordance to 'The Anglo-Saxon Poetic Records.'*" *Mediaevalia* 8 (1982): 9–52.

Bergson, Henri. *Creative Evolution*. Translated by Arthur Mitchell. New York: H. Holt, 1911.

Bergsveinn Birgisson. *Inn i skaldens sinn: Kognitive, estetiske og historiske skatter i den norrøne skaldediktingen*. Bergen: University of Bergen, 2008.

———. "What Have We Lost by Writing? Cognitive Archaisms in Skaldic Poetry." In *Oral Art Forms and Their Passage into Writing*, edited by Else Mundal and Jonas Wellendorf, 163–81. Copenhagen: Museum Tusculanum, 2008.

Best, Stephen, and Sharon Marcus. "Surface Reading: An Introduction." *Representations* 108 (2009): 1–21.

Bibire, Paul. "North Sea Language Contacts in the Early Middle Ages: English and Norse." In *The North Sea World in the Middle Ages: Studies in the Cultural History of North-Western Europe*, edited by T. R. Liszka and L. E. M. Walker, 88–107. Dublin: Four Courts Press, 2001.

Bitterli, Dieter. *Say What I Am Called: The Old English Riddles of the Exeter Book and the Anglo-Latin Riddle Tradition.* Toronto: University of Toronto Press, 2009.

Bjarni Einarsson. *Skáldasögur: Um uppruna og eðli ástaskáldasagnanna fornu.* Reykjavík: Bókaútgáfa Menningarsjóðs, 1961.

Bjarni Guðnason. *Um Skjöldungasögu.* Reykjavík: Bókaútgáfa Menningarsjóðs, 1963.

———, ed. *Sǫgur Danakonunga.* Íslenzk fornrit 35. Reykjavík: Hið íslenzka fornritafélag, 1982.

Bjork, Robert E. "Grímur Jónsson Thorkelin's Preface to the First Edition of *Beowulf*, 1815." *Scandinavian Studies* 68 (1996): 290–320.

———. "Scandinavian Relations." In *A Companion to Anglo-Saxon Literature*, edited by Phillip Pulsiano and Elaine Treharne, 388–99. Oxford: Blackwell, 2001.

———. "Speech as Gift in *Beowulf*." *Speculum* 69 (1994): 993–1022.

Bjork, Robert E., and John D. Niles, eds. *A Beowulf Handbook.* Lincoln: University of Nebraska Press, 1997.

Björn Magnússon Ólsen, ed. *Den tredje og fjærde grammatiske afhandling i Snorres Edda tilligemed de grammatiske afhandlingers prolog og to andre tillæg.* Copenhagen: Knudtzon, 1884.

Bliss, Alan J. *The Metre of "Beowulf."* Rev. ed. Oxford: Blackwell, 1967.

Blockley, Mary. *Aspects of Old English Poetic Syntax: Where Clauses Begin.* Urbana: University of Illinois Press, 2001.

Bloomfield, Morton W. "'Interlace' as a Medieval Narrative Technique with Special Reference to *Beowulf*." In *Magister Regis: Studies in Honor of Robert Earl Kaske*, edited by Arthur Groos, 49–59. New York: Fordham University Press, 1986.

———. "Stylistics and the Theory of Literature." *New Literary History* 7 (1976): 271–311.

Boer, Richard C. *Die Sagen von Ermanarich und Dietrich von Bern.* Halle an der Saale: Weisenhaus, 1910.

———. "Studier over Skjoldungedigtningen." *Aarbøger for nordisk Oldkyndighed og Historie*, 3rd ser., 12 (1922): 133–266.

Borges, Jorge Luis. "Die Kenningar." In Borges, *Das Eine und die Vielen: Essays zur Literatur*, translated by Karl August Horst, 17–34. Munich: Hanzer, 1966.

———. "Pierre Menard, Author of the *Quixote*" (1939). Reprinted in *The Garden of Forking Paths* (1941). Translated by Andrew Hurley in Borges, *Collected Fictions*, 88–95. London: Penguin, 1998.

Borroff, Marie. "Systematic Sound Symbolism in the Long Alliterative Line in *Beowulf* and *Sir Gawain*." In *English Historical Metrics*, edited by C. B. McCully and J. J. Anderson, 120–33. Cambridge: Cambridge University Press, 1996.

Borst, Arno. *Der Turmbau von Babel*. 6 vols. Stuttgart: Hiersemann, 1957–63.

Bosworth, Joseph. *The Elements of Anglo-Saxon Grammar*. London: Harding, Mavor, and Lepard, 1823.

Bouman, A. C. *Patterns in Old English and Old Icelandic Literature*. Leiden: Leiden University Press, 1962.

Bracher, Frederick. "Understatement in Old English Poetry." *PMLA* 52 (1937): 915–34. Reprinted in *Essential Articles for the Study of Old English Poetry*, edited by Jess B. Bessinger and Stanley J. Kahrl, 228–54. Hamden, CT: Archon, 1968.

Brady, Caroline. "Weapons in *Beowulf*: An Analysis of the Nominal Compounds and an Evaluation of the Poet's Use of Them." *Anglo-Saxon England* 9 (1979): 79–141.

Brady, Lindy. "Death and the Landscape of *The Fortunes of Men*." *Neophilologus* 98 (2014): 325–36.

Brandl, Alois. "Die angelsächsische Literatur." In *Grundriss der germanischen Philologie*, 3 vols., 2nd ed., edited by Hermann Paul. Strassburg: Trübner, 1901–9. Issued separately as *Geschichte der altenglischen Literatur*. Strassburg: Trübner, 1908.

Bredehoft, Thomas A. *Authors, Audiences, and Old English Verse*. Toronto: University of Toronto Press, 2009.

———. *Early English Metre*. Toronto: University of Toronto Press, 2005.

———. "Estimating Probabilities and Alliteration Frequencies in Old English Verse." *Old English Newsletter* 34 (2000): 19–23.

———. "Old English and Old Saxon Formulaic Rhyme." *Anglia* 123 (2005): 204–29.

———. "OE *yðhengest* and an Unrecognized Passage of Old English Verse." *Notes & Queries* 54 (2007): 120–22.

———. "Secondary Stress in Compound Germanic Names in Old English Verse." *Journal of English Linguistics* 31 (2003): 199–220.

Breeze, Andrew. "*Maldon* 68: *Mid Prasse Bestodon*." *English Studies* 73 (1992): 289–91.

Bremmer, Rolf H. "The Importance of Kinship: Uncle and Nephew in *Beowulf*." *Amsterdamer Beiträge zur älteren Germanistik* 15 (1980): 21–38.

Brodeur, Arthur Gilchrist. *The Art of "Beowulf."* Berkeley: University of California Press, 1971.

Brooks, Kenneth R., ed. *Andreas and the Fates of the Apostles*. Oxford: Clarendon, 1961.

Brown, Penelope, and Stephen C. Levinson. *Politeness: Some Universals in Language Usage*. Cambridge: Cambridge University Press, 1987.

Browne, Sir Thomas. *Religio Medici and Hydriotaphia, or Urne-Buriall*. Edited by Stephen Greenblatt and Ramie Targoff. New York: New York Review of Books, 2012.

Bugge, Sophus. *Bidrag til den ældste skaldedigtnings historie*. Christiania [Oslo]: Aschehoug, 1894.

Bullough, Donald A. *Carolingian Renewal: Sources and Heritage*. Manchester: Manchester University Press, 1991.

Bunting, Basil. *Complete Poems*. Edited by Richard Caddel. Newcastle upon Tyne: Bloodaxe Books, 2000.

Butterfield, Ardis. "Medieval Genres and Modern Genre Theory." *Paragraph* 13 (1990): 184–201.

Byrhtferth of Ramsay. *Byrhtferth's Enchiridion*. Edited and translated by Peter S. Baker and Michael Lapidge. Early English Text Society, supplementary series 15. Oxford: Oxford University Press, 1955.

———. *Byrhtferth of Ramsay: The Lives of St Oswald and St Ecgwine*. Edited and translated by Michael Lapidge. Oxford: Oxford University Press, 2009.

Cable, Thomas M. *The English Alliterative Tradition*. Philadelphia: University of Pennsylvania Press, 1991.

———. "Metrical Simplicity and Sievers' Five Types." *Studies in Philology* 69 (1972): 28–88.

———. "Progress in Old English Metrics." In *Old English Tradition: Essays in Honor of J. R. Hall*, edited by Lindy Brady, 53–70. Tempe, AZ: Medieval and Renaissance Texts and Studies, 2021.

Calder, Daniel G. *Cynewulf*. Boston: Twayne, 1981

———. "Histories and Surveys of Old English Literature: A Chronological Review." *Anglo-Saxon England* 10 (1982): 201–44.

———. "The Study of Style in Old English Poetry: A Historical Introduction." In *Old English Poetry: Essays on Style*, edited by Daniel G. Calder, 1–65. Berkeley: University of California Press, 1979.

Calvino, Italo. *Six Memos for the Next Millennium*. The Charles Eliot Norton Lectures, 1985–86. Cambridge, MA: Harvard University Press, 1988.

Camden, William. *Remaines of a Greater Worke, Concerning Britain* (London, 1605). 7th ed. Reprint, London: J. R. Smith, 1870.

Cameron, Esther, and Quita Mould. "Saxon Shoes, Viking Sheaths? Cultural Identity in Anglo-Scandinavian York." In *Land, Sea and Home: Proceedings of a Conference on Viking-Period Settlement*, edited by John Hines et al., 457–66. Leeds: Maney, 2004.

Campbell, Alistair, ed. *The Battle of Brunanburh*. London: Heinemann, 1938.

———, ed. and trans. *The Chronicle of Æthelweard*. London: Nelson, 1962.

———. *Skaldic Verse and Anglo-Saxon History*. The Dorothea Coke Memorial Lecture in Northern Studies. London: Lewis, 1971.

Cannon, Christopher. *The Grounds of English Literature*. Oxford: Oxford University Press, 2008.

Carr, Charles T. *Nominal Compounds in Germanic*. London: Oxford University Press, 1939.

Carroll, Lewis. *Alice's Adventures in Wonderland* and *Through the Looking Glass*. Edited by Donald J. Gray. New York: Norton, 1971.

———. *Refectory Umbrella and Mischmasch*. 2nd ed. Edited by Florence Milner. New York: Dover, 1971.

———. *The Annotated Alice: Alice's Adventures in Wonderland and Through the Looking Glass*. Notes by Martin Gardner. New York: Bramhall House, 1960.

Carruthers, Mary. "Inventional Mnemonics and the Ornaments of Style: The Case of Etymology." *Connotations* 2 (1992): 103–14.

Carson, Anne. *Economy of the Unlost (Reading Simonides of Keos with Paul Celan)*. Princeton, NJ: Princeton University Press, 1999.

Cavell, Megan. *Weaving Words and Binding Bodies: The Poetics of Human Experience in Old English Literature*. Toronto: University of Toronto Press, 2016.

Caxton, William. *The History of Reynard the Fox*. Edited by Norman F. Blake. London: Oxford University Press, 1970.

Chambers, R. W. *Beowulf: An Introduction to the Study of the Poem with a Discussion of the Stories of Offa and Finn*. 3rd ed., with supplement by C. L. Wrenn. Cambridge: Cambridge University Press, 1959.

———. *Beowulf with the Finnsburg Fragment*. Cambridge: Cambridge University Press, 1914. Rev. ed. of Alfred J. Wyatt, *Beowulf*. Cambridge: Cambridge University Press, 1894.

———. *Widsith: A Study in Old English Heroic Legend*. Cambridge: Cambridge University Press, 1912.

Chapman, Don. "Composing and Joining: How the Anglo-Saxons Talked about Compounding." In *Verbal Encounters: Anglo-Saxon and Old Norse Studies for Roberta Frank*, edited by Antonina Harbus and Russell Poole, 39–54. Toronto: University of Toronto Press, 2004.

———. "'You Belly-Guilty Bag': Insulting Epithets in Old English." *Journal of Historical Pragmatics* 9 (2008): 1–19.

Chase, Colin, ed. *Two Alcuin Letter-Books*. Toronto: Pontifical Institute of Mediaeval Studies, 1975.

Chase, Martin. "*Concatenatio* as a Structural Element in the Christian *Drápur*." Workshop Papers, 1:115–29. The Sixth International Saga Conference, Helsingør, 1985.

———, ed. *Eddic, Skaldic, and Beyond: Poetic Variety in Medieval Iceland and Norway*. New York: Fordham University Press, 2014.

Chaucer, Geoffrey. *The Riverside Chaucer*. 3rd ed. Edited by Larry Dean Benson. Boston: Houghton Mifflin, 1987.

Chickering, Howell D., Jr., ed. and trans. *Beowulf: A Dual-Language Edition*. New York: Random House, 1977. 2nd ed., New York: Anchor Books, 2006.

Cicero. *De Oratore, Books 1 and 2*. Translated by E. W. Sutton and H. Rackham. Loeb Classical Library 348. Cambridge, MA: Harvard University Press, 1942.

———. *Cicero's Letters to His Friends.* Translated by D. R. Shackleton Bailey. London: Penguin, 1978.

Clark, David. "Notes on the Medieval Ideal of Dying with One's Lord." *Notes & Queries* 58 (2011): 475–84.

Clark, David, and Nicholas Perkins, eds. *Anglo-Saxon Culture and the Modern Imagination.* Cambridge: D. S. Brewer, 2010.

Clark, David, and Carl Phelpstead, eds. *Old Norse Made New: Essays on the Post-Medieval Reception of Old Norse Literature and Culture.* London: Viking Society for Northern Research, 2007.

Clark Hall, J. R. *Beowulf and the Fight at Finnsburg: A Translation.* London: Allen & Unwin, 1958.

Classen, Ernest. *Vowel Alliteration in the Old Germanic Languages.* Manchester: University Press, 1913.

Clayton, Mary. "An Edition of Ælfric's *Letter to Brother Edward.*" In Treharne and Rosser, eds., *Early Medieval English Texts,* 263–83.

Clemoes, Peter. *Rhythm and Cosmic Order in Old English Christian Literature.* Cambridge: Cambridge University Press, 1970.

Clover, Carol J. "The Germanic Context of the Unferþ Episode." *Speculum* 55 (1980): 444–68.

———. "Regardless of Sex: Men, Women, and Power in Early Northern Europe." *Speculum* 68 (1993): 363–87.

———. "Skaldic Sensibility." *Arkiv för nordisk filologi* 93 (1978): 68–81.

Clunies Ross, Margaret. *A History of Old Norse Poetry and Poetics.* Cambridge: D. S. Brewer, 2005.

———. *The Norse Muse in Britain, 1750–1820.* Trieste: Edizione Parnaso, 1998.

———. *The Old Norse Poetic Translations of Thomas Percy: A New Edition and Commentary.* Turnhout: Brepols, 2001.

———. "Style and Authorial Presence in Skaldic Mythological Poetry." *Saga-Book of the Viking Society* 20 (1978): 276–304.

———. "Stylistic and Generic Definers of the Old Norse Skaldic Ekphrasis." *Viking and Medieval Scandinava* 3 (2007): 161–85.

Clunies Ross, Margaret, and Jonas Wellendorf, eds. and trans. *The Fourth Grammatical Treatise.* London: Viking Society for Northern Research, 2014.

Colman, Fran. *The Grammar of Names in Anglo-Saxon England: The Linguistics and Culture of the Old English Onomasticon.* Oxford: Oxford University Press, 2014.

———. "The Name-Element *Æðel-* and Related Problems." *Notes & Queries* 28 (1981): 295–301.

Connell, Bruce. "Downstep: Suprasegmental and Prosodic Phonology." In *The Blackwell Companion to Phonology,* edited by Marc van Oostendorp et al., 4:824–47. Malden, MA: Wiley-Blackwell, 2011.

Connor, Patrick W. *Anglo-Saxon Exeter: A Tenth-Century Cultural History.* Woodbridge: Boydell, 1993.

Conybeare, John Josias, with William Daniel Conybeare. *Illustrations of Anglo-Saxon Poetry*. London: Harding and Lepard, 1826.

Copeland, Rita. "Grammar, Rhetoric, and Figurative Language: Learned Innovations and Vernacular Receptions." In *Intellectual Culture in Medieval Scandinavia, c. 1100–1350*, edited by Stefka Georgieva Eriksen, 213–42. Turnhout: Brepols, 2016.

Cornelius, Ian. *Reconstructing Alliterative Verse: The Pursuit of a Medieval Meter*. Cambridge: Cambridge University Press, 2017.

Cosijn, Peter J. "Anglosaxonica." *Tijdschrift voor nederlandsche Taal- en Letterkunde* 1 (1881): 143–58.

Craigie, Sir William. *The Northern Element in English Literature*. Toronto: University of Toronto Press, 1931.

Creed, Robert P. "The *Beowulf*-Poet: Master of Sound Patterning." In *Oral Traditional Literature: A Festschrift for Albert Bates Lord*, edited by John Miles Foley, 194–216. Bloomington, IN: Slavica, 1981.

———. *Reconstructing the Rhythm of Beowulf*. Columbia: University of Missouri Press, 1990.

Crépin, André. *Old English Poetics: A Technical Handbook*. Paris: Publications de l'Association des médiévistes de l'enseignement supérieur, 2005.

Cronan, Dennis. "Alliterative Rank in Old English Poetry." *Studia Neophilologica* 58 (1986): 145–58.

———. "The Poetics of Poetic Words in Old English." In Neidorf et al., eds., *Old English Philology*, 256–75.

Cross, J. E. "On *The Wanderer* Lines 80–84: A Study of a Figure and a Theme." *Vetenskaps-societeten i Lund, Arsbok* 35 (1959): 77–110.

Cross, James E., and Jennifer Morrish Tunberg, eds. *The Copenhagen Wulfstan Collection: København, Kongelige Bibliotek Gl. Kgl. Sam. 1595*. Early English Manuscripts in Facsimile, 25. Copenhagen: Rosenkilde and Bagger, 1993.

Cross, Katherine. *Heirs of the Vikings: History and Identity in Normandy and England, c. 950–c. 1015*. Woodbridge: York Medieval Press, 2018.

Culler, Jonathan. *Theory of the Lyric*. Cambridge, MA: Harvard University Press, 2015.

Cunningham, Valentine. "The Dead (and Live) Poets' Society." *The Times Higher Educational Supplement*, November 12, 1999, 25.

Damico, Helen. *Beowulf's Wealhtheow and the Valkyrie Tradition*. Madison: University of Wisconsin Press, 1984.

Dance, Richard. "*The Battle of Maldon* line 91 and the Origins of *Call*: A Reconsideration." *Neuphilologische Mitteilungen* 100 (1999): 143–54.

———. "North Sea Currents: Old English-Old Norse Relations, Literary and Linguistic." *Literature Compass* (2004): 1–10.

———. "*Þær wearð hream ahafen*: A Note on Old English Spelling and the Sound of *The Battle of Maldon*." In *The Power of Words: Anglo-Saxon Studies*

Presented to Donald G. Scragg on his Seventieth Birthday, edited by Hugh Magennis and Jonathan Wilcox, 278–317. Morgantown: West Virginia University Press, 2006.

———. *Words Derived from Old Norse in Early Middle English: Studies in the Vocabulary of the South-West Midland Texts*. Tempe: Arizona Center for Medieval and Renaissance Studies, 2003.

Dane, Joseph A. "The Notion of Ring Composition in Classical and Medieval Studies: A Comment on Critical Method and Illusion." *Neuphilologische Mitteilungen* 94 (1993): 61–67.

Daniélou, Jean. *Sacramentum futuri: Études sur les origins de la typologie biblique*. Paris: Beauchesne, 1950. Translated by Wulstan Hibberd as *From Shadows to Reality: Studies in the Biblical Typology of the Fathers*. London: Burrs and Oates, 1960.

Davies, Joshua. "The Literary Languages of Old English: Words, Styles, Voices." In *The Cambridge History of Early Medieval English Literature*, edited by Clare Lees, 257–77. Cambridge: Cambridge University Press, 2013.

Davis, Kathleen. "Periodization and the Matter of Precedent." *postmedieval: a journal of medieval cultural studies* 1 (2010): 354–60.

Davis-Secord, Jonathan. *Joinings: Compound Words in Old English Literature*. Toronto: University of Toronto Press, 2016.

Delanty, Greg, and Michael Matto, eds. *The Word Exchange: Anglo-Saxon Poems in Translation*. New York: Norton, 2011.

de Man, Paul. "Conclusions: Walter Benjamin's 'The Task of the Translator.'" In de Man, *The Resistance to Theory*, 73–105. Minneapolis: University of Minnesota Press, 1986.

Denno, Jerry. "Oppression and Voice in Anglo-Saxon Riddle Poems." *CEA Critic* 70 (2007): 35–47.

Dietrich, Franz. "Die Räthsel des Exeterbuchs: Würdigung, Lösung und Herstellung." *Zeitschrift für deutsches Altertum* 11 (1859): 448–90.

Dimrock, E. "The Name of Odysseus." *The Hudson Review* 9 (1956): 52–70.

DiNapoli, Robert. *A Far Light: A Reading of Beowulf*. Newcastle upon Tyne: Cambridge Scholars Publishing, 2016.

Dodwell, C. R. *Anglo-Saxon Art: A New Perspective*. Manchester: Manchester University Press, 1982.

Donaldson, Talbot. *Beowulf: A Prose Translation*. New York: Norton, 1975.

Donoghue, Daniel. *Lady Godiva: A Literary History of the Legend*. Oxford: Blackwell, 2003.

———. "The Philologer Poet: Seamus Heaney and the Translation of *Beowulf*." In Heaney, *Beowulf: A Verse Translation*, edited by Daniel Donoghue, 237–47. New York: Norton, 2002.

———. *Style in Old English Poetry: The Test of the Auxiliary*. New Haven, CT: Yale University Press, 1987.

Doyle, Sir Arthur Conan. "The Boscombe Valley Mystery." In *The Adventures and Memoirs of Sherlock Holmes*, 69–93. Harmondsworth: Penguin, 2001.

Dronke, Ursula, ed. and trans. *The Poetic Edda*. Vol. 3, *Mythological Poems* 2. Oxford: Clarendon, 2011.

Drout, Michael, and Nelson Goering. "Terrified the Heruli." *Modern Philology* 117 (2020): 285–300.

Dumitrescu, Irina, and Eric Weiskott, eds. *The Shapes of Early English Poetry: Style, Form, History*. Kalamazoo: Medieval Institute Publications, Western Michigan University, 2019.

Earl, James W. "The Forbidden *Beowulf*: Haunted by Incest." *PMLA* 125 (2010): 289–305.

———. "The Swedish Wars in *Beowulf*." *Journal of English and Germanic Philology* 114 (2015): 32–60.

Edwards, Diana C. "Clause Arrangement in Skaldic Poetry. 1. Clause Arrangement in the *dróttkvætt* Poetry of the Ninth to Fourteenth Centuries; 2. Clause Arrangement in the Poetry of Arnórr jarlaskáld." *Arkiv för nordisk filologi* 98 (1983): 123–75.

Egeler, Matthias. *Avalon, 66° Nord. Frühgeschichte und Rezeption eines Mythos*. Berlin: De Gruyter, 2015.

Ekwall, Eilert. *English River-Names*. Oxford: Clarendon, 1928.

Ellard, Donna Beth. *Anglo-Saxon(ist) Pasts, postSaxon Futures*. Goleta, CA: Punctum Books, 2019.

Ellis, George. *Specimens of the Early English Poets, to which is Prefixed an Historical Sketch of the Rise and Progress of the English Poetry and Language*. 3 vols. 2nd ed. London: Nicol and Wright, 1801; 3 vols. 3rd ed. London: W. Bulmer, 1803.

Elstob, Elizabeth. *The Rudiments of Grammar for the English-Saxon Tongue. First given in English with an Apology for the Study of Northern Antiquities*. London: J. Bowyer, 1715.

Emerson, Oliver Farrar. "Transverse Alliteration in Teutonic Poetry." *Journal of Germanic Philology* 3 (1900–1): 127–37.

Engster, Hermann. *Poesie einer Achsenzeit: Der Ursrung der Skaldik im gesellschaftlichen Systemwandel der Wikingerzeit*. Frankfurt: Lang, 1983.

Erasmus, Desiderius. *Colloquia* (1517), translated by C. R. Thompson. In *Collected Works of Erasmus*, vols. 39–40. Toronto: University of Toronto, 1997.

Erhardt-Siebold, Erika von. *Die lateinischen Rätsel der Angelsachsen: Ein Beitrag zur Kulturgeschichte Altenglands*. Heidelberg: Winter, 1925. Reprint, Amsterdam: Swets and Zeitlinger, 1974.

Even-Zohar, Itamar. "Polysystem Theory" and "Laws of Literary Interference." *Poetics Today* 11 (1990): 9–25; 53–72.

Falk, Hjalmar. *Altnordische Waffenkunde*. Kristiania [Oslo]: Dybwad, 1914.

———. "Med hvilken ret kaldes skaldesproget kunstigt? 1. Homonymiens rolle. 2. De saakaldte halfkenningar. 3. Personnavnes indflydelse paa mands- og kvindekenningar. 4. Oversigt over det poetiske udtryks udvikling." *Arkiv för nordisk filologi* 5 (1889): 245–77.

Farr, Carol. "Style in Late Anglo-Saxon England: Questions of Learning and Intention." In *Anglo-Saxon Styles*, edited by Catherine E. Karkov and George Hardin Brown, 115–30. Albany: State University of New York Press, 2003.

Faulkes, Anthony. *Poetical Inspiration in Old Norse and Old English Poetry*. The Dorothea Coke Memorial Lecture in Northern Studies. London: Viking Society for Northern Research, 1997.

———. *What Was Viking Poetry For?* Inaugural Lecture. Birmingham: University of Birmingham School of English, 1993.

Fear, Andrew, and Jamie Wood, eds. *Isidore of Seville and His Reception in the Early Middle Ages*. Amsterdam: Amsterdam University Press, 2016.

Feist, Sigmund. *Etymologisches Wörterbuch der gotischen Sprache*. Halle: Niemeyer, 1923.

Ferhatović, Denis. *Bound Objects and the Art of Poetry: Spolia in Old English Verse*. Manchester: Manchester University Press, 2019.

Fidjestøl, Bjarne. *The Dating of Eddic Poetry: A Historical Survey and Methodological Investigation*. Edited by Odd Einar Haugen. Bibliotheca Arnamagnæana 41. Copenhagen: Reitzel, 1999.

———. "'Har du høyrt eit dyrare kvæde?' Litt om økonomien bak den eldste fyrstediktinga" ["Have you heard a poem worth more?" A note on the economic background of early skaldic praise-poetry]. In *Festskrift til Ludvig Holm-Olsen*, edited by B. Fidjestøl et al., 61–73. Øvre Ervik: Alvheim og Eide, 1984. Reprinted in Fidjestøl, *Selected Papers*, 117–32.

———. "Kenningsystemet. Forsøk på ein lingvistisk analyse" [The kenning system: An attempt at a linguistic analysis]. *Maal og Minne* (1974): 5–50. In Fidjestøl, *Selected Papers*, 16–67.

———. *Det norrøne fyrstediktet*. Øvre Ervik: Alvheim og Eide, 1982.

———. *Selected Papers*. Edited by Odd Einar Haugen and Else Mundal. Translated by Peter G. Foote. Odense: Odense University Press, 1997.

Firth, John Rupert. *Papers in Linguistics, 1934–1951*. London: Oxford University Press, 1957.

———. *The Tongues of Men and Speech*. London: Oxford University Press, 1964.

———. "The Use and Distribution of Certain English Sounds." *English Studies* 17 (1935): 8–18.

Fischer, Andreas. *Engagement, Wedding and Marriage in Old English*. Heidelberg: Winter, 1986.

Fischer, Frank. *Die Lehnwörter des Altwestnordischen*. Palaestra 85. Berlin: Mayer & Müller, 1909.

Foote, Peter. "Beginnings and Endings: Some Notes on the Study of Scaldic Poetry" (1976). In Foote, *Aurvandilstá: Norse Studies*, edited by Michael Barnes et al., 236–48. Odense: Odense University Press, 1984.

———. "Skandinavische Dichtung der Wikingerzeit." In *Neues Handbuch der Literaturwissenschaft* 6, *Europäisches Frühmittelalter*, edited by Klaus von See, 317–30. Wiesbaden: AULA-Verlag, 1985.

Foucault, Michel. *The Archaeology of Knowledge*. Translated by A. M. Sheridan Smith. New York: Pantheon, 1972.

Fowler, Henry W. *A Dictionary of Modern English Usage*. New York: Oxford University Press, 1926.

Frank, Roberta. "Anglo-Scandinavian Poetic Relations." *American Notes and Queries*, n.s., 3 (1990): 74–79.

———. "*Beowulf* and the Intimacy of Large Parties." In *Dating Beowulf: Studies in Intimacy*, edited by Daniel C. Remein and Erica Weaver, 54–72. Manchester: Manchester University Press, 2020.

———. "The Boar on the Helmet." In *Aedificia Nova: Studies in Honor of Rosemary Cramp*, edited by Catherine E. Karkov and Helen Damico, 76–88. Kalamazoo, MI: Medieval Institute Publications, 2008.

———. "Conversational Skills for Heroes." In *Narration and Hero: Recounting the Deeds of Heroes in Literature and Art of the Early Medieval Period*, edited by Victor Millet and Heike Sahm, 19–43. Berlin: De Gruyter, 2014.

———. "Did Anglo-Saxon Audiences Have a Skaldic Tooth?" *Scandinavian Studies* 59 (1987): 338–55.

———. "The Discreet Charm of the Old English Weak Adjective." In *Anglo-Saxon Styles*, edited by Catherine E. Karkov and George Hardin Brown, 239–52. Albany: State University of New York Press, 2003.

———. "Dróttkvætt." Special issue "In Brief," edited by Irina Dumitrescu and Bruce Holsinger, *New Literary History* 50 (2019): 393–98.

———. "Germanic Legend in Old English Literature." In *The Cambridge Companion to Old English Literature*, edited by Malcolm Godden and Michael Lapidge, 88–106. Cambridge: Cambridge University Press, 1991. 2nd rev. ed. 2013, 82–100.

———. "The Ideal of Men Dying with Their Lord in *The Battle of Maldon*: Anachronism or Nouvelle Vague." In *People and Places in Northern Europe 500–1600: Essays in Honour of Peter Hayes Sawyer*, edited by Ian Wood and Niels Lund, 95–106. Woodbridge: Boydell & Brewer, 1991.

———. "The Incomparable Wryness of Old English Poetry." In *Inside Old English: Essays in Honour of Bruce Mitchell*, edited by John Walmsley, 59–73. Oxford: Blackwell, 2006.

———. "King Cnut in the Verse of His Skalds." In *The Reign of Cnut, King of England, Denmark and Norway*, edited by Alexander F. Rumble, 106–24. Leicester: Leicester University Press, 1994.

———. "Late Old English *þrymnys* 'Trinity': Scribal Nod or Word Waiting to Be Born?" In *Old English and New: Studies in Language and Linguistics in Honor of Frederic G. Cassidy*, edited by Joan H. Hall, Nick Doane, and Dick Ringler, 97–110. New York: Garland, 1992.

———. "The Lay of the Land in Skaldic Praise Poetry." In *Myth in Early Northwest Europe*, edited by Stephen O. Glosecki, 175–96. Turnhout: Brepols, 2007.

———. "Like a Bridge of Stones." *The Yale Review* 99 (2011): 170–77.

———. "Marketing Óðinn's Mead in a Strange Land." In *The Morton Bloomfield Lectures, 1989–2005*, edited by Daniel Donoghue, James Simpson, and Nicholas Watson, 246–72. Kalamazoo, MI: Medieval Institute Publications, 2010.

———. "North-Sea Soundings in *Andreas*." In Treharne and Rosser, eds., *Early Medieval English Texts*, 1–11.

———. *Old Norse Court Poetry: The Dróttkvætt Stanza*. Islandica 42. Ithaca, NY: Cornell University Press, 1978.

———. "Old Norse Memorial Eulogies and the Ending of *Beowulf*." *The Early Middle Ages, Acta* 6 (1979): 1–19.

———. "Onomastic Play in Kormakr's Verse: The Name Steingerðr." *Mediaeval Scandinavia* 3 (1970): 7–30.

———. "*Quid Hinieldus cum feminis*? The Hero and Women at the End of the First Millennium." In *La Funzione dell'Eroe germanico: Storicità, Metafora, Paradigma*, edited by Teresa Pàroli, 7–25. Atti del Convegno internazionale di studio. Rome: Calamo, 1995.

———. "Reading *Beowulf* with Isidore's *Etymologies*." In *By Definition: Studies in Medieval Literature and Lexicology in Honor of Antonette diPaolo Healey*, edited by Maren Clegg-Hyer, Haruko Momma, and Samantha Zacher, 245–59. Cambridge: Boydell & Brewer, 2020.

———. "The Search for the Anglo-Saxon Oral Poet." *Bulletin of the John Rylands University Library of Manchester* 75 (1993): 11–36. Reprinted (with new postscript) in *Textual and Material Culture in Anglo-Saxon England: Thomas Northcote Toller and the Toller Memorial Lectures*, edited by Donald Scragg, 137–60. Woodbridge: Boydell and Brewer, 2003.

———. "Sex in the *Dictionary of Old English*." In *Unlocking the Wordhord: Anglo-Saxon Studies in Memory of Edward B. Irving, Jr*, edited by Mark C. Amodio and Katherine O'Brien O'Keeffe, 302–12. Toronto: University of Toronto Press, 2003.

———. "Some Uses of Paronomasia in Old English Verse." *Speculum* 47 (1972): 207–26.

———. "A Taste for Knottiness: Skaldic Art at Cnut's Court." *Anglo-Saxon England* 47 (2018 [2020]): 197–217.

———. "To Commemorate Friendship: The Life and Times of Old English *Wine*." In *Old English Tradition: Essays in Honor of J. R. Hall*, edited by Lindy Brady, 3–19. Tempe, AZ: Medieval and Renaissance Texts and Studies, 2021.

———. "Viking Atrocity and Skaldic Verse: The Rite of the Blood Eagle." *English Historical Review* 99 (1984): 332–43.

Frege, Gottlob. "Negation" (1919). In *The Frege Reader*, edited by Michael Beaney, 346–61. Oxford: Blackwell, 1997.

Frotscher, Antje G. "Treasure and Violence: Mapping a Conceptual Metaphor in Medieval Heroic Literature." *Neophilologus* 97 (2013): 753–74.

Fulk, R. D. *A History of Old English Meter*. Philadelphia: University of Pennsylvania Press, 1992.

———. "Inductive Methods in the Textual Criticism of Old English Verse." *Medievalia et Humanistica*, n.s., 23 (1996): 1–24.

———. "On Argumentation in Old English Philology with Particular Reference to the Editing and Dating of *Beowulf*." *Anglo-Saxon England* 32 (2005): 1–26.

———. "Six Cruces in *Beowulf*." In O'Brien O'Keeffe and Orchard, eds., *Latin Learning and English Lore*, 1:349–67.

Gade, Kari Ellen. "Ælfric in Iceland." In *Learning and Understanding in the Old Norse World: Essays in Honour of Margaret Clunies Ross*, edited by Judy Quinn, Kate Heslop, and Tarrin Wills, 321–39. Turnhout: Brepols, 2007.

———. "The Dating and Attribution of Verses in the Skald Sagas." In *Skaldsagas: Text, Vocation, and Desire in the Icelandic Sagas of Poets*, edited by Russell G. Poole, 50–74. Berlin: De Gruyter, 2001.

———. "On the Recitation of Old Norse Skaldic Poetry." In *Studien zum Altgermanischen*, edited by Heiko Uecker, 126–51. Berlin: De Gruyter, 1994.

———. *The Structure of Old Norse Dróttkvætt Poetry*. Islandica 49. Ithaca, NY: Cornell University Press, 1995.

Gallagher, R. "Latin Acrostic Poetry in Anglo-Saxon England: Reassessing the Contribution of John the Old Saxon." *Medium Ævum* 86 (2017): 249–74.

Garmonsway, G. N., and Jacqueline Simpson. *Beowulf and Its Analogues*. New York: Dutton, 1968.

Garrison, Mary. "Quid Hinieldus cum Christo?" In O'Brien O'Keeffe and Orchard, eds., *Latin Learning and English Lore*, 1:237–59.

Gauger, Hans-Martin. "Zur Frage des Stils." In *Stilfragen*, edited by Willi Erzgräber et al., 9–27. Tübingen: Gunter Narr, 1992.

Genette, Gérard. *Mimologiques*. Paris: Seuil, 1976.

Getty, Michael. *The Metre of Beowulf: A Constraint-Based Approach*. Berlin: De Gruyter, 2002.

Ghosh, Shami. *Kings' Sagas and Norwegian History: Problems and Perspectives*. Leiden: Brill, 2011.

Gísli Brynjúlfsson. "Oldengelsk og oldnordisk." *Antikvarisk tidskrift för Sverige* 4 (1852–54): 81–143.

Glosecki, Stephen O. *Shamanism and Old English Poetry*. New York: Garland, 1989.

Gneuss, Helmut, and Michael Lapidge. *Anglo-Saxon Manuscripts: A Bibliographical Handlist of Manuscripts and Manuscript Fragments Written or Owned in England up to 1100*. Toronto: University of Toronto Press, 2014.

Godden, Malcolm. "Literary Language." In *The Cambridge History of the English Language*, Vol. 1, *The Beginnings to 1066*, edited by Richard M. Hogg, 490–535. Cambridge: Cambridge University Press, 1992.

Goeres, Erin Michelle. *The Poetics of Commemoration: Skaldic Verse and Social Memory c. 890–1070*. Oxford: Oxford University Press, 2015.

Golston, Chris. "Old English Feet." In *Versatility in Versification: Multidisciplinary Approaches to Metrics*, edited by Tonya Kim Dewey and Frog, 105–22. New York: Peter Lang, 2009.

Gombrich, Ernst Hans. *Art and Illusion: A Study in the Psychology of Pictorial Representation*. Princeton, NJ: Princeton University Press, 1960.

Graham, Stephen. "So What Did the Danes Feel? Emotion and Litotes in Old English Poetry." In *Anglo-Saxon Emotions: Reading the Heart in Old English Language, Literature and Culture*, edited by Alice Jorgensen, Frances McCormack, and Jonathan Wilcox, 75–90. London: Routledge, 2015.

Gräslund, Bo. *Beowulfkvädet: Den nordiska bakgrunden*. Uppsala: Kungliga Vitterhetsakademien, 2018.

Greenfield, Stanley B. *The Interpretation of Old English Poems*. London: Routledge & Kegan Paul, 1972.

Gregory the Great. *Moralia in Iob*. 3 vols. Edited by Marc Adriaen. Corpus Christianorum, Series Latina 143, 143A, 143B. Turnhout: Brepols, 1979–85.

Gretsch, Mechthild. *The Intellectual Foundations of the English Benedictine Reform*. Cambridge: Cambridge University Press, 1999.

Grice, H. Paul. "Logic and Conversation." In *Speech Acts*, edited by Peter Cole and Jerry L. Morgan, 41–58. New York: Academic Press, 1975. Reprinted in Grice, *Studies in the Way of Words*, 22–40. Cambridge, MA: Harvard University Press, 1989,

Griffith, Mark. "Alliterating Finite Verbs and the Origin of Rank in Old English Poetry." In Neidorf et al., eds., *Old English Philology*, 103–21.

———. "Alliterative Licence and the Rhetorical Use of Proper Names in *The Battle of Maldon*." In *Prosody and Poetics in the Early Middle Ages: Essays in Honour of C. B. Hieatt*, edited by M. J. Toswell, 60–79. Toronto: University of Toronto Press, 1995.

———. "Convention and Originality in the Old English 'Beasts of Battle' Type-scene." *Anglo-Saxon England* 22 (1993): 179–99.

———. "Extra Alliteration on Stressed Syllables in Old English Poetry: Types, Uses and Evolution." *Anglo-Saxon England* 47 (2018 [2020]): 69–176.

———, ed. *Judith*. Exeter: University Press of Exeter, 1997.

———. "Old English Poetic Diction Not in Old English Verse or Prose—and the Curious Case of Aldhelm's Five Athletes." *Anglo-Saxon England* 43 (2014): 99–131.

———. "On the Lexical Property Termed 'Rank' in Old English Poetry and Its Later Development." *Notes & Queries* 60 (2013): 1–14.

———. "Poetic Language and the Paris Psalter: The Decay of the Old English Tradition." *Anglo-Saxon England* 20 (1991): 167–86.

———. "The Register of Divine Speech in *Genesis A*." *Anglo-Saxon England* 41 (2013): 63–78.

———. "Some Difficulties in *Beowulf*, lines 874–902: Sigemund Reconsidered." *Anglo-Saxon England* 24 (1995): 11–41.

———. "Verses Quite Like *cwen to gebeddan* in *The Metres of Boethius*." *Anglo-Saxon England* 34 (2005): 145–67.

Grinda, Klaus. "Pigeonholing Old English Poetry: Some Criteria of Metrical Style." *Anglia* 102 (1984): 305–22.

Grønlie, Siân E. *The Saint and the Saga Hero: Hagiography and Early Icelandic Literature*. Cambridge: D. S. Brewer, 2017.

Grønvik, Ottar. "Runeinnskriften på gullhornet fra Gallehus." *Maal og Minne* (1999): 1–18.

Grove, Jonathan. "Recreating Tradition: Sigvatr Þórðarson's *Víkingarvísur* and Óttarr svarti's *Hǫfuðlausn*." In *Á Austrvega. Preprint Papers of the 14th International Saga Conference, Uppsala, 9–15 August 2009*, edited by Agneta Ney, Henrik Williams, and Fredrik Charpentier Ljungqvist, 1:327–35. Gävle: University of Gävle Press, 2009.

Grundtvig, Nikolai F. S. "Et par ord om det nys udkomme angelsaeksiske Digt." *Nyeste Skilderie af Kjøbenhavn* 60 (1815): cols. 945–52.

Guðrún Nordal. *Tools of Literacy: The Role of Skaldic Verse in Icelandic Textual Culture of the Twelfth and Thirteenth Centuries*. Toronto: University of Toronto Press, 2001.

Gullbekk, Svein H. "Coins and Epigraphy: Comments on Literacy in Eleventh-Century Norway." In *Epigraphy in an Intermedial Context*, edited by Alessia Bauer, Elise Kleivance, and Terje Spurkland, 43–58. Dublin: Four Courts Press, 2018.

Gummere, Francis B. *Germanic Origins: A Study in Primitive Culture*. New York: Scribner, 1892.

———. *A Handbook of Poetics for Students of English Verse*. Boston: Ginn, 1885.

Gwara, Scott. "Paradigmatic Wisdom and the Native Genre *giedd* in Old English." *Studi Medievali* 53 (2012): 783–851.

———. "A Record of Anglo-Saxon Pedagogy: Aldhelm's *Epistola ad Heahfridum* and Its Gloss." *Journal of Medieval Latin* 6 (1996): 84–134.

Haber, Tom Burns. *A Comparative Study of the "Beowulf" and the "Aeneid."* Princeton, NJ: Princeton University Press, 1931.

Hadley, Dawn M. "In Search of the Vikings." In *Vikings and the Danelaw: Select Papers from the Proceedings of the Thirteenth Viking Congress*, edited by James Graham-Campbell et al., 13–30. Oxford: Oxbow Books, 2001.

Hahn, J., and S. Munzel. "Knochenflöten aus dem Aurignaien des Geissenklösterle bei Blaubeuren, Alb-Donau-Kreis." *Fundberichte aus Baden-Württemberg* 20 (1995): 1–12.

Hall, J. R. "*Exodus* 166b, *cwyldrof*; 162–67, the Beasts of Battle." *Neophilologus* 74 (1990): 112–21.

———. "*Exodus* 449a: *beorhhliðu*." *American Notes and Queries* 22 (1984): 94–97.

———. "*Mansceaðan*: Old English *Exodus* 37." *Neophilologus* 66 (1982): 145–48.

———. "Old English *sæbeorg*: *Exodus* 442a, *Andreas* 308a." *Papers on Language and Literature* 25 (1989): 127–34.

Hammerich, Frederik. *De episk-kristelige oldkvad hos de gotisk folk*. Copenhagen: Gyldendal, 1873.

Harmon, William. "Rhyme in English Verse: History, Structure, Functions." *Studies in Philology* 84 (1987): 365–93.

Harmon, William, and C. H. Holman. *A Handbook to Literature*. 7th ed. Upper Saddle River, NJ: Prentice Hall, 1996.

Harris, A. Leslie. "Litotes and Superlative in *Beowulf*." *English Studies* 69 (1988): 1–11.

Harris, Joseph C. "*Brunanburh* 12b-13a and Some Skaldic Passages." In *Magister Regis: Studies in Honor of Robert Earl Kaske*, edited by Arthur Groos et al., 61–68. New York: Fordham University Press, 1986.

———. "Elegy in Old English and Old Norse." In *The Old English Elegies*, edited by Martin Green, 46–56. Rutherford, NJ: Fairleigh Dickinson University Press, 1983.

———. "The Rök Stone through Anglo-Saxon Eyes." In *Anglo-Saxons and the North*, edited by Matti Kilpiö et al., 11–45. Tempe: Arizona Center for Medieval and Renaissance Studies, 2009.

Harris, Richard L. *A Chorus of Grammars: The Correspondence of George Hickes and His Collaborators on the "Thesaurus linguarum septentrionalium."* Publications of the Dictionary of Old English 4. Toronto: Pontifical Institute of Mediaeval Studies, 1992.

Harris, Sara. "*Tam Anglis quam Danis*: 'Old Norse' Terminology in the *Constitutiones de foresta*." *Anglo-Norman Studies* 37 (2014): 131–48.

———. *The Linguistic Past in Twelfth-Century Britain*. Cambridge: Cambridge University Press, 2017.

Hartman, Megan E. *Poetic Style and Innovation in Old English, Old Norse, and Old Saxon*. Richard Rawlinson Center Series for Anglo-Saxon Studies. Berlin: De Gruyter, 2020.

Hatto, A. T. "Snake-swords and Boar-helms in *Beowulf*." *English Studies* 38 (1957): 145–60.

Haugen, Einar. *The First Grammatical Treatise: The Earliest Germanic Phonology*. 2nd ed. London: Longman, 1972.

Hawk, Brandon W. "Isidorian Influence in Ælfric's Preface to Genesis." *English Studies* 95 (2004): 357–66.

Heaney, Seamus. *Beowulf: A New Verse Translation*. New York: Norton, 2000.

———. *The Spirit Level*. London: Faber & Faber, 1996.

Heinzel, Richard. "Über die Hervararsaga." In *Sitzungsberihte der Österreichischen (Kaiserlichen) Akademie der Wissenschaften in Wien*, Phil.-hist. Klasse 114, 417–519. Vienna, 1887.

———. "Über den Stil der altgermanischen Poesie." In *Quellen und Forschungen zur Sprach- und Kulturgeschichte der germanischen Völker*, 10:1–54. Strassburg: Trübner, 1875.

Heller-Roazen, Daniel. *Dark Tongues: The Art of Rogues and Riddlers*. New York: Zone, 2013.

———. *Echolalias: On the Forgetting of Language*. New York: Zone, 2005.

———. *No One's Ways: An Essay on Infinite Naming*. New York: Zone, 2017.

Helm, Karl. "Hansa." *Beiträge zur Geschichte der deutschen Sprache und Literatur* 29 (1903): 194–96.

Henry of Huntingdon. *Historia Anglorum*. Edited and translated by Diana Greenway. Oxford: Clarendon, 1996.

Heusler, Andreas. *Die altgermanische Dichtung*. Berlin: Athenaion, 1923.

———. *Deutsche Versgeschichte, mit Einschluss des altenglischen und altnordischen Stabreimverses*. Berlin: De Gruyter, 1925.

Hiatt, Alfred. "Genre without System." In *Middle English: Twenty-First Century Approaches to Literature*, edited by Paul Strohm, 277–94. Oxford: Oxford University Press, 2007.

Hickes, George. *Linguarum veterum septentrionalium thesaurus grammatico-criticus et archæologicus*. 2 vols. Oxford: Sheldonian Theatre, 1703–5.

Hieatt, Constance B. "Alliterative Patterns in the Hypermetric Lines of Old English Verse." *Modern Philology* 71 (1974): 237–42.

———. "Envelope Patterns and the Structure of *Beowulf*." *English Studies in Canada* 1 (1975): 249–65.

Hill, John M., ed. *On the Aesthetics of Beowulf and Other Old English Poems*. Toronto: University of Toronto Press, 2010.

Hill, Joyce. "Ælfric's Use of Etymologies." *Anglo-Saxon England* 17 (1988): 35–44.

———, ed. *Old English Minor Heroic Poems*. Rev. ed. Durham: Durham Medieval Texts, 1994.

Hill, Thomas D. "Invocation of the Trinity and the Tradition of the *Lorica* in Old English Poetry." *Speculum* 56 (1981): 259–67.

———. "The Myth of the Ark-born Son of Noe and the West-Saxon Royal Genealogical Tables." *Harvard Theological Review* 80 (1987): 379–83.

Hines, John. "The *Benedicite* Canticle in Old English Verse: An Early Runic Witness from Southern Lincolnshire." *Anglia* 133 (2015): 257–77.

Hinton, Leanne, Johanna Nichols, and John J. Ohala, eds. *Sound Symbolism*. Cambridge: Cambridge University Press, 1994.

Hoffmann, M. E. *Negatio contrarii: A Study of Latin Litotes*. Assen/Maastricht: Van Gorcum, 1987.

Hofmann, Dietrich. *Nordisch-englische Lehnbeziehungen der Wikingerzeit*. Bibliotheca Arnamagnæana 14. Copenhagen: Munksgaard, 1955.

———. *Die Versstrukturen der altsächsischen Stabreimgedichte Heliand und Genesis*. 2 vols. Heidelberg: G. Winter, 1991.

Hollander, Lee M. "Litotes in Old Norse." *PMLA* 53 (1938): 1–33.

———. "Observations on Skaldic Rime Usage with Special Reference to the *dunhent* and *liðhent* Varieties of *dróttkvætt*." *PMLA* 61 (1946): 891–909.

———. *The Skalds: A Selection of their Poems, with Introduction and Notes*. Princeton, NJ: Princeton University Press, 1945.

Hollmérus, Ragnar. *Studier över allitterationen i Eddan*. Helsingfors: Mercator, 1936.

Holmberg, Per, Bo Gräslund, Olof Sundqvist, and Henrik Williams. "The Rök Runestone and the End of the World." *Futhark: International Journal of Runic Studies* 9–10 (2018–19): 7–38.

Holthausen, Ferdinand. *Altenglisches etymologisches Wörterbuch* (1934). 3rd ed. unrev. Heidelberg: Winter, 1991.

Holtsmark, Anne. "Gevjons plog." *Maal og Minne* (1944): 169–79; reprinted in Holtsmark, *Studier in norrøn diktning*, 162–76. Oslo: Gyldendal, 1956.

Honegger, Thomas. "Form and Function: The Beasts of Battle Revisited." *English Studies* 79 (1998): 289–98.

Hoover, David L. *A New Theory of Old English Meter*. New York: Lang, 1985.

Hopkins, Gerard Manley. *The Collected Works of Gerard Manley Hopkins*. Vol. 2, *Correspondence 1882–1889*. Edited by R. K. R. Thornton and Catherine Phillips. Oxford: Oxford University Press, 2013.

Horn, C. R. "Zur Metrik des Heliand." *Beiträge zur Geschichte der deutschen Sprache und Literatur* 5 (1878): 164–91.

Horn, Laurence R. "Lie-toe-tease: Double Negatives and Unexcluded Middles." *Philosophical Studies* 174 (2017): 79–103.

———. "Multiple Negation in English and Other Languages." In *The Expression of Negation*, edited by Laurence R. Horn, 111–48. Berlin: De Gruyter, 2010.

———. *A Natural History of Negation*. Chicago: University of Chicago Press, 1989.

———. "Uncovering the Un-word: A Study in Lexical Pragmatics." *Sophia Linguistica* 49 (2002): 1–64.

Housman, A. E. *Collected Poems and Selected Prose of A. E. Housman*. Edited by Christopher Ricks. London: Lane, 1988.

Howard, Edwin J. "Old English Tree Climbing: *Christ* vv. 678–79." *Journal of English and Germanic Philology* 30 (1931): 152–54.

Howe, Nicholas. "Aldhelm's *Enigmata* and Isidorian Etymology." *Anglo-Saxon England* 14 (1985): 37–59.

———. "The New Millennium." In *A Companion to Anglo-Saxon Literature*, edited by Phillip Pulsiano and Elaine Treharne, 496–505. Oxford: Blackwell, 2001.

———. "What We Talk about When We Talk about Style." In *Anglo-Saxon Styles*, edited by Catherine E. Karkov and George H. Brown, 169–78. Albany: State University of New York Press, 2003.

Howlett, David R. *British Books in Biblical Style*. Dublin: Four Courts Press, 1997.

Hreinn Benediktsson, ed. *The First Grammatical Treatise*. Reykjavík: Institute of Nordic Linguistics, 1972.

Hübner, Alfred. *Die mhd. Ironie oder die Litotes im Altdeutschen*. Palaestra 170. Leipzig: Mayer & Müller, 1930.

Hultgård, Anders. "Midgardbrinner: Ragnarök i religionshistorisk belysning." *Acta Academiae Regiae Gustavi Adolphi* 196 (Uppsala, 2017): 171–75.

Hussey, Matthew T. "Dunstan, Æthelwold, and Isidorean Exegesis in Old English Glosses: Oxford, Bodleian Library Bodley 319." *Review of English Studies*, n.s. (2009): 681–704.

Hutcheson, B. R. "Accidental Alliteration in Old English Poetry: A Reconsideration." *English Language Notes* 30 (1992): 1–10.

———. *Old English Poetic Metre*. Cambridge: D. S. Brewer, 1995.

Ingalls, Daniel H. H., ed. and trans., with Jeffrey Moussaieff Masson and M. V. Patwardhan. *The "Dhvanyāloka" of Ānandavardhana with the "Locana" of Abhinavagupta*. Cambridge, MA: Harvard University Press, 1990.

Irvine, Susan, ed. *Chronicle E*. The Anglo-Saxon Chronicle: A Collaborative Edition, 7. Cambridge: D. S. Brewer, 2004.

Irving, Edward B. "The Charge of the Saxon Brigade: Tennyson's 'Battle of Brunanburh.'" In *Literary Appropriations of the Anglo-Saxons from the Thirteenth to the Twentieth Century*, edited by Donald Scragg and Carole Weinberg, 174–93. Cambridge: Cambridge University Press, 2000.

———. "Heroic Experience in the Old English Riddles." In *Old English Shorter Poems: Basic Readings*, edited by Katherine O'Brien O'Keeffe, 199–212. New York: Garland, 1994.

Isaacs, Neil D. "Up a Tree: To See *The Fates of Men*." In *Anglo-Saxon Poetry: Essays in Appreciation. For John C. McGalliard*, edited by Lewis E. Nicholson and Dolores Warwick Frese, 363–75. Notre Dame, IN: University of Notre Dame Press, 1975.

Isidore of Seville. *Etymologiarum sive Originum libri XX*. 2 vols. Edited by W. M. Lindsay. Oxford: Clarendon, 1911.

———. *The Etymologies of Isidore of Seville*. Translated by Stephen A. Barney, W. J. Lewis, J. A. Beach, and Oliver Berghof with Muriel Hall. Cambridge: Cambridge University Press, 2006.

Itó, Tsukusu. "The Gosforth Fishing Stone and *Hymiskviða*: An Example of Inter-Communicability between Old English and Old Norse Speakers." *Scripta Islandica* 60 (2009): 137–57.

Jackson, Peter. "Det urnordiska namnelementet *–gastiz*. Några språk- og religionshistoriska sonderingar." *Studia anthroponymica Scandinavica: Tidskrift för nordisk personnamnsforskning* 30 (2012): 5–18.

Jacob, Georg. *Arabische Berichte von Gesandten an germanische Fürstenhöfe aus dem 9 und 10 Jahrhundert*. Quellen zur deutschen Volkskunde 1. Berlin and Leipzig: De Gruyter, 1927.

Jakob Benediktsson. "Icelandic Traditions of the Scyldings." *Saga-Book of the Viking Society* 15 (1957–61): 48–66.

Jakobson, Roman. "Linguistics and Poetics" and "What Is Poetry?" In Jakobson, *Language and Literature*, edited by Krystyna Pomorska and Stephen Rudy, 62–94; 368–78. Cambridge, MA: Belknap, 1987.

———. "On the So-Called Vowel Alliteration in Germanic Verse," with an appendix by Sigrid Valfells. *Zeitschrift für Phonetik, Sprachwissenschaft und Kommunikationsforschung, Festgabe für Otto von Essen* 16 (1963): 85–94.

Jauss, Hans Robert. "Theory of Genres and Medieval Literature." In *Modern Genre Theory*, edited by David Duff, 127–47. London: Longman, 2000.

Jellinek, Max. "Ein Kapitel aus der Geschichte der deutschen Grammatik." In *Abhandlungen zur germanischen Philologie: Festgabe für Richard Heinzel*, edited by Ferdinand Detter, 31–111. Halle an der Saale: Niemeyer, 1898. Reprint, Hildesheim: Olms, 1985.

Jesch, Judith. "Eagles, Ravens and Wolves: Beasts of Battle, Symbols of Victory and Death." In *The Scandinavians from the Vendel Period to the Tenth Century*, edited by Jesch, 251–80. Woodbridge: Boydell, 2001.

———. "Knútr in Poetry and History." In *International Scandinavian and Medieval Studies in Memory of Gerd Wolfgang Weber*, edited by Michael Dallapiazza et al., 243–56. Trieste: Parnaso, 2000.

———. "The Norse Gods in England and the Isle of Man." In *Myths, Legends, and Heroes: Essays on Old Norse and Old English Literature*, edited by Daniel Anlezark, 11–24. Toronto: University of Toronto Press, 2011.

———. "The Norse Gods in Scotland." In *Scandinavian Scotland—Twenty Years After*, edited by Alex Woolf, 49–73. St. Andrews: Committee for Dark Age Studies, 2009.

———. "Scandinavians and 'Cultural Paganism' in Late Anglo-Saxon England." In *The Christian Tradition in Anglo-Saxon England*, ed. Paul Cavill, 55–68. Cambridge: D. S. Brewer, 2004.

———. *Ships and Men in the Late Viking Age: The Vocabulary of Runic Inscriptions and Skaldic Verse*. Woodbridge: Boydell, 2001.

———. "Skaldic Verse in Scandinavian England." In *Vikings and the Danelaw: Select Papers from the Proceedings of the Thirteenth Viking Congress*, edited by James Graham-Campbell et al., 313–25. Oxford: Oxbow Books, 2001.

———. *The Viking Diaspora*. London: Routledge, 2015.

Jesperson, Otto. *Negation in English and Other Languages*. Copenhagen: Høst, 1917.

Johnson, Eleanor. *Practicing Literary Theory in the Middle Ages: Ethics and the Mixed Form in Chaucer, Gower, Usk, and Hoccleve*. Chicago: University of Chicago Press, 2013.

Johnston, Andrew James. "*Beowulf* as Anti-Virgilian World Literature." In Dumitrescu and Weiskott, eds., *The Shapes of Early English Poetry*, 37–58.

Jón Helgason. *Handritaspjall.* Reykjavík: Mál og Menning, 1958.

Jones, Chris. *Fossil Poetry: Anglo-Saxon and Linguistic Nativism in Nineteenth-Century Poetry.* Oxford: Oxford University Press, 2018.

———. *Strange Likeness: The Use of Old English in Twentieth-Century Poetry.* Oxford: Oxford University Press, 2006.

Kahle, Bernhard. *Die Sprache der Skalden auf Grund der Binnen- und Endreime verbunden mit einem rimarium.* Strassburg: Trübner, 1892.

Karasawa, Kazutomo, ed. *The Old English Metrical Calendar* [*Menologium*]. Cambridge: D. S. Brewer, 2015.

Karkov, Catherine E. *The Art of Anglo-Saxon England.* Woodbridge: Boydell, 2011.

———. "Hagar and Ishmael: The Uncanny and the Exile." In *Imagining the Jew in Anglo-Saxon Literature and Culture*, edited by Samantha Zacher, 197–218. Toronto: University of Toronto Press, 2016.

Karlsen, Espen. "Fragments of Patristic and Other Ecclesiastical Literature in Norway from c. 1100 until the Fifteenth Century." In *Latin Manuscripts of Medieval Norway: Studies in Memory of Lilli Gjerløw*, ed. Espen Karlsen, 215–69. Oslo: Novus, 2013.

Kemble, John Mitchell. *The Poetry of the Codex Vercellensis with an English Translation.* London: Taylor, 1843.

Kendall, Calvin B. *The Metrical Grammar of Beowulf.* Cambridge: Cambridge University Press, 1991.

———. "The Prefix *un-* and the Metrical Grammar of *Beowulf.*" *Anglo-Saxon England* 10 (1982): 39–52.

Ker, N. R. *Catalogue of Manuscripts Containing Anglo-Saxon.* Oxford: Clarendon, 1957; reissued 1990.

Ker, W. P. *The Dark Ages.* Edinburgh: Blackwood, 1904.

———. *Epic and Romance: Essays on Medieval Literature.* London: Macmillan, 1897.

Kermode, Frank. *The Sense of an Ending: Studies in the Theory of Fiction.* Oxford: Oxford University Press, 1967.

Kershaw, Jane F. "Culture and Gender in the Danelaw: Scandinavian and Anglo-Scandinavian Brooches." *Viking and Medieval Scandinavia* 5 (2009): 295–325.

Kershaw, Nora. *Anglo-Saxon and Norse Poems.* Cambridge: Cambridge University Press, 1922.

Keynes, Simon. "The Declining Reputation of King Æthelred the Unready." In *Ethelred the Unready: Papers from the Millenary Conference*, edited by David Hill, 227–53. Oxford: British Archaeological Reports, 1978.

Kintgen, Eugene R. "*Lif*, *Lof*, *Leof*, *Lufu*, and *Geleafa* in Old English Poetry." *Neuphilologische Mitteilungen* 78 (1977): 309–16.

Klaeber, Friedrich, ed. *Beowulf and the Fight at Finnsburg.* 3rd ed. Lexington, MA: D. C. Heath, 1936; supplemented 1941 and 1950.

Klinck, Roswitha. *Die lateinische Etymologie des Mittelalters*. Munich: Fink, 1970.

Klingenberg, Heinz. *Runenschrift—Schriftdenken—Runeninschriften*. Heidelberg: Winter, 1973.

Kluge, Friedrich. "Zur Geschichte des Reimes im Altgermanischen." *Beiträge zur Geschichte der deutschen Sprache und Literatur* 9 (1884): 422–50.

Knörk, Fritz. *Die Negation in der altenglischen Dichtung*. PhD diss., University of Kiel, 1907.

Kock, Ernst Albin. *Notationes Norrœnæ: Anteckningar till edda- och skaldediktning*. Lunds Universitets årsskrift, new series 1. Lund: Gleerup, 1923–44.

Kopár, Lilla. *Gods and Settlers: The Iconography of Norse Mythology in Anglo-Scandinavian Sculpture*. Turnhout: Brepols, 2012.

Krackow, Otto. *Die Nominalkomposita als Kunstmittel im altenglischen Epos*. Berlin: Mayer & Müller, 1903.

Krause, Arnulf. *Die Dichtung des Eyvindr skáldaspillir: Edition–Kommentar—Untersuchungen*. Leverkusen: Literaturverlag Norden Mark Reinhardt, 1990.

Krause, Arthur. *Litotes und ähnliche Figuren im Nibelungenliede*. Berlin: Ebering, 1913.

Krause, Wolfgang. *Die Kenning als typische Stilfigur der germanischen und keltischen Dichtersprache*. Halle: Niemeyer, 1930.

Kreutzer, Gert. *Die Dichtungslehre der Skalden: Poetologische Terminologie und Autorenkommentare als Grundlage einer Gattungspoetik*. 2nd ed. Meisenheim am Glan: Hain, 1977.

Kristján Árnason. "Alliteration in Iceland: From the Edda to Modern Verse and Pop Lyrics." In *Alliteration in Culture*, ed. Jonathan Roper, 123–40. London: Palgrave Macmillan, 2011.

———. "On the Principles of Nordic Rhyme and Alliteration." *Arkiv för nordisk filologi* 122 (2007): 79–114.

———. *The Rhythms of Dróttkvætt and Other Old Icelandic Metres*. Reykjavík: University of Iceland, 1991.

Krömmelbein, Thomas, ed. *Die Dritte Grammatische Abhandlung: Der isländische Text nach den Handschriften*. Oslo: Novus, 1998.

———. *Skaldische Metaphorik: Studien zur Funktion der Kenningsprache in skaldischen Dichtungen des 9. und 10. Jahrhunderts*. Kirchzarten: Burg-Verlag, 1983.

Kubouchi, Tadao. "Wulfstan's Scandinavian Loanword Usage: An Aspect of the Linguistic Situation in the Late Old English Danelaw." In *Inside Old English: Essays in Honour of Bruce Mitchell*, edited by John Walmsley, 134–52. Oxford: Blackwell, 2006.

Kuhn, Hans. "Anlautend *p*- im Germanischen." *Zeitschrift für Mundartforschung* 28 (1961): 1–31. Reprinted in Kuhn, *Kleine Schriften: Aufsätze und Rezensionen aus den Gebieten der germanischen und nordischen Sprach-, Literatur- und Kulturgeschichte*, Vol. 1, *Sprachgeschichte, Verskunst*, 361–89. Berlin: De Gruyter, 1969.

———. *Das Dróttkvætt.* Heidelberg: Winter, 1983.

———. "Vor tausend Jahren: Zur Geschichte des skaldischen Innenreims." In *Speculum Norroenum: Norse Studies in Memory of Gabriel Turville-Petre*, edited by Ursula Dronke et al., 293–309. Odense: Odense University Press, 1981.

———. "Westgermanisches in der altnordischen Verskunst." *Beiträge zur Geschichte der deutschen Sprache und Literatur* 63 (1939): 178–236.

Lactantius. *L. Caeli Firmiani Lactanti Opera omnia.* Edited by Samuel Brandt and Georg Laubmann. Corpus scriptorium ecclesiasticorum Latinorum 19, 27. Vienna: Tempsky, 1890–97..

Lanham, Richard. *Analyzing Prose.* 2nd ed. New York: Continuum, 2003.

Lapidge, Michael. "Aldhelm's Latin and Old English Verse." *Comparative Literature* 31 (1979): 249–314.

———. *The Anglo-Saxon Library.* Oxford: Oxford University Press, 2006.

———. "An Aspect of Old English Poetic Diction: The Postpositioning of Prepositions." In *Inside Old English: Essays in Honour of Bruce Mitchell*, edited by John Walmsley, 153–80. Oxford: Blackwell, 2006.

———. "An Isidorian Epitome from Early Anglo-Saxon England." *Romanobarbarica* 10 (1988–89): 443–83. Reprinted in Lapidge, *Anglo-Latin Literature, 600–899*, 183–223. London: Hambledon, 1996.

———. "Old English Poetic Compounds: A Latin Perspective." In *Intertexts: Studies in Anglo-Saxon Culture Presented to Paul E. Szarmach*, edited by Virginia Blanton and Helene Scheck, 17–32. Tempe: Arizona Center for Medieval and Renaissance Studies, 2008.

———. "The School of Hadrian and Theodore." *Anglo-Saxon England* 15 (1986): 45–72. Reprinted in Lapidge, *Anglo-Latin Literature, 600–899*, 141–68 and 502–3. London: Hambledon, 1996.

———. "Some Latin Poems as Evidence for the Reign of Athelstan." *Anglo-Saxon England* 9 (1981): 61–98. Reprinted in Lapidge, *Anglo-Latin Literature, 900–1066*, 49–86. London: Hambledon, 1993.

———. "Theodore and Anglo-Latin Octosyllabic Verse." In Lapidge, *Anglo-Latin Literature, 600–899*, 225–45. London: Hambledon, 1996.

Larkin, Philip. *Collected Poems.* Edited by Anthony Thwaite. London: Faber & Faber, 1988.

———. *Selected Letters of Philip Larkin, 1940–1985.* Edited by Anthony Thwaite. London: Faber & Faber, 1992.

———. *Whitsun Weddings.* London: Faber & Faber, 1964.

Larrington, Carolyne. *Winter Is Coming: The Medieval World of "Game of Thrones."* London: Tauris, 2015.

Lattimore, Richard, trans. *The Odyssey of Homer.* New York: Harper, 1999.

Lawrence, John. *Chapters on Alliterative Verse.* London: Frowde, 1893.

Lefkowitz, Mary R. *The Lives of the Greek Poets.* 2nd ed. Baltimore: Johns Hopkins University Press, 2012,

Lehmann, Winfred P. *The Alliterations of Old Saxon Poetry*. Oslo: Aschehoug, 1953.

Lendinara, Patrizia. "L'episodio di Sigemund nel *Beowulf* (vv. 874b–915)." In *La tradizione nibelungico-volsungica*, Atti del XXXVI Convegno dell'Associazione Italiana di Filologia Germanica, edited by M. Giovanna Arcamone and Marco Battaglia, 157–92. Pisa: ETS, 2010.

Leneghan, Francis. *The Dynastic Drama of Beowulf*. Cambridge: D. S. Brewer, 2020.

———. "Making the Psalter Sing." In *The Psalms and Medieval Literature: From the Conversion to the Reformation*, edited by Tamara Atkin and Francis Leneghan, 173–97. Cambridge: D. S. Brewer, 2017.

Le Page, R. B. "Alliterative Patterns as a Test of Style in Old English Poetry." *Journal of English and Germanic Philology* 58 (1959): 434–41.

Lerer, Seth. "The Endurance of Formalism in Middle English Studies." *Literature Compass* 1 (2003): 1–15.

Lewis, Charlton M. "Notes on Transverse Alliteration." *Modern Language Notes* 16 (1901): 43–44.

Lewis, Richard A. "Plurilinear Alliteration in Old English Poetry." *Texas Studies in Literature and Language* 16 (1975): 589–602.

———. "Old English Poetry: Alliteration and Structural Interlace." *Language and Style* 6 (1973): 196–205.

Leyerle, John. "The Interlace Structure of *Beowulf*." *University of Toronto Quarterly* 37 (1967): 1–17.

Liberman, Anatoly. Review of *The Verse and Language of Old Germanic Poetry* by O. A. Smirnitskaia. *Scandinavian Studies* 70 (1998): 87–108.

Liebermann, Felix, ed. *Die Gesetze der Angelsachsen*. 3 vols. Halle: Niemeyer, 1897–1916. Reprint, Aalen: Scientia, 1960,

Lie, Hallvard. *"Natur" og "unatur" i skaldekunsten*. Oslo: Aschehoug, 1957. Reprinted in Lie, *Om sagakunst og skaldskap: Utvalgte avhandlinger*, 201–315. Øvre Ervik: Alvheim & Eide, 1982.

———. "Skaldestil-studier." *Maal og Minne* (1952): 1–92. Reprinted in Lie, *Om sagakunst og skaldskap*, 109–200.

Liggins, Elizabeth. "Irony and Understatement in *Beowulf*." *Parergon* 29 (1981): 3–7.

Lindow, John. "Narrative and the Nature of Skaldic Poetry." *Arkiv för nordisk filologi* 97 (1982): 94–121.

Lindqvist, Sune. *Gotlands Bildsteine 1*. Stockholm: Wahlström & Widstrand, 1941–42.

Liu, Alan. "The Power of Formalism." *English Literary History* 56 (1989): 721–71.

Liuzza, Roy M. *Beowulf: A New Verse Translation*. Toronto: Broadview Press, 2000.

———. "Iron and Irony in *Beowulf*." In *Beowulf at Kalamazoo: Essays on Translation and Performance*, edited by Jana K. Schulman and Paul E. Szarmach, 50–68. Kalamazoo, MI: Medieval Studies Publications, 2012.

Lochrie, Karma. "Anglo-Saxon Morning Sickness." *Neophilologus* 70 (1986): 316–18.
Lockett, Leslie. *Anglo-Saxon Psychologies in the Vernacular and Latin Traditions.* Toronto: University of Toronto Press, 2011.
———. "The Role of Grendel's Arm in Feud, Law, and the Narrative Structure of *Beowulf*." In O'Brien O'Keeffe and Orchard, eds., *Latin Learning and English Lore*, 1:368–88.
Longfellow, Henry Wadsworth. "Anglo-Saxon Literature." *North American Review* 47 (1839): 90–134.
Losquino, Irene Garcia. *The Early Runic Inscriptions: Their Western Features*. New York: Peter Lang, 2015.
Louviot, Elise. *Direct Speech in Beowulf and Other Old English Narrative Poems.* Cambridge: D. S. Brewer, 2016.
Machan, T. W. "Snorri's *Edda*, Mythology, and Anglo-Saxon Studies." *Modern Philology* 113 (2016): 295–309.
Macrae-Gibson, O. D., ed. *The Old English Riming Poem*. Cambridge: D. S. Brewer, 1983.
Magennis, Hugh. "'No Sex Please, We're Anglo-Saxons': Attitudes to Sexuality in Old English Prose and Poetry." *Leeds Studies in English* 26 (1995): 1–27.
Magnús Fjalldal. *Anglo-Saxon England in Icelandic Medieval Texts*. Toronto: University of Toronto Press, 2005.
Magnus, Margaret. *Gods of the Word: Archetypes in the Consonants*. Kirksville, MI: Thomas Jefferson University Press, 1999.
Magoun, Frank P. "The Theme of the Beasts of Battle in Anglo-Saxon Poetry." *Neuphilologische Mitteilungen* 56 (1955): 81–90.
Major, Tristan. *Undoing Babel: The Tower of Babel in Anglo-Saxon Literature.* Toronto: University of Toronto Press, 2018.
Males, Mikael. "Applied *Grammatica:* Conjuring Up the Native *Poetae*." In *Intellectual Culture in Medieval Scandinavia, c. 1100–1350*, edited by Stefka Georgieva Eriksen, 263–301. Turnhout: Brepols, 2016.
———, ed. *Etymology and Wordplay in Medieval Literature*. Turnhout: Brepols, 2018.
———. *The Poetic Genesis of Old Icelandic Literature*. Berlin: De Gruyter, 2020.
Malkiel, Yakov. *Diachronic Problems in Phonosymbolism*. Philadelphia: J. Benjamins, 1990.
Malm, Mats. "Two Cultures of Visual(ized) Cognition." In *Intellectual Culture in Medieval Scandinavia, c. 1100–1350*, edited by Stefka Georgieva Eriksen, 309–30. Turnhout: Brepols, 2016.
———. "Varför heter det kenning?" In *Snorres Edda in europeisk og islandsk kultur*, edited by Jon Gunnar Jørgensen, 73–90. Reykholt: Snorrastofa, 2009.
Malone, Kemp, ed. *Widsith*. Copenhagen: Rosenkilde and Bagger, 1962.
Marenbon, John. "Les sources du vocabulaire d'Aldhelm." *Archivum Latinitatis Medii Aevi (Bulletin du Cange)* 41 (1979): 75–90.

Maring, Heather. *Signs That Sing: Hybrid Poetics in Old English Verse*. Gainesville: University Press of Florida, 2017.

Markey, Thomas. "HlewagastiR Exposed." In *Vox Germanica: Essays in Germanic Languages and Literatures in Honor of James E. Cathey*, edited by Stephen J. Harris et al., 89–105. Tempe: Arizona Center for Medieval and Renaissance Studies, 2012.

Marlowe, Frank W. *The Hadza: Hunter-Gatherers of Tanzania*. Berkeley: University of California Press, 2010.

Marold, Edith. "Karlevi. §2: Runenkundliches." In *Reallexikon der Germanischen Altertumskunde*, edited by Heinrich Beck et al., 16:275–80. Berlin: De Gruyter, 2000.

———. *Kenningkunst: Ein Beitrag zu einer Poetik der Skaldendichtung*. Berlin: De Gruyter, 1983.

———. "Ragnarsdrápa und Ragnarssage: Versuch einer Interpretation der Ragnarsdrápa." In *Germanic Dialects: Linguistic and Philological Investigations*, edited by Bela Brogyanyi and Thomas Krömmelbein, 427–57. Amsterdam and Philadelphia: J. Benjamins, 1986.

———. "Runeninschriften als Quelle zur Geschichte der Skaldendichtung." In *Runeninschriften als Quellen interdisziplinäres Forschung*, edited Klaus Düwel and Sean Nowaki, 667–93. Berlin: De Gruyter, 1998.

———. "Der Skald und sein Publikum." In *Studien zum Altgermanischen*, edited by Heiko Uecker, 462–76. Berlin: De Gruyter, 1994.

———. "Vers oder nicht Vers? Zum metrischen Charakter von Runeninschriften im älteren Futhark." *Futhark* 2 (2012): 63–102.

———. "Das Walhallbild in den *Eiríksmál* und den *Hákonarmál*." *Mediaeval Scandinavia* 5 (1972): 19–33.

Mastrelli, Carlo. "La Formula Germanica: 'Sotto l'Helmo.'" *Annali dell'Instituto Universitario Orientale, Napoli, Studi nederlandesi, Studi nordici* 22 (1979): 177–93.

Mayer, C. A. "Die vokalische Allitteration im Heliand." *Zeitschrift für deutsches Altertum* 47 (1904): 413–20.

McKinnell, John. "Eddic Poetry in Anglo-Scandinavian Northern England." In *Vikings and the Danelaw: Select Papers from the Proceedings of the Thirteenth Viking Congress*, edited by James Graham-Campbell et al., 327–44. Oxford: Oxbow, 2001.

———. "*Vǫlundarkviða*: Origins and Interpretation." In *Essays on Eddic Poetry*, edited by Donata Kick and John D. Shafar, 221–48. Toronto: University of Toronto Press, 2014.

Mees, Bernard. "Style, Manner and Formula in Early Germanic Epigraphy." *North-Western European Language Evolution* 54/55 (2008): 63–98.

Meissner, Rudolf. *Die Kenningar der Skalden: Ein Beitrag zur skaldischen Poetik*. Bonn and Leipzig: Schroeder, 1921. Reprint, Hildesheim: Olms, 1984.

Mendelson, Edward. *Early Auden*. London: Faber & Faber, 1981.

Meredith, William. *Partial Accounts: New and Selected Poems*. New York: Knopf, 1987.

Metcalfe, Frederick. *The Englishman and the Scandinavian; or, A Comparison of Anglo-Saxon and Old Norse Literature*. London: Trübner, 1880.

Meyer, Marc. "The Queen's Demesne in Later Anglo-Saxon England." In *The Culture of Christendom: Essays in Medieval History in Memory of Denis L. T. Bethel*, edited by M. Meyer, 75–114. London: Hambledon, 1993.

Meyer, Richard M. *Die altgermanische Poesie nach ihren formelhaften Elementen beschrieben*. Berlin: W. Hertz, 1889.

Mieder, Wolfgang. "All Roads Lead to 'perverbs': Harry Mathews' *Selected Declaration of Dependence*." *Proverbium* 36 (2019): 183–216.

Mikkelsen, Egil. *Looting or Missioning: Insular and Continental Sacred Objects in Viking-Age Contexts in Norway*. Oxford: Oxbow, 2019.

Miller, D. A. *Hidden Hitchcock*. Chicago: University of Chicago Press, 2016.

Miller, J. Hillis. "Poetics Today." *University of Toronto Quarterly* 88 (2019): 101–11.

Milton, John. *Complete Prose Works of John Milton*. 8 vols. Edited by Don M. Wolfe. New Haven, CT: Yale University Press, 1953–82.

Miner, Earl. *Comparative Poetics: An Intercultural Essay on Theories of Literature*. Princeton, NJ: Princeton University Press, 1990.

Minkova, Donka. *Alliteration and Sound Change in Early English*. Cambridge: Cambridge University Press, 2003.

———. "Prosody-Meter Correspondences in Late Old English and *Poema Morale*." In Neidorf et al., eds., *Old English Philology*, 122–43.

Mitchell, Bruce. *Old English Syntax*. 2 vols. Oxford: Clarendon, 1985.

Mitchell, Bruce, and Fred Robinson. *Guide to Old English*. 8th ed. Oxford: Wiley-Blackwell, 2012.

Mize, Britt. *Traditional Subjectivities: The Old English Poetics of Mentality*. Toronto: University of Toronto Press, 2013.

Mohr, Wolfgang. *Kenningstudien: Beiträge zur Stilgeschichte der altgermanischen Dichtung*. Stuttgart: W. Kohlhammer, 1933.

Momma, Haruko. *The Composition of Old English Poetry*. Cambridge: Cambridge University Press, 1997.

———. "Old English Poetic Form: Genre, Style, Prosody." In *The Cambridge History of Early Medieval English Literature*, edited by Clare Lees, 278–308. Cambridge: Cambridge University Press, 2013.

Mone, Franz Joseph. "Zur Kritik des Gedichts vom *Beowulf*." In Mone, *Untersuchungen zur Geschichte der teutschen Heldensage*. Vol. 1 of 2nd series of the Bibliothek der gesammten deutschen National-Literatur, 129–36. Quedlingburg and Leipzig: G. Basse, 1836.

Moretti, Franco. *Distant Reading*. London: Verso, 2013.

———. *Graphs, Maps, Trees: Abstract Models for Literary History.* New York: Verso, 2007.

Morgan, Edwin. *Beowulf: A Verse Translation into Modern English.* Hythe, Kent: Hand and Flower Press, 1952.

———. *Collected Poems.* Manchester: Carcanet, 1997.

Morris, Richard, ed. and trans. *The Blickling Homilies.* 3 vols. EETS o.s. 58, 63, 73. London: Trübner, 1874–80. Reprinted as one volume, London: Oxford University Press, 1967.

Morris, Richard. *Time's Anvil: England, Archaeology and the Imagination.* London: Weidenfeld and Nicolson, 2012.

Mueller Report. Report on the Investigation into Russian Interference in the 2016 Presidential Election, by Special Counsel Robert S. Mueller. 2 vols. 2019.

Myrvoll, Klaus Johan. "The Authenticity of Gísli's Verse." *Journal of English and Germanic Philology* 119 (2020): 220–57.

———. "The Constitutive Features of the *Dróttkvætt* Metre." In *Approaches to Nordic and Germanic Poetry*, edited by Kristján Árnason et al., 229–56. Reykjavík: University of Iceland Press, 2016.

———. "Kronologi i skaldekvæde. Distribusjon av metriske og språklege drag i høve til tradisjonell datering og attribuering." PhD diss., University of Oslo, 2014.

Naumann, Hans-Peter. "English Keywords in Old Norse Literature." In *Words, Words, Words: Philology and Beyond: Festschrift for Andreas Fischer*, edited by Sarah Chevalier and Thomas Honegger, 109–25. Tübingen: Francke, 2012.

———. "*Hann var manna mestr óníðingr*: Zur Poetizität metrischer Runeninschriften." In *Studien zum Altgermanischen: Festschrift für Heinrich Beck*, edited by Heiko Uecker, 490–502. Berlin: De Gruyter, 1994.

———. *Metrische Runeninschriften in Skandinavien.* Tübingen: Narr Francke, 2018.

Neckel, Gustav. "Die kriegerische Kultur der heidnischen Germanen." *Germanisch-romanische Monatsschrift* 7 (1919): 26–33.

Neckel, Gustav, and Hans Kuhn, eds. *Edda: Die Lieder des Codex Regius nebst verwandten Denkmälern.* Vol. 1, *Text.* 5th ed. Heidelberg: Winter, 1983.

Neidorf, Leonard, and Rafael J. Pascual. "Old Norse Influence on the Language of *Beowulf*: A Reassessment." *Journal of Germanic Linguistics* 31 (2019): 298–322.

Neidorf, Leonard, Rafael J. Pascual, and Tom Shippey, eds. *Old English Philology: Studies in Honour of R. D. Fulk.* Cambridge: D. S. Brewer, 2016.

Neville, Jennifer. "Fostering the Cuckoo: *Exeter Book Riddle 9*." *Review of English Studies* 58 (2007): 431–46.

———. "Hrothgar's Horses: Feral or Thoroughbred?" *Anglo-Saxon England* 35 (2006): 131–57.

Nielsen, Hans Frede. "The Linguistic Status of the Early Runic Inscriptions of Scandinavia." In *Runeninschriften als Quellen interdisziplinären Forschung*, Abhandlungen des Vierten Internationalen Symposiums über Runen und Runeninschriften in Göttingen, 4–9 August 1995, edited by Klaus Düwel, 539–55. Berlin: De Gruyter, 1998.

———. *Old English and the Continental Germanic Languages: A Survey of Morphological and Phonological Interrelations.* 2nd ed. Innsbruck: Institut für Sprachwissenschaft der Universität Innsbruck, 1985.

Niles, John D. *Beowulf: The Poem and Its Tradition.* Cambridge, MA: Harvard University Press, 1983.

———. "Compound Diction and the Style of *Beowulf.*" *English Studies* 62 (1981): 489–503.

———. *God's Exiles and English Verse: On the Exeter Anthology of Old English Poetry.* Exeter: University of Exeter Press, 2019.

———. *The Idea of Anglo-Saxon England 1066–1901: Remembering, Forgetting, Deciphering, and Renewing the Past.* Oxford: Wiley-Blackwell, 2015.

———. *Old English Enigmatic Poems and the Play of the Texts.* Turnhout: Brepols, 2006.

———. "On the Danish Origins of the *Beowulf* Story." In *Anglo-Saxon England and the Continent*, edited by Joanna Story and Hans Sauer, 41–62. Tempe: Arizona Center for Medieval and Renaissance Studies, 2018.

———. "Ring Composition and the Structure of *Beowulf.*" *PMLA* 94 (1979): 924–35.

———. "Skaldic Technique in *Brunanburh.*" *Scandinavian Studies* 59 (1987): 356–66.

Niles, John D., and Mark Amodio, eds. *Anglo-Scandinavian England: Norse-English Relations in the Period before the Conquest.* Lanham, MD: University Press of America, 1989.

Niles, John D., and Marijane Osborn, eds. *Beowulf and Lejre.* Tempe: Arizona Center for Medieval and Renaissance Studies, 2007.

Nolan, Maura. "The Invention of Style." *Studies in the Age of Chaucer* 41 (2019): 33–71.

Nordal: see Guðrún; Sigurður.

Noudelmann, François. *Penser avec les oreilles.* Paris: Max Milo, 2019.

Novacich, Sarah Elliott. "The Old English *Exodus* and the Read Sea." *Exemplaria* 23 (2011): 50–66.

Nuttin, J. M. "Narcissism beyond Gestalt and Awareness: The Name-Letter Effect." *European Journal of Social Psychology* 15 (1985): 353–61.

Nyquist, Cole Erik. "Compositional Techniques and Perceptions of Authorship in Skaldic Poetry: Alliterative and Hending Word Constellations." Master's thesis, University of Oslo, 2014.

O'Brien O'Keeffe, Katherine. "Diction, Variation, the Formula." In Bjork and Niles, eds., *A Beowulf Handbook*, 85–104.

———. "*The Wife's Lament* and the Poetics of Affect." In *Old English Tradition: Essays in Honor of J. R. Hall*, edited by Lindy Brady, 37–51. Tempe, AZ: Medieval and Renaissance Texts and Studies, 2021.

———. O'Brien O'Keeffe, Katherine, and Andy Orchard, eds. *Latin Learning and English Lore: Studies in Anglo-Saxon Literature for Michael Lapidge*. 2 vols. Toronto: University of Toronto Press, 2005.

Obst, Wolfgang. *Der Rhythmus des Beowulf: Eine Akzent- und Takttheorie*. Heidelberg: C. Winter, 1987.

O'Camb, Brian. "Isidorean Wolf Lore and the *felafæcne deor* of *Maxims I.C.*: Some Rhetorical and Legal Contexts for Recognising Another Old English *wulf* in Sheep's Clothing." *English Studies* 97 (2016): 687–708.

O'Donnell, Daniel Paul. *Cædmon's Hymn: A Multimedia Study, Archive and Edition.* Cambridge: D. S. Brewer, 2005.

O'Donoghue, Heather. *English Poetry and Old Norse Myth: A History.* Oxford: Oxford University Press, 2014.

———. "Owed to Both Sides: W. H. Auden's Double Debt to the Literature of the North." In *Anglo-Saxon Culture and the Modern Imagination*, edited by David Clark and Nicholas Perkins, 51–69. Cambridge: D. S. Brewer, 2010.

———. *Skaldic Verse and the Poetics of Saga Narrative*. Oxford: Oxford University Press, 2005.

O'Hara, James J. *True Names: Vergil and the Alexandrian Tradition of Etymological Wordplay.* Ann Arbor: University of Michigan Press, 1996..

Oliver, Lisi. *The Beginnings of English Law.* Toronto: University of Toronto Press, 2012.

Ollett, Andrew. *Language of the Snakes: Prakrit, Sanskrit, and the Language Order of Premodern India.* Oakland: University of California Press, 2017.

Olrik, Axel. *Danmarks heltedigtning: En oldtidsstudie*. Vol. 1, *Rolf Krake og den ældre Skjoldungrække*. Copenhagen: Gad, 1903. Translated by Lee M. Hollander as *The Heroic Legends of Denmark.* New York: American-Scandinavian Foundation, 1919.

Olsen, Alexandra Hennessey. *Speech, Song, and Poetic Craft: The Artistry of the Cynewulf Canon.* New York: Lang, 1984.

Omberg, Margaret. *Scandinavian Themes in English Poetry, 1760–1800.* Uppsala: Almqvist & Wiksell, 1976.

Opelt, Ilona. "Etymologie." In *Reallexikon für Antike und Christentum: Sachwörterbuch zur Auseinandersetzung des Christentums mit der antiken Welt*, edited by Theodor Klauser, Georg Schöllgen, and Franz Joseph Dölger, vol. 6, cols. 797–844. Stuttgart: Hiersemann, 1965.

Opland, Jeff. *Anglo-Saxon Oral Poetry: A Study of the Traditions*. New Haven, CT: Yale University Press, 1980.

Orchard, Andy. "Alcuin and Cynewulf: The Art and Craft of Anglo-Saxon Verse." *Journal of the British Academy* 8 (2020): 295–399.

———. "Artful Alliteration in Anglo-Saxon Song and Story." *Anglia* 113 (1995): 429–63.

———. "Both Style and Substance: The Case for Cynewulf." In *Anglo-Saxon Styles,* edited by Catherine E. Karkov and George H. Brown, 271–305. Binghamton: State University of New York Press, 2003.

———. *A Critical Companion to Beowulf.* Cambridge: D. S. Brewer, 2003.

———. "Enigma Variations: The Anglo-Saxon Riddle Tradition." In O'Brien O'Keeffe and Orchard, eds., *Latin Learning and English Lore,* 1:284–304.

———. "Old English and Anglo-Latin: the Odd Couple." In *The Blackwell Companion to British Literature,* Vol. 1, *The Medieval Period,* edited by Robert DeMaria Jr., Heesok Chang, and Samantha Zacher, 273–92. Oxford: Blackwell, 2014.

———. "The Originality of *Andreas.*" In Neidorf et al., eds., *Old English Philology,* 331–70.

———. *The Poetic Art of Aldhelm.* Cambridge: Cambridge University Press, 1994.

———. "The Word Made Flesh: Christianity and Oral Culture in Anglo-Saxon Verse." *Oral Tradition* 24 (2009): 293–318.

Orel, Vladimir. *Handbook of Germanic Etymology.* Leiden: Brill, 2003.

Orton, Fred. "Rethinking the Ruthwell and Bewcastle Monuments: Some Deprecation of Style; Some Consideration of Form and Ideology." In *Anglo-Saxon Styles,* edited by Catherine Karkov and George H. Brown, 31–67. Binghamton: State University of New York Press, 2003.

Orton, Peter. "Anglo-Saxon Attitudes to Kuhn's Laws." *Review of English Studies* 50 (1999): 287–303.

———. *The Transmission of Old English Poetry.* Turnhout: Brepols, 2000.

Orwell, George. "Politics and the English Language." In *The Collected Essays, Journalism, and Letters of George Orwell,* edited by Sonia Orwell and Ian Angus, 4:127–39. New York: Harcourt, Brace, and World, 1968.

Osborn, Marijane. *Beowulf: A Verse Translation with Treasures of the Ancient North.* Berkeley: University of California Press, 1983.

———. "Legends of Lejre, Home of Kings." In Niles and Osborn, eds., *Beowulf and Lejre,* 235–54.

———. "The Lejre Connection in *Beowulf* Scholarship." In Niles and Osborn, eds., *Beowulf and Lejre,* 287–93.

Overing, Gilliam R. "*Beowulf*: A Poem in Our Time." In *The Cambridge History of Early Medieval English Literature,* edited by Clare Lees, 309–31. Cambridge: Cambridge University Press, 2012.

Paetzel, Walther. *Die Variationen in der altgermanischen Alliterationspoesie.* Berlin: Mayer & Müller, 1913.

Page, Denys L. *Poetae Melici Graeci: Alcman, Stesichoris, Ibycus, Anacreon, Simonides and Corinna.* Oxford: Clarendon, 1962.

Page, R. I. *Chronicles of the Vikings: Records, Memorials, Myths.* Toronto: University of Toronto Press, 1995.

———. *"A Most Vile People": Early English Historians on the Vikings.* Dorothea Coke Memorial Lecture in Northern Studies. London: Viking Society for Northern Research, 1987.

———. Review of *The Vikings*, edited by R. Farrell. *Saga-Book of the Viking Society* 21 (1982–85): 308–11.

Parks, Ward W. "Ring Structure and Narrative Embedding in Homer and *Beowulf.*" *Neuphilologische Mitteilungen* 89 (1988): 237–51.

———. *Verbal Duelling in Heroic Narrative: The Homeric and Old English Traditions.* Princeton, NJ: Princeton University Press, 1990.

Parsons, David. "How Long Did the Scandinavian Language Survive in England?" In *Vikings and the Danelaw*, edited by James Graham-Campbell et al., 299–312, Oxford: Oxbow Books, 2001.

Pascual, Rafael J. "Bliss's Rule and Old English Metrics." *American Notes and Queries* 32 (2019): 209–13.

Pasternack, Carol Braun. *The Textuality of Old English Poetry.* Cambridge: Cambridge University Press, 1995.

Paterson, Don. *The Poem: Lyric, Sign, Metre*. London: Faber & Faber, 2018.

———. *Rain.* London: Faber & Faber, 2009.

Patria, Bianca. "Quotations with a Twist: Aware Intertextuality in Skaldic Verse." *Quaestio Insularis: Selected Proceedings of the Annual Cambridge Colloquium on Anglo-Saxon, Norse and Celtic* (2018): 70–91.

Patterson, Lee. "The Heroic Laconic Style: Reticence and Meaning from *Beowulf* to the Edwardians." In *Medieval Literature and Historical Inquiry: Essays in Honour of Derek Pearsall*, edited by David Aers, 133–57. Cambridge: D. S. Brewer, 2000. Reprinted in Patterson, *Acts of Recognition: Essays on Medieval Culture*, 155–80. Notre Dame, IN: University of Notre Dame Press, 2010.

Peacock, Thomas Love. *The Complete Novels.* Edited by David Garnett. London: Harvest Books, 1963.

Pelteret, David A. E. *Slavery in Early Mediaeval England: From the Reign of Alfred until the Twelfth Century.* Woodbridge: Boydell, 1995.

Peradotto, John. *Man in the Middle Voice: Name and Narration in the Odyssey.* Princeton, NJ: Princeton University Press, 1990.

Percy, Thomas. *Five Pieces of Runic Poetry Translated from the Icelandic Language*. London: R. and J. Dodsley, 1763.

———. *Reliques of Ancient English Poetry: Consisting of Old Heroic Ballads, Songs, and Other Pieces of Our Earlier Poets . . .* 3 vols. London: J. Dodsley, 1765.

Perloff, Marjorie, and Craig Dworkin, eds. "Introduction." In *The Sound of Poetry/ The Poetry of Sound*, 1–17. Chicago: University of Chicago Press, 2009.

Peters, Hans. "Zum skandinavischen Lehngut im Altenglischen." *Sprachwissenschaft* 6 (1981): 85–124.

Peterson, Lena. *Nordiskt runnamnslexikon*. 5th rev. ed. Uppsala: Institutet för Språk och Folkminnen, 2007.

Pfeifer, J. D. "Early Anglo-Saxon Glossaries and the School of Canterbury." *Anglo-Saxon England* 16 (1987): 17–44.

Pindar: Nemean Odes, Isthmian Odes, Fragments. Edited and translated by William H. Race. Loeb Classical Library 485. Cambridge, MA: Harvard University Press, 1997.

Plumer, Danielle Cunniff. "The Construction of Structure in the Earliest Editions of Old English Poetry." In *The Recovery of Old English: Anglo-Saxon Studies in the Sixteenth and Seventeenth Centuries*, edited by Timothy Graham, 243–79. Kalamazoo, MI: Medieval Institute Publications, 2000.

Pollock, Sheldon. *A Rasa Reader: Classical Indian Aesthetics*. New York: Columbia University Press, 2016.

Pons-Sanz, Sara M. *The Lexical Effects of Anglo-Scandinavian Linguistic Contact on Old English*. Turnhout: Brepols, 2013.

———. *Norse-Derived Vocabulary in Late Old English Texts: Wulfstan's Works, A Case Study*. Odense: University Press of Southern Denmark, 2007.

Poole, Russell G. "Crossing the Language Divide: Anglo-Scandinavian Language and Literature." In *The Cambridge History of Early Medieval English Literature*, edited by Clare Lees, 579–606. Cambridge: Cambridge University Press, 2013.

———. "*Cyningas sigefæste þurh God*: Contributions from Anglo-Saxon England to Early Advocacy for Óláfr Haraldsson." In *Old English Literature and the Old Testament*, edited by Michael Fox and Manish Sharma, 266–91. Toronto: University of Toronto Press, 2012.

———. "Ekphrasis: Its 'Prolonged Echoes.'" *Viking and Medieval Scandinavia* 3 (2007): 245–67.

———. "*Liðsmannaflokkr*: The Campaigns of Knútr and Þorkell in England." In Poole, *Viking Poems on War and Peace: A Study in Skaldic Narrative*, 86–115. Toronto: University of Toronto Press, 1991.

———. "Metre and Metrics." In *A Companion to Old Norse-Icelandic Literature and Culture*, edited by Rory McTurk, 264–84. Oxford: Blackwell, 2005.

———. *Old English Wisdom Poetry*. Annotated Bibliographies of Old and Middle English Literature 5. Cambridge: D. S. Brewer, 1998.

———. "Scholars and Skalds: The Northwards Diffusion of Carolingian Poetic Fashions." *Gripla* 24 (2013): 7–44.

———. "In Search of the Partar." *Scandinavian Studies* 52 (1980): 264–77.

———. "Skaldic Verse and Anglo-Saxon History: Some Aspects of the Period 1009–16." *Speculum* 62 (1987): 265–98.

———, ed. *Skaldsagas: Text, Vocation, and Desire in the Icelandic Sagas of Poets*. Berlin: De Gruyter, 2001.

———. "Some Examples of the Adverbial Genitive in Skaldic Poetry." *Mediaeval Scandinavia* 14 (2004): 115–31.

———. "Some Southern Perspectives on Starcatherus." *Viking and Medieval Scandinavia* 2 (2006): 141–66.

Pope, John C. *Eight Old English Poems*. 3rd ed., revised by R. D. Fulk. New York: Norton, 2001.

Porck, Thijs. *Old Age in Early Medieval England: A Cultural History*. Cambridge: D. S. Brewer, 2019.

Porter, David W. "Isidore's *Etymologiae* at the School of Canterbury." *Anglo-Saxon England* 43 (2014): 7–44.

Purvis, Meghan. *Beowulf*. London: Penned in the Margins, 2013.

Puttenham, George. *The Arte of English Poesie* (London: Richard Field, 1589). Edited by Frank Whigham and Wayne A. Rebhorn. Ithaca, NY: Cornell University Press, 2007.

Quinn, Judy. "*Eddu list*: The Emergence of Skaldic Pedagogy in Medieval Iceland." *Alvíssmál* 4 (1994): 69–72.

Quinn, Judy, and Margaret Clunies Ross. "The Image of Norse Poetry and Myth in Seventeenth-Century England." In *Northern Antiquity: The Post-Medieval Reception of Edda and Saga*, edited by Andrew Wawn, 189–210. Enfield Lock: Hisarlik Press, 1994.

Quintilian. *The Orator's Education* [*Institutiones oratoriae*]. Edited and translated by D. A. Russell. Loeb Classical Library 124–127. Cambridge, MA: Harvard University Press, 2002.

Quirk, Randolph. "Poetic Language and Old English Metre." In *Early English and Norse Studies Presented to Hugh Smith*, edited by Arthur Brown and Peter Foote, 150–71. London: Methuen, 1963. Reprinted in Quirk, *Essays on the English Language*, 1–19. London: Longmans, 1968

Raffel, Burton. *Beowulf: A New Translation with an Introduction*. New York: New American Library, 1963.

Ragnar Ingi Aðalsteinsson. "Ljóðstafurinn s í íslenskum kveðskap." *Són: Tímarit um óðfræði* 3 (2005): 59–85.

Reichardt, Konstantin. *Studien zu den Skalden des 9. und 10. Jahrhunderts*. Palaestra 159. Leipzig: Mayer & Müller, 1928.

Reinhard, Mariann. *On the Semantic Relevance of the Alliterative Collocations in "Beowulf."* Bern: Francke, 1976.

Remein, Daniel C. "Auden, Translation, Betrayal: Radical Poetics and Translation from Old English." *Literature Compass* 8/11 (2011): 811–29.

Riedinger, Anita R. "The Formulaic Relationship between *Beowulf* and *Andreas*." In *Heroic Poetry in the Anglo-Saxon Period: Studies in Honor of Jess B. Bessinger Jr*, edited by Helen Damico and John Leyerle, 283–312. Kalamazoo, MI: Medieval Institute Publications, 1993.

Rieger, Max. "Die alt- und angelsächsische Verskunst." *Zeitschrift für deutsche Philologie* 7 (1876): 1–64.

Rigg, A. G. "Henry of Huntingdon's Metrical Experiments." *Journal of Medieval Latin* 1 (1991): 60–72.

Roach, Levi. *Æthelred the Unready*. New Haven, CT: Yale University Press, 2016.

Roberts, Jane. "Some Anglo-Saxon Psalters and Their Glosses." In *The Psalms and Medieval Literature: From the Conversion to the Reformation*, edited by Tamara Atkin and Francis Leneghan, 37–71. Cambridge: D. S. Brewer, 2017.

Robinson, Fred C. "Anglo-Saxon Onomastics in the Old English *Andreas*." *Names* 21 (1972): 133–36.

———. *"Beowulf" and the Appositive Style*. Knoxville: University of Tennessee Press, 1985.

———. "God, Death, and Loyalty in *The Battle of Maldon*." In *J. R. R. Tolkien, Scholar and Storyteller: Essays in Memoriam*, edited by Mary Salu and Robert T. Farrell, 76–98. Ithaca, NY: Cornell University Press, 1979.

———. "Lexicography and Literary Criticism: A Caveat." In *Philological Essays: Studies in Old and Middle English Literature in Honour of Herbert Dean Meritt*, edited by James Rosier, 99–110. The Hague: Mouton, 1970.

———. "Metathesis in the Dictionaries: A Problem for Lexicographers." In *Problems of Old English Lexicography*, edited by Alfred Bammesberger, 243–65. Reginsburg: Pustet, 1983. Reprinted in Robinson, *The Editing of Old English*, 131–48. Oxford: Blackwell, 1994.

———. "Personal Names in Medieval Narrative and the Name of Unferth in *Beowulf*." *Essays in Honor of Richebourg Gaillard McWilliams*, edited by Howard Creed. *Birmingham-Southern College Bulletin* 63, no. 2 (1970): 43–48.

———. "Sigemund's *fæhðe ond fyrena: Beowulf* 879a." In *To Explain the Present*, edited by T. Nevalainen and L. Kahlas-Tarkka, 201–8. Helsinki: Société néophilologique, 1997.

———. "The Significance of Names in Old English Literature." *Anglia* 86 (1968): 14–58.

———. "Some Aspects of the *Maldon* Poet's Artistry." *Journal of English and Germanic Philology* 75 (1976): 25–40.

———. "Some Uses of Name-Meanings in Old English Poetry." *Neuphilologische Mitteilungen* 69 (1968): 161–71.

———. "A Sub-Sense of Old English *fyrn*(-)." *Neuphilologische Mitteilungen* 100 (1999): 471–75.

———. *The Tomb of Beowulf and Other Essays on Old English*. Oxford: Blackwell, 1993.

Robinson, Fred C., and E. G. Stanley, eds. *Old English Verse Texts from Many Sources*. Early English Manuscripts in Facsimile 23. Copenhagen: Rosenkilde and Bagger, 1991.

Ross, A. S. C. "Philological Probability Problems." *Journal of the Royal Statistical Society, B* 12 (1950): 19–59.

Rowe, Elizabeth Ashman. "Irony in the Old Norse and Old English Interrogative Situation." *Neophilologus* 73 (1989): 477–79.

Rubin, David C. *Memory in Oral Traditions: The Cognitive Psychology of Epic, Ballads, and Counting-out Rhymes*. Oxford: Oxford University Press, 1995.

Ruff, Carin. "Aldhelm's Jewel Tones." In *Anglo-Saxon Styles*, edited by Catherine E. Karkov and George Hardin Brown, 223–38. Albany: State University of New York Press, 2003.

Ruggerini, Maria Elena. "Alliterative Lexical Collocations in Eddic Poetry." In *A Handbook to Eddic Poetry: Myths and Legends of Early Scandinavia*, edited by Carolyne Larrington, Judy Quinn, and Brittany Schorn, 310–30. Cambridge: Cambridge University Press, 2016.

Rühs, Christian Friedrich. *Über den Ursprung der isländischen Poesie aus der angelsächsischen nebst vermischten Bemerkungen über die nordische Dichtkunst und Mythologie*. Berlin: Reimer, 1813.

Russom, Geoffrey. "A Bard's-eye View of the Germanic Syllable." *Journal of English and Germanic Philology* 101 (2002): 305–28.

———. *Beowulf and Old Germanic Metre*. Cambridge: Cambridge University Press, 1998.

———. *The Evolution of Verse Structure in Old and Middle English Poetry*. Cambridge: Cambridge University Press, 2017.

———. *Old English Meter and Linguistic Theory*. Cambridge: Cambridge University Press, 1987.

Salmon, P. "Anomalous Alliteration in Germanic Verse." *Neophilologus* 42 (1958): 223–41.

Saltzman, Benjamin A. *Bonds of Secrecy: Law, Spirituality, and the Literature of Concealment in Early Medieval England*. Philadelphia: University of Pennsylvania Press, 2019.

Salvador-Bello, Mercedes. *Isidorian Perceptions of Order: The Exeter Book Riddles and Medieval Latin Enigmata*. Morgantown: West Virginia University Press, 2015.

Sanders, Willy. "Grundzüge und Wandlungen der Etymologie." In *Etymologie*, edited by Rüdiger Schmitt, 7–49. Darmstadt: Wissenschaftliche Buchgesellschaft, 1977.

Sauerländer, Willibald. "From Stilus to Style: Reflections on the Fate of a Notion." *Art History* 6 (1983): 253–70.

Saussy, Haun. "Jueju." *New Literary History* 50 (2019): 453–56.

Saxo Grammaticus Gesta Danorum: The History of the Danes. Edited by Karsten Friis-Jensen. Translated by Peter Fisher. Oxford Medieval Texts. Oxford: Clarendon, 2015.

Sayers, William. "Scarfing the Yard with Words (*Fóstbrœðra saga*): Shipbuilding Imagery in Old Norse Poetics." *Scandinavian Studies* 74 (2002): 1–18.

Schaefer, Ursula. "Rhetoric and Style." In Bjork and Niles, eds., *A Beowulf Handbook*, 105–24.

Schlosser, Horst Dieter, ed. *Althochdeutsche Literatur: Eine Textauswahl mit Übertragungen*. Berlin: Schmidt, 1998.

Scholtz, Hendrik van de Merwe. *The Kenning in Anglo-Saxon and Old Norse Poetry*. Utrecht: Dekker, 1927.

Schrøder, Ludvig. *Om Bjovulfs drapen: efter en række foredrag på folkehöjskolen i Askov*. Copenhagen: Schønberg, 1875.

Schuchardt, Richard. *Die Negation im "Beowulf." Berliner Beiträge zur germanischen und romanischen Philologie* 38 (1910): 1–149.

Schücking, Levin L. *Untersuchungen zur Bedeutungslehre der angelsächsischen Dichtersprache*. Heidelberg: C. Winter, 1915.

———. "Wann entstand der *Beowulf*? Glossen, Zweifel und Fragen." *Beiträge zur Geschichte der deutschen Sprache und Literatur* 42 (1917): 347–410.

Scragg, Donald G. "The Nature of Old English Verse." In *The Cambridge Companion to Old English Literature*, edited by Malcolm Godden and Michael Lapidge, 55–70. Cambridge: Cambridge University Press, 1991.

Seaton, Ethel M. *Literary Relations of England and Scandinavia in the Seventeenth Century*. Oxford: Clarendon, 1935.

See, Klaus von. *Germanische Verskunst*. Stuttgart: Metzler, 1967.

———. "Hastings, Stiklastaðir und Langemarck: Zur Überlieferung vom Vortrag heroischer Lieder auf dem Schlachtfeld." *Germanisch-romanische Monatsschrift* 57, n.s., 26 (1976): 1–13.

———. "*Húskarla hvǫt*: Nochmals zum Alter der *Bjarkamál*." In *Speculum Norroenum: Norse Studies in Memory of Gabriel Turville-Petre*, edited by Ursula Dronke et al., 421–36. Odense: Odense University Press, 1981.

———. *Skaldendichtung: Eine Einführung*. Munich: Artemis, 1980.

———. "Skop und Skáld: Zur Auffassung des Dichters bei den Germanen." *Germanisch-romanische Monatsschrift* 45 (1964): 1–14.

———. "*Skothending*: Bemerkungen zur Frühgeschichte des skaldischen Binnenreims." *Beiträge zur Geschichte der deutschen Sprache und Literatur* 90 (1968): 217–22.

See, Klaus von, Beatrice La Farge, Eve Picard, and Katja Schulz. *Kommentar zu den Liedern der Edda*. 7 vols. Heidelberg: Winter, 1997–2019.

Shanzer, Danuta. "The Tale of Frodebert's Tail." In *Colloquial and Literary Latin*, edited by E. Dickey and F. Chaboud, 376–405. Cambridge: Cambridge University Press, 2010.

Shippey, T. A. "Names in *Beowulf* and Anglo-Saxon England." In *The Dating of Beowulf: A Reassessment*, edited by L. Neidorf, 58–78. Cambridge: D. S. Brewer, 2014.

———. *Old English Verse*. London: Hutchison, 1972.

Shippey, T. A., and Andreas Haarder, eds. *Beowulf: The Critical Heritage*. London: Routledge, 1998.

Shuman, R. Baird, and H. Charles Hutchins. "The *un*-Prefix: A Means of Germanic Irony in *Beowulf*." *Modern Philology* 57 (1960): 217–22.

Sievers, Eduard. *Altgermanische Metrik*. Halle: Niemeyer, 1893.

———. "Zur Rhythmik des germanischen Alliterationsverses." *Beiträge zur Geschichte der deutschen Sprache und Literatur* 10 (1885): 209–314, 451–545; 12 (1886): 454–82.

Sigurður Nordal, ed. *Egils saga Skalla-Grímssonar*. Íslenzk fornrit 2. Reykjavík: Hið íslenzka fornritafélag, 1933.

Simensen, Erik. "The Old Nordic Lexicon." In Bandle et al., eds., *The Nordic Languages*, 1:951–62.

Simpson, James, and Brian Cummings, eds. *Cultural Reformations: Medieval and Renaissance in Literary History*. Oxford: Oxford University Press, 2010.

Simpson, Michael. "*Odyssey* 9: Symmetry and Paradox in Outis." *The Classical Journal* 68 (1972): 22–25.

Skeat, Walter W. "An Essay on Alliterative Poetry." In *Bishop Percy's Folio Manuscript: Ballads and Romances*, edited Frederick J. Furnivall and John W. Hales, 3:xi–xxxix. London: Trübner, 1867–68.

Smith, A. H. "The Early Literary Relations of England and Scandinavia." *Saga-Book of the Viking Society for Northern Research* 11 (1928–36): 215–32.

Smith, Barbara Herrnstein. *Poetic Closure*. Chicago: University of Chicago Press, 1968.

Smith, Ted Johnson, ed. and trans. *Historia de Sancti Cuthberti: A History of Saint Cuthbert and a Record of his Patrimony*. Cambridge: D. S. Brewer, 2002.

Snorri Sturluson, *Edda. Háttatal*. 2nd ed. Edited by Anthony Faulkes. London: Viking Society for Northern Research, 2007.

———. *Edda. Skáldskaparmál*. 2 vols. Edited by Anthony Faulkes. London: Viking Society for Northern Research, 1998.

Spaeth, John Duncan. *Old English Poetry: Translations into Alliterative Verse, with Introduction and Notes*. Princeton, NJ: Princeton University Press, 1921.

Spurkland, Terje. *Norwegian Runes and Runic Inscriptions*. Translated by Betsy van der Hoek. Woodbridge: Boydell and Brewer, 2005.

Stafford, Pauline. *Queen Emma and Queen Edith: Queenship and Women's Power in Eleventh-Century England*. Oxford: Blackwell, 1997.

Stanley, Eric. "Aesthetic Evaluations of the Sound of Old English: 'About the Anglo-Saxon tongue there was the strength of iron, with the sparkling and the beauty of burnished steel.'" In *Essays for Joyce Hill on Her Sixtieth Birthday*, edited by Mary Swan, *Leeds Studies in English*, n.s., 37 (2006): 451–72.

———. "Alliterative Ornament and Alliterative Rhythmical Discourse in Old High German and Old Frisian Compared with Similar Manifestations in Old

English." *Beiträge zur Geschichte der deutschen Sprache und Literatur* 106 (1984): 184–217.

———. *A Collection of Papers with Emphasis on Old English Literature.* Publications of the *Dictionary of Old English* 3. Toronto: Pontifical Institute of Mediaeval Studies Press, 1987.

———. "Courtliness and Courtesy in *Beowulf* and Elsewhere in Medieval English Literature." In *Words and Works: Studies in Medieval English Language and Literature in Honour of Fred C. Robinson*, edited by Peter S. Baker and Nicholas Howe, 67–103. Toronto: University of Toronto Press, 1998.

———. "*Geoweorþa*: 'Once Held in High Esteem.'" In *J. R. R. Tolkien: Scholar and Storyteller, Essays in Memoriam*, edited by M. Salu and R. T. Farrell, 99–119. Ithaca, NY: Cornell University Press, 1979. Reprinted in Stanley, *A Collection of Papers*, 318–35.

———. *In the Foreground: Beowulf.* Cambridge: D. S. Brewer, 1994.

———. "The Narrative Art of *Beowulf*." In *Medieval Narrative: A Symposium*, edited by Hans Bekker-Nielsen et al., 58–81. Odense: Odense University Press, 1979. Reprinted in Stanley, *A Collection of Papers*, 170–91.

———. "Notes on Old English Poetry, iv, A Long Unit of Old English Verse and Modern Editorial Punctuation: *Beowulf*, lines 864–917a." *Leeds Studies in English*, n.s., 20 (1989): 330–34.

———. "Old English Poetic Diction and the Interpretation of *The Wanderer*, *The Seafarer*, and *The Penitent's Prayer*." *Anglia* 73 (1955): 413–66. Reprinted in Stanley, *A Collection of Papers*, 234–80.

———. "The Oldest English Poetry Now Extant." *Poetica* (Tokyo) 2 (1974): 1–24. Reprinted in Stanley, *A Collection of Papers*, 115–38.

———. "Playing upon Words, I and II." *Neuphilologische Mitteilungen* 102 (2001): 339–56, 451–68.

———. "Rhymes in English Medieval Verse: From Old English to Middle English." In *Medieval English Studies Presented to George Kane*, edited by Edward D. Kennedy, Ronald Waldron, and Joseph S. Wittig, 19–54. Cambridge: D. S. Brewer, 1988.

———. "Studies in the Prosaic Vocabulary of Old English Verse." *Neuphilologische Mitteilungen* 72 (1971): 385–418.

Starobinski, Jean. *Les mots sous les mots: Les anagrammes de Ferdinand de Saussure.* Paris: Gallimard, 1971.

———. "Les mots sous les mots: Textes inédits des *Cahiers* d'anagrammes de Ferdinand de Saussure." In *To Honor Roman Jakobson: Essays on the Occasion of His Seventieth Birthday*, 3:1906–17. The Hague: De Gruyter Mouton, 1967.

———. "Lettres et syllabes mobiles: Complément à la lecture des *Cahiers* d'anagrammes de Ferdinand de Saussure." *Littérature* 99 (1995): 7–18.

Stavnem, Rolf. "The Kennings in *Ragnarsdrápa*." *Mediaeval Scandinavia* 14 (2004): 161–84.

Steen, Janie. *Verse and Vertuosity: The Adaptation of Latin Rhetoric in Old English Poetry.* Toronto: University of Toronto Press, 2008.

Stévanovitch, Colette. "Envelope Patterns in *Genesis A* and *B*." *Neophilologus* 80 (1996): 465–78.

———. "Envelope Patterns and the Unity of the Old English *Christ and Satan*." *Archiv für das Studium der neueren Sprachen und Literaturen* 233 (1996): 260–67.

Stjerna, Knut. "Hjälmar och svärd i *Beovulf*." In *Studier tillägnade Oscar Montelius*, edited by Sune Ambrosiani et al., 99–120. Stockholm: Norstedt, 1903.

Stoppard, Tom. *The Invention of Love.* London: Faber and Faber, 1997.

Storch, Theodor. *Angelsächsische Nominalcomposita.* Strassburg: Trübner, 1886.

Storms, Godfrid. "The Subjectivity of the Style of *Beowulf*." In *Studies in Old English Literature in Honor of Arthur G. Brodeur*, edited by Stanley Greenfield, 171–86. Eugene: University of Oregon Press, 1963.

Strohm, Paul. "Middle English Narrative Genres." *Genre* 13 (1980): 379–88.

Sutherland, John. "Newly Unoriginal: The Inter-knittedness of Writing." *The Times Literary Supplement* 6090 (December 20, 2019): 36.

Suzuki, Seiichi. "In Defense of Resolution as a Metrical Principle in *Beowulf*." *English Studies* 46 (1995): 20–33.

———. *The Meters of Old Norse Poetry.* Ergänzungsbände zum Reallexikon der Germanischen Altertumskunde 86. Berlin: De Gruyter, 2014.

———. *The Metre of Old Saxon Poetry: The Remaking of Alliterative Tradition.* Cambridge: D. S. Brewer, 2004.

———. *The Metrical Organization of Beowulf: Prototype and Isomorphism.* Berlin: De Gruyter, 1996.

Sweet, Henry. "Sketch of the History of Anglo-Saxon Poetry." In Thomas Warton, *The History of English Poetry from the Close of the Eleventh Century to the Commencement of the Eighteenth Century*, 4th rev. ed. by W. Carew Hazlitt et al., 2:1–19. London: Reeves and Turner, 1871.

Swenson, K. "Death Appropriated in *The Fates of Men*." *Studies in Philology* 88 (1991): 25–35.

Swift, Jonathan. *Letter to a Young Gentleman Lately Entered into Holy Orders.* 2nd ed. London: Roberts, 1721.

Syrett, Martin. *The Vikings in England: The Evidence of Runic Inscriptions.* Cambridge: Department of Anglo-Saxon, Norse and Celtic, 2002.

Taine, Hippolyte. *Histoire de la littérature anglaise.* Paris: L. Hachette, 1863. Translated by H. Van Laun as *History of English Literature.* 2 vols. Edinburgh: Edmonston & Douglas, 1871.

Taylor, Paul Beekman. "Onomastics and Propaganda in *Brunanburh*." *American Notes and Queries* 7 (1994): 67–88.

Temple, Sir William. *Miscellanea, The Second Part in Four Essays.* London: Tonson, 1690.

Terasawa, Jun. *Old English Metre: An Introduction.* Toronto: University of Toronto Press, 2011.

Theodoricus monachus. Historia de antiquitate regum Norwgensium: An Account of the Ancient History of the Norwegian Kings. Translated by David McDougall and Ian McDougall. London: Viking Society for Northern Research, 1998.

Þorgeir Sigurðsson. "Rímstuðlar Um tengsl ríms, atkvæðaskiptingar og stuðla í íslenskum skáldskap." *Íslenskt mál og almenn málfræði* 23 (2001): 215–27.

Thornbury, Emily V. "Æthilwulf poeta." In *Latinity and Identity in Anglo-Saxon Literature*, edited by Rebecca Stephenson and Emily V. Thornbury, 54–72. Toronto: University of Toronto Press, 2016.

———. *Becoming a Poet in Anglo-Saxon England.* Cambridge: Cambridge University Press, 2014.

———. "Light Verse in Anglo-Saxon England." In *The Shapes of Early English Poetry: Style, Form, History*, edited by Irina Dumitrescu and Eric Weiskott, 85–106. Kalamazoo: Medieval Institute Publications, Western Michigan University, 2019.

———. "*Ða Gregorius gamenode mid his wordum*: Old English Versions of Gregory's Bilingual Puns." *Leeds Studies in English* 38 (2007): 17–30.

Tiller, Kenneth. "Anglo-Norman Historiography and Henry of Huntingdon's Translation of *The Battle of Brunanburh.*" *Studies in Philology* 109 (2012): 173–91.

Tolkien, J. R. R. "*Beowulf*: The Monsters and the Critics." *Publications of the British Academy* 22 (1936): 245–95.

———. *Beowulf: A Translation and Commentary, together with Sellic Spell.* Edited by Christopher Tolkien. Boston: Houghton Mifflin Harcourt, 2014.

Tolkien J. R. R., and Joan Turville-Petre, eds. and trans. *The Old English "Exodus."* Oxford: Clarendon, 1981.

Tolman, Albert H. "The Style of Anglo-Saxon Poetry." *Transactions of the Modern Language Association of America* (1887): 17–41.

Tonsfeldt, H. Warn. "Ring Structure in *Beowulf.*" *Neophilologus* 61 (1977): 443–62.

Toswell, M. J. *The Anglo-Saxon Psalter.* Turnhout: Brepols, 2014.

———. "The Translation Techniques of the Old English Metrical Psalter, with Special Reference to Psalm 136." *English Studies* 75 (1994): 393–407.

Townend, Matthew. *Antiquity of Diction in Old English and Old Norse Poetry.* E. C. Quiggin Memorial Lectures 17. Cambridge: Department of Anglo-Saxon, Norse and Celtic, 2015.

———. "Cnut's Poets: An Old Norse Literary Community in Eleventh-Century England." In Tyler, ed., *Conceptualizing Multilingualism*, 197–215.

———. "Contextualizing the *Knútsdrápur*: Skaldic Praise-Poetry at the Court of Cnut." *Anglo-Saxon England* 30 (2001): 145–79.

———. "Ella: An Old English Name in Old Norse Poetry." *Nomina* 20 (1997): 23–35.

———. *English Place-Names in Skaldic Verse.* English Place-Name Society, extra series 1. Nottingham: English Place-Name Society, 1998.

———. "Knútr and the Cult of St Óláfr: Poetry and Patronage in Eleventh-Century Norway and England." *Viking and Medieval Scandinavia* 1 (2005): 251–79.

———. *Language and History in Viking Age England: Linguistic Relations between Speakers of Old Norse and Old English.* Turnhout: Brepols, 2002.

———. "Norse Poets and English Kings: Skaldic Performance in Anglo-Saxon England." *Offa* 58 (2001): 269–75.

———. "Pre-Cnut Praise-Poetry in Viking Age England." *Review of English Studies* 51 (2000): 349–70.

———. "Viking Age England as a Bilingual Society." In *Cultures in Contact: Scandinavian Settlement in England in the Ninth and Tenth Centuries*, edited by Dawn M. Hadley and Julian D. Richards, 89–105. Turnhout: Brepols, 2000.

Townend, Matthew, T. O'Donnell, and E. M. Tyler. "European Literature and Eleventh-Century England." In *The Cambridge History of Early Medieval English Literature*, edited by Clare A. Lees, 607–36. Cambridge: Cambridge University Press, 2013.

Townsend, David. "Latinities, 893–1143." In *The Cambridge History of Early Medieval English Literature*, edited by Clare A. Lees, 530–53. Cambridge: Cambridge University Press, 2013.

Tranter, Stephen. "Medieval Icelandic *artes poeticae*." In *Old Icelandic Literature and Society*, edited by Margaret Clunies Ross, 140–60. Cambridge: Cambridge University Press, 2000.

Treharne, Elaine, and Susan Rosser, eds. *Early Medieval English Texts and Interpretations: Studies Presented to Donald G. Scragg.* Tempe, AZ: Medieval and Renaissance Texts and Studies, 2002.

Trilling, Renée R. *The Aesthetics of Nostalgia: Historical Representation in Old English Verse.* Toronto: University of Toronto Press, 2009.

Tripp, Raymond P. "Odin's Powers and the Old English Elegies." In *The Old English Elegies: New Essays in Criticism and Research*, edited by Martin Green, 57–68. Toronto: Associated University Presses, 1983.

Tucker, Herbert F. "Unsettled Scores: Meter and Play in Two Music Poems by Browning." *Critical Inquiry* 41 (2014): 24–52.

Tupper, Frederick, ed. *The Riddles of the Exeter Book.* Boston: Ginn, 1910.

Turner, Ken, and Laurence Horn, eds. *Pragmatics, Truth, and Underspecification: Towards an Atlas of Meaning.* Leiden: Brill, 2018.

Turner, Sharon. *The History of the Anglo-Saxons from the Earliest Period to the Norman Conquest.* 2 vols. 2nd ed. London: Longman, Hurst, Rees and Orme, 1807; 2 vols. 6th ed. Philadelphia: Carey & Hart, 1841.

Turville-Petre, Gabriel. *Scaldic Poetry.* Oxford: Clarendon, 1976.

Tyler, Elizabeth M. *Old English Poetics: The Aesthetics of the Familiar in Anglo-Saxon England.* York: York Medieval Press, 2006.

———, ed. *Conceptualizing Multilingualism in Medieval England, c. 600–c. 1250.* Turnhout: Brepols, 2011.

Tynjanov, Jury. "The Literary Fact." In *Modern Genre Theory*, edited by David Duff, 29–49. London: Longman, 2000.

Underwood, Ted. *Why Literary Periods Mattered: Historical Contrast and the Prestige of English Studies.* Stanford, CA: Stanford University Press, 2013.

Urquhart, Jane. *The Underpainter.* Toronto: McClelland and Stewart, 1997.

Viðar Hreinsson, ed. *The Complete Sagas of Icelanders*. Reykjavík: Leifur Eiríksson, 1977.

Vogrin, Valerie. "The Unceasing Call of Style: A Novelist's Perspective." In *On Style: An Atelier*, edited by Eileen A. Joy and Anna Klosowska, 111–20. Brooklyn: Punctum Books, 2013.

Vogt, Walther H. "Binnenreime in der Edda." *Acta Philologica Scandinavica* 12 (1937–38): 228–62.

Vries, Jan de. *Altnordische Literaturgeschichte*. 2 vols. 2nd ed. Berlin: De Gruyter, 1964–67. 3rd ed. with a foreword by Stefanie Würth, 1999.

———. *Altnordisches etymologisches Wörterbuch*. 2nd rev. ed. Leiden: Brill, 1977.

Walde, Alois. *Vergleichendes Wörterbuch der indogermanischen Sprachen*. 3 vols. Edited and revised by Julius Pokorny. Berlin: De Gruyter, 1929–32.

Wallace, David, ed. *The Cambridge History of Medieval English Literature*. Cambridge: University of Cambridge Press, 1999.

Wärtli, Hans. *Stilistische Dämpfung als Mittel der Ausdruckssteigerung und der Ausdrucksmilderung im Altenglischen und im Neuenglischen (Litotes and Understatement)*. Zürich: Leeman, 1935.

Warton, Thomas. *The History of English Poetry, from the Close of the Eleventh to the Commencement of the Eighteenth Century, etc etc*. 3 vols. London: Dodsley, etc., 1774–81.

Watkins, Calvert, ed. *The American Heritage Dictionary of Indo-European Roots.* 3rd rev. ed. Boston: Houghton Mifflin Harcourt, 2011.

Wawn, Andrew. *The Anglo Man: Þorleifur Repp, Philology and Nineteenth-Century Britain.* Studia Islandica 49. Reykjavík: Bókaútgáfa Menningsjóðs, 1991.

———. "Anglo-Saxon Poetry in Iceland: The Case of *Brúnaborgar Bardaga Quida*." In *Essays for Joyce Hill on Her Sixtieth Birthday*, edited by Mary Swan, *Leeds Studies in English*, n.s., 37 (2006): 473–90.

———. "The Cult of 'Stalwart Frith-thjof' in Victorian Britain." In *Northern Antiquity: The Post-Medieval Reception of Edda and Saga*, edited by Wawn, 211–54. Enfield Lock: Hisarlik Press, 1994.

———. "The Post-Medieval Reception of Old Norse and Old Icelandic Literature." In *A Companion to Old Norse-Icelandic Literature and Culture*, edited by Rory McTurk, 320–37. Oxford: Blackwell, 2005.

Weber, Benjamin D. "Sworn Swords: The Germanic Context of *Beowulf* 2064, *aðsweord*." *Anglo-Saxon England* 47 (2019): 177–96.

Weber, Gerd Wolfgang. "Of Trees and Men: Some Thoughts on Kennings and Metaphors—and on Ludvig Holberg's Arboresque Anthropology." In *Twenty-Eight Papers Presented to Hans Bekker-Nielsen on the Occasion of His Sixtieth Birthday, 28 April 1993*, edited by Hans Frede Nielsen and Erik Hansen, 419–46. Odense: Odense University Press, 1993.

Webster, Leslie. "Style: Influences, Chronology, and Meaning." In *The Oxford Handbook of Anglo-Saxon Archaeology*, edited by Helena Hamerow, David A. Hinton, and Sally Crawford, 460–500. Oxford: Oxford University Press, 2011.

Wehlau, Ruth, ed. *Darkness, Depression, and Descent in Anglo-Saxon England.* Kalamazoo, MI: Medieval Institute Publications, 2019.

Weiskott, Eric. *English Alliterative Verse: Poetic Tradition and Literary History.* Cambridge: Cambridge University Press, 2016.

———. *Meter and Modernity in English Verse, 1350–1650.* Philadelphia: University of Pennsylvania Press, 2021.

———. "Old English Poetry, Verse by Verse." *Anglo-Saxon England* 44 (2016): 95–130.

———. "The *Paris Psalter* and English Literary History." In Dumitrescu and Weiskott, eds., *The Shapes of Early English Poetry*, 107–134.

———. "Three *Beowulf* Cruces: *healgamen, fremu, Sigemunde*." *Notes & Queries* 58 (2011): 3–7.

———. "Three-Position Verses in *Beowulf*." *Notes & Queries* 60 (2013): 483–85.

Wellek, René. *The Rise of English Literary History.* Chapel Hill: University of North Carolina Press, 1941.

Wessén, Elias. "Theoderikmyt eller hjältesaga? Svar till professor Höfler." *Arkiv för nordisk filologi* 79 (1964): 1–20.

Westcott, R. W. "Linguistic Iconism." *Language* 47, no. 2 (1971): 416–28.

Weyman, Carl. "Studien über die Figur der Litotes." *Jahrbücher für classische Philologie*, 15th supplementary vol. (1887): 453–556.

Whatley, Gordon. "Old English Onomastics and Narrative Art: *Elene* 1062." *Modern Philology* 73 (1975): 109–20.

Whitelock, Dorothy. *The Audience of Beowulf.* Oxford: Clarendon, 1951.

———. *From Bede to Alfred: Studies in Early Anglo-Saxon Literature and History.* London: Variorum Reprints, 1980.

Whitman, F. H. *A Comparative Study of Old English Metre.* Toronto: University of Toronto Press, 1993.

Wieland, Gernot R. "A New Look at the Poem 'Archalis clamare triumuir.'" In *Insignis Sophiae Arcator: Medieval Latin Studies in Honour of Michael Herren on His 65th Birthday*, edited by G. R. Wieland, C. Ruff, and R. G. Arthur, 178–92. Turnhout: Brepols, 2006.

Wilcox, Jonathan. "'Tell Me What I Am': The Old English Riddles." In *Readings in Medieval Texts: Interpreting Old and Middle English Literature*, edited by

David F. Johnson and Elaine Treharne, 46–59. Oxford: Oxford University Press, 2005.

William of Malmesbury. *Gesta Regum Anglorum.* 2 vols. Edited and translated by R. A. B. Mynors, R. M. Thomson, and M. Winterbottom. Oxford: Oxford University Press, 1998.

Williamson, Craig. *The Old English Riddles of the Exeter Book.* Chapel Hill: University of North Carolina Press, 1977.

Wilton, David. "What Do We Mean by *Anglo-Saxon*? Pre-Conquest to the Present." *Journal of English and Germanic Philology* 119 (2020): 425–54.

Wine, Joseph D. *Figurative Language in Cynewulf: Defining Aspects of a Poetic Style.* New York: Lang, 1993.

Withycombe, E. G. *The Oxford Dictionary of English Christian Names.* 3rd ed. Oxford: Clarendon, 1977.

Wolff, Ludwig. "Über den Stil der altgermanischen Poesie." *Deutsches Vierteljahrschrift* 1 (1923): 214–29.

Wolfson, Susan. "Reading for Form." *Modern Language Quarterly* 61 (2000): 1–16.

Woolf, Rosemary. "The Ideal of Men Dying with Their Lord in the *Germania* and in *The Battle of Maldon*." *Anglo-Saxon England* 5 (1976): 63–81.

Worm, Ole [Olaus Wormius]. *Runir seu Danica literatura antiquissima, vulgo Gothica dicta luci reddita . . . cui accessit De prisca Danorum poesi dissertatio.* Copenhagen: M. Martzan, 1636.

Wright, Charles D. "*Genesis A* ad litteram." In *Old English Literature and the Old Testament*, edited by Michael Fox and Manish Sharma, 121–71. Toronto: University of Toronto Press, 2012.

———. "More Old English Poetry in Vercelli Homily XXI." In Treharne and Rosser, eds., *Early Medieval English Texts*, 245–62.

Wright, Thomas. "On Anglo-Saxon Poetry." *Fraser's Magazine* 12 (1835): 76–88.

Würth, Stefanie. "Skaldic Poetry and Performance." In *Learning and Understanding in the Old Norse World: Essays in Honour of Margaret Clunies Ross*, edited by Judy Quinn et al., 263–81. Turnhout: Brepols, 2007.

Wyatt, David. *Slaves and Warriors in Medieval Britain and Ireland, 800–1200.* Leiden: Brill, 2009.

Wyld, Henry Cecil. "Diction and Imagery in Anglo-Saxon Poetry." *Essays and Studies* 11 (1925): 49–91.

Yakovlev, Nicolay. "The Development of the Alliterative Metre from Old to Middle English." D.Phil. diss., University of Oxford, 2008.

Zacher, Samantha. "Cynewulf at the Interface of Literacy and Orality: The Evidence of the Puns in *Elene*." *Oral Tradition* 17 (2002): 346–87.

———. "Multilingualism at the Court of King Æthelstan: Latin Praise Poetry and *The Battle of Brunanburh*." In Tyler, ed., *Conceptualizing Multilingualism*, 77–103.

———. "Views on Circumcision in Old English Literature." In *Old English Literature and the Old Testament*, edited by Michael Fox and Manish Sharma, 89–118. Toronto: University of Toronto Press, 2012.

Zamboni, Alberto. *L'etimologia.* Bologna: Zanichelli, 1976.

Ziolkowski, Jan M. "Obscenity in the Latin Grammatical and Rhetorical Tradition." In *Obscenity: Social Control and Artistic Creation in the European Middle Ages*, edited by Jan M. Ziolkowski, 41–59. Leiden: Brill, 1998.

Zipf, G. K. *Human Behavior and the Principle of Least Effort: An Introduction to Human Ecology.* Cambridge, MA: Addison-Wesley, 1949.

Zumthor, Paul. *Toward a Medieval Poetics.* Translated by Philip Bennett. Minneapolis: University of Minnesota Press, 1992.

INDEX

Note: The index lists modern Icelandic and medieval Norse persons by given name; items beginning with Þ appear at the end of the index. References to poems by a named skald are absorbed into that skald's entry.

ROBERTA FRANK is the Marie Borroff Professor Emerita of English at Yale University. Over the past half century, she has published many essays on the style, form, and history of Old English and Old Norse poetry. Her first sole-authored book was *Old Norse Court Poetry.*

Lightning Source UK Ltd.
Milton Keynes UK
UKHW021830220422
401869UK00003B/161